Ontology Without Borders

Ontology Without Borders

JODY AZZOUNI

UNIVERSITY PRESS

Oxford University Press is a department of the University of Oxford. It furthers the University's objective of excellence in research, scholarship, and education by publishing worldwide. Oxford is a registered trade mark of Oxford University Press in the UK and certain other countries.

Published in the United States of America by Oxford University Press
198 Madison Avenue, New York, NY 10016, United States of America.

© Oxford University Press 2017

First issued as an Oxford University Press paperback, 2020

All rights reserved. No part of this publication may be reproduced, stored in a retrieval system, or transmitted, in any form or by any means, without the prior permission in writing of Oxford University Press, or as expressly permitted by law, by license, or under terms agreed with the appropriate reproduction rights organization. Inquiries concerning reproduction outside the scope of the above should be sent to the Rights Department, Oxford University Press, at the address above.

You must not circulate this work in any other form
and you must impose this same condition on any acquirer.

CIP data is on file at the Library of Congress
ISBN 978-0-19-062255-8 (hardcover); 978-0-19-007873-7 (paperback)

CONTENTS

Acknowledgments   vii
General Introduction   ix

PART I | Ontological Commitment

1   Transcendence and Immanence   3

2   The Transcendence of the Natural-Language "Exist" When Used to Assert or Deny Ontological Commitment   30

3   Ontological Neutrality in Natural Languages   55

4   Truth and Bivalence   73

5   Applications of Neutrality   100

Conclusion to Part I   129

PART II | What There Is

Introduction to Part II   135

6   The Master Argument Against Ontological Borders   143

7   Feature-Characterization Languages   171

8 Focusing in on (Some of) the Real   194

9 Constructing "Objects"   224

   General Conclusion   250

   Bibliography   257
   Index   269

ACKNOWLEDGMENTS

MY THANKS TO MY SEMINAR class on objects (Spring 2014), where we studied the "penultimate" version of this book while I worked up yet another final version—and not for the last time, it turned out. I'm indebted not only to the attending students but also to everyone else who graciously sat in. In an order innocent of significance, my thanks to Anthony Adrian, Stefano Boscolo, Pedro Carné, Nat Carter, Corey Dethier, Dave Gottlieb, Justis Koon, David Laprade, George E. Smith, and Isaac Wilhelm. I thank Otávio Bueno and Jeff McConnell for discussions on these topics over several years; I thank Yvonne Raley for several valuable (emailed) suggestions in June and July 2014, and John Collins for the same, plus another valuable email in January 2016. I thank Eric Dean for pages of helpful detailed, and substantial, comments on the entire manuscript in late 2015 and in the first half of 2016, while I was doing final preparations.

Some help is targeted enough to acknowledge with footnotes, but most came in ineffable or global ways hard to be footnote-specific about. For example, chapter 6 came under pressure during several classes. The result was substantial modifications in presentation and content. Chapter 7 is also material generated because members of the class requested additional details about feature-presentation languages. George Smith was especially concerned (and helpful) about how relations are interpreted in these languages.

Valuable suggestions from several members of the class (among them Corey Dethier, Dave Gottlieb, Justis Koon, and Isaac Wilhelm) induced me to *remove* items. But you can't thank someone by dropping footnotes into what's otherwise the middle of nowhere: *Thanks to So-and-so for a much-needed lacuna* right here.

I especially want to thank Michael Glanzberg for a very generous set of searching comments, questions, and objections. While working on the manuscript (during the winter of 2015 and the spring of 2016), I rewrote a great deal of it as a result. (There are footnotes to this effect throughout the book.)

My thanks to an anonymous referee who reviewed the book for Oxford in 2015 for raising several concerns that I responded to.

I thank both the Philosophy Department and the Deans of Arts and Sciences at Tufts University for introducing a special program of classes that incorporate students into the professor's research process. I hope my students found this as valuable as I did. (Back in 1994, I thanked the Philosophy Department at Tufts for providing a near-perfect environment in which to do philosophy. Remarkably, this is still true.)

GENERAL INTRODUCTION

I.1 Ontological Neutrality

One theme of my earlier work is that the quantifiers of formal languages and the corresponding terms of natural languages are *ontologically neutral*. Quantifiers don't *require* ontological commitments to what they quantify over. Call this *quantifier neutralism*.[1] Quantifier neutralism is an empirical thesis when applied to natural languages: it's sensitive to language-usage evidence. For formal languages, however, quantifier neutralism is a theorem: nothing about formal languages, or the semantics for such languages, *forces* an ontologically committing interpretation of their quantifiers. (I'm excluding, of course, stipulatively *imposing* an ontological interpretation on formal quantifiers; but this doesn't require a special *kind* of semantics.) In the appendix to this introduction, I sketch the proof of quantifier neutralism for various formal languages and their many possible semantics; I also discuss the usage evidence for the quantifier neutralism thesis when it's applied to natural languages.

I first endorsed, in Azzouni (1994), an ontology-free interpretation of first-order formal languages—even when accompanied by standard objectual (Tarskian) semantics. I there characterized mathematical practice as families of formal axiom systems that don't require ontological commitments.

---

[1] I owe this label to William Lane Craig (2011). It was used earlier to describe my position (or positions seen as resembling it), but Craig was the first to directly press me to adopt it.

Quantifier neutralism equalizes the burdens of proof between nominalists and Platonists—indeed, it levels the playing field between ontological minimizers *of all sorts* and their opponents. Literal quantification over fictional entities, properties, and so on need raise no fears that *on that basis alone* ontological commitments to these things arise. Their existence can be supported by *metaphysical* reasons, of course. *Quantifier neutralism* only denies that quantifier languages and their semantics *force* commitments. Easy extensions of the arguments given in the appendix show this is true of *any* terms—formal or natural—that proponents hope carry ontological commitments because of their *semantics*. I discuss singular terms, specifically, next.

In Azzouni (2010a), I gave an argument (first sketched in Azzouni 2004a) that the ontological neutrality thesis applies to singular expressions. When it comes to names, like "Hercules" and "Barack Obama," or to our use of terms such as "this" while demonstrating something seen, natural languages impose no semantic requirement that something real be targeted. Formal languages follow suit with a theorem: no semantics for languages containing singular terms *requires* ontological commitments.

Although I stressed the ontological neutrality of standard Tarskian objectual quantification subsequent to its tacit presupposition in Azzouni (1994)—for example, in Azzouni (1997)—only in Azzouni (2004a) did I use ontological neutrality to support nominalism. I coupled neutralism with a metaphysical mind- and language-independence criterion for what exists. Quantifier neutralism is about formal and informal quantifier *languages*; it's compatible with all sorts of *metaphysical* positions, not just ones I like. I say more about this in the appendix.

I've applied ontological neutrality results in previous work to talk of what *isn't*. I've argued for an "easy road" deflationary nominalism, one that abjures ontological commitments to Platonic objects without rewriting mathematical or scientific discourse to eliminate empty quantifications and empty singular terms.

The just-used "easy road" terminology is Colyvan's (2010). The phrase "deflationary nominalism," to label the brand of nominalism I like, is Bueno's (2010). Notice, however, that "nominalism" in philosophy of mathematics refers to positions that deny Platonic objects. In metaphysics generally, it labels denials of universals, properties, and the like. My metaphysical deflationism is broader than this. Not only do I reject Platonic objects, universals, and properties; I also reject fictional entities, hallucinated entities, Meinongian creatures, and possible worlds. My full deflationary project should be described, therefore, as *pure deflationary metaphysics*.[2]

---

[2] "*Pure*," because Meinongians might also advertise themselves as "deflationary metaphysicians." See Azzouni (2012a, 2014b).

Quantifier neutralism, however, is even more illuminating about what there is, and that's the aim of this book. One recent debate concerns "quantifier variance," that unrestricted quantifiers with different domains have different "meanings" and that despite this they can be equally good.[3] Philosophers have variously claimed that implications of this are conceptual relativity, or anti-realism, or that ontological debates are purely verbal. Others feel threatened by ontological incommensurability, an inability to make sense of ontological disagreements.

I show in part I that these worries arise from artificially tying the ordinary existence notion to the technical formalism of first-order quantifiers—as Quine and Carnap originally did, and as nearly everyone continues to do.[4] Everything straightens out once this unnecessary linkage goes.

Part I aims to make quantifier neutralism *visible*. Not just philosophical inertia prevents this. The popularity of Quine's criterion is a symptom of natural (and probably innate) cognitive mechanisms that prevent philosophers from seeing why quantifier neutralism is even *possible*. What seems possible, instead, are positions close to but different from quantifier neutralism. Meinongians are *certainly* affected this way, as I'll illustrate shortly, but all metaphysicians are.

I.2 The Aboutness Illusion

One cognitive phenomenon that blinds philosophers to quantifier neutralism is the "aboutness illusion." In talking or thinking about something *that we know doesn't exist*—Hercules, say—we involuntarily experience ourselves as nevertheless talking or thinking about a *something* that's different from other nonexistent somethings we could be thinking of or talking about instead, for example Pegasus. Cartwright (1960, 24) depicts the deeply entrenched aboutness illusion, and the bewilderment it causes:

> It is at least disturbing to be told that when we finally tell our children that Santa Claus does not exist, we say nothing about Santa Claus. Presumably they *expect* to hear something about him—the truth about him, one way or the other. ... Nor is it much consolation (to us or to them) to be told that we say

---

[3] See Hirsch (2011a). The idea dates back through Putnam's work (e.g., 1990) to Carnap (1956b).
[4] Some philosophers—Hirsch (2011a) and Cameron (2010) are examples—use quantifier variance to *partially* emancipate themselves from Quine's criterion. But they don't systematically work out the implications of this semantic liberation.

nothing about him *in the same sense* as that in which we say something about Caesar when we say he crossed the Rubicon; for it is not clear that "about" has an appropriately different sense.

"About," surely, doesn't have an appropriately different sense. We can say "We've been talking about Santa Claus *and* Barack Obama." This indicates that—in this respect—language parallels cognition. Nevertheless, we really are talking about nothing at all (and we *know* it) when we're talking about what we know doesn't exist.

Aboutness illusions prevent us from seeing that when we describe quantifiers as "ranging over things that don't exist," we don't need those "things in the domain" otherwise metaphysically characterized. Talk of "domains" is a sheer (and philosophically misleading) metaphor for a technical device, "objectual truth conditions for quantifiers": truth conditions for object-language quantifiers given via metalanguage quantifiers rather than some other way—by substituting terms for quantifier variables, for example. This means that whatever is ranged over by object-language quantifiers corresponds to—is "contained in"—whatever is ranged over by the metalanguage quantifiers. Philosophers searching for objects won't find more in the metalanguage than this linkage between the *quantifiers* of two languages. Objects *may be* ranged over by metalanguage quantifiers (and therefore ranged over by object-language quantifiers); but, of course, this needn't happen. And regardless, objectual semantics is unaffected. This is why (objectual) quantifiers are ontologically neutral.

So we needn't engage in "domain metaphysics." There's no need to explain how things "in the domain" that don't exist are different from other things ("in the domain") that don't exist; we needn't posit that things "in the domain" have properties their possession of which makes true, or false, assertions about them (e.g., "Santa wears red"); nor, finally, must we characterize the "domain" of these quantifiers as containing items like "the objects of thought" or "intentional objects" and so on. This isn't required, anyway, *to make sense of the semantics.* (See the appendix to this introduction for a more extensive discussion.)

Although talk of domains is metaphorical *and* philosophically misleading, I'll nevertheless *extensively* use it—especially in part I. That's because it's a metaphor that can be *completely unpacked* in technical terms, and because it's *much* easier to state facts using this metaphor than the technical terms it stands for. To say, for example, that "the quantifiers of two languages L_1 and L_2 have the same domain" is to (really) say that there is a metalanguage interpretation of the quantifiers of those two languages L_1 and L_2, so that

$(x)_{L_1}(\exists y)_{L_2}(x=y)$ & $(x)_{L_2}(\exists y)_{L_1}(x=y)$—where $(x)_{L_1}$, $(\exists y)_{L_1}$ and $(x)_{L_2}$, $(\exists y)_{L_2}$, respectively, are metalanguage quantifiers restricted, appropriately, to the domains of L_1 and L_2; that is, $(x)_{L_1}(\text{—})$ stands for $(x)(R_1 x \to \text{—})$, where R_1 is the characterization of the domain of the quantifiers of L_1 (and so on, at considerably more length). Anyone who understands this introduction—especially the appendix—will not be misled by talk of "domains," and will appreciate the brevity of such talk.

1.3 Near-Miss Positions

There is an empirical question—of linguistics—whether our uses of particular phrases semantically exemplify ontological neutrality or instead force ontological commitment. Investigating this empirical question presupposes *seeing* quantifier neutralism first, and what makes *that* hard is the aboutness illusions that bewitch us into thinking that talk about something (or reference to something) presupposes a *particular* something (even if it's Mickey Mouse).

Meinongians try to capture the evident fact that Santa Claus and Hercules don't exist, while nevertheless (and incompatibly) satisfying the cognitive illusion that if we're thinking about Santa Claus, we aren't thinking about the *same thing* as when we're thinking about Hercules. That's why we're told strange things by Meinongians, such as Santa Claus and Hercules (who don't exist) nevertheless have different properties, or have different forms of being, or even that they are distinguishable "intentional" beings that we're talking about in some very robust sense of "about." This isn't right—this isn't even *sensible*—unless these claims are metaphors for "*Words* like 'Santa Claus' and 'Hercules' have different properties, and because of this, the *sentences* these words appear in can have different truth values; but how those sentences acquire their truth values has nothing to do with the *things* these words refer to" (because, after all, there are *no* things *these* words refer to).[5]

Part I is about making quantifier neutralism visible. One way is to distinguish the view from the other views I've been mentioning. Another is to notice how usage supports quantifier neutralism but not its competitors. I discuss the nature of this usage evidence in the appendix to this introduction.

---

[5] These points can be made with "thoughts" and "concepts" instead of "words" and "sentences." Notice also that "refer," as used here, is a technical coinage: as the word is ordinarily used, "Hercules" refers to Hercules and not to Pegasus. The word "about" is similar. See Azzouni (2012b) for a description of the *regimentations* that straighten this out.

I.4 Object Projectivism

Once philosophers see quantifier neutralism, a doctrine about *language*, they'll be able to see a second distinctive and perhaps shocking *metaphysical* position. This is *object projectivism*—the topic of part II. Think of an object as shaped out of material, the way a statue is shaped out of marble. Describe the two Aristotelian-flavored components of objects as, first, their ontological boundaries (their contours in space and time) and, second, the stuff they're composed of.[6] The object projectivist claims that neither ontological *boundaries* (ontological *contours*) nor *stuffs* are *worldly*. They are both projected onto the world by *us*. (By humans.) What's left—what I call "features"—*are* in the world. (We project some features too—in my view. But not *all* features.)

Several psychological mechanisms cue us (involuntarily) to project objects (boundaries and stuff) on the world. There are, for example, the many ways that *perception* cues so much around us as objects. Not all our senses impose object-experiences on us; smell probably doesn't, but sight surely does. Apart from that, language contains numerous "reification" practices. Finally (but I'm not exhaustively characterizing object cues), objects are invoked—intuitively, but not just intuitively—by our methods of scientifically and commonsensically explaining and understanding events (phenomena) in the world. More dramatically, our understanding of explanation is deeply entangled with the projection of objects. I discuss this a little bit in section 4.5, section 6.9, and section 9.4, but this topic—really—deserves a book of its own.

I.5 Vagueness and Stability Positions in Metaphysics

The phenomenon of vagueness is an important indicator that object projectivism is right. The object projectivist *expects* vagueness because object borders are human projections and human projections needn't be exact. In any case, vagueness—heap problems—is, like talking about nothing, among the earliest philosophical puzzles: ancient Greeks worried about both.

Vagueness continues to drive contemporary debates by forcing them to "stability positions." Here's a recipe of *many* philosophers. Presume, first,

---

[6] Mathematical points are thought of as objects despite missing stuff; and stuff—water or butter, say—is usually seen as missing contours (although we don't experience stuffs as objects). I'm not offering a necessary condition on objects (ontological contours plus composition out of stuff); I'm just trying to provide an easy way to see what object projectivism denies.

that ontological borders are worldly. Next, claim that any object has determinate borders. Finally, force philosophers into metaphysical commitments to (and only to) objects that aren't vague.

Avoiding vague objects isn't the only factor motivating stability positions, although it is one of the more important ones.[7] *Chairs* are puzzling, for example, because it's not clear (i) what's included in the chair at a time and what's not (that is, which chair-bordering molecules are, and which aren't, in the chair), and (ii) exactly when, during the manufacturing of a chair, it comes to be, and when, during its subsequent destruction, it ceases. Call these "ontological contour questions" (or "contour questions"). What's taken as required are principled (non-arbitrary) grounds for answering contour questions. The apparent impossibility of principled answers to contour questions about chairs motivates denying that chairs exist. Stability positions posit only those kinds of objects for which principled answers to contour questions are available.

Monist positions (e.g., Horgan and Potrč 2008) are one family of stability positions: all (purported) ontological borders are denied except for the outermost boundary around everything. Another set of stability points are "nihilist" positions (examples are Unger 1979, Unger 1980, van Inwagen 1990, Merricks 2001, and Dorr 2005). Its purported objects are "simples," as they're usually called—hypothesized entities that aren't composed of anything smaller and that have sharp spatiotemporal borders.[8] Both sorts of positions are "eliminativist" positions insofar as they deny some or all commonsense entities that are composed of other entities.

A third position (mereological universalism)—variously called "universalism" (van Inwagen 1990), "Explosionism" (Sosa 1999), or "Amorphous Lumpism" (Eklund 2008)[9]—handles vagueness by multiplying entities in every possible way. Any possible ontological border is *actual*. Every way that an object *could be* ontologically contoured is a way that some object *is*

---

[7] It's the main (and acknowledged) maneuver of, for example, van Inwagen (1990) and Horgan and Potrč (2008). See the warning in Lowe (2012, 92–93) about using vagueness as a tool of argument. As I show in this book, object projectivism has the resources to diagnose and tame vagueness; but vagueness *isn't* used to make the case for the position. Other standard tools used by metaphysicians to force stability positions (that the object projectivist rejects) are "arguments from explanatory redundancy," "arguments from arbitrariness," and "arguments from bruteness." (I borrow this terminology from Korman 2009, 251.) I discuss why object projectivists avoid these other argumentative tools in chapter 6.
[8] Van Inwagen (1990) isn't exactly a nihilist because he argues for additional objects—living beings—apart from simples. Someone could take space-time points as "simples."
[9] Dummett's (1973, e.g., 563) "amorphous lumpism" isn't this. It's "stuff" metaphysics: object contours are imposed on the world, rather than the different versions of possible object already being out there. For object projectivism, by contrast, "stuffs" are projections too.

ontologically contoured. Mereological sums of objects are objects too. This is stable because no exclusionary decisions are made: all choices are ontologically significant.[10]

These positions, notice, assume *there are* objects (object boundaries are worldly), and go on to offer arguments for why some contour conditions determine objects while others don't (or an argument for why *every* contour condition does). Usually overlooked (in the sense of not being recognized as even a *possibility*) is object projectivism: that no heavy metaphysical lifting determines which purported borders between objects are genuine and which aren't—because *none* are genuine, *none* are metaphysically real.

I.6 Getting Our Minds Around Object Projectivism

The primary reason for the invisibility of object projectivism is the involuntary nature of our projection of objects on the world that's a ubiquitous aspect of our psychology. We experience ourselves as surrounded by objects; we constantly talk about objects using language that seems to have objecthood truth conditions. It's extremely hard to systematically think through all this into recognizing the possibility of object projectivism.

One point. Eliminativist philosophers who deny commonsense objects—like the metaphysical nihilists and monists cited above—must embrace a central corollary of object projectivism: we project (linguistically or psychologically) *commonsense* ontological borders. The *real* borders of objects (these philosophers say) aren't where we speak of them (or experience them). They are where these philosophers have "proven" them to be. One major (but intuitive) piece of evidence for the existence of ontological borders, however, is that we experience them. These views, therefore, are evidentially on all fours with object projectivism—at least as far as ordinary intuitions are concerned. The same holds of mereological universalism, since we *don't* experience all the numerous ontological boundaries that there are (on this view) but only a minuscule subset of them. Mereological universalism, thus, is also on all fours with object projectivism—again, at least as far as ordinary intuitions are concerned.

It's tempting to say object projectivism denies the existence of objects altogether. There are no objects "out there." This thought induces ontological *vertigo*. One thinks the object projectivist's universe is a "buzzing blooming

---

[10] Another stability position is argued for by Heller (1990). All "filled" space-time *regions* are objects—and nothing else is. The position is close to (or identical to) mereological universalism.

confusion"—a *fuzzy* ontological *mess*. No, it's not. Characterize object projectivism this way instead: Start with the world as *you* currently imagine it—all its objects interacting in the various ways that you experience and conceptualize and talk about them as doing. Object projectivism requires two steps. First, erase *all* (and *only*) the ontological boundaries. Claim: *everything out there, nevertheless, is still the same.* (It's not that, grossly, all the *insides* of the various former objects are now spilling out all over the place and intermingling together.) "Everything is still the same" because all the *relational* occurrences, all the *property* occurrences, all the *lawlike* shifts of those property and relation occurrences (over time), and all the causal *effectings* are still there. *All* that's missing are ontological borders around chunks of what's going on, so that we can say: here is one object, here is another object. ... The object boundaries as originally perceived are limitations *imposed* on the real, not features *of* the real. We could *draw* such (four-dimensional area-enclosing) perimeters on the world, of course, but they aren't there to begin with. And drawing them adds nothing new to the world, although it does add something to our discourse. Some philosophers convey this by talk of "carving"—but I'll largely avoid such language because it misleadingly suggests the world is being modified by the process. (I should probably avoid "chunking" or "slicing" too.)

The second step is a little harder to imagine. Removing object boundaries leaves intact an impression of *stuff* that can *flow*. We can imagine this stuff *here* is later that stuff *there*. Think of the water in a river moving along a riverbed, or sand moving through an hourglass.[11] Now remove the projection of identifying foreground movements of the "same stuff" against a background. What are left are *features*, or *feature-occurrences*, at various times and places with no identifications of these across times and places.[12]

Another way to "get one's mind around" object projectivism is this. Imagine God creates everything in the universe. He creates *ways of being*: property and relation occurrences that are here, there (and everywhere). It's better to use feature-placing sentences (Strawson 1953–54, 1959) to describe what God

---

[11] Van Inwagen (1996, 58 n. 2) briefly considers a universe of "pure" butter, but that's implicitly ruled out for him by an indispensability argument: talk of objects *of some sort* is required. See Horgan and Potrč (2008) for a description of their "jello-world." I've mentioned Dummett (1973), but also relevant is Putnam (e.g., 1987, 19), who often spoke of "slicing the same dough" to convey his—at that time—conceptual relativism. I discuss conceptual relativism later in this introduction, and explain why it too isn't object projectivism.
[12] Imagine the motion of a car depicted on a computer screen. Pixels in different places on the screen (at different times) are lighting up and dimming, as well as changing colors. Now remove the pixel as the lower-limit unit of space that shifts over time in its features to make this analogy fit object projectivism better.

actually creates. At this point, everything that *could* be in a world is there—there's nothing more for God to do (or that he could do) to further distinguish objects from one another (and there's nothing more for him to do to add "stuffs" into the world either).

I can, finally, put the matter this way. One thing *not* found in the world is what Sider (2011) describes as "distinguished structure," what others have also described as "quantificational joints,"[13] but what's more illuminatingly described as *ontological borders*. Ontological borders (or contours) are *not* worldly, I argue. They are imposed on the world; more accurately, they are the many ways *we* experience—and describe—things to be in the world and to be distinguished from one another.

As I'll show, there are many ways to project ontological borders; this latitude can be captured formally by quantifiers having different domains. It might seem, therefore, that object projectivism is *existential relativism* (Sosa 1999, 133): "what ... exists relative to one conceptual scheme may not do so relative to another." No—the views should be distinguished.

Existential relativism is motivated this way. Start with "quantifier immanence": domains for different quantifiers (in distinct languages) arise by slicing the same world differently. The object projectivist agrees. Presume next these different quantifier domains are why sentences with these quantifiers have ontological commitments to different kinds of objects. This last step licenses conceptual relativity. It also presupposes what object projectivism denies: these specialized domains contain different *objects*. The object projectivist only accepts that the domains of the differing quantifiers contour the world differently: they contour different *topics* for "conversation." This *doesn't* introduce different *objects*.

Here's another way to make the point. To be true, "what ... exists relative to one conceptual scheme may not do so relative to another" requires that "exist" is understood so that "A shoe exists" is false if the *contours* demarcating the shoely areas of space-time aren't *themselves* worldly—despite the feature distribution being the same. *This* is rejected by object projectivists: they think features *exist*, and they don't see why the truth or falsity of a genuine metaphysical existence claim should turn on projected contours.[14]

---

[13] Sider (2004, 646) writes that "existence is a logical joint in reality." Also see Cameron (2010, 15) on "natural" "quantificational structure" and "the meaning for the quantifier that carves the world at its quantificational joints."

[14] Avoiding existential relativism this way, and also the response to the charge that object projectivism falsifies ordinary ontological claims about concrete objects, will be developed in chapter 7. Object projectivists thus avoid an issue facing monists who accept the cogency of quantification depending on ranging over objects. Since such monists think the "blobject" (the one big thing) is the only object there is, they need Byzantine truth conditions to "indirectly" connect truths

Object projectivism isn't a relativist position. Although it describes object boundaries and stuffs as *our* projections, this *isn't* to say that the "objects" resulting from such boundaries and stuffs are "relative to us." For one thing, the features of objects are still left in the world after removing the projected borders and stuffs. There *are* features in the world, the object projectivist thinks, even if we're not right about all of them. But, further, it's misleading to describe what we project as "relative to us." Consider a border stipulated between two countries. Should we say that such a border is out there "relative to us"? The object projectivist disagrees with the object realist about what's really in the world. This is a genuine metaphysical disagreement, and it muddies the debate to bring in talk of "relative to." This is *not* to deny that borders in a clear sense are *our* stipulations. This is why borders are our "projections."

I.7 An Analogy Between Ontological and Geographic Borders

The border between two geographic entities can be abstract, but *in practice* it's often a meandering bit of fence, the beginnings of a mountain range, a riverbank, and so on. *Real geographic features* often function as borders, or as parts of borders. We *could* say borders are metaphysically supervenient on geographic features; we could even describe a "border" as a second-order notion (or property). It's better to say instead that, when imposing borders, we sometimes use features as borders; and sometimes the border (or some of it) occurs undistinguished, abstractly marking out a region of space without anything in that space distinguishing the border. There are no necessary and sufficient conditions implicitly inducing particular geographic features as borders.

Geographic borders, some might think, are legal conventions. Not always: we *do* experience certain geographic regions as having natural boundaries. Indeed, we *experience* certain geographic items—rivers, mountain ranges, ponds, fields, forests, and so on—as bordered. Experiencing geographic objects as bordered, of course, is compatible with being unable to determine precisely (or sometimes even roughly) where those natural borders are. Nevertheless, the experience of such natural borders can't be

---

about the way the "blobject" *really is* to ordinary quantificational claims like "there are shoes." See Horgan and Potrč (2008, especially section 6.4) on what they call "particularist" truth conditions. See Schaffer (2012) and Lowe (2012) for criticisms of Horgan and Potrč's undeveloped discussion of truth conditions.

denied. So we might persist in thinking of certain geographic regions as having *natural borders*.

Mistakes are possible. One might think natural features are projected the way legal borders are. They aren't. Natural features are *there*. Apart from certain epistemic challenges that I won't raise in this book, we can be taken as seeing objective aspects of the world when we see such features, as, for example, the changes in physical qualities where a mountain range ends, or the changes in mass and material at a river's edge.

The second mistake is to think that somehow such natural features implicitly reveal definitive conditions, *necessary and sufficient conditions*, that characterize the where and when of geographic regions. No. A border seen at a certain level of grain (viewing the edge of a forest from an airplane) may turn fuzzy at a different level of grain (viewing that edge from the ground). If necessary and sufficient conditions were implicitly in place for a particular geographical area (for a forest, say), changing the grain of viewpoint wouldn't raise puzzles about where that area begins and ends.

The third mistake is thinking our stipulative legal practices must respect natural borders insofar as we experience them. Not so. Our stipulative legal practices can incorporate or *ignore* natural borders. For example, our legal practices governing the borders of countries often take advantage of our experience of natural borders. Nevertheless, the official borders of an area may meander independently of those natural borders.

In all these ways our experiences and practices with geographic borders are quite close to our experiences and practices with object borders.

I.8 Object Projecting and "Deep Metaphysics"

Object projecting is deep. It's deep not just because it's basic to cognition—that's true, of course—but because it operates in many *independent* ways. As I've indicated, it arises not only because our senses seem to present us with objects but because language induces object projecting as well. Although I won't say *everything* in part II about the mechanisms of object projection, I think I'll say enough for the purposes of this book.

Hirsch often describes the commonsense notion of an object as a mess, and his rhetoric can get quite emphatic. He writes, for example:

> Our ordinary referential apparatus is not just vague, it is incredibly *messy* in various ways. If you try to divide up the totality of (actual and possible) successions of bits of matter into those which common sense does, and those

which common sense does not, count as constituting a "unitary object," you don't seem to find any kind of neat set of necessary and sufficient conditions on which this division is based. Rather you seem to find something more on the order of a "complicated network of family resemblances" vaguely marking off the "unitary objects." ... No one could possibly look at the vague mess of our concept of an object and say: "*That* is the uniquely correct concept of an object." (Hirsch 1999, 43–44, italics his)

And he also writes:

> Our common-sense selection function [a function that determines what, according to common sense, is an object and what isn't], as far as one can make it out, seems to be an amorphous and intractably complex mess, containing in all likelihood disjunctive conditions and grue-like exceptions. (Hirsch 2004, 138)

Conceding that the commonsense notion of an object lacks necessary and sufficient conditions, however, doesn't yield its complete incoherence—that nothing systematic is at work. I'll illustrate in this book the several aspects to our experience of ordinary objects: the sometimes conflicting inputs from our visual faculties—from our senses more generally—and those from our language (and theorizing practices). These conflicting *faculties* contribute to the appearance of intractable complexity and vagueness of the commonsense notion of an object. (I'd prefer to say the notion is *tractably* complex and vague.) Indicating the various projective mechanisms of our object-notion makes clear why it has been an intellectual trap for so long.

The old philosophical issues about objects are still with us: among them, when what are *prima facie* two objects is actually one, what "dynamic cohesion" relations objects at particular times have to themselves later, what "constitution" and "persistence" conditions objects obey. These issues appear in new forms, however. We now need to explain the principles at work when we project contour boundaries on the world. This subject area is still recognizable as what Hirsch (2011a) derisively labels "deep ontology," except that it now incorporates psychology and language. Object projectivism Kantifies ontology. But only partially: Kant's view, notoriously, made characterization and understanding of "the thing in itself" impossible *in principle*. That's false of object projectivism: we can—*in principle*—determine what's projected and what's not. Our contribution and the world's contribution are *factorable*.

1.9 More "Near Miss" Philosophical Positions

First, there are pure idealist or constructivist positions. Many philosophers, including Kant, Goodman, Carnap, Putnam, and Quine—not to mention nineteenth-century and early twentieth-century idealists—treat our and the world's contributions as *unfactorable*. One way to motivate *metaphysical unfactorability* is to deny that metaphysically real predication survives the demise of the metaphysically real object. Objects *and* the properties and relations attributed *to* such objects, some may argue, are a conceptually indivisible package. If objects are projections, then the relations and properties attributed to objects are projections too. Predication needs both objects *and* what's predicated of objects.

Maybe so. But dumping the whole package doesn't leave us mute, unable to describe what's in the world. For we can understand a distribution of worldly *features* unaccompanied by worldly object boundaries: we can understand (although not *experience*) the world as the same—with respect to features, with respect to "how it is"—without objects. *How so?* some may protest. *You just used the phrase "how it is."* Rejoinder: Sure, but "it" is pleonastic, just as it is in weather talk. We say "It's cold outside," or "It's raining."

This is a radical metaphysical move, and it motivates new terminology that I'll give in chapter 7. Objects, properties/relations, *and* the predication relation *are rejected*. Instead of predication there is an "is at" relation. This radical metaphysical move *appears* to be accompanied by radical changes in the logic/syntax of natural and formal languages. No—at least as far as logic and language are concerned, the result is pretty conservative. Not so of the metaphysics. In any case, this is why object projectivism doesn't collapse into idealism.

Talk of distributed features invites comparison to a second set of near-miss philosophical positions. Many philosophers deny spatiotemporal objects, or what they call "substances," just as the object projectivist does. They instead invoke properties and relations, or tropes—items they call "entities" or "constituents," which they construct everything else out of, including what other philosophers call "objects." This "bundling" is either set-theoretical or mereological, or whatever.[15] Properties and relations (or tropes) function as

---

[15] See, e.g., Simons (1994, 1998), Paul (2012, 2013). Paul (2012, 251) writes: "I have described my properties as 'qualitative natures,' and taken them to be a kind of repeatable universal, perhaps akin [to] Aristotle's nonsubstantial forms. Properties are located in virtue of being qualitatively fused to spatiotemporal relations or relational properties. They are the basic constituents of the world, hence all universals are instantiated, where this just means that they exist and are parts of the world-whole." She regularly calls these things "entities" (e.g., Paul 2012, 244). Simons (1994,

objects on these views—but the object projectivist is a pure metaphysical deflationist who denies properties and relations, or tropes, or anything metaphysically like these. I'll illustrate the differences in viewpoint in the next two paragraphs.

Suppose the universe is a spread of features. We can, it seems, adopt any of several positions. Perhaps what's distributed in the universe are particulars—tropes—that resemble one another (the way that two exemplifications of Red resemble one another). Or perhaps, instead, there are properties—Redness and Greenness, for example—that are exemplified here and there: Redness can repeatedly occur in different places at the same time. Furthermore, perhaps constructions of various sorts exist too—bundles of these properties or tropes, or mereological sums of them, or set-theoretical constructions of them. These are rich enough—this is the view of some metaphysicians—to supplant objects or substances completely.

The object projectivist denies these existence claims. The feature distribution of the world isn't itself (composed of) tropes, particulars, (immanent) universals, or anything like that. Relatedly, *either* to say that features multiply occur in various places *or* to deny this (by calling them tropes) and to say instead that they occur uniquely but resemble one another, is—from the object projectivist's point of view—to offer competing *identity* conditions for what are mistakenly taken to be objects. Consider a red-feature in two places. The object projectivist claims that both a two-place feature *and* one-place features are at the two places; but it's illegitimate to ask whether *in reality* it's the *same* one-place feature (Red) that appears and that bears the identity relation to itself or two *different* one-place features (Red_1 and Red_2) that bear the resemblance relation to one another. Either choice treats features as themselves objects and dictates particular object-boundary contours for *them*. Of course, to *impose* one or the other identity condition on features is the same as introducing ontological contours into the world; nothing stops us, but we must recognize that we are projecting. Similarly, although object projectivists allow (non–ontologically committing) quantification over these things (if it's useful), and consequently also allow set-theoretical and/or mereological

---

565) writes: "We should not . . . take seriously the view that tropes, whether they are ways or not, are not entities at all. Clearly a bundle theorist cannot, because then he would be building entities out of non-entities. Ways and other tropes are not nothing, hence they are something, hence they are entities. But they are not THING-like, if by that we mean substance-like. They are not *res*, they are *rei* or *rerum*." Still, he writes: "It is prudent not to be too dogmatic about the gulf in being between substances and tropes." Dasgupta (2009) also has a metaphysics of universals without individuals—but his view about individuals is eliminativist rather than constructivist. My thanks to Anthony Adrian for stressing the importance of distinguishing these substantial metaphysical positions from object projectivism.

constructions out of them, they deny these quantifications induce a requirement of supplying identity conditions.[16] I discuss this in section 7.2.

1.10 The Notion of an Object

I take "deep ontology" seriously: the claims I've announced in this introduction, and which I subsequently justify, are about *how the world is*, as well as about how we project. Nevertheless, there is still a sense in which these claims are metaphysically *shallow*. Our notion of "object," more significantly the notion of "existence" that "object" is conceptually connected to, could have been different. *It could have been* that our concept of an object had necessary and sufficient conditions; *it could have been* that laws of "dynamic cohesiveness" apply if something at one time can be identified with something at a different time. In the same way, to resurrect the analogy with geographic regions and their borders, it could have been that we *defined* borders in terms of human artifacts, such as fences. More dramatically, our *experience* of objects could have been this quite different way. If we cognitively project objects on the world one way, we could have cognitively projected objects on the world some other way—subject to constraints on brain engineering, of course.

This observation requires discussing at least three points. It must be shown, first, that the *meanings* of words like "exist" or "object" are free of such necessary and sufficient conditions. (This discussion is in chapter 3.) Second, the (possibly contingent historical/biological) reasons must be sketched for why our notion of an object has its particular semantic properties. (I do some of that in chapter 9, but the discussion is promissory because this turns on empirical results we don't have yet.) And third, it must be indicated why we shouldn't "regiment away" our ordinary notion altogether: replace it with a newly minted, better-behaved one. (Some of that discussion also takes place in chapter 3.)

One reason for retaining our notion of *object* could be that the already-in-place notion is indispensable. Or it could be optimal: anything else (in particular, anything accompanied by necessary and sufficient conditions) has major drawbacks. This will, somewhat, be looked into in the course of this book.

Notice these considerations are *conceptual*. They aren't about *metaphysics*: what the concept corresponds to. To make this clear, imagine that we actually

---

[16] For contrasting sentiments, see Simons, as cited in footnote 15.

understood "ontological border" to mean "such-and-such necessary and sufficient contour conditions on concreta." Suppose that we always experienced *objects* (the ontological borders of objects) as obeying those specific necessary and sufficient conditions. That, nevertheless, *wouldn't* be a universe with genuine ontological borders. It would be a universe with a certain feature distribution where we *understood* "ontological border" to pick out certain configurations (in space and time) as objects; it wouldn't be a universe where in addition to physical configurations (of such-and-such sorts) there was *something else*: ontological borders.

I.11 Mistakes About Language Engendering Mistakes About Metaphysics

G. E. Moore (1903) hypothesized that goodness was something in the world—a non-natural property that we experience. His view, with what in hindsight looks like a pretty dubious epistemology, was subsequently worked out in detail by ethical intuitionists. In retrospect, it may be thought (*I* think this) that all this was due to a misunderstanding of normative words. Whether or not this is true of Moore and his immediate philosophical descendants, misunderstandings of ordinary words *are* widely at work in contemporary ontology.

Many contemporary ontologists (and metaontologists), on the contrary, are proud of their emancipation from the twentieth-century linguistic turn. They take themselves to no longer mistakenly confuse ontology with ontological language.[17] But nothing in *philosophy* is that easy to pull off. If we don't get our *language practices* with certain words right, we won't get ontology right either. We'll distort metaphysics because of misunderstandings of the words needed to *do* ontology and metaontology. An important, and related, confusion is one between metaphysics and semantics. Semantic considerations (for example, about truth conditions and the like) are often misinterpreted in ways that legislate unjustified metaphysical conclusions. This must also be straightened out if we're to become clear about what there is and what it's like.

As I've been stressing, object projectivism can't be seen if the position isn't developed along with quantifier neutralism. Nevertheless, if *you* grasp quantifier neutralism well enough to apply it systematically, then you can skip part I. (You can skip the appendix to this introduction as well.)

---

[17] See Cameron (2010) for discussion of the "ontological turn" and "ontological turners."

I've described object projectivism as (currently) invisible. That isn't exactly true: it has been characterized in at least two papers (and thus seen fairly clearly by at least *three* philosophers), although their failure to defend the position adequately betrays the lesson of the last two paragraphs. "Ontological nihilism" is described as a position that "repudiates ontology altogether" (O'Leary-Hawthorne and Cortens 1995, 145) or one that claims "there is nothing at all" (Turner 2011, 3). The second formulation is surely wrong; but the former is too. Far worse, however, is that both papers don't explore the so-called nihilist position much at all but instead worry about the cogency of various paraphrase projects because of the overwhelming concern (in both cases) to capture the expressive capacities of (first-order) quantifiers without importing existential commitments. Such papers, therefore, are unintendedly ironic explorations of how badly "ontological nihilism" is served when quantifier neutralism is overlooked. A corollary lesson of these two papers is this: Get clear about the mechanisms of language—of quantifier languages in particular—*before* engaging in metaphysics.[18]

Here's a dramatic proclamation of one of the main theses of this book: *To restrict oneself to expressively impoverished interpretations of formalisms—and, worse, to demand that our understanding of natural language only be seen in those terms—is to drastically restrict the options for how we can conceive reality to be.* Object projectivism is a way that reality might be that eludes metaphysicians not because of genuine challenges to the position but only because of entrenched false views about logical formalisms and language.

Last point. At the moment this book is being published, there is a lot of excitement in certain metaphysical circles about what's variously called "grounding," "ontological dependence," or "ontological priority." Some things (sets, modes or tropes, fictional characters, etc.) are taken to "ontologically depend" on other things (the objects the sets are of, the substances or things the modes or tropes are the modes or tropes of, fictional artifacts such as books and movies, etc.). A deflationary metaphysician can't take this seriously—for want of the appropriate categories of *things*. (See Azzouni 2012a.) So I'll have—pretty much—nothing to say about this family of notions. There's nothing in the world, according to the object projectivist, to be the relata *at both ends* of this supposed grounding relation. Something interesting is going on in the *neighborhood*, however, that I'll discuss—especially in chapter 9. This is that, on the basis of what there is, we often generate further object-*talk* that in turn impels additional object-experiences.

---

[18] My thanks to Nat Carter for drawing my attention to these papers, and for discussion.

In doing so, our talk induces apparent ontological-dependence relations—like that of sets to the items they are the sets of. There actually *would be*, for example, metaphysically exciting ontological dependence relations between sets and what they are sets of ... *if only there were sets*. But there aren't.

Effingham (2012) thinks the differences between pure deflationary metaphysicians and grounding proponents are terminological. What pure deflationary metaphysicians describe as "mere talk" about what doesn't exist still has to be grounded in what these metaphysicians take to be real, just as the grounding proponent (e.g., Cameron 2010, Schaffer 2009) has to ground what she thinks isn't fundamental in what is fundamental; once the unreal is assimilated to the not fundamental and the real to the fundamental, the projects look indistinguishable. Not so, as I show in chapter 4. Proponents of grounding, like their ancestors—fact-correspondence theorists—must provide object-to-object reductions (of some sort) or at least sentence-to-fact reductions: they require something that deserves the name *grounding*. The appropriate model for our talk, however—according to the pure deflationary metaphysician—isn't grounding but holistic and global *coherence*. Talk about nothing is indispensable for various reasons (among them our inability to talk directly about all and only what exists). But this doesn't imply what in any case isn't true: that there is a sentence-to-sentence (or object-to-object) grounding relation between our talk of what doesn't exist and the "real content" that is its truth-conditional ground.

Appendix

A Sketch of Proofs for the Ontological Neutrality of Semantics for Formal Languages, a Description of the Empirical Evidence for Ontological Commitment in the Vernacular, and the "I Don't Understand Neutral Quantifiers" Objection

A.1 Formal Languages and Ontology

Quine's criterion for ontological commitment uses an artifact of formal notation—the existential quantifier. His influence (as well as that of the logical tradition he belonged to) makes talk of ontological commitment in terms of existential quantifiers natural—the recent doctrine of "quantifier variance," for example, terminologically focuses on quantifiers. But it's more accurate, both for the first-order formalisms interpreted by Tarskian objectual semantics and for other traditions for interpreting natural-language quantifiers (for example, the generalized-quantifier tradition), to target instead "the domain" or "the universe" that quantifiers "range over." I can, in this way, make the case for ontological neutrality in a general setting that covers both the Tarskian semantic tradition and other ones.

Consider a first-order formalism accompanied by Tarskian semantics. This is a first-order language—quantifier expressions, predicate expressions, variables, and so on. A domain D is given, on the basis of which an interpretation I is defined for the above expressions—the one-place predicates are interpreted by I as subsets of D, the individual constants are interpreted by I as individuals in D, and so on. A recursive definition of the truth (or falsity) of every sentence of the formalism, in turn, follows from I and the syntax of that formalism. If, for example, a predicate P is assigned a non-empty subset of D by I, then the sentence $(\exists x)Px$ is true under I.[19] Quinean ontological commitments are to the *kinds* of things a discourse is committed to. Kinds of things, in turn, are characterized by one-place predicate expressions (both primitive and defined) Qx that a language can express. And ontological commitment to Qs occurs when such an expression holds of something in the domain—that is, when $(\exists x)Qx$ is true of the domain.

The ontological neutralist challenges the ontologically committing role of the existential quantifier in first-order formalisms by challenging the idea that the domains D *must be* understood as containing existing things. Opponents of neutralism correspondingly deny that a domain D (partially or fully) containing nonexistent things makes sense. A "domain" intrinsically contains *things*; if a domain is "given," objects (that exist) must be what's "in" it.[20]

So why *must* Tarskian semantics "give domains" that contain existing *things*? This turns on the language of the semantics (the "metalanguage") when a domain D is "given." This language is also a first-order language, and the domain D is the extension of a predicate R; that is, the domain D is given by some sentence of the form $(\exists X)RX$ of the metalanguage.[21]

Domains, therefore, aren't "given" outright (whatever that could mean); they are *characterized descriptively* by sentences of the metalanguage. In particular, they are characterized descriptively by sentences of exactly the same

---

[19] I abuse use and mention here, and throughout the book, as is customary now.
[20] "I do not know what a domain can be other than a domain of existing things," someone might say. I thank an anonymous referee for this way of putting the objection.
[21] In general, $(\exists X)\neg RX$ is true as well because more is often needed for the semantics of a first-order language than the quantifier commitments of that first-order language: often a richer background set theory is involved, and is therefore part of the domain of the metalanguage.

form as sentences that occur in the language the semantics is for: sentences that descriptively characterize collections of objects, for example, $(\exists x)Px$.

The result is straightforward. That it *doesn't* make sense for a domain D to contain what *doesn't* exist is equivalent to: It *doesn't* make sense for an existential sentence in the metalanguage, of the form $(\exists X)RX$, *not* to be ontologically committing. We have just traveled in a very small circle. Nothing about objectual semantics for first-order languages—specifically the invocation of domains—reveals *additional* resources for opponents of ontological neutrality beyond what they had to begin with. If an argument succeeds that "domains" D, to make sense, *must be* composed of existing objects, then the same argument succeeds about any ordinary sentence, such as "There are Ps," where this is something we take to be true. (And so any reference to domains or to the objectual semantics of first-order languages in this argument is idle.)

Someone might respond that the literal meaning of quantifiers is given in terms of domains. And so the response I just gave sends the problem upstairs by insisting that the metalanguage quantifiers can be interpreted neutrally as well. But then we face the same issue of intelligibility we did before, though now in terms of the metametalanguage.[22] This way of putting my response, however, misrepresents its force. The response to the intelligibility worry isn't that the quantifiers of the metalanguage can be interpreted neutrally; that's true, of course, but not central to the response. Central to the response is that talk of "domains" is metaphorical, and when the metaphor is unpacked in terms of what objectual semantics really does, it reduces to the claim that the opponent can't make sense of a certain set of metalanguage sentences unless they are interpreted as ontologically committing. Invoking domains is rhetorically effective but not a genuine observation about *objectual semantics*. To say, for example, that the objects *themselves* "are there to be used in reasoning in the metalanguage"[23] is to commit a use/mention error. What's in the metalanguage is only what's in the object language, which is sentences and characterizations—and that's what we reason with, not objects! Thus the intelligibility demand has returned to where it began after a short epicycle generated by talk of "domains": as a concern with whether certain *sentences* can be understood without interpreting them as about what exists.

It might be thought that this is a tie. No. The neutralist has claimed that nothing about the Tarskian objectual semantics of first-order languages

---

[22] My thanks to an anonymous referee for raising this objection.
[23] Again, I thank an anonymous referee for putting the objection this way.

requires a true interpreted sentence, $(\exists x)Px$, to be ontologically committing. Nothing *requires* its truth to involve existing somethings that it's interpreted in terms of. The opponent claims *specifically of domains* that they don't make sense unless they only contain existing things. This begs the question against the neutralist since a domain is *fully* characterized by a true interpreted sentence of the form $(\exists X)RX$. If considerations exist that require domains to make sense only if they contain existing things, those considerations have to go beyond both formalisms and their semantics to how formalisms *must be* applied to natural languages, and to how sentences of those formalisms *must be* understood when so applied. I take this up in the next section.

Notice, meanwhile, that these points generalize to generalized-quantifier formalisms because these formalisms are interpreted by metalanguages quantifying over sets.[24] As before, a domain (or "universe") D is given, the various predicates are interpreted as subsets of the appropriate cross-products of the domain D (for example, a three-place relation R is a subset of the cross-product $D \times D \times D$), and the various quantifiers are defined as operations on the set-theoretic extensions that predicates are interpreted in terms of.

Consider, for example, statements such as "At least five Ps are Qs" ("At least five of these apples are rotten") or "There are infinitely many Ps that are Qs" ("There are infinitely many numbers that are prime"):

(at least five)$_D$(P, Q) $\Leftrightarrow$ $|P \cap Q| \geq 5$,
(infinitely many)$_D$(P, Q) $\Leftrightarrow$ $P \cap Q$ is infinite.

That the semantics of generalized-quantifier formalisms don't force ontological commitments on generalized quantifiers is easily established in one of two ways. One is to notice that (in general) the background set theory of these semantic theories is first-order. So the neutrality of the generalized-quantifier formalism follows from the already established fact that the "domain" D of the (first-order) metalanguage is "given" by a first-order sentence of the form $(\exists X)RX$ that needn't be ontologically committing. The second way is to do it directly. If we presume that the quantifiers of the background set theory are themselves generalized quantifiers, we can replicate the first-order formalism argument about the "domain" D in their terms. The same argument goes through without difficulty.

---

[24] See, e.g., Peters and Westerståhl (2006), Keenan and Westerståhl (1997). For a nice introduction, see Westerståhl (2011).

These two arguments similarly extend to languages with indexical expressions, such as "I" or "you," where the metalanguage is presumed either to be first-order or to have the same devices as the language the semantics is for. Imagine, for example, that a language contains the phrase "That [noun phrase]," which is accompanied by a gesture. Consider the uttered statement "That vase is ugly." A standard truth condition is this:

> An utterance u, at time t, by speaker s, of "That vase is ugly" is true iff there is an object (a vase) o, designated by s by her use of "that vase," at time t, and o is ugly.

Because a first-order quantifier (here transcribed as "there is") is used in the truth conditions, and this idiom is neutral (that is, the "domain" D that the quantifier ranges over needn't contain anything real), the use of "that vase" is neutral as well. If, on the other hand, a truth condition is given that employs the same idioms in the metalanguage that appear in the object language, for example, "that vase," then the truth condition will be something like:

> "That vase is ugly" is true iff that vase is ugly.

Here the phrase "that vase" is accompanied by the same gesture (in the same context) in both clauses. And if the phrase "that vase" is neutral in one case, it's neutral in other.[25]

To conclude: If an argument against ontological neutrality can be made, it isn't via the ontological requirements of semantic theories; it can't be the argument that the technical device of domains doesn't make sense unless it contains only what exists. I turn now to exploring other possible resources for the opponents of ontological neutrality.

A.2 A Description of the Empirical Evidence for Ontological Commitment in the Vernacular

Raw empirical data rarely plays an evidential role all by itself. It's usually accompanied by theory. The erratic orbit of Uranus, for example, wasn't data *all by itself* for the existence of a planet with such-and-such a trajectory and mass (Neptune). Uranus's orbit being characterized as "erratic," to begin

---

[25] Azzouni (2010a) contains a more extensive discussion of the neutrality of the various semantics for demonstrative and indexical expressions.

with, required an already-in-place theory of orbital motion that described what the trajectory of Uranus's orbit should be, given the other known massive bodies in the solar system. Sometimes, though, theory can't bear directly and decisively on an issue, and raw empirical data has to do a lot of the work. The previous discussion of semantic theories—that such theories don't impose ontological commitments on any of the terms they provide the semantics for—shows this is the case for the empirical question of whether the neutralist is right about natural languages.

It would be different if "domains"—as they technically operate in semantic theories—could be shown to *require* existing entities to be made sense of. Then a direct argument from the general form of semantic theories to how terms in the vernacular must be interpreted would be available.[26] This aside, the relative plausibility of alternative theories about how ontological commitment operates in the vernacular *is* affected by other constraints arising from linguistic theory. For example, ambiguity views about the word "exist" are made plausible (or implausible) by how similar "exist" is to other ambiguous expressions.

But, linguistic theory aside, what does the *data* look like? Speaking of theories of natural-language syntax, Chomsky (1986, 36) describes linguistic data this way:

> In actual practice, linguistics as a discipline is characterized by attention to certain kinds of evidence that are, for the moment, readily accessible and informative: largely, the judgments of native speakers. Each such judgment is, in fact, the result of an experiment, one that is poorly designed but rich in the evidence it provides.

This was equally true for semantics at the time—as Chomsky explicitly states—and it remains true for both subjects to this day. That means that empirical data has to take the form, nearly enough, of numbered sentences on a page alongside the author's indication that the items exhibited are acceptable, unacceptable, or questionable. McNally (2011, 1835) recently writes:

> Williams (1984) argues that if the coda were the main predicate, it should be able to extract like a main predicate. But as the contrast between (16a-b) shows, it does not.

---

[26] This was the dream of Davidson, and the numerous philosophers influenced by him.

What follows is the evidence:

(16) a. How sick were the children?
b. *How sick were there the children?

McNally adds: "Such reduced acceptability under extraction is characteristic of adjuncts."

Evidence of exactly this kind appears absolutely everywhere in the linguistics literature. It takes the form of a numbered list of sentences that evoke impressions in readers. In this case, because readers (it's presumed) share the impression of "reduced acceptability," the numbered sentences are evidence of the claim of the author.

It's philosophically misleading to describe this evidence as "intuitions"—if only because the word "intuition" is so vague. Rather, the data in question is a prediction (based on the linguist's competence as a language user) of usage acceptability. Provided that the linguist's idiolect sufficiently matches those of other speakers, the evidence generalizes beyond the linguist's individual case. If not, the evidence isn't falsified; it's restricted to a special case.[27]

This makes clear why the questionnaire studies that experimental philosophers like aren't informative or even relevant. Such studies *may* show that the data in question is restricted in its scope (restricted, even, not to the linguist, but to the linguist in special circumstances)—but that's something that can otherwise be verified without introducing the additional artifact-dangers that questionnaire design poses.

I'll provide plenty of usage data in part I. It will essentially be of the form that I've described here.

A.3 The "I don't understand neutral quantifiers" Objection

This is a family of objections that haven't, to my knowledge, made it into print, but which I've repeatedly run across nevertheless—in informal conversation as well as in anonymous referee reports. Among philosophers, the "I don't understand" objection rhetorically operates in several different ways; it's important to separate these in this particular case. There are, first, objections based on premises the neutralist is directly challenging. If the opponent refuses to relinquish these premises, the result begs the question against

---

[27] One way that linguists avoid narrowing the relevance of their data is to test it on others.

the neutralist. For example, there is the charge, rebutted in section A.1 of this appendix, that a domain that contains things that don't exist "makes no sense." A similar begging of the question is a refusal to raise objections to the neutralist position—as it's stated—but instead reinterpreting it in the opponent's favorite alternative formalism. So, for an example pertinent to this case, the opponent may refuse to take the neutralist position as it's stated (e.g., as applying to the case of Tarskian objectual quantifiers) but instead take it as a version of free logic or as involving a semantics of inner and outer domains (where predicates that are taken to hold only of existing items correspondingly have extensions restricted to the inner domains).[28]

There is, second, the *genuine* puzzlement engendered by aboutness illusions. The philosopher who *can't* believe that to think of Hercules and Pegasus *isn't* to think of two different things will be forced to accept that it's impossible to think of (or talk about) what doesn't exist. Even in this case, it's possible to get that philosopher to understand that one can sincerely disagree, and so an interpretation of statements like "Hercules doesn't exist" along neutralist lines is *possible* despite that philosopher's inability to "understand" it. Furthermore, it's clear that this issue of understanding is independent of whether there is an internal problem with the neutralist viewpoint or whether it faces a problem accommodating linguistic data.

Finally, there is the non-negligible point that when a philosopher claims not to "understand" something, this often means only that the philosopher has an objection. To *this* philosopher, I can only say that there are plenty of meetings of objections in this book. I tell a pretty full story in part I about the neutralist approach. Included are: a discussion of truth, a discussion of what makes statements true, resolutions of vexing issues such as Geach's Hob-Nob problem, and much else.

A.4 Applying Neutral Quantifiers

It's important that the issue of the neutrality of interpreted formal languages and the question of the neutrality of natural languages come neatly apart. The argument given in section A.1 of this appendix (first given in Azzouni 2004a) has become widely recognized as decisive.[29] This isn't true of the

---

[28] This type of begging the question is used, most notably, by Lewis (1990) against Routley's version of quantification. For a response, see Azzouni and Armour-Garb (2005).

[29] See, for example, Bueno (2014), Collins (2011), Craig (2011), Crane (2013), Fine (2009), Raley and Burnor (2011), and others. Neutral quantification, as I mentioned earlier, doesn't foreclose on any particular metaphysics. Unsurprisingly, therefore, there isn't much overlap in metaphysics between me and other philosophers who have recognized the cogency of neutral quantification.

neutrality claims I made (also in 2004a) about natural languages. Those claims continue to be mired in controversy.[30]

This means, however, that regardless of my claims about the ontological neutrality of the idioms of natural language, the semantic-neutrality-for-interpreted-formalisms result increases enormously the flexibility of how formal languages can be applied. An analogy will help.[31] Until the late nineteenth century, Euclidean geometry was understood to be a theory (or description) of actual space. This interpretation of it explicitly restricted how it could be applied: one only used "straight" applications. Once non-Euclidean geometries were invented, and especially after Euclidean geometry was rejected as a theory of actual space, it was recognized that geometries can be applied quite usefully in many different ways. When Euclidean geometry is applied to a tabletop, for example, it isn't that the actual geometry of that tabletop is presumed to be Euclidean. "Non-straight" applications of geometry are extremely useful, and this is why Euclidean geometry, in particular, hasn't been discarded but continues to be as useful for us as it was when it was taken to be a theory of actual space.

Even if my claims about the ontological neutrality of natural-language idioms are empirically refuted, this won't fault the applications of the insights of neutrality to metaphysics that occur in part II of this book.

---

[30] See, for example, Asay (2010), Hofweber (2007b, 2009), Raley (2009), Schaffer (2009), and others.
[31] I owe this analogy to Eric Dean.

I | Ontological Commitment

The ontology to which an (interpreted) theory is committed comprises all and only the objects over which the bound variables of the theory have to be construed as ranging in order that the statements affirmed in the theory be true.

—W. V. Quine (1951a, 11)

1 | Transcendence and Immanence

1.1 Introduction

First, a required bit of terminology. A *context-restricted use of a quantifier* (implicitly) understands that quantifier to range over a contextually-restricted subset of the relevant domain. An example is an utterance of "There are no chairs," when used to indicate there are no chairs in the room the speaker is in. A *context-unrestricted use of a quantifier* has no contextually induced restrictions.

I start off by characterizing the immanent and transcendent perspectives on interpretations of *unrestricted* quantifiers *across* different first-order languages. According to the *immanent* perspective, unrestricted first-order quantifiers of different languages differ arbitrarily in their domains. They have different "quantifier meanings," as it's often put these days. The *transcendent* perspective requires unrestricted first-order quantifiers across different first-order languages to have one domain.

The immanent perspective seems explicit in Carnap (1956b), in his general presentation of "linguistic frameworks." "The world of things," "the system of numbers," and "the system of propositions," for example, are frameworks explicitly stipulated to be different languages because of what their unrestricted quantifiers range over, and not just because of their differing non-logical vocabulary. Contemporary philosophers who couch metaphysical issues within the quantifier-variantist framework, such as Bennett, Eklund, Hirsch, and Sider, also take the immanent perspective.

I make the case in section 1.2.2 that there is sufficient textual evidence to attribute the transcendent perspective toward the (first-order objectual) quantifiers to Quine—at least by 1960. The difference between Quine's and Carnap's perspectives toward quantifiers is due to Quine having adopted by that time a single-language-bound natural-language perspective, as opposed to Carnap's free-ranging artificial-language perspective. This difference in attitude toward formal languages, in turn, isn't because of the issues that Quine and Carnap famously sparred over, that is, the analytic/synthetic distinction and the internal/external distinction. Rather, Quine's later naturalism holds that we're trapped within our natural language (although we can *regiment* it with formal devices). According to Carnap, on the other hand, we can easily adopt any of a wide number of artificial languages.[1]

In section 1.2, I characterize these language-bound and language-free perspectives, and from them I deduce a difference in attitude toward quantifiers. Hirsch (2011a), interestingly, splits the difference between Quine and Carnap by adopting the immanent viewpoint toward the quantifiers while simultaneously ridiculing the suggestion that we can desert the language we speak. In section 1.3, I discuss Hirsch's complex views as well as some objections to his views raised by critics, and then give my own objections.

I conclude the chapter with a discussion of ontological debates. Although they can be straightforwardly understood given the transcendent perspective, they seem impossible given the immanent perspective. This discussion also prepares us for the evaluation of quantifier onticity that takes place in later chapters.

"Quantifier immanence" is new terminology. I'll connect it to the widely used expression "quantifier variance." "Quantifier variance" is slippery, but it's largely used as Hirsch (2011b, xii) uses it: *There is no uniquely best ontological language with which to describe the world.* Quantifier immanence is weaker: it allows varying quantifier domains without any comparisons of the values of domain choices. Quantifier immanence is presupposed by quantifier variance. The reason it hasn't been distinguished heretofore from quantifier variance is because recent participants in ontological debates are more interested in grander issues—whether there is (or isn't) a *best* ontology for a set of quantifiers.

One last preliminary point. The forthcoming metaontological discussion reveals an important difference between how I approach quantifier variance and how much of the literature does. My discussion is restricted to the first-order context: I'm disallowing plural quantification, and *largely* disallowing supplementary formalizations of one or another kind of modal idiom that *some* of these philosophers help themselves to. The reason *isn't* that this was

---

[1] For a subtle and nuanced presentation of the evolution of Carnap's views on artificial languages, see Carus (2007). The adjective "easily" is probably inaccurate. But it certainly applies to the "Carnap" of the contemporary philosopher—especially the contemporary metaphysician—who invokes him whenever an anticipation of quantifier variance is needed. See Eklund (2008), Hirsch (2011a), Putnam (1990), and many others.

how Quine framed his debate with Carnap (although that's true). The reason is that Quine's criterion, which remains a touchpoint in this literature, becomes murky when non-first-order resources are introduced. Although they clearly increase the expressive powers of the languages they occur in, many philosophers insist they are ontologically innocent. This is debatable.[2] But in any case, first, conflicts between the different views of quantifier domains can be seen clearly in the first-order context; second, the cogency of the various objections to those different views can also be seen clearly in that context; and third, philosophical results about first-order quantifiers generalize without changing much in character when additional formal apparatus is added.

Nevertheless, these aren't the primary considerations. Rather, once quantifier neutralism is motivated in chapter 4, the bearing of beyond-first-order-logic on questions of the ontological commitments of discourse and even on questions about how to interpret the ontological commitments of others (when those ontological commitments differ from the ontological commitments of the interpreters) will be seen to *vanish*.

1.2 Immanent and Transcendent Quantifiers: Carnap and Quine

I first present the immanent and transcendent perspectives on the quantifiers.[3] *The immanent perspective* takes quantifier domains—when quantifiers are unrestricted—as language-specific. First-order languages, therefore, are individuated not just by their non-logical vocabulary but also by what their unrestricted quantifiers range over. There is a similar individuation of the "metalanguages," as the languages characterizing the semantics of specific target languages (the "object languages") are called.[4]

To characterize the contrasting *transcendent* viewpoint of unrestricted first-order quantifiers, it's best to focus on a specific *family* of first-order languages. Then the unrestricted quantifiers of all such languages are taken to

---

[2] Worse than debatable. It's wrong *on technical grounds* to think plural quantifiers or higher-order logics don't induce additional Quinean ontological commitments, *pace* Boolos, Lewis, van Inwagen, and many others. See Azzouni (2015), where I give tools that measure the Quinean commitment costs of plural-quantifier formalisms (and other formalisms as well). But as what I momentarily say shows, I don't have to establish this *now*.
[3] This distinction is derived from—but not identical to—one that Quine (1986, 19) draws. He writes: "A notion is immanent when defined for a particular language; transcendent when directed to languages generally."
[4] The ur-text for all this is Tarski (1983a).

have the same domain. The two perspectives, therefore, can be distinguished by considering any two languages L_1 and L_2, and considering a metalanguage M of *both* of them where the range of the quantifiers of M includes the ranges of the quantifiers of L_1 and L_2. If M contains equality, and $(x)_{L1}$, $(\exists y)_{L1}$ and $(x)_{L2}$, $(\exists y)_{L2}$, respectively, are metalanguage quantifiers appropriately restricted to the domains of L_1 and L_2, then $(x)_{L1}(\exists y)_{L2}(x=y)$ & $(x)_{L2}(\exists y)_{L1}(x=y)$ is true on the transcendent view; it needn't be on the immanent view. In practice, a moderate version of transcendence is usually *induced* in a specific language by using (and only allowing) Tarskian tools to interpret any alternative language: one's own language is the metalanguage of the alternatives. The domain of any alternative set of quantifiers, as a result, must be a *subset* of one's own quantifier domain. An extra bit of argument is needed if a philosopher wants full transcendence, as we'll see Quine does.

1.2.1 Carnap's immanent quantifiers

As I've indicated in section 1.1, it's easy—on textual grounds—to credit Carnap with the immanent view. Apart from characterizing different linguistic frameworks in terms of their differing vocabularies, Carnap also distinguishes them by their "different variables." For example, Carnap (1956b, 209) begins his discussion of "the system of propositions" by writing: "New variables, '*p*', '*q*', etc., are introduced. . . ."

Also, although Carnap accepts Quine's criterion for what a discourse is committed to, he resists considering this being old-fashioned "ontology." He writes:

> Quine has repeatedly pointed out the important fact that, if we wish to find out what kind of entities somebody recognizes, we have to look more at the variables he uses than at the constants and closed expressions. . . . I am essentially in agreement with this view, as I shall presently explain. [But] I should prefer not to use the word '*ontology*' for the recognition of entities by the admission of variables. This use seems to me to be at least misleading; it might be understood as implying that the decision to use certain kinds of variables must be based on ontological metaphysical convictions [whereas] the decision to use certain types of variables is a practical decision like the choice of an instrument. (Carnap 1956a, 42–43)

He also writes:

> We may still speak (and have done so) of "the acceptance of the new entities" since this form of speech is customary; but one must keep in mind that

this phrase does not mean for us anything more than acceptance of the new framework, i.e., of the new linguistic forms. Above all, they must not be interpreted as referring to an assumption, belief, or assertion of "the reality of the entities." There is no such assertion. An alleged statement of the reality of the framework of entities is a pseudo-statement without cognitive content. (Carnap 1956b, 214)

Quine's criterion, for Carnap, functions as a language-internal indicator of the kind of variables involved in a language—specifically about how the variables in a language are functioning. They indicate nothing extralinguistic. Talk of reality, apart from the practical choices made in choosing variables, are "pseudo-statements devoid of cognitive meaning."

1.2.2 Does Quine interpret the quantifiers transcendentally?

That Quine's view of the quantifiers is the transcendent one is harder to establish.[5] My primary evidence is the shift Quine exhibited from the early 1950s to the publication of his *Word and Object* in 1960b: the emergence of his "naturalism." Accompanying this naturalism was the requirement to start "with ordinary things." As Quine puts it near the beginning of his book:

> Neurath has likened science to a boat which, if we are to rebuild it, we must rebuild plank by plank while staying afloat in it. . . . If we improve our understanding of ordinary talk of physical things, it will not be by reducing that talk to a more familiar idiom; there is none. It will be by clarifying the connections, causal or otherwise, between ordinary talk of physical things and various further matters which in turn we grasp with the help of ordinary talk of physical things. (1960b, 3)

This should be seen for what it really is: a rejection of artificial languages (*Carnap's* artificial languages) as various *alternative* languages that we can adopt (while deserting ordinary language). Esperanto is a utopian ideal; so is the idea that we can replace ordinary language with something else—an artificial language in the style of Carnap.[6]

---

[5] I once wrote (2004a, 126): "On Quine's view, our quantifiers range over what exists, not over what we merely take to exist." Peñaranda (2013, 686 n. 4) criticizes me for interpreting Quine this way. I can still make the case that I'm right—but not in the easy way I earlier thought it would go. My thanks to Juan Peñaranda for making it clear (in emails) that this bit of Quinean exegesis isn't *obvious*.

[6] There are complex issues here that neither Quine nor Putnam ever explored—although both philosophers pushed "no cosmic exile" throughout their careers. What's called for is an *empirical* exploration of the possible role(s) of artificial languages in our cognitive and social lives—logical languages in particular, but also various computer languages. Can (and do) we actually *use* these

This may be a surprising interpretation of *Quine*: he never seemed to like ordinary language philosophy.[7] But this is because Quine saw himself as acknowledging the creative *regimentation* of natural languages, whereas he saw ordinary language philosophy as rooted in an unchanging atavism. Regimentation, for Quine, utilizes the resources of contemporary logic to *modify* otherwise murky aspects of natural language; it's *not* a full-scale replacement of the natural language we speak with something else.

Is this, ultimately, a distinction without a difference? Don't both Carnap and Quine aim for a formal language that's in some way interpreted?[8] One important difference is that Quine—at first pass—is aiming at *a* formal language, but Carnap offers us *many*. This is a first pass because Quine is always aware that we must continue to reason with vocabulary only partially or unsuccessfully regimented at any given time—if that vocabulary is essential to science, as propositional-attitude vocabulary is. The task of regimentation is never done. Carnap's languages are restricted in their vocabularies, depending on the scientific applications needed. Quine thinks the entire language often has to play a role. That's why our natural language can't be *fully* formalized.

The impossibility of "cosmic exile" has a corollary. Alternative languages can't be interpreted *except by* reconstruing them in one's own language. Because Quine restricts "one's own language" to a(n under-construction) first-order language, this is *very hard*. Quine (1960b, 1986) offers extended exhibitions of both regimentations of ordinary language *and* attempts to interpret or translate alternative ways of speaking into ways that *we* speak.

In "On What There Is," Quine still endorses studying various artificial languages, in the "let many flowers bloom" spirit of Carnap, and he even

---

languages—in the sense of speaking them (or something akin to this)? Or is it that we only talk *about* these languages within natural language? This is an important issue, not just intrinsically but also because some contemporary ontologists glibly talk of deserting our natural-language idioms for a new language—"Ontologese," an artificial formal language some philosophers think they speak when practicing metaphysics—and they seem to think this is *easy*: just stipulate that your ontic idioms have the needed referential properties! (See, e.g., Dorr 2005. Also see Sider 2011, 74–77, 172, on introducing "Ontologese.") I won't spar over this now. However, I explore (Azzouni 2006, 2008a, 2008b, 2009a, 2009b, 2011) pragmatic constraints on regimentation and proxying—both being methods of changing or reinterpreting natural language expressions. In Azzouni (2013a), I explore the ways we seem "trapped" in natural languages.

Quine could have argued, although he never did, that how Carnap (1956b) presents artificial languages illustrates the impossibility of "cosmic exile." He presents them, after all, in natural language. This isn't just a practical matter; *sui generis* presentation of the semantics of these language frameworks seems impossible if we're supposed to *understand* them.

[7] See Quine (1969), a somewhat dismissive discussion of Austin's work.
[8] My thanks to Michael Glanzberg for this question.

describes the question of what ontology to adopt as "still open," pending a choice of language framework (1953, 19). But in *Word and Object* (1960b) and thereafter, Quine is no longer open-minded. Ontological questions can still *pend*—subject to how regimentation techniques develop—but this isn't to choose between different language frameworks. It's a matter of how to best regiment a class of expressions in *our* (developing) natural language.

This exegesis of Quine probably requires more textual attention to make it convincing.[9] I want, instead, to sketch why his general approach seems to force transcendence: since you are stuck with how your language currently operates, your quantifiers can only range over what they range over (given how your language is *now*). But then, you have no *choice* but to interpret alien quantifier domains as subsets of your *own* quantifier domain. That subsets of your own quantifier domain are the only choices for interpreting alien quantifier domains seems to follow, anyway, if you agree with Quine that your own language is restricted in its extra-quantifier resources (for example, that there are no operators that can be applied to quantified expressions to shift what their bound variables range over, that the only truth predicates available to you can be applied to the expressions of alien discourse only after those expressions have been translated to your own language, and so on).[10]

---

[9] Nevertheless, I should connect this disagreement with their official ones, if only in a footnote. The Quine-Carnap debate focused on Carnap's internal/external distinction and his talk of "frameworks," on one hand, and his adherence to the analytic/synthetic distinction, on the other. As Yablo (1998, 122–23) notes, these issues aren't close, even though Carnap and Quine *agree* that their debate over analyticity is the source of their dispute about frameworks. But how can this be right? It's true that artificial-language frameworks are set up by "analytic" principles, according to Carnap. It's true that Quine doesn't think there are analytic principles. But how does this bear on *frameworks*? It doesn't follow from there being no analytic principles that there are no artificial-language frameworks. What follows is the uninteresting conclusion that we can't call the principles used to set up a framework "analytic." Quine thinks he's scored a point against Carnap because he thinks he's undercut Carnap's artificial-language frameworks. He hasn't (not by *this* argument, anyway). Undercutting Carnap's artificial-framework approach has to be done directly—as Quine does (by the time of *Word and Object*): we're stuck in one framework (one language). We can't, as Carnap thinks, hop from one formal language to another; we have to regiment the one *we're in*. From this, with a supplementary assumption, it follows there are no analytic truths. And the supplementary assumption is that any purported analytic truth can be regimented away; Quine hopes to show this with the history of applied mathematics. It's only *after* artificial-language frameworks have been *ruled* out that Quine's holism can undercut analyticity, not before—as he is so often interpreted. This is important, since Quine admits that Carnap is a holist too, and explicitly draws his holism *from* Carnap. (Yablo stresses this last point [1998, 124 n. 20].) I should note that for Quine, "ruling out artificial frameworks" doesn't mean they don't exist. As formal *uninterpreted* language frameworks, they do exist; living speakers (i.e., ourselves) just can't inhabit them.

[10] "*Seems* to follow," because Hirsch offers additional resources—term-independent sentence-to-sentence mappings—that, if successful, deflect this result. See section 1.3.

There is one bit left. The foregoing seems to show that Quine's approach requires all first-order quantifiers (of any language) to range over the *actual* domain that one *takes* one's *own* quantifiers to range over. (If *you* think (∃*x*) Unicorn*x* is *true*, then Unicorn*x* holds of something in *your* domain.) That's not right. Quine announces his fallibilism as often as he announces his naturalism. We can always be wrong. Couple this fallibilism with Quine's criterion and it follows that we can be wrong about our own quantifier domain. Quine thus takes our quantifier domain to be what *exists*, not what we (or anyone else) "take" to exist. This makes no difference *to us*, however, unless we change our minds about what *does* exist. It always matters, though, when interpreting alien quantifiers. Since all quantifiers are taken by Quine to range over all and only what exists, he can't accept moderate transcendence. *And*, since we presume (until proven otherwise) that our own ontology is correct, we take all quantifiers (of any language) to range over what our own quantifiers range over.

It's remarkable that neither Quine nor Carnap ever characterized their disagreements this way.[11] This may simply be because neither of them (nor anyone else) *distinguishes* the two possible interpretations to begin with (let alone diagnoses a disagreement in their terms). Cartwright (1987) and some of Quine's other critics *presuppose* the transcendent viewpoint; the objections they raise to Quine's criterion aren't cogent otherwise. It's similarly striking that much of the subsequent literature in philosophy of language and logic takes the transcendent approach to the quantifiers as sacrosanct: the quantifiers range over *what there is*.[12] This is even true of Meinongians, who extend the quantifier domain to include the odder denizens of Irreal Estate.

One last point about the relationship between the two interpretations of the quantifiers and realism/irrealism issues: they are independent.[13] I explain why in the next four paragraphs.

---

[11] Huw Price (2009) *does* characterize the Carnap-Quine disagreement as being over quantifiers. He focuses not on the transcendent/immanent distinction, however, but on the disagreement Quine (1951b) focuses on over different styles of variables versus one kind of variable. This difference (which Quine uses to press the idea that the disagreement is over the analytic/synthetic distinction) is superficial and, as Price notes, doesn't enable Quine to score points against Carnap.

[12] As Hirsch (1999, 41–42) notes. I eventually explain this tendency as due to our understanding of the ordinary-language word "exist," when used to ontologically commit. See chapter 3.

[13] Hirsch (e.g., 2009, 220) repeatedly observes this about the immanent interpretation of the quantifiers, to distinguish his "quantifier variance" from the "anti-realisms" of Carnap and Putnam. He seems unaware, however, that the transcendent perspective on the quantifiers—one he sometimes attributes to Sider—*doesn't* require a "metaphysically privileged sense of the quantifier." (See Hirsch 2002, 82–83.)

Carnap (1956b), notoriously, is a dismissivist about ontological debates.[14] He doesn't reject ontological realism or anti-realism; he denies the debate is coherent. The immanent interpretation of the quantifiers, however, seems quite natural for anti-realists and idealists because if there is no independent world constraining language, then the quantifiers (of different languages) can differ arbitrarily in their domains. (What they range over being determined independently by the world makes no sense to anti-realists nor to idealists.) The transcendent perspective, on the other hand, seems naturally wedded to a strong realism about what objects there are and aren't in the world.

To show otherwise, suppose a philosopher is convinced that any interpretation of foreign quantifier domains must treat them as subsets of her own quantifier domains because she thinks no cosmic exile is possible, her own language is first-order, and her only tool of interpretation is using her own language as a Tarskian metalanguage. Moderate transcendence follows. Nevertheless, that philosopher could reject Quine's criterion and draw an internal distinction between those things quantified over that she takes to exist and those things quantified over that she *doesn't* take to exist. For that matter, she could be a Kantian about the objects her own quantifiers range over—they are *not* "things in themselves." An anti-realist but nevertheless modest transcendence results from rejecting Quine's criterion while still accepting Quine's austerity about available language resources. Additional presumptions are needed, of course, to get full transcendence, but these don't have to be realist ones. A Kantian may take the "objects" in her domain to be interconnected in such a way that the entire domain must be quantified over if the resulting language is to be cogent.

This should be no surprise. Why would a constraint (for whatever reason, other than a metaphysical one) that one's understanding of alien quantifier domains requires interpreting them as subsets of one's own quantifier domain *all by itself* imply anything metaphysical?

The same is true of the immanent interpretation. Pending resolution of what sorts of semantics are compatible with the immanent interpretation of the quantifiers, it does seem possible to accept a realist view of the most ordinary sort (for example, that there are such-and-such objects in the world with quite specific properties) and yet allow that quantifiers, in general, needn't range over such objects. This requires tweaking the semantics of quantifiers to allow them to range over something other than what exists; the question

---

[14] This lovely term is Bennett's (2009).

whether that's possible isn't *metaphysical*, but just a matter of what semantic mechanisms are possible for quantifiers. (I develop and evaluate tools to allow this in chapter 3.)

1.3 Immanent Quantifiers: Hirsch's View and Objections to it

In various essays, remarkably, Hirsch (2011a) seems to work out a position where immanent quantifiers sit comfortably with the Quinean requirement that we remain within our current language ("English") while being ontologically committed only to those objects that our English (or, more broadly, natural-language) quantifiers range over. Hirsch seems to achieve this without invoking additional expressive resources—plural quantification, modality, and so on—that Quine would have opposed. Moreover, Hirsch seems to have established an important distinction between purely verbal and substantial ontological debates. The purely verbal ontological debates between opponents A and B are revealed by the presence of term-independent sentence-to-sentence mappings from sentences that A takes to be true (but that B would take to be false) to sentences that B takes to be true; substantial debates are revealed by the absence (or impossibility) of such mappings.

I show that Hirsch's ambitious and sophisticated attempt to manage this conceptual wedding fails. The problem, quite simply, is that Hirsch doesn't prove that the needed term-independent sentence-to-sentence mappings exist. A related problem is that if the term-independent sentence-to-sentence mappings do exist, it doesn't seem possible for ontological debaters to find them. One last issue with Hirsch's attempt is that the immanent view of the quantifiers doesn't seem compatible with ontological debates of any sort—substantial or otherwise. This last issue provides some motivation for detaching ontology altogether from how quantifier domains are interpreted, as the neutralist urges, and as we'll see in later chapters.

1.3.1 Hirsch's claim that some ontological debates are purely verbal

How is the purely verbal status of certain ontological debates established? Hirsch borrows an informally described—but nevertheless technical—maneuver of Putnam's (for example, as presented in Putnam 1990). This is to enable *our* interpretation of the sentences of an alien language (with an alien quantifier domain different from our quantifier domain) by means of *sentence-to-sentence* mappings between their sentences and ours. The mappings that Hirsch always discusses are structurally induced by one or another *object-parts mapping* of the respective quantifier domains of the two languages. These sentence-to-sentence mappings are "truth-preserving" in the following sense: what the alien speakers take to be true (respectively, false) is mapped to what we take to be true (respectively, false). Hirsch often calls these "coarse-grained truth-conditional equivalences" (as in Hirsch 2011b, xi) or "coarse-grained truth-conditions" (as in Hirsch 2002, 92–93, and 2005, 158–159).

Hirsch's point in calling these "coarse-grained" is to indicate that, as far as the respective ontological opponents are concerned, these mappings *aren't* to be characterized in a standard Tarskian compositional manner, recursively mapping sentences to sentences via mappings of the non-logical vocabulary to the non-logical vocabulary of the respective languages—for example, mappings of the non-logical predicates of the respective languages to each other. That's why I call these "term-independent sentence-to-sentence mappings," or "sentence-to-sentence mappings," for short.

These mappings disperse the appearance of disagreement between ontological opponents. What one group says (and describes as true) is something, relative to the interpretation of what they say by means of a sentence-to-sentence mapping, that their apparent opponents agree with.

Hirsch (2002, 76–77) offers these sentence-to-sentence mappings as "translations," claiming further that they are *finitary* theories "of truth." Hirsch's point is clear, even though sentence-to-sentence mappings aren't supposed to be Tarski-style theories of truth. In either language, one can define truth for the other language by using these mappings. If S_2 is a sentence of L_2, M is a one-to-one onto mapping of the sentences of L_1 to the sentences of L_2, and T_2 is the truth predicate of L_2, a speaker of L_2 can define the truth of the sentences of L_1 this way: $T_1 S_1$ iff$_{df}$ $T_2 M S_1$. (A speaker of L_1 can proceed similarly.) Speaking of a different example (where he claims a sentence-to-sentence mapping is also available), Hirsch (2005, 158) describes the mapping as satisfying "the demand for a compositional semantics in the only sense in which such a demand has any clear force." He means: truth conditions—by this maneuver—have a finite (recursive) characterization.[15]

---

[15] It may seem that compositional semantics is motivated by more than the need for a finite characterization condition: it's supposed to capture how sentences are understood by speakers in terms of their understanding of those sentence's meaningful subsentential parts—in particular, terms. I won't beg the question against Hirsch (as I claim, later, that Eklund and Hawthorne do) by imposing, a priori, strong conditions on how speakers of one language are to "understand" the sentences of another language. I take Hirsch's approach at his word and directly show its problems. This *isn't* to deny that an argument can be brought against Hirsch

I'll illustrate the maneuver with two types of examples. The first type modifies persistence conditions of objects; the second involves mereological sums. Hirsch (2011a) gives more than one version of each type in various places.[16]

One example of the first type is Hirsch's incar-outcar. In this alien language, cars aren't individuated as we individuate them; an incar, rather, has persistence conditions so that there are no incars outside garages; outcars, correspondingly, don't exist inside garages. Should someone drive her car out of a garage (according to us), what's happening (according to them) is that an incar is vanishing into nothing at the door of the garage and an outcar is spontaneously emerging from it just outside the door of the garage. Another example of the first type is the shree, which, similarly, is a treelike object that spontaneously loses its branches each dusk (although trees don't) and regains its branches at dawn. That is, the persistence conditions of shrees is such that after dusk the branches attached to them are no longer parts of them, but after dawn those branches *are* parts of them.

In a perfectly clear sense, incars, outcars, and shrees are the results of tampering with, respectively, the persistence conditions of cars and trees; alternatively, this can be described as a well-defined (and finite) characterization of an *object-parts mapping* of the parts of the objects corresponding to the terms of one language to the parts of the objects of a different kind corresponding to the terms of the other language. (I'm here allowing that an object-parts mapping maps whole objects as well as parts of those objects.) Furthermore, this object-parts mapping *induces* (Tarski-style) a finite (recursive) characterization of a truth-preserving sentence-to-sentence mapping.

Notice that the apparently deeply peculiar beliefs of the aliens in incars and outcars are, according to the sentence-to-sentence mappings, perfectly ordinary beliefs. There is no real disagreement. For example, the alien sentence "Julie drove her incar from time t_o to time t_m and drove her outcar from time t_m to t_n."—when, during that time, her car emerges from a garage—is mapped to the ontologically unexceptionable sentence "Julie drove her car

---

that the understanding of the sentences of any language requires it be done via an understanding of the meaningful subsentential parts of those sentences—including terms. Hirsch clearly opposes this condition on understanding, and bringing any such argument against him is nontrivial. Nevertheless, I *do* eventually undermine the claim that speakers can discover Hirsch's sentence-to-sentence mappings on the grounds that they don't have access to the object-parts mappings that structurally underlie those mappings. This, perhaps, can be transformed into an argument that the understanding of sentences requires understanding terms—but how to do this isn't obvious. (My thanks to Michael Glanzberg for prompting this footnote.)

[16] These examples—incars and outcars, in particular—seem to first appear in Hirsch (1982, 32).

from time t_0 to time t_n," or perhaps "Julie drove her car out of her garage from time t_0 to time t_n."[17]

The second type of example involves alien quantifiers ranging over various mereological sums. Here too, Hirsch provides a well-defined object-parts mapping that induces a sentence-to-sentence mapping. Consider Clinton's nose and the Empire State Building. This is a disconnected single object (according to this alien language). But a sentence in this language, "Clinton's nose/the Empire State Building is multicolored," is mapped to our ordinary sentence "Clinton's nose is colored c_1 and the Empire State Building is colored c_2."[18] What appears to be a deep ontological disagreement, like before, turns out to be—according to the truth-preserving sentence-to-sentence mapping—just a different way of speaking.

Because of the object-parts mappings involved, it's clear why Hirsch thinks such apparently alternative languages nevertheless describe the world in equivalent ways, where neither way seems superior. It's similarly clear why he describes these particular ontological disputes, over cars versus incars/outcars, or those over ordinary objects versus mereological sums of such, as purely verbal in nature. On the other hand, it's also clear why opponents think the mere *exhibition* of such examples doesn't prove much. For perhaps the most important thing—that there *are* cars and that there *aren't* either incars or outcars—is missing from the comparison between these two languages that yields their supposed equivalence. This metaphysical issue will be taken up in detail in part II of this book, although I'll raise the point again (and do some work with it) in section 1.3.5.

1.3.2 The semantic objection

An *interpretational* rejoinder to Hirsch's views has surfaced (Hawthorne 2006, Eklund 2008, 2009) that I'll call—following Eklund—the "semantic objection." Before discussing its shortcomings, I'll briefly recap the earlier-mentioned presuppositions of Carnap and Hirsch. Carnap offers many languages that vary in their vocabulary and quantifier domains. He is disinterested in how speakers of one language are supposed to interpret the

---

[17] There are complications I'm skipping in the interests of not *suffocating* the exposition—in particular that incars and outcars don't appear and vanish instantaneously but only over periods of time. This can be accommodated either by having incars and outcars vanish and appear instantaneously or by introducing more complicated sentences and correspondingly more complicated sentence-to-sentence mappings.

[18] I'm skipping complications again—in particular, that both an object-parts mapping *and* a corresponding *property* mapping are needed to induce the appropriate sentence-to-sentence mapping. It's easy to see how this goes.

other ones. The point of such languages is only to meet various scientific needs. Hirsch similarly allows quantifier immanence—languages with different quantifier domains. Hirsch, however, *is* interested in how speakers of one language are supposed to interpret other languages. He explicitly introduces term-independent sentence-to-sentence mappings to handle interpretational cases that Tarskian interpretation can't handle. On the basis of the presence or absence of such mappings, he introduces a distinction between substantial ontological debates and purely verbal ones. The debate between car-believers and incar/outcar-believers he takes to be a purely verbal debate because of a truth-preserving sentence-to-sentence mapping between the languages of the debaters. Similarly for lovers of the mereological sum of Clinton's nose and the Empire State Building and their opponents. A debate between Platonists and nominalists, however, is a substantial ontological debate because a truth-preserving sentence-to-sentence mapping between the languages of those debaters *isn't* available.[19]

There is much to be challenged here, and I'll challenge it later. But what's unacceptable is begging the question against Hirsch's assumptions. Nevertheless, the "semantic objection" that both Eklund (2008, 2009) and Hawthorne (2006) raise does exactly that by ignoring Hirsch's sentence-to-sentence mappings altogether and instead *imposing* a requirement that an interpretation of one language by another *must be* Tarskian.

Davidson (1984) notoriously *required* the utilization of a Tarski-style theory of truth for the interpretation of *other* languages. Eklund (2008, 2009) presses Davidson's demand polemically against Hirsch, Putnam, and Carnap. Eklund sometimes formulates the demand directly by arguing that the *semantics* for a language B in a language A requires that truth (for that language B) be connected to the references of the terms of B, and sometimes he formulates the demand indirectly by arguing that languages shouldn't be "expressively impoverished"—which he claims they would be if they couldn't supply a Tarskian semantics (one that connects truth to reference) for *other* languages.

I've already cited Hirsch (2005, 158) as arguing that term-independent sentence-to-sentence mappings satisfy the demand "for a compositional

---

[19] The required mapping doesn't exist if Platonistic commitments are rich enough. Hirsch *doesn't* think the Platonist/nominalist debate is purely verbal, and he *doesn't* demand a charitable truth-preserving interpretation of opponents in substantial ontological debates. He writes (2005, 150–51): "If we pick almost any intuitively substantive dispute, and set ourselves the task of finding some plausibly charitable assignment of truth conditions that will make both sides come out right in their associated languages, we generally find that we have not the faintest idea of how to proceed." See Hirsch 2009, 239–46 on Eklund and the Platonist/nominalist debate.

semantics in the only sense in which such a demand has any clear force." Speaking of another example where he regards the ontological dispute as purely verbal, Hirsch says (2005, 158) that the burden is on the philosopher who denies that these examples provide sentence-to-sentence mappings that supply an "intelligible" interpretation just because they resist "a particular kind of semantic analysis." Those (like Davidson) who say that a Tarskian compositional approach is *required* are clearly being targeted.

It's not responsive to Hirsch, therefore, to *stipulate* that the semantics for a language B in a language A requires that truth (for that language B) be connected to the references of the terms of B. This, after all, is what Hirsch has denied by offering his term-independent sentence-to-sentence mappings to begin with. *One needs to show why Hirsch's alternative is unacceptable.* Eklund never does this. Similarly, it's not an objection to Hirsch (or to Carnap, for that matter) to label a language "expressively impoverished" (Eklund 2009) if it can't manage Tarskian semantics for other languages. So-called expressive impoverishment is an assumption of the quantifier variance setup to begin with. If languages have different quantifier domains, then—except under special circumstances—they can't be used to interpret one another via Tarskian semantics.

Hawthorne (2006) also begs the question against Hirsch. He develops a lengthy example of two angels with different quantifier domains, and asks how "Gabriel" is to interpret the claims of "Michael." Gabriel, Hawthorne presumes, adopts the following principle of interpretation:

> Ref: Sentences of the form "That is F" [in the language to be interpreted] are true only if [something is referred to] by "that"

and he comments, in a footnote (2006, 59, n. 20), that Ref is drawn from Tarski's approach. Hawthorne *doesn't* argue that adopting Ref is a *requirement* on interpretation, as Eklund does. He suggests, rather, that we might discover that an angelic proponent ("Gabriel") *of an otherwise apparently austere ontology* uses this principle along with charity (a "transcendent" truth predicate) in his interpretation of those with more ample ontological presuppositions. It's hard to see why this example (where an interpreter insists on using Tarskian interpretational tools) bears against Hirsch at all. Isn't it irrelevant that someone might try to interpret others using Tarskian tools rather than the sentence-to-sentence mappings that Hirsch explicitly offers for this purpose?

Here's the takeaway lesson. The important question is this preliminary one: *must* Tarskian (term-linked) tools be used to interpret alien languages with different quantifier domains, or can Hirsch's term-independent sentence-to-sentence mappings be used where the former are inapplicable? This question is the one to be answered *first* if we are to evaluate the success of Hirsch's characterization of "purely verbal" ontological disputes.

1.3.3 The finite characterization objection

I've intimated that there are serious problems with Hirsch's sentence-to-sentence approach. Here's the worst one: Hirsch requires such mappings to be *finitely characterizable*. That's what enables ontological proponents to use those mappings as theories of truth for the sentences of their opponents. Furthermore, because Hirsch assumes the respective ontological opponents don't have access to each other's quantifier domains (that's why this is a situation of "quantifier variance"), these characterizations can't recursively operate through terms of each language that refer to the items in these quantifier domains—that is, these characterizations can't be compositional in the sense that they involve term-to-term mappings, where the terms refer to the items in the respective quantifier domains. Unfortunately, Hirsch never *exhibits* the *finite characterizations* of the sentence-to-sentence mappings that he claims are available. This matters because if a finite characterization of a sentence-to-sentence mapping *that includes* a recursion over a mapping of terms exists, it doesn't follow *from that* that a finite characterization exists of that sentence-to-sentence mapping *that's restricted purely to sentences* (and doesn't include a recursion through the object-parts mapping of the quantifier domains).

Hirsch does nothing, that is, to reassure us that his "coarse-grained" truth conditions *exist*.[20] He always (only) alludes to them via antecedent descriptions of the object-parts mappings that induce them, and that he *is* explicit about. It's clear, of course, that the full package of object-parts mappings plus the induced sentence-to-sentence mappings yields a finite characterization of a theory of truth because this mapping helps itself to standard compositional

---

[20] Hirsch clearly intends to understand truth primitively (instead of—as Tarski does with some languages—derivatively in terms of other notions such as reference). And he intends to similarly understand truth conditions in terms of this notion of truth. Hirsch writes: "One thing we need to bear in mind is that our primary focus is on the truth conditions of sentences rather than on the reference of terms" (2005, 156). And he notes: "It must be borne in mind that I have defined the notion of 'truth conditions'—and consistently use it here—in the coarse-grained unstructured sense" (Hirsch 2002, 78 n. 15). Also: "Our concept of 'reference' varies with our concept of 'what exists,' but it should be emphasized that our concept of 'truth' does not thereby vary. Whether we speak [edurantist]-English or [perdurantist]-English we mean the same by 'The sentence S is true in the language L'" (Hirsch 2009, 239).

Tarskian theories of truth for *both* languages. Although Hirsch never does the technical work of showing this (or even sketching how it would go), we can easily see how it works. First we are given a finite characterization of the object-parts mapping between the two domains. Then we induce a mapping of the full compositional Tarskian theory of truth of one language onto the other one on the basis of the Tarskian truth recursion clauses for each language.

But notice that this *requires access to the objects in the domains of both languages*. The problem (again) is that we don't know that a finite (recursive) characterization of this sentence-to-sentence mapping exists that doesn't help itself to the respective domains—unless Hirsch explicitly tells us what it is. A second problem has emerged. Let's say that such a finite characterization of the needed term-independent sentence-to-sentence mapping does exist—after all, I'm not arguing these things *don't* exist. How do the respective populations discover them? (How are *we* supposed to discover them? After all, *we* don't know how to do it either.)[21]

Note the flavor of *these* objections to Hirsch. I'm not imposing access to the reference relation of an alien language a priori as a condition on interpretation and using that condition against Hirsch. I'm taking him at his word: what's required is only finite characterizations of the needed sentence-to-sentence mappings that don't involve terms that refer to the objects of both domains. I'm asking: on what grounds has Hirsch shown that such finite characterizations of his sentence-to-sentence mappings exist? This question is an acute one for Hirsch because his own exposition of these examples *always* utilizes object-parts mappings.

We *lucky philosophers*—who seem to possess *discourse omniscience*, who live (anyway) in a kind of verbal *heaven* from where we can look down on *both* languages and, more importantly, from where we have access to *both* sets of objects—see at a glance that the object-parts mappings (Hirsch describes) induce *compositionally* (and therefore in a finite way) the needed sentence-to-sentence mappings. But usually, in Hirsch's exposition, "we" are supposed to belong to one group of language speakers—English-speakers—and so our

---

[21] There's no reason to think that any finite characterization of a sentence-to-sentence mapping *must be* compositional in the sense of operating recursively on the basis of a mapping of the *terms* that refer to the items in the respective domains. That's why Hirsch's project isn't a nonstarter to begin with. But that any such finite characterization must operate off of the syntax of the respective languages in some way is surely a given (otherwise it won't be a *finite* characterization). One of the reasons Tarski's compositional approach is celebrated is because it's so hard to see how finite characterizations of truth are available apart from his approach.

quantifiers (by assumption) don't range over incars, outcars, perdurantist objects, or any *other* weird stuff.

Hirsch officially intends to detach the requirements on characterizing the truth of the sentences of (some) alien discourses from any requirement on characterizing the "references" of the terms of those discourses, and more generally, from characterizations of the purported ontology of what those discourses are about. This is why the truth predicate that's involved can be understood to correspond to *our* ordinary notion of truth. (Hirsch never speaks of "as-if" truth.) Reference and existence in other languages, on the other hand (and on his view), go dim: they become "as-if" reference and "as-if" existence. Alien speakers do something that *looks like* reference (as in Hirsch 1999). And that's why demanding (as a condition on "interpretation") that reference be taken account of, as Eklund and Hawthorne do, misses the target. The right way to proceed is to notice that Hirsch himself continually invokes referential facts (about *both* domains) to indicate (to us) a finite characterization of the sentence-to-sentence mappings, and then to press him for reasons why a finite characterization of the sentence-to-sentence mappings exists that can be had by either community who can't utilize Hirsch's particular (reference-based) finite characterization.

1.3.4 Characterizing sentence-to-sentence mappings that provide truth conditions without including the object-parts mappings that underlie them

Hirsch (2005) offers a different way of recognizing finite characterizations of sentence-to-sentence mappings to provide truth conditions other than by means of the object-parts mappings that underlie them. He considers a debate between mereological essentialists (who think no object survives the replacement of any of its parts) and four-dimensionalists (who think any arbitrary collection of objects can compose an object and further that any temporal part of an object is an object), and he considers an attempted interpretation of four-dimensional discourse by mereological essentialists. So consider, from the viewpoint of mereological essentialists, the ontologically unproblematic four-dimensional statement

> (1) There is something in the room that is brown, and later there is something in the room that is pink.

There is in the room, imagine, first a brown pencil, and later a pink rubber ball. This statement, by assumption, occurs in both languages—or, more accurately, the mereological essentialists have no problem translating this sentence to one of their own that unproblematically has the same truth conditions. And consider the quite puzzling (to mereological essentialists) four-dimensional statement

(2) There is something in the room that is first brown and later pink.

Again, there is in the room first a brown pencil, and later a pink rubber ball. Four-dimensionalists think these are two temporal parts of the same object. Imagine that the mereological essentialists are groping for a sentence-to-sentence mapping of the four-dimensional language to theirs that includes a mapping of (2) to their version of (1). How do they manage this? Well, they can use the claim of the four-dimensionalists *themselves*, that the *four-dimensional* versions of (1) and (2) are closely linked enough ("a priori necessary") that—in the four-dimensional language—(1) could be used (successfully) to provide the truth conditions for (2). This is enough, that is, for the mereological essentialists to use *their* version of (1) to provide the truth conditions for their versions of (1) *and* (2).[22]

Notice that this works—even if explicit account is taken of the fact that mereological essentialists need a finite characterization of the relevant sentence-to-sentence mapping as well as the fact that they don't have access to everything in the domain of the four-dimensionalists. For we can assume that the four-dimensionalists themselves have a *finite* (domain-compositional) characterization of the mapping between these two kinds of sentences. The mereological essentialists can borrow this internal four-dimensional sentence-to-sentence mapping *even though they don't understand it referentially*; for them it's a finite characterization of a purely syntactic operation on sets of sentences of the language of the four-dimensionalists.

Unfortunately, this maneuver is too *specialized* because it's inapplicable in circumstances that are very close (metaphysically speaking) to other ontological debates. Consider a closely related ontological debate between, instead, mereological essentialists and *variant* four-dimensionalists: the latter think that whenever (1) holds, (2) holds, but that sometimes the reverse *doesn't happen*. (These "restricted" four-dimensionalists think some object-sums don't *decompose* into parts that are *objects*; although they're committed to some objects that are pencil-like early on and are pink-rubber-ball-like later on, they refuse to accept the existence of the relevant temporal slices of pencils

---

[22] See Bennett (2009) for a nice discussion of this strategy of Hirsch's. I'm analyzing the case in a very different way.

and rubber balls, or perhaps any temporal slices of pencils and rubber balls, *as objects*.) In *this* case, there may be *no sentences* that are "necessarily a priori" linked in the four-dimensional language that can be used to provide the needed internal four-dimensional sentence-to-sentence mapping; therefore, there may be *no sentences* that enable a finite characterization of a term-independent sentence-to-sentence mapping of four-dimensional discourse to mereological-essentialist discourse.

Hirsch (2005, section III) allows both mereological essentialists and four-dimensionalists to have access to *set-theoretical* constructions (such as ordered pairs composed of objects and temporal ranges). This gives both groups ample expressive powers, and—assuming (in addition) that both groups are committed to "a priori necessary" linking principles between their own statements about concreta and about various abstracta—finite characterizations of sentence-to-sentence mappings between the discourses are available to both parties.

But consider instead two communities that are committed to cars, on one hand, and incars and outcars, on the other. It's not hard to imagine that such communities may (respectively) refuse to believe in the existence of the other community's objects and, worse, *may be nominalists as well*. Since both communities are composed of nominalists, they won't have access to ordered pairs—of objects and temporal spreads, for example—that speakers of the respective languages might otherwise regard as "a priori necessarily" equivalent to their claims about cars or incars and outcars, respectively, and which the other communities might use to construct sentence-to-sentence mappings between the languages.

In this case, therefore, "a priori necessary" within-language linkages between sentences that will provide the respective communities the needed sentence-to-sentence mappings will be absent from *both* languages. This is despite the impression that an ontological debate shouldn't shift from being purely verbal (in Hirsch's sense) to one that's substantial (in Hirsch's sense) just because we've modified our thought experiments about these communities by imagining them to have fewer ontological commitments (but *without* otherwise affecting the ontological commitments under *dispute* between the communities).

I have to stress that I'm *speculating* about how Hirsch's various claims—about purely verbal ontological debates—link up. Neither he nor his critics approach his discussion as I've done here. Hirsch never seems to address, in his own work, the problem of how the needed finite characterizations of the sentence-to-sentence mappings are available to those speakers trapped within the more austere ontologies. Correspondingly, Hirsch never officially offers the "a priori necessity" move as a solution to *this* problem, as I've presented it. Rather, he offers the "a priori necessary" condition as the "simplest paradigm of a verbal dispute" (2005, 162); but this leaves entirely open how we're supposed to recognize the other cases—the ones he's described as purely verbal (such as car/incar-outcar debates)—as purely verbal if his "a priori necessary" linking conditions aren't available in the respective languages. The articles critical of Hirsch that raise issues in the neighborhood of the ones I've just raised either argue against his simplest paradigm case or beg the question by invoking the semantic objection.

1.3.5 Representing opponent metaphysical views

I've been discussing what Hirsch regards as purely verbal ontological disagreements, and evaluating his tools for identifying such disagreements. Let's focus now on something I've taken for granted: that ontological debates can take place *at all*. According to Hirsch, as I mentioned, these can be either *substantial* or purely verbal. Although the transcendent approach to the quantifiers straightforwardly accommodates ontological debate, such debates—at least prima facie—make no sense if the immanent approach is taken.

There seem to be three *minimal requirements* on an ontological debate (and a debate, moreover, that both parties *understand* is a debate):

 (i) They are disagreeing about something they can describe in common.
 (ii) They can *represent* the statements of their opponents that they disagree with.
 (iii) They can attribute different truth values to those statements.

I'll start by describing how this is supposed to go according to quantifier transcendentalists. Imagine the disagreement is over Bigfoot. There are a number of statements about Bigfoot, statements of the form, let's say, $(\exists x)$Bigfoot$x$, and perhaps additional uniqueness clauses (depending on the beliefs) as well as statements of the form (x)(Bigfoot$x \to Px$) for various predicates P. Bigfoot believers and disbelievers disagree about the truth values of the existential statements about Bigfoot. This satisfies clauses (i)–(iii). The quantifier transcendentalist, in addition, describes one and only one of these opponents as right. This is because there is one domain they share in common and $(\exists x)$Bigfoot$x$ is either true or false of that domain.

In order to apply this simple paradigm of ontological debate to the cases that Hirsch (and other contemporary metaphysicians) are concerned with, let's start by recollecting something I slid by you when I first discussed Hirsch's examples.

I wrote in section 1.3: "The purely verbal ontological debates between opponents A and B are revealed by the presence of term-independent sentence-to-sentence mappings from sentences that A takes to be true (but that B would take to be false) to sentences that B takes to be true." But where is this *debate*, exactly? If A doesn't have access to B's vocabulary, the only way A can interpret B's sentences is by Hirsch's truth-preserving sentence-to-sentence mapping. The same, of course, is true of B. So in what language is their "debate" to be couched? B "would take" the sentences of A to be false exactly *how*? We outsiders, who have access to both domains, can characterize a potential ontological debate between them—if only there were some way for these participants to find common ground *for* a disagreement. But all they seem to have for mutual interpretation is Hirsch's purported truth-preserving sentence-to-sentence mapping, and in that case they will only detect agreement.

The solution looks to be easily within reach. The languages must be augmented so that the languages of A and B have the same vocabulary items. The vocabulary for incars and outcars, cars, mereological sums, or Platonistic objects must appear in the language of disbelievers of incars and outcars, cars, mereological sums, or Platonistic objects. In this way, statements can be formed in the respective languages of the ontological opponents that they can disagree over.

Augmenting the vocabulary in this way is disallowed by Carnap—but Carnap, of course, isn't interested in ontological *debate* at all. Augmenting the vocabulary of ontological opponents so that they can deny truth to the statements of their ontological opponents seems (all things considered) a minor move.

Transcendentalists and immanentists split on the next step. I'll take on transcendentalists first. Transcendental ontological opponents take each other to have the same quantifier domain. Their disagreement—as they would put it—is about what's *in* that domain. I believe cars are there, but not incars or outcars. I can list the various statements about incars and outcars that my opponent believes are true, but I will assign them truth values in accord with how I take the quantifier domain to be. $(\exists x)\text{Incar} x$ is false, in my view, and $(x)(\text{Incar} x \rightarrow Px)$ is vacuously true for every predicate P. I can also recognize that my opponent assigns these sentences different truth values in accord with what she believes. Introduce into my language a two-place relation between sentences and truth values, $B(p, v)$, that characterizes the truth values that my opponent assigns to these sentences. If I know exactly what my opponent and I disagree over, as far as the domain is concerned, the truth conditions of $B(p, v)$ can be given compositionally Tarski-style.[23]

---

[23] This is, actually, easy to see. The crucial issue is only the characterization of the base clauses. Presumably, the disagreements over the instantiations of the primitive expressions can be finitely characterized. Modify one's own Tarskian characterization (of one's own language) in

As I said, the transcendentalist and the immanentist split on their strategies here. Here's what Hirsch writes:

> The quantificational apparatus in our language and thought—such expressions as "thing," "object," "something," "(there) exists"—has a certain variability or plasticity. There is no necessity to use these expressions in one way rather than various other ways, for the world can be correctly described using a variety of concepts of "the existence of something." One of [Putnam's] favorite examples concerns a disagreement between mereologists and anti-mereologists as to how many objects there are in some domain. Suppose we are evaluating the truth of the sentence, "There exists something that is composed of Clinton's nose and the Eiffel Tower." Mereologists will accept this sentence, whereas anti-mereologists will reject it. Putnam's doctrine of quantifier variance implies that the expression "there exists something" can be interpreted in a way that makes the sentence true or in a way that makes the sentence false. Since both interpretations are available to us, we have a choice between operating with a concept of "the existence of something" that satisfies the mereologist or operating with a different concept that satisfies the anti-mereologist. (2002, 68–69)

Now presume I'm an immanentist. The first step is to change my attitude toward the sentences I was disagreeing with my ontological opponent over. In particular, she's *right* about Bigfoot: $(\exists x)\text{Bigfoot}x$ is true. For that matter, so is $(\exists x)\text{Incar}x$, if we're disagreeing about that. In general, the following clause holds for all sentences p if I'm an immanentist: $B(p,t) \rightarrow p$. But wait: don't I think that it's false that there are incars? So how am I supposed to think that my opponent is *right*?

Hirsch gives the solution when he writes of "a variety of concepts of 'the existence of something.'" I'm disagreeing, let's say, with someone about shrees and trees. "Trees exist," I say, "shrees don't exist." "Shrees exist," she says back, "trees don't exist." It *looks* like we're in a fight. (If we're *married*, it's a really bad sign that we're fighting over *this*.) But this misconstrues what's going on. She's not using the same concept of existence that I am. She's using the concept, say, of *shxistence*. I'm saying that trees exist, and that shrees don't; she's saying that shrees shxist and that trees don't. There's no disagreement here at all. For that matter, Platonists and nominalists don't

---

terms of one's own domain to accommodate these. For example, normally the formula Px is satisfied by a mapping of the variables and primitive relations to the domain iff x is in the subset of the domain corresponding to P. Instead let Px be so satisfied, unless B($\exists x$Px,f), and then it isn't. Treat the rest of the truth clauses standardly. Notice the resulting compositional characterization isn't of the truth of these statements (on the transcendental view); it's of what one's opponent *takes to be true*, or thinks is true, given her differing view of the quantifier domain.

disagree either. Nominalists say that numbers don't exist and Platonists think they do exist. But nominalists are talking about nomxistence, whereas Platonist are talking about platxistence. There's no ontological debate here *either*. The picture turns out to be very close to Carnap's. Ontological debate has ceased to make sense.

Hirsch does repeatedly speak of "debates," and he distinguishes substantial ontological debates from purely verbal ones, as I've indicated. But if quantifier variance is pressed seriously, it's hard to see how this can be. All ontological debate has evaporated: everyone is talking past everyone else.

This is sad because there really *is* something intuitively compelling about Hirsch's distinction between purely verbal and substantial debates nevertheless. The Platonist and the nominalist really do seem to be engaged in what looks like an important argument about the status of numbers, for example. On the other hand, the same world *really does* seem to be correctly described—in some sense—by both the mereologist *and* the anti-mereologist. Here is how Hawthorne tries to convey the intuition that certain ontological debates are purely verbal:

> I bring a watch to a watchmaker, who dismantles it. Two communities look on. When I go back to the watchmaker the following week members of one community say "He is picking up his old watch," while members of the other say "He is picking up a new watch, one made of the same pieces that his old watch was made from." Which of them is correct? Many of us are inclined towards reconciliation, unable to take very seriously the thought that one of the communities is ontologically more attuned than the other. (2006, 53)

We can find in Sider (2011) a way of resurrecting ontological debate within the immanent paradigm. This is to presume (against Carnap, in particular) that it makes sense to ask the metaphysical question: Which quantifier domain *really* corresponds to the way the world is? Call this *the correspondence question*. The world itself, that is, divides into objects in a certain way (and not other ways), and more generally, there are (or aren't) certain kinds of objects in the world. If the quantifier domain of a language corresponds to the world (perhaps, even, *is* the world), then that language is "metaphysically correct." Sider would describe such a language—at least as far as the quantifiers are concerned—as carving the world correctly at its joints, whereas other quantifiers (because of their domains) don't.

Whether Hirsch would accept this is unclear to me. (I'll give reasons at the end of this section for why he shouldn't accept it.) It's clear that Hirsch is willing to let the idea that an ontological debate is genuine vanish with respect to *some* debates, but not with respect to others. Unless this correspondence idea is adjoined to the immanent view, I don't see how the immanent view can capture the idea of ontological debate *at all*. But even granting the cogency of the correspondence question, Hirsch still faces a problem distinguishing substantial from purely verbal debates because of the finite-characterization problem his term-independent sentence-to-sentence mappings face.

This is a shame because Hawthorne's quote given above suggests something that Hirsch's discussion of his examples suggests as well. This is the impression that, in some sense, the claim that in some cases there is no genuine ontological debate *doesn't* turn on there being a (term-independent) sentence-to-sentence mapping of a certain sort between languages. It turns, instead, on facts about how the *same domain* is being treated by ontological opponents. But that suggests, in turn, that the "different quantifier domains" approach to these debates is misguided to begin with. In these purely verbal debates the "same world" is being chopped up in different ways, and the debaters are disagreeing about whether different ways of placing boundaries within that same world yield objects *that exist*. This means that the transcendentalist is in a better position to try to capture Hirsch's distinction between purely verbal and substantial debates than the immanentist is.

It might seem that the immanentist can capture the distinction if we allow the ontological opponents additional resources and we accept the cogency of the correspondence question. In Hawthorne's watch case, we have the two different kinds of watches (with different individuation conditions), one in each quantifier domain, but there are also the parts of the watches, and these are shared across the domains. Similarly, the anti-mereologist quantifies over Clinton's nose and the Eiffel Tower, but not their sum. The mereologist shares Clinton's nose and the Eiffel Tower with the anti-mereologist, but his domain contains, in addition, the sum of Clinton's nose and the Eiffel Tower. Their disagreement must include the fact that Clinton's nose and the Eiffel Tower in the anti-mereologist's domain *are* the same objects as the ones in the mereologist's domain.

Are Clinton's nose and the Eiffel Tower in *both* domains? Are the parts of the watch in *both* domains? There is nothing in the doctrine of quantifier variance, as Hirsch presents it, to indicate an answer to this question one way or another. If we treat the opponents as speaking different languages, or as invoking quantifiers that have different meanings because they have different quantifier domains, we can treat the domains as *not* overlapping. Or otherwise. To treat distinctive quantifier domains as indicative of the respective quantifiers having different meanings doesn't require one way or the other that they be disjoint.

Does treating such domains as overlapping in some of their contents secure Hirsch's claim that the debate is purely verbal? There are two problems with this. First, consider the kind of case I've been describing, where the domains overlap. Even accepting this still leaves the impression that the debate isn't purely verbal because at stake is a correspondence question just like the one posed between nominalist and Platonists. The mereologist thinks there is (in the world) a sum of Clinton's nose and the Eiffel Tower; the anti-mereologist disagrees. They are disagreeing, both might agree, on where the borders between objects *are*. But why is *that* debate purely verbal? For one thing, it leads to disagreements about how many objects *there are*. An argument is needed that a debate—in this context—over how many objects there are is itself purely verbal; Hirsch never gives one. The reason for the rider "in this context" is because the Platonist and the nominalist also disagree over how many objects there are, and yet Hirsch doesn't take this to be a purely verbal debate.

But quantifier domains needn't overlap at all, and in general won't. That is, opponents might not want the additional resources I mentioned above because those resources are additional ontological commitments. Ontological opponents, that is, might quantify over, respectively, trees and shrees or cars and incars/outcars, *without* simultaneously quantifying over anything that either they or outsiders would regard as commonly believed to exist. Nothing like the matter in common between trees and shrees, or space-time points, and so on need be in both of their quantifier domains. Or they may disagree about the properties of that matter or those space-time points, so that the space-time points or matter that is in these quantifier domains isn't shared either. The issue is that anything in their quantifier domains is something they take to exist, and they may radically disagree over the correspondence question about what really exists. After all, they need only disagree about something in one respect in order to force disjointness in their domain with respect to that something. This shows that the metaphysical reconciliation intuitions that Hawthorne pumps rely on an artifact about the case: that the parts of the watch are *objects* both communities take to exist.

There is, I think, a worse problem. In accepting the cogency of the correspondence question, the immanentist, in effect, is adopting a transcendent existence concept. After all, what "really" exists in any quantifier domain is what corresponds to what's in the world. This suggests that the immanentist must either reject the cogency of ontological debates or give up his position altogether.

1.4 Some Concluding Remarks

Perhaps this is a small issue, but it's an issue nonetheless. On the immanent view, the impression that certain debates are *only* over how ontological borders are being drawn in the world is one that seems to be deeply sensitive to the other ontological commitments of the ontological debaters. That ontological borders are what the disagreement is over can be seen by both parties to the debate if they are arguing over Hawthorne's watch *and* they agree that the parts of the watch exist. In turn, they may (or may not) feel that a debate that's only over such borders is in some sense purely verbal. But this can't be seen as what's at stake if they don't agree about the parts of the watch—that is, if the parts of the watch aren't in both of their quantifier domains. So too, an ontological debate about trees and shrees can be seen as one that's only over ontological borders provided both debaters are committed to something that the trees and shrees have in common.

So that's one issue. Another is this: some philosophers have the powerful intuition that debates over ontological borders are purely verbal (e.g., Hirsch 2011a, Hawthorne 2006). Of course, some philosophers don't share this intuition—or, at least, they argue as if they don't (e.g., Sider 2011). This second issue is the topic of part II.

The third and most important issue is that quantifier variance (because of quantifier immanence) can't make sense of ontological debate to begin with. Capturing the idea of debate by introducing the cogency of the correspondence question amounts to deserting the variance view. If ontological debate is to be taken seriously, quantifier immanence (and therefore quantifier variance) must be rejected. That is the major conclusion of this chapter. In later chapters I explore a particularly neat way of taking ontological debate seriously: combining a transcendent existence predicate with a neutral interpretation of quantifier domains.

2 | The Transcendence of The Natural-Language "Exist" When Used to Assert or Deny Ontological Commitment

2.1 Introduction

When do non-philosophers *make* or *deny* ontological commitments? Contemporary philosophers have pretty much accepted Quine's complex answer—even those who deny significant aspects of his picture. Non-philosophers, Quine says, rarely think about ontological commitment.[1] Despite this, they *make* (and *deny*) ontological commitments all the time—whenever what they say imposes those commitments (or imposes negations of those commitments). That is, when non-philosophers express sentences they're committed to the truth of, they *ontologically* commit themselves (or deny *ontological* commitments) whenever the locutions used in those sentences force ontological commitments, or their denials.

On views like this, certain locutions, typically used, force ontological commitments: "there ...," as in "There are rabbits in Australia, but not in the Arctic" or "There are angels"; "exist," as in "God exists" or (as pagans claim) "gods exist." Negations of these are ontological denials. But natural-language users also ontologically commit themselves using neither locution, as with "*Dogs* are on the lawn again" or "The raccoons around here will eat the garbage if it's left out."

Despite how these sentences are usually regimented in first-order languages (with (∃x)), in none of them do natural-language *quantifiers* appear. What are properly regarded as natural-language quantifiers, however, *also*

---

[1] He says something stronger (1981b, 9): "Ontological concern is not a correction of a lay thought and practice; it is foreign to the lay culture, though an outgrowth of it."

induce ontological commitments or denials according to this picture. "Some eggs are in the refrigerator," "Most toads have four appendages," and even "All apples are edible" are ontologically committing. Not all these sentences are first-order regimentable, but many are. More importantly, the semantics of these natural-language sentences are typically characterized using one or another version of domain semantics—as I described them in the appendix to the general introduction. Thus, the transcendence/immanence issue of chapter 1 arises in natural languages with respect to every locution that induces ontological commitment—whether or not they're (natural-language) quantifiers.

The Quinean, recall, codes ontological commitment (in first-order languages) via existential sentences semantically interpreted Tarski-style by a domain viewed transcendentally. Quine applies this to natural languages by first-order-regimenting amenable natural-language sentences. Given a domain semantics of natural-language locutions, a generalization of Quine's characterization of ontological commitment is available for natural languages without detouring through first-order formal languages—by a transcendent interpretation of that domain.

Opponents of Quinean transcendence can transpose the quantifier-variance terminology to natural languages—including the phrase "quantifier variance" itself—because "domains" are the nub of the disagreement. I'll go along with this to fruitfully engage with metaphysicians in this tradition. I'll speak of different "quantifier meanings," as they do, even for uses of "there is" and "exists"—neither of which is a quantifier. I'll also speak of the transcendent and immanent views of natural-language "quantifiers." So-called domains—as I just indicated—are semantically relevant not only to natural-language quantifiers but to all locutions that induce ontological commitments in natural languages—specifically "there is" and "exist." (The remarks in this paragraph should prevent anyone sensitive to "exist" and "there is" *not* being natural-language quantifiers from being misled by the quantifier terminology already used by many metaphysicians.)

I'm challenging this tidy Quinean-inspired picture. I deny "domains" *must* contain what exists. I stressed in the general introduction that this metaphor is *treacherous*. "Domains" aren't collections of *things*; the word metaphorically (and misleadingly) indicates a specific linkage between the metalanguage and the object language that does not, in fact, depend on there being *things* involved. If we characterize ontological commitment in natural language as the application of a natural-language "existence concept," as I recommend, the issues devolve to two: "What properties does the natural-language existence concept have?" and "How are domains relevant?"

I'm challenging Quine's legacy in a second way. He distorts ontological commitment among non-philosophers both by diminishing its presence *and* by augmenting it. He understates the significance of ontological concerns among non-philosophers by suggesting non-philosophers don't care about ontology.[2] Many philosophers agree with Quine and Carnap that non-philosophers don't care about ontology, noticing that non-philosophers don't care about what moves *philosophers*: Is Platonism right? Are there universals? Tropes? Even worries about the ontological status of species or fictional objects don't interest non-philosophers.

This ignores the ontological debates non-philosophers are *deeply* concerned with. Prominent are arguments about God's existence, and other similar debates. Did Jesus exist? Did Buddha? Does Bigfoot exist? Do angels? Are there intelligent extraterrestrial humanoid creatures on other planets? Among us? Non-philosophers don't merely debate these questions; they *kill* one another over them.

Quine also overstates the presence of ontological commitment among non-philosophers. There are definitely ontological *debates*, wherein non-philosophers *assert* and *deny* ontological commitments. God *exists*; God doesn't *exist*. In just those words. *There are* extraterrestrial aliens among us. *There aren't* extraterrestrial aliens among us; indeed, *there aren't* extraterrestrial aliens at all. In just *those* words. Let's draw a distinction between (i) *asserting* ontological commitments and (ii) saying something true about something we *are* ontologically committed to. I think cars exist. I also think cars were invented by Karl Benz. I don't think Mickey Mouse exists. Nevertheless, I *do* think Mickey Mouse was invented by Walt Disney. (This is a truth about Mickey Mouse; it's not a truth about something else—Mickey Mouse cartoons or Mickey Mouse thoughts.) If we can commit ourselves to truths about things that don't exist (or that we deny exist), then space has been created for a distinction between asserting ontological commitments and saying something true about something to which one may (or may not) have an ontological commitment. To say As were invented by B isn't, by

---

[2] Recall note 1. Carnap agrees, writing (1956b, 207), "This question [of the reality of the thing world] is raised neither by the man in the street nor by scientists, but only by philosophers. Realists give an affirmative answer, subjective idealists a negative one, and the controversy goes on for centuries without ever being solved." Kant disagreed (1783, 121): "That the human mind would someday entirely give up metaphysical investigations is just as little to be expected, as that we would someday gladly stop all breathing so as never to take in impure air. There will therefore be metaphysics in the world at every time, and what is more, in every human being, and especially the reflective ones; metaphysics that each, in the absence of a public standard of measure, will carve out for themselves in their own manner." Kant is right.

virtue of saying *that*, to undertake an ontological commitment to As (or B). I argue further for this in chapter 3.

Meanwhile, notice that this *is* a very natural distinction, and that it restricts the expressions for *assertion* or *denial* of ontological commitments. "God *exists*," I can say (with an emphasis that indicates I mean this *ontologically*). "Aliens don't *exist*," I can also say (with a similarly meaningful emphasis). "There ..." is the same: "There *are* extraterrestrial aliens," I can say with emphasis, or "There are *no* extraterrestrial aliens."

Consider, though, "Some eggs are in the refrigerator," "The raccoons around here will eat garbage if it's left out," or "A cow is in the barn." These sentences don't allow a stress to enable us to *assert* an ontological commitment by means of them; similarly, these aren't sentences that can state ontological positions in ontological debates. I can certainly stress that *some* eggs are in the refrigerator, that *the raccoons* around *here* will eat garbage if it's left out, or that *a cow* is in the barn. But these aren't the kinds of stress that arise in ontological debates.[3] "Exist," "there is," "real," and "object" or "thing" *can* be used to assert (or deny) ontological commitment: "There *are* unicorns," "Vampires *aren't* real," "Some heroes *are* real," and "Shrees aren't *things*" are *ontological* commitments (and denials).

Whether any genuine natural-language quantifiers can be used to *assert* or *deny* ontological commitments isn't clear. Consider, for example, a debate about the existence of extraterrestrial aliens, and imagine that during this debate a rocket ship lands on the lawn. (We've all seen movies like *this*.) The proponent can slyly respond to the naysayer, rolling his eyes, "Extraterrestrial aliens are on the lawn *again*." This *doesn't* look like an ontological *assertion*, however; it looks like a Gricean *implicature* of an ontological assertion. The matter is complicated; I discuss it further in chapter 3.

The narrowing of ontological assertion to the contexts of ontological debate requires justifying that we can assert truths about what we aren't ontologically committed to. I show this in chapter 3. Meanwhile (in this chapter) I adopt the premise that ontological debates are the primary places of ontological *assertions* and *denials*. Assuming this enables a focus on "exist," the central word of such debates. Questions can be asked about the properties of this word—"exist"—when used in ontological debates. Furthermore, ontological assertions/denials using "there is," "real," "objects," and "exist"

---

[3] Notice the point. What are called "existential quantifiers" in English, among them the indefinite "a" and the two quantifiers sometimes glossed as "some" and "sm," are *not* naturally used to *assert* ontological commitments or ontological denials. My thanks to Michael Glanzberg for pressing me on this.

are transposable into assertions/denials using the other phrases: "Vampires aren't real," "Vampires don't exist," "There are no vampires," "No objects are vampires." These statements are, pretty much, the ones Quine treats (after first-order regimentation) as ontologically committing or denying, and these are the statements that quantifier variantists are speaking of when they claim, as Hirsch (2002, 68) does, that

> the quantificational apparatus in our language and thought—such expressions as "thing," "object," "something," "(there) exists"—has a certain variability or plasticity. There is no necessity to use these expressions in one way rather than various other ways, for the world can be correctly described using a variety of concepts of "the existence of something."

It is this concept of "the existence of something" that's deployed during ontological debates, and that's explored by asking how "exist" operates in such debates.

Certain philosophers—Hirsch, Hofweber, and Thomasson are three—draw substantial conclusions about ontology and ontological commitments on the basis of claims about the ordinary words "exist," "there is," and "object." It seems to matter *a lot*, therefore, as I illustrate in this chapter and chapter 3, that they're wrong about these words. It's also important what properties ordinary-language locutions that express the existence concept *have* if we're restricted to natural languages, or even—less dramatically—if we're restricted in how much we can change the semantic properties of natural-language phrases by regimentation or replacement. Only believers in "Ontologese"—an artificial formal language some philosophers think they speak when practicing metaphysics—can ignore properties of these natural-language words.

In section 2.2, I evaluate usage evidence for the immanent viewpoint toward, specifically, "exist." I conclude (contrary to Hirsch) that it's transcendent in ontological assertions and denials. That is, we take its extension to be the same in every language; the result, therefore, can be extended to "there is," "real," and "object" when these are also used to make ontological assertions and denials. Hirsch (2011a) presumes us to be speakers of natural languages. But this and quantifier variance are inconsistent. Not shown by this is that we *can't* change natural languages (through regimentation) to allow other languages to have different "existence concepts." Recall the conclusion of chapter 1: we can do this, it seems, only at the cost of making ontological debate incoherent. Some philosophers don't mind that cost (see the discussion of Thomasson in section 2.3), but I think it's too great, and too much of a deviance from the non-philosophical understanding of the matter. (It's too much because it rules out a philosophical concern—one of the few ones left nowadays—that philosophers *share* with non-philosophers.)

2.2 Establishing Natural-Language Transcendence

Hirsch motivates quantifier variance by analogizing differing quantifier domains to meaning differences exhibited by homonyms like "bank." If—after counting marbles—we disagree about the number of objects, and I realize you're counting marbles *and* mereological fusions of marbles, I should conclude (according to Hirsch) that your word "object" has a "different meaning" than mine does. Similar claims apply to "there is" and "exists."

Notice a powerful *observational implication* of domain variation being *meaning* difference, that I used in chapter 1. Ontological *disagreement* vanishes. *This is a general fact about perceived meaning differences.* If A and B think "bear" has one meaning, then their disagreement about whether bears eat people is an ontological issue about *bears that eat people*. Are there *any*? If they use *different* words (with different meanings), then their disagreement isn't about *bears*. Perhaps bears$_1$ eat people and bears$_2$ don't. This observational implication was used to put pressure on immanence in chapter 1. Call it *the ontological debate test*. Two individuals (or populations) think they're using a word W with the *same* public meaning only if they can disagree over whether *there are* Ws in this way.

The presence or absence of ontological debates with certain words is *empirical evidence* of similarity or difference in the public meaning of those words. It's also empirical evidence if ontological arguments evaporate whenever participants recognize (or decide) they are using words "in different ways." This evidence, of course, can be verified by sociological studies, but it can also be anecdotally confirmed by competent language users.

In speaking about differences in "public meaning"—apart from the word "public"—I'm following the literature, Hirsch in particular. But what sort of notion of "meaning" *is* this? Is it *lexical meaning*, as semanticists understand it?[4] Nothing claimed in this book requires answering this thorny theoretical question. Here's why. Consider the widespread impression that tomatoes are vegetables, and the scientific correction that tomatoes, in fact, are fruits. This is one of a large number of examples I discuss in section 2.2.1. It exemplifies our collective practice of using certain words to classify items (and attribute

---

[4] My thanks to Michael Glanzberg, who raised this question.

properties to them), although we'll accept corrections by authority figures—usually called "experts"—that doing so is wrong.[5]

The *public meaning* of words such as "tomato," "banana," "emerald," and so on takes our use of them as defeasible.[6] There are two empirical possibilities for how public meaning relates to lexical meaning. The first is that these are (more or less) identical. Any fact about public meanings is about *lexemes*; any empirical result about public meanings bears directly on lexical semantics. That so many English-speakers wrongly classify tomatoes as vegetables, for example, is because of other factors: psychologically innate tendencies to so structure mental concepts, perhaps, or cultural factors; but in neither case is lexical meaning, per se, indicated. Another option is that lexical meaning *does* entail that tomatoes are vegetables—but we override this entailment (learn to call it a "mistake") because we accept the authority of specialists about certain words. Public meaning, on this view, separates from lexical meaning the way "good grammar" taught in schools separates from the real syntax of the language students speak.

Issues about the transcendence/immanence of domains are about public meaning—and only according to certain linguistic theories do they relate to lexical semantics. In turn, the thought experiments and other evidence—such as the ontological debate test—that verify facts about public meaning only indirectly imply results about lexical meaning (via theories about the relation of public meaning to lexical meaning).

As I said, nothing in this book turns on how "public meaning" as I use it (and how Hirsch and other metaphysicians use "meaning") relates to the theoretical notion of "meaning" emerging in linguistics.[7] There is no doubt linguistic meaning, specifically lexical meaning, importantly contributes to public meaning. The point is only that it needn't be the sole factor. More important is that "public meaning" is what's relevant to "quantifier meaning" issues—specifically, whether speakers experience "what exists" as something to be argued over. This is because public meaning is directly operationalized

---

[5] The nomenclature of gems, in particular, is dictated by professionals sensitive to economic factors as much as, or more than, they're sensitive to facts about chemical makeup. Emeralds, for example, are *stipulated* to be green beryls. We *know* that emeralds aren't grue because that has been ruled out by *stipulation*. (I thank Yvonne Raley for this example.)

[6] Who is this "us," exactly? The evidence I give in section 2.2.1 indicates "us" to be people who take science and certain other institutions seriously. The parameters of "us" can be tested along the lines of, for example, Machery, Mallon, Nichols, and Stich (2004).

[7] For a survey of the complexity of the lexical-semantics literature, see the recent Gasparri and Marconi (2016).

in terms of ontological debate possibilities. I'll often drop the word "public" in what follows and speak simply of "meaning."

Let's return to Hirsch's analogy between distinctive quantifier domains and perceived ambiguities in words such as "bank." Because homonyms such as "bank$_1$" (a financial institution) and "bank$_2$" (a side of a river) have different public meanings, "bank" flunks the ontological debate test—arguments over whether there are banks that adjoin rivers derail once it's realized both parties are right. As we'll see, this is false of disagreements over quantifier domains—more naturally put, false of debates about what exists. I'll use this *datum* in my brief that the ordinary-language phrases "there is," "exist," and so on are transcendent when used for ontological commitment. My counterclaim is: *English* (or its users) demands that words corresponding to "exist" and "there is" in other languages—when used to ontologically commit or deny—range over all and only what these words range over in English.

Just *stating* my counterclaim invites the rejoinder that quantifier immanence looks like a truism—impossible to argue against (let alone describe as false). Why *couldn't* "there is" and "exist" have different meanings in other languages? How could *English-speakers* demand the ranges of these words in *other languages* be restricted to the range of the corresponding English words? Response: the suggestion (despite its prominence in the history of philosophy) that there are different notions of *existence* is metaphysically bizarre. A notion of "existence" genuinely different in meaning from our notion wouldn't be a notion of *existence*, but something else. Taking witches to exist and denying witches exist don't involve different notions of existence; they involve a disagreement over *what* exists, a difference in what people *take* to exist.

In the rest of section 2, I'll first draw a preliminary distinction between *criterion-transcendent* and *criterion-immanent* words.[8] I'll present and motivate this public-meaning distinction, and then I'll show how quantifier immanence is undercut by the criterion transcendence of "exists," "there is," and similar terms when used for ontological commitment and denial.

I apologize for the potentially confusing terminology. The criterion-transcendence/immanence distinction isn't the same as the transcendence/immanence distinction in perspectives toward quantifier domains. The latter distinction concerns *different* languages. The former—with respect to ontological debate—is a characterization of words *within* a language.

---

[8] See Azzouni (2000 and 2010b).

2.2.1 Criterion transcendence and criterion immanence

Philosophers have long noticed that words such as "vixen," "bachelor," "sibling," "square," and so on have entailments that non-philosophers recognize and that are necessary or sufficient conditions for such words. If something is a brother, it's a sibling (necessary condition for "brother"; sufficient condition for "sibling"). More rarely, these entailments induce "necessary and sufficient" conditions—something is a square if and only if it's an equilateral equiangular quadrilateral. If "exist"—when used in ontological debate—has entailments that induce necessary and sufficient conditions, this yields a "criterion" for what exists. Such perceived entailments constrain when changes in usages are recognized as changes in public meanings.

We can test perceived entailments of ordinary words. Consider a purported entailment G → H between kind-terms G and H. The ontological debate test is applied by imagining scenarios where we discover we're wrong about the items called Gs: we thought they were Hs, but they're not.[9] Do Gs exist, given this scenario? If yes, then the purported entailment isn't one. Otherwise the entailment stands.

Consider the purported entailment "Domestic cats are mammals." Imagine we discover all the animals we call "domestic cats" are examples of evolutionary convergence. They're *birds*. We'd say we'd discovered domestic cats are birds; we wouldn't say we'd discovered domestic cats don't exist. That we think of this scenario as a *discovery about domestic cats* (instead of a discovery that *there are no* domestic cats) indicates the purported entailment from "domestic cat" to "mammal" isn't understood as constraining the public meaning of "domestic cat."

I've described the confirmation of this claim about public-meaning entailments as using a "thought experiment." This is how many philosophers describe these examples originally given by Putnam and Kripke. The confirmations are described as relying on "intuitions"—in particular, "intuitions" about the lexical meanings of certain words—and some philosophers have become uneasy about this form of confirmation.[10] This is misleading. Putnam and Kripke's insights should be more minimally characterized as recognitions (in print) of a widespread practice with nomenclature—both in the sciences and in ordinary life. For a large class of terms G—described

---

[9] See Putnam (1975) and Kripke (1980) for influential examples. Also see Austin (1962, 122 n. 1) for anticipation of the Putnam-Kripke view about natural-kind terms, and Carnap (1963, 920) for anticipation of the empirical *test* used to establish the view.
[10] See, for example, the opening paragraph of Machery, Mallon, Nichols, and Stich (2004). Instead of "thought experiment," they use the word "story."

by philosophers as "natural-kind terms"—if (i) G is taken to apply to certain items, if (ii) H is taken to apply to anything that's a G, and if (iii) it's discovered that the items that are purportedly Gs aren't Hs, there are two choices: deny (i) or deny (ii). Deny the items are Gs, or deny Gs are Hs. Putnam and Kripke recognized that under a wide range of circumstances we (collectively) deny (ii) rather than (i).

That Putnam and Kripke are *right* is *easily* shown and doesn't require thought experiments. Consider the article "20 Foods (and Drinks) That Aren't What They Seem" (Spar 2015). The subtitle is "Everything You Thought About These Foods Has Been Wrong." We learn (the article indicates) quinoa isn't a grain, it's a seed; bananas are "giant herbs"; avocados, sweet peppers, squash, cucumbers, and chile peppers are fruits; eggplants are berries; peanuts are beans; strawberries aren't berries. Another article is equally revelatory: blackberries and raspberries aren't berries, and watermelons (gasp!) *are* berries (Spiegel 2014).

A more dramatic-sounding "discovery" could have been: *There are no bananas, avocados, sweet peppers, watermelons, raspberries,* and so on. *So many foods don't exist.* This *isn't* how the popular literature goes—and this is generally true of an enormous class of terms, as Putnam and Kripke recognized. In the cases of "sweet peppers," "raspberries," and so on, what's behind these "discoveries" is an application of the (sometimes homophonic) botanical terminology to what non-botanists use these words to pick out. Botanists define a fruit as the portion of a flowering plant that develops from the ovary. Botanical subcategories in the fruit family with specialized definitions include citrus, berry, stone fruit, and drupe. Some of these terms, co-opted by botanists—"fruit" and "berry," among them—long predate botanical intrusions into the nomenclature. Nevertheless, the popular literature doesn't complain that "berry" and "fruit" have homonyms that are used differently by botanists and everyone else. Nor that botanists are wrong.

As those familiar with popular (or sophisticated) science know, "widespread practice" is no exaggeration. The same is true of *most* other nomenclature—both scientific and ordinary. Coral was thought to be a plant until Herschel used a microscope to establish that coral cells had the thin-cell membranes of an animal cell—this is how the history is depicted, not that Herschel discovered something new that wasn't coral (because there isn't any *coral*). Tuataras, we learn, were "misclassified" as lizards until 1867. There are numerous other examples, from materials science, chemistry, gemology, and so on. There can be no doubt that the phenomenon Putnam and Kripke described in thought experiments is real and widespread. What can, and should, be doubted are the conclusions they drew, both about linguistic meaning and about metaphysics:

> (i) That the extensions of such words conform to the microstructural similarities of substances, biological entities, and so on (as these will eventually be discovered by science).
>
> (ii) That such words are metaphysically "rigid."

Therefore:

> (iii) That such words, in identities, yield a posteriori necessary truths.

And:

> (iv) That science discovers essences.

Almost all the literature subsequent to Putnam and Kripke's work targets these semantical and metaphysical doctrines. New thought experiments, and other evidence about the intricate and complex relationships between natural-language kind-words and the specialized kind-words of the sciences, have been brought against these views, which are, collectively, variously described as "the new theory of reference," "the discovery picture," or "the causal picture."[11]

There is, however, a semantically and metaphysically modest view that's been sadly buried alive because of its association with these substantial claims—claims it's distinct from because it's untouched by the many counterexamples to (i)–(iv). Kind-words such as "gold," "cat," "water," and so on are *criterion-transcendent*. We take such words as continuing to be used *with the same public meaning* despite changes in what seemed to be *de facto* necessary and/or sufficient conditions on that usage. If a kind-word is criterion-transcendent, it disallows entailments of certain sorts. We can't generally *reason* from something not being yellow to its not being a lemon. We can't generally *reason* from something being a bird to its not being a cat.

This point is subtle and needs more discussion. Most of our ordinary reasoning is defeasible: we draw conclusions given certain background

---

[11] See, for example, Dupré (1981), who shows that (i) is false of biological terms; and LaPorte (1996), who shows that (i) is false of minerals and gemstones. Both philosophers, by the way, give many illustrations of what I've already stressed about the public meaning of these words—what Putnam (1975) called "the linguistic division of labor."

assumptions that we presume are in place—often tacitly. We can definitively reason from something being a circle to its being a locus of points in the same plane equidistant from a point—if we're competent with "circle." We can similarly (and definitively) reason from something being a refrigerator to its being an artifact designed to keep food cold—if we're competent with "refrigerator." But we can't similarly (definitively) reason about zebras, water, rubies, lemons, or gold. We can be competent with these words, and right that the samples these words are linked to *really are* uniform in their properties and *really do* project to a well-defined collection of things. We're just wrong about the properties we attribute to these things. The Putnam/Kripke thought experiments (and copious examples from popular literature and the history of science) illustrate the phenomenon: under the circumstances specified, most of us accept that we would have been *wrong* about the properties that porcupines, lemons, gold, and so on have. We would have, that is, continued to apply the kind-words to the items in the samples (and to other items taken to belong to the same kinds as those items); we would have regarded such continued application of these words as the continued use of them as they were used before. We would instead change our views about the properties of the things that the words in question apply to, rather than regard ourselves as having changed the public meanings of the words themselves.

Criterion-transcendent kind-words contrast with *criterion-immanent* kind-words such as "notarized document" or "refrigerator." Criterion transcendence is manifested by our treating the application of a kind-word—in certain *changed* epistemic circumstances—as *strongly retroactive*: when the criteria we associate with a criterion-transcendent kind-word change, we presume that the items that don't fit with the new criteria don't belong, *nor have ever belonged*, to the extension of that word. (We describe these changes as "discoveries.") Retention of the word "gold" after discovering gold is an organic substance—somewhat like amber (say)—is accompanied by characterizing earlier speakers as *"mistaken."* Earlier speakers are "mistaken" in their commitments both to earlier characterizations and to certain objects fitting those characterizations (if those objects are now revealed to fit instead current characterizations).[12] This practice contrasts with a practice we *don't* have: retaining "gold" but treating its reference as changed, so that what the previous word "gold" referred to is different from what the current word "gold" refers to. Contrast the criterion-immanent term "legal tender."

---

[12] People who continue to describe strawberries and raspberries as "berries" are "mistaken."

Changes in criteria for legal tender *aren't* applied retroactively: items once regarded as legal tender aren't legal tender any longer but are described as *having been* legal tender.

Mistakes in the use of "refrigerator," "notarized document," or "legal tender" can occur because individual usage mismatches community usage (see Burge 1979). Criterion-transcendent terms are open to these mistakes as well. The difference between the two types of term is that retroactive correction of previous reference occurs with criterion transcendence but not with criterion immanence. These two aspects of criterion transcendence and criterion immanence are linked. Criterion-transcendent terms can't have public-meaning entailments: these would interfere with strong retroactivity. Criterion-immanent terms aren't strongly retroactive: this is compatible with such words having public-meaning entailments.

Haven't I gone beyond the evidence by claiming criterion-transcendent terms can't have public-meaning entailments? Isn't what has been shown merely that it's not obvious (not *as* obvious as some philosophers once thought) what these entailments are? If something's a horse, it isn't a planet; surely *that's* an entailment.[13]

I'm afraid I'm not budging on this. We can get things pretty wrong—at least in principle. It's true that there's too much that we currently know about horses and planets and the way the universe works that rules out the possibility that some horses are planets (although these are things that the ancient Greeks, for example, *didn't know* about constellations). But I think we can recognize that such background knowledge doesn't support public entailments.

2.2.2 "Exists"—when used in ontological debates—is criterion-transcendent

I've described the differences between criterion-transcendent and criterion-immanent terms. I've indicated my commitment to—but not yet shown—"exist" being in the former category (when used in ontological debate). I turn to this and the prior task of showing "criterion transcendent" and "criterion immanent" apply beyond "natural kinds" and certain "artifact kinds."[14]

---

[13] I owe this example to Eric Dean.
[14] "Certain" because *many* artifactual terms are criterion-transcendent: "polystyrene" and "bread" are examples. Eric Dean protests (email August 2016): "If someone showed me something that looked like bread but wasn't edible I'd just say it wasn't bread, or if someone said that the word now referred to something inedible, I'd say it wasn't the same word." Again, I disagree. A cute example can be found in Marx (1967, 174–75 n. 3), where he describes the kind of stuff that was put into bread and sold to poor people, stuff that made the bread inedible. "Inedible,"

According to the Putnam-Kripke discovery picture, criterion transcendence is due to the semantics of such words being determined by *real* structural similarities the items of a kind share. The metaphysically modest view is neutral—both about metaphysics and about how meaning properties of public expressions are related to lexical-semantic properties.[15] In any case, criterion transcendence applies broadly. "True," "refer," "good," "right," and "exist" are criterion-transcendent terms, even though metaphysical correspondence needn't be particularly relevant. Recognition of criterion transcendence first occurred with "normative" words, such as "good."[16] Overinterpreting a word's criterion transcendence—reading it as picking out a kind that's "real" in some sense *by virtue of criterion transcendence alone*—occurs in philosophy of language *and* value theory.

Let's return to "exist," to establish its criterion transcendence when it occurs in ontological debate. Philosophers *engaged in ontology* have argued that what exists are (all and only) items in space and time, or are causally efficacious, or are mind- and language-independent, et cetera. Applying the ontological debate test, notice that these suggestions, and the various arguments offered, aren't suggestions for how the public meaning of "exist" should *change*. If "exist" were not criterion-transcendent, this is how these debates would have gone. Unger's 1979 paper is titled "Why I Do Not Exist." This paper argues that Unger—and other people too—don't exist. Unger doesn't argue (nor has he ever been seen as arguing) that the meaning of "exist" should be changed so that, given the word's new meaning, one can now correctly claim no people exist. That these debates are universally understood as about what (really) exists, and not about changing the meaning of "exist," illustrates the same phenomenon that occurs with "cat," "berry," and so on. Thus, "exist"—when understood ontologically—is criterion-transcendent.

Consider an alternative position—"actual quantifier variance"[17]—about the word "exist." Our language has different "existence concepts." One way

---

after all, applies to *food* that can make someone sick or even die: "That bread is inedible" isn't contradictory. What about "baked"? Can bread still be bread if it's not baked? Yes, it can. What if it isn't made of grain of some sort? (Sure—especially because the word "grain" is criterion-transcendent too. Quinoa bread is *bread*.) It's the category of criterion-immanent words that I'm worried about; I *think* I have cases of such words, but I think, generally, that category is very small.

[15] Many criterion-transcendent terms of the vernacular that look like "natural-kind" words don't have "natural-kind" extensions—at least from the point of view of the relevant science, e.g., "ant," "porcupine," "oak," etc. (see, e.g., the citations in note 11). Nothing in our practices with these words requires them to have metaphysically robust extensions.

[16] See Moore (1903) on the "naturalistic fallacy."

[17] The label is Hirsch's (2002, 80). He opposes the position. Putnam (1990) seems to embrace the position at the end of the paper, although in passing.

to flavor the view is for "exist" to be context-sensitive, corresponding to various existence concepts appropriate to different contexts. When speaking of fictional objects, people (implicitly) use one existence concept; when speaking of the fundamental constituents of matter, a different existence concept is used.

This suggestion fits badly with usage. Non-philosophers *do* apply "exist" to strategies for circumventing anger, waltzes designed to last more than ten hours, and fictional talking mice. For example:

(1) Strategies for circumventing anger exist. Many are found in self-help books.
(2) Waltzes designed to last more than ten hours exist, but no one ever dances them.
(3) Fictional mice that talk do exist in many Disney cartoons, but there are no talking yaks.

If an ontological debate context is introduced, speakers don't recognize different uses of "exist" in play. Instead, they do what's predicted they'll do if they take themselves to have one word "exist" that's criterion-transcendent: either they embrace ontological commitment ("Fictional beings really exist! They just don't exist in our world!") or they repudiate ontological commitment by backtracking. Backtrackers say, for example:

(4) Mickey Mouse exists in cartoons—but he doesn't *really* exist.
(5) The bogyman isn't real; he *only* exists in your mind.

The different-meaning view works with words such as "bank" not only because different "meanings" are contextually activated but also because speakers are *aware* of shifts in the concepts in different contexts. This awareness is patently absent with "exist." Speakers instead embrace or backtrack. They *don't* backtrack when they perceive meaning differences as involved: they *don't* say of a financial institution, "That's not really a bank," if they have a riverbank in mind. They instead say, "That's not the kind of bank I had in mind." No one says, "That's not the kind of existence I had in mind."

Related evidence against actual quantifier variance includes sentences like:

(6) Cartoon characters, and people who look like them, exist.

That this and other similar sentences (designed by varying noun phrases arbitrarily) are completely natural things to say shows that "exist," whatever it's appended to, doesn't change in what's perceived as its meaning.

2.2.3 De facto versus de jure criteria for what exists

Hirsch (2011a), especially when arguing against revisionary ontologists, gives *ordinary-people-would-be-amazed-and-outraged-if-you-said-that* arguments. He offers these as usage evidence for the presence and absence in English of various quantifier meanings: people are outraged by imputations of weird meanings to the terms "exist" and "there is." These arguments fail because Hirsch overlooks the criterion transcendence of these words used in the ontological disagreements he describes. I briefly illustrate this.

When speaking of the non-philosopher's reaction to shrees, Hirsch (2002, 87) writes:

> If we explain to ordinary people that the "brown wooden thing" in question need not be any kind of familiar thing, it need not be an interesting thing or the sort of thing one would normally talk about, they ... regard the sentence ["There exists a brown wooden thing in the yard that keeps losing its branches every night and gaining them back every morning."] as insanely false. ... For they take it for granted that there is no brown wooden thing in the yard *of any sort whatever* that keeps gaining and losing branches.

Hirsch (2003, 107) jokingly warns of possible aggressive behavior against philosophers with peculiar ontological views. For if such a philosopher tries to get someone to recognize as an object something that is first a white piece of wood and then a different brown piece of wood, saying (somewhat condescendingly) that

> you [keep] restricting your attention to just one sort of thing even though you were told not to. The correct answer is that any early part of this [piece of wood] together with any later part of [that other piece of wood] make up a wooden thing that is first white and then brown,

the likely outcome is that the person will "throw you out the window."[18]

---

[18] Hirsch elsewhere (1999, 42) jokingly warns philosophers about somewhat milder repercussions they're in danger of: "if you try to tell ordinary folk about the gerrymandering objects which ... they are supposedly committed to, they will look for the nearest place to commit you to."

Let's grant these sociological predictions. If true, they show that people don't think there are objects like the ones these philosophers are contemplating; they show that people (and some philosophers too, it turns out) think it's pretty ridiculous to suggest there *are* such objects. But this doesn't show that the *meaning* of "exist" excludes such objects.

The reason it doesn't is that when non-philosophers perceive shocking violations of meaning, they have "huh?" reactions, not violent disagreement reactions; and these aren't the same. (This is an application of the ontological debate test.) If I say to someone that I think cups of water are going extinct (because poachers are exterminating them for their horns), and if she stays in the conversation long enough to see what's gone wrong, she'll hypothesize I'm (weirdly) confused about what "cup of water" means. Similarly with "A lot more squares than people realize are actually circles" or "Many chairs, it surprisingly turns out, are irrational numbers." This is because non-philosophers *do* distinguish between when it strikes them that the public meaning of a word is being violated and when instead it's their beliefs about the things a word designates that are being disturbed.

To summarize, it's true (and Hirsch's thought experiments illustrate this) that *there are* general conditions on what people take to exist. Such conditions (whatever they are) exclude shrees and arbitrary object fusions. Speakers recognize this isn't due to what "exist" *publicly means*, however sure they are about there not *being* any such objects. One piece of evidence for this, as just mentioned, is that their reactions to weird philosophical options aren't similar to their reactions when the meanings of words seem (to them) to be violated. Another piece of evidence is that they *accept* weird options when presented by the right authorities. Contrary to their tendencies to throw *philosophers* out windows or into asylums, they avidly read about *scientific developments* that reveal strange facts about objects (and their properties), and *they accept them*. This is just what's predicted if "exist" is criterion-transcendent and, furthermore, if numerous other words are criterion-transcendent as well.

2.2.4 Transcendence across languages?

Still to be established is that "exist" is transcendent; that speakers understand "exist" in *other* languages to have the same range as it has in their own language. Criterion transcendence places a condition on *previous usage* (that it's strongly retroactive). Criterion transcendence also affects the relations of current usage to future usage. We speak of being wrong about what we thought existed.[19] This (given an identification of the extension of "exist" with the "domain") is understood as our accepting the possibility that we're wrong about what our quantifiers (currently) range over. We *think* they range over As, but they don't. Quantifier transcendence, however, is a condition on the *concurrent* range of quantifier domains in other languages. What shows *this*?

What shows this is that we *agree* or *disagree* when we take others as making claims about what exists or doesn't exist.[20] It's unnatural (virtually impossible, really) for the non-philosopher to entertain, during ontological disagreements, that "exist" and "real" are being used differently. Alert non-philosophers *will* spontaneously consider that someone is using "tree" differently—especially after it's explained what "trees" are supposed to do according to that someone: cease possessing their branches each evening, but regain possession of them each morning.[21] Non-philosophers *don't* extend this sort of possibility to "exist."

Consider, first, a purported language that differs from English only in what "exist" ranges over. If non-philosophers think they once spoke that language, they won't treat "exist" as ranging over something different from what their current word "exist" ranges over. They'll think, rather, that they were wrong about what they once *took* the word "exist" to apply to. (We once thought witches existed, but witches *didn't* exist—not even back *then*.) So why would we treat current speakers of this other language (that's identical to our former one) as *right* about what their word "exist" applies to?

Suppose it's explained to a non-philosopher that "there is" and "exist" in this other language are *different*. Here's the cool thing, we say: these people are *right* about what *they* think their terms "there is" and "exist" range over. The alert non-philosopher will find this a pretty dubious suggestion: why do *these people* get to have words *just like* our words "exist" and "there is" except that they *can't* be wrong about what their words range over? Using jargon such as "semantics" on non-philosophers won't help: saying (authoritatively) that the "semantics" of these alien words "exist" and "there is" are different won't convince *anyone*. The non-philosopher will just shake his head and say: "Look, I just don't get it. You're telling me their words are the same

---

[19] Books and articles on the fossil record indicate this: much of it concerns animals we thought existed and the reasons we now think they didn't exist (as of the dates of those books and articles).
[20] My thanks for comments from Otávio Bueno, Eli Hirsch, and Ted Sider on this and the next four paragraphs during a presentation of an earlier version of this material at the 2012 Central APA session on realism and anti-realism.
[21] People *are* capable of considering this possibility, especially if told: "This is a *definition*: shrees are ..." They will still, of course, consider such a definition, and any talk about such objects, as *silly*. And they will strongly resist the idea that these things *exist*—even with a definition that characterizes these things successfully and that's projectable. I've *tested* this; you can *too*.

except that it's built into their words that they can't be wrong. But of course they *can be* wrong."

In defense against the non-philosopher's viewpoint, much as Hirsch does, *general principles* of charity and interpretation can be invoked: we should interpret the speakers of this other language to make them *right*. But this argumentative strategy will be as successful with non-philosophers as the metaphysician is when he uses general metaphysical principles against the non-philosopher's intuitions that rocks and people exist.[22] As soon as it's clear the alien language is supposed to be like English *except for* phrases like "there is" and "exist" ranging over witches (even though there aren't any), the non-philosopher will resist and say, "Well, not only are these people just wrong—their language is wrong *too*." (No one thinks speaking a *different language* gives anyone license to be *right* about *there being* shrees or incars—or witches or Bigfoot, for that matter.)[23]

Notice that using incars instead of witches doesn't change reactions. Non-philosophers won't care whether the nonexistent items are open to Hirschian sentence-to-sentence truth conditions or not; they won't care whether the debates are "purely verbal," in Hirsch's sense, or substantial. This is because "there is" and "exist" (when used to ontologically commit or deny) are criterion-transcendent. The bank analogy has no echo in the non-philosopher's experience of words such as "exist" and "there is."

One aspect of Hirsch's approach to quantifier variance is that he characterizes the English notion of *truth* as transcendent: charity is built into the interpretative mechanism that we apply to other languages. But, contrary to Hirsch's quantifier variantist, non-philosophers accompany their transcendent notion of truth with a transcendent notion of existence. We evaluate what others claim to exist against what we think exists, and what they think is true against what we think is true. Truth and existence attributions belong together *in this way*; they can't be separated in the way that quantifier immanence needs them to be separated.[24]

---

[22] See Hirsch (2005, 164–70) on burden-shifting issues vis-à-vis commonsense object realism vs. general metaphysical "axioms" that cut against it.

[23] We *can* say: their word has a different meaning. They'll accept that until we further explain: it's their *existence notion*. (Again, this is easily testable. Suggesting the meaning is different even though the word is still about existence is very hard to get across to non-philosophers—let alone convince them of it. I've found it *impossible*.)

[24] They can, however, be separated in a different way, as I show in chapter 3: it's possible for sentences about what doesn't exist to nevertheless be true (or false).

2.3 Thomasson on Ontology

2.3.1 Putnam's stereotypes versus Thomasson's application and coapplication conditions

Pertinent to differences between my views on "exist" and those of Amie L. Thomasson (2009, 2007) are differences about terms *other* than ontological ones. Thomasson claims that each term (each "sortal") comes with (i) "frame-level application conditions" that, very broadly, describe in which situations that term is properly applied or refused and (ii) "coapplication conditions" that describe when a term may be applied again.

Her claim about "sortals" motivates her view of ontological terms and ontology. "Specific existence questions"—for example, *whether an N exists or not*—are determined by the frame-level application conditions for N. If we wonder whether tables exist, we must "first [determine] what application conditions are associated with the sortal 'table,' and then [examine] whether or not they are fulfilled ... if they are, then tables exist" (2009, 455). There are strong intimations of the internal leg of Carnap's internal/external distinction, as well as echoes of verificationism.

Thomasson contrasts well-defined and meaningful "specific existence questions" with "generic existence questions." The latter utilize certain terms, "object," "thing," and the like, in a "purportedly" generic way. Thomasson is skeptical of the cogency of generic existence questions because she argues that the words "object," "thing," and so on are only legitimately used in ways that don't allow generic existence questions; only a "defective" neutral use of these words is left to allow space for such questions.

Thomasson recognizes two legitimate classes of uses of words such as "object" and "thing". The first is the class of "sortal uses," where speakers use these terms with specific application and coapplication conditions (although there is a lot of variation in the specific application and coapplication conditions). The second class of uses is "covering uses," when "object" and "thing" act as "placeholders" for genuine sortal terms. Covering uses are often restricted placeholder roles—not every sortal term (during such a use) may substitute for "object" or "thing." Notice that when words such as "object" and "thing" are used as Thomasson alleges they are in the above two kinds of cases, genuine metaphysical debate isn't possible: if something fits the specific application and coapplication conditions (or the family of such) in play, then it's an example of the objects or things in question. Otherwise not.

This leaves only the third possibility of an "alleged neutral use" of the words "object" or "thing" that doesn't tie the words to specific sortals (or delineated families of such). Genuine ontological debates, if there are any, are possible if ontological idioms, such as "object" and "thing," have such conditions-detached uses. Thomasson (2009, 462) denies this:

> For if "thing" and "object" are being used in ways that entirely lack application conditions of their own, and are not guaranteed to apply given the application of some genuine sortal term(s) (which do have application conditions), then it seems competent speakers would have no idea of under what sorts of conditions these terms should be applied and when they should be refused. Indeed, there seems nothing to determine whether or not these terms refer, and no way to evaluate the truth-values of existence claims that use these terms. And if simple existence claims made using these terms are not truth-evaluable, then the very generic existence questions on which so much of ontology is based turn out to be unanswerable questions.

My disagreement with Thomasson over ontological terminology is rooted in a disagreement over sortals. Thomasson has issued a challenge to any opponent of the idea that sortals come with application and coapplication conditions. If they don't, then, paraphrasing Thomasson, competent speakers would have no idea when these terms should be applied or refused. There seems to be nothing that might determine whether or not these terms refer, and no way to evaluate the truth values of existence claims that use these terms.

Thomasson is ignoring a possibility. Recall from section 2.2.1 my discussion of the distinction between criterion-transcendent and criterion-immanent words. Criterion-immanent words, on my view—"refrigerator," "screwdriver," "notarized document," and so on—fit Thomasson's characterization of *all* sortals: these words seem to come fixed with "frame-level application conditions" and "coapplication conditions."[25]

We've already seen, however, that "zebra," "coral," "water," "rubies," "berries," and "gold" aren't like this. In many circumstances, we relinquish the properties we attributed to what these terms refer to; correspondingly, we relinquish the "frame-level application conditions" and "coapplication conditions" generated by those purported properties without (as a result) being unable to use those terms.

Putnam's (1975, 247–52) earlier "stereotypes" handle Thomasson's challenge. The use of "gold," for example, is grounded in various *defeasible*

---

[25] When I first offered the criterion transcendent/immanent distinction (Azzouni 2000), I called these "criteria."

stereotypic property attributions to gold: being yellow, metal, et cetera. That such attributions are defeasible doesn't defeat the impression that because someone shares our stereotypes about "gold," we understand what that someone means by "gold." Mutual understanding based on shared stereotypes, thus, is compatible with recognizing that these stereotypes don't license *entailments* about what the words "mean"—part of the mutual understanding of a word is sharing expectations about how it will shed old stereotypes for new stereotypes under various conditions. (Thomasson's "frame-level application conditions" and "coapplication conditions," it seems to me, *are* Putnam's "stereotypes.") In the same way, Hirsch's examples illustrate the stereotypes speakers have about "objects" and "things" that make them resist shrees and incars being "things."

Competence with criterion-transcendent terms doesn't require these terms to be *individuated* by frame-level application and coapplication conditions. At most what's required is such terms have *purported* (defeasible) application and coapplication conditions. Our grip on usage survives (even massive) changes in these conditions; this is indicated by our taking the referents (and public meanings) of such terms to be unchanged even if the application and coapplication conditions have *drastically* altered.

A term's application and coapplication conditions are *not* understood as determining its reference. This is most obvious, again, with scientific terms and with certain commonsense terms (such as "lead") the recognition procedures of which are deeply infiltrated by scientific methods; but it's largely true of every criterion-transcendent term. There are always "false positives" and "false negatives": cases of good reasons to deny that the term actually refers according to the conditions in question.[26]

Notice if Thomasson is right about the "covering use" of words such as "object" and "thing," then these words—straightaway—inherit their criterion transcendence (given this use of them, anyway) from the criterion

---

[26] In Azzouni (2000), I used "criteria," and "procedures," e.g., "recognition-procedures," where Thomasson instead uses "conditions." Otherwise the notions seem similarly meant to describe the same methods of word application. The felt plausibility of Thomasson's view of sortals is due to commonsense terms seeming far more wedded to the procedures (conditions) associated with them than they in fact are. This illusion is engendered by overlooking our substantial deference to the knowledge of others about whether something is an N or not. It's nontrivial to determine how much gold an item has in it; it's equally nontrivial to recognize whether a stove is (really) leaking gas, whether the diamonds in a necklace are real, or even whether *that* is an ugly couch or (instead) an unpleasant work of art. One factor is that we're quite ignorant of (and experts quite knowledgeable about) the false positives and negatives that the recognition procedures associated with our terms have. But, in addition, only a little study reveals both that there are many different kinds of recognition procedures associated with our terms, and that they're constantly changing.

transcendence of ordinary sortals. But in any case, it's clear that ontologically committing uses of words such as "object" and "thing" are criterion-transcendent—apart from any purported "covering use" they supposedly have. Philosophical debates about whether shrees or arbitrary mereological fusions are objects, whether any object must be causally efficacious or in space and time, whether points can be objects, and so on show this. If these words did come with Thomassonian application and coapplication conditions, those conditions would run interference with these being *debates*. (This is another application of the ontological debate test.) Right on the surface of the usage of these words is that such debates don't strike anyone as violating the meanings of these words.

Terms used to assert or deny ontological commitments, such as "object," "thing," and so on, float free of Thomasson-style conditions just as (criterion-transcendent) sortals do—at least as far as public meaning is concerned. We allow the possibility that some *objects*—in the most serious ontological sense of "object" that we can muster—might not be in space and time, might not have causal powers, and so on.[27]

Thomasson needs to explain this away. Her only tool is an error theory: some philosophers are confused about words such as "thing" and "object," and *so* confused that they don't experience what they would otherwise experience if they witnessed a debate (say) about whether squares are circular. Putnam's defeasible-stereotype approach, on the other hand, gets the practice with these words *right*: application and coapplication conditions don't operate as entailments. These various conditions that we understand to govern these words are defeasible.

2.3.2 Pragmatic reasons for the criterion transcendence of (certain) terms

As I noted in section 2.2.1, Putnam and Kripke drew metaphysical and semantic conclusions (about "natural kinds") on the basis of criterion transcendence. We should ask instead what public-language utility criterion transcendence serves. I suggest that individuating public-word meanings by application/coapplication conditions would force constant terminological revisions. This is because, most obviously with scientific terms (but this is also true of commonsense terms), application/coapplication conditions associated with (criterion-transcendent) sortals are driven by epistemic factors, and these constantly change. Consider "lead." A major and ongoing

---

[27] Again, the evidence for this—*outside of philosophy*—shows up in the popular literature.

project in chemical science is the invention and development of *new* "frame-level application conditions" and "coapplication conditions" for various substances, including lead.[28] The same point, without Thomasson's jargon, is this: chemists develop new methods for recognizing the presence of lead in all the many places that lead might turn up. And "lead" is hardly exceptional.

Language, as it were, solves this problem by allowing us to treat the relevant terms as not fixed by (or individuated in terms of) the procedures or conditions stereotypically associated with them, but instead as flexible or open-ended in their associations. The unappealing alternative would instead be a constant introduction of new terms corresponding to the invention of new application and coapplication conditions, as well as the constant elimination of old terms.

2.4 Concluding Remarks

This chapter has concerned itself solely with establishing the transcendence of words when used to ontologically commit or deny. Indirectly shown (as I'll indicate in chapter 3) is the transcendence of quantifier domains—when they too are invoked by the language we use to make ontological commitments or denials.

Even with these qualifications, what has been shown here shouldn't be overstated. Quantifier immanence hasn't been ruled out, for we can certainly try to impose it as a practice (as a regimentation) on how we interpret others. What chapter 1 has shown, however, is that quantifier immanence offers pretty much nothing as a tool to illuminate ontological debate. And once the value of quantifier neutrality is described in chapters 4 and 5, no motivation will remain for characterizing ontological disagreements in terms of quantifier variance.

There's a lesson that I've been pushing in the foregoing that should be brought out more explicitly. Suppose that Hirsch is right about natural languages; suppose that Thomasson is right about natural languages. What follows? I've already suggested, in the case of Hirsch, that the answer is: not much. It isn't obvious that we can regiment ontologically committing language to understand it *immanently*—not if we want to retain the coherence of ontological *debate*.

---

[28] An example of a pertinent journal is *Analytical Chemistry*; but there are lots of pertinent journals. And rather a lot of pertinent articles are published each year: *thousands*, actually.

But suppose we *could* regiment natural language this way. Doing this wouldn't affect the outcome of a different—*metaphysical*—question. Namely: is there an ontologically weighty characterization of "existence" that's independent of issues of language? Given such a notion, howsoever it's established, we can ask if a particular set of immanent quantifiers have as their quantifier domain what exists (in this sense); we can ask whether the extension of "exist," as used in this imagined language, is coextensive with the language's quantifier domain. Hirsch, I suggested in the conclusion to chapter 1, is *not* in a good position to rule out a notion like this because he takes substantial ontological disagreements seriously. And taking these disagreements "seriously" can't *just be* that different quantifier domains can't be trivialized by sentence-to-sentence mappings; more has to be involved than *that*.

It can be argued, similarly, that even if Thomasson is right, there can still be an ontologically weighty notion of existence that we can introduce into natural language by a characterization of it. For example, we might introduce a *criterion for what exists* justified not on the basis of words such as "exist" and "there is," but instead because it tracks a metaphysically important distinction. An example of such a criterion is *mind- and language-independence*. We can argue that there is an important metaphysical distinction between what we "make up" and what we don't. We make up unicorns; we don't make up horses. If this distinction is robust, issues about "exist" and the like in natural language can be sidestepped altogether.

This isn't my strategy in the rest of part I. The reason is that it can be shown—as I have in this chapter, and as I'll continue to do in chapter 3—that Hirsch and Thomasson (and other philosophers) are wrong about natural languages. We *already have* the words to express important metaphysical distinctions, and we already use those words—at times—to express when we think something does (or doesn't) exist in this robust sense. I turn to establishing this in chapters 3, 4, and 5.

3 | Ontological Neutrality in Natural Languages

3.1 Introduction

Central to this chapter and chapters 4 and 5 is the distinction between *quantifier onticity* and *quantifier neutralism*. The widely believed quantifier onticity view takes quantifiers to be operators on subsets of domains of things that *exist*; consequently, their contribution to the truth conditions of the sentences those quantifiers appear in is *essentially* related to ontology. This essential connection to ontology is extended to other expressions in natural languages—"there ... ," "exist," "real," "object"; consequently, if these appear in certain appropriate positions in sentences, then those sentences are taken to convey ontological commitments or denials.[1]

Proponents of quantifier immanence (e.g., Hirsch) presuppose quantifier onticity. Different quantifier domains (in different languages), despite differing in what they contain, also have their distinctive quantifiers operating on subsets of "objects"; the same ontological view is extended to the expressions "there ... ," "exist," and so on of *those* languages. Different existence concepts are taken as corresponding to different quantifier domains.

Quantifier neutralism takes its start from what's established in the appendix to the general introduction. No semantic theory that utilizes the technical apparatus labeled informally as "domains" requires objects of any sort to function successfully. Crucial to understanding quantifier neutralism is the stress on *neutrality*. Although nothing that exists need be involved in the

---

[1] I'm describing natural language from the generalized-quantifier perspective. It can be described from the first-order perspective instead. The issues are the same.

linkages between object languages and metalanguages, things that exist *can be* so involved. If they are, then the language-world relations indicated in the metalanguage are transferred by these linkages to object-language terms; otherwise, not. Picturesquely put, domains can contain no objects that exist, some objects that exist, or only objects that exist.

If I speak of "objects that don't exist," I'm *not* contradicting myself; I'm using natural language as we normally do. (See section 3.3 on the contrastive role of "exist.") This is important. When philosophers accept that an argument fails if pitched against a position at the object-language level, they sometimes try the same argument at a meta-level. But the very tools of natural language that enable talking about nothing are tools that can be used to talk about nothing with respect to the semantics of natural languages as well. The next few chapters illustrate this point in detail.

This chapter provides some usage evidence for quantifier neutrality in natural languages. I show two theses about usage. First, I exhibit sentences that we assert and take to be true, although the background discourse domains for these sentences needn't contain anything. I show, second, that the expressions used in ontological debates—to ontologically commit and deny—are themselves neutral. I mean by this that these expressions (without differing in meaning or being used metaphorically) are also used to state truths (or what speakers take to be truths) without functioning in those sentences to either ontologically commit or deny. I also indicate some obstacles facing opponents of these two neutrality theses. In particular, I explore usage that undercuts ambiguity/polysemy views of natural language ontologically committing (and denying) expressions.

3.2 Natural-Language Quantifiers

Here are some things we can (and do) say:

(1) All the cows in these barns are sick.
(2) All the orcs in these books are evil.
(3) Three-fourths of the tiles in the brown boxes are chipped.
(4) Three-fourths of the deities in the Indian pantheon are female.
(5) A mugger is a frightening thing.
(6) A dragon is a frightening thing.
(7) Some critics only admire one another.
(8) Some mythological creatures only admire one another.
(9) Politicians are universally depicted as asking favors of wealthy constituents.

(10) Witches are universally depicted as owning books of magic spells.
(11) Most cats have been owned by women.
(12) Most cartoon characters have been invented by women.
(13) Hillary Clinton is depicted by the *New York Times* as more civilized than Donald Trump.
(14) Sherlock Holmes is depicted by the *New York Times* as more intelligent than Mickey Mouse.
(15) Nearly all the houses that people own they can't afford to pay for.
(16) Nearly all the houses people intend to build they can't afford to pay for.
(17) Few books are planned to be read by people these days.
(18) Few books are planned to be written by people these days.
(19) No professional except Louise came to the meeting.
(20) No Roman god except Janus has two faces.
(21) It's important to know the differences between brownstones, townhouses, and carriage houses.
(22) It's important to know the differences between elfstones, witchmeads, and warlock wands.
(23) The red table has four legs.
(24) The average star has 2.4 planets.[2]

The standard view of generalized quantifiers takes a relevant discourse universe as the background quantifier domain; noun and verb phrases have sets of that universe as their extensions. The determiner denotes a binary relation between sets of the discourse universe that exemplifies the meaning of the determiner (e.g., "most," "every," "at least five," and so on).[3]

Truism: people disagree over what exists. They disagree about what they're willing to ontologically commit themselves to. I've chosen the above twenty-four sentences so that the odd-numbered ones contain noun phrases—"marbles," "muggers," "cats," and so on—the instances of which *most* people think exist (disagreements among people aside); the even-numbered ones, however, contain noun phrases (and some verb phrases) with instances that *most* people don't think exist: "Roman gods," "dragons," "mythological creatures," "average stars," "owns books of magic," and so on.

---

[2] Although it's easy to characterize definite descriptions in the generalized-quantifier formalism, there is some controversy whether that characterization is true of definite descriptions in natural languages.

[3] See, e.g., Peters and Westerståhl (2006), and references. For an introduction to the topic, see Westerståhl (2011). I'm simplifying somewhat.

Many of these things—Roman gods, dragons, and so on—some *philosophers* argue *do* exist. Some philosophers, for example, think that fictional entities *exist*; they think they're abstracta, or concreta in possible worlds. They give arguments for these claims; the results are sophisticated debates based on contentious assumptions. The above list, however (and that it can be extended arbitrarily by substitutions of noun and verb phrases), indicates that a person's ontological predilections don't affect her ability to utter truths, or what she takes to be truths, about objects she also denies the existence of. The odd- and even-numbered sentences have identical grammatical forms, and appear semantically identical as well.

Furthermore, as the appendix to the general introduction makes clear, the semantic formalism of discourse universes, determiners, and noun and verb phrases *doesn't require* that discourse universes contain what exists. The most straightforward application of the mathematics of generalized quantifiers to natural language, therefore, is neutral: the metalanguage *needn't require* language-world connections.

The burden of proof falls on the shoulders of the non-neutralist. To salvage the claim that discourse domains *do* contain only what exists, various strategies are needed. When a speaker uses a locution to make a claim about something she doesn't think exists—(20), for example—she can be taken as saying something that (i) is nonliteral or (ii) involves an implicit intensional context that provides truth conditions different from those of (19). More generally, an ambiguity/polysemy strategy can be deployed to separate the meanings of the otherwise identical determiner + noun phrases in each case. Also possible is (iii) she, despite herself, is talking about something that exists. These strategies have substantial costs.[4] The crucial cost they all share, however, is that they ignore the semantic and syntactic parallels these statements exhibit, parallels respected by a neutral application of semantics. This alone should motivate exploring the neutrality approach.

Consider (18): "Few books are planned to be written by people these days." This seems to require "book" to have in its extension books that exist *and* ones that don't. This is important because it's one illustration (there are many) of how we simultaneously talk about things we take to exist and things we don't using the same phrases. (I'll give more examples in section 3.4.)

---

[4] I've extensively discussed these strategies and their drawbacks elsewhere. See, for example, Azzouni (2004a), Azzouni (2010a), and Azzouni (2012b).

3.3 Ontological Assertions and Denials

Let's turn to explicit assertions and denials of what exists. Here are several about real and unreal reptiles:

(25) Turtles exist.
(26) Dragons don't exist.
(27) Komodo dragons are real.
(28) Fire-breathing dragons aren't real.
(29) There are turtles.
(30) There are no fire-breathing dragons.

Statements like these are regularly asserted during ontological debates: Bigfoot doesn't exist; there is no Bigfoot; Bigfoot isn't real. (Or, if someone believes otherwise about hobbits: Hobbits *do* exist! Hobbits *are* real!) Are statements containing actual natural-language quantifiers used to ontologically commit or deny? It seems so. Consider this debate:

"Bears eat people."
"No, they don't. Bears don't eat people. No bears eat people. Bears that eat people don't exist."

The last sentence, "Bears that eat people don't exist," looks like both an ontological denial and an emphasis of what the earlier sentences express: "Bears don't eat people" and "No bears eat people." Similarly, "*Some* bears eat people" looks like an ontological assertion, and one that can be followed by ontological assertions using "there is" or "exist": "There *are* bears that eat people," "Bears that eat people exist." On the other hand, "Most bears eat people" *doesn't* naturally transpose to ontological assertion or denial, stressed or otherwise—even though it's clear it can imply an ontological assertion: "Bears that eat people exist." It's also hard to see how "Most bears eat people" would (directly) show up in an ontological debate—as opposed to a debate about what bears *do*. What properties, that is, (most) bears have.

This, I think, is the key. To actually assert or deny ontological commitments is to use "exist," "real," "object," or some version of "is."[5] Saying

---

[5] We can't say in English, "Bears that eat people are," or "Vampires aren't." ("Bears that eat people are what?" "Vampires aren't what?" This is how people will respond because they think the thought hasn't been fully expressed.) We have to say, instead, "There are bears that eat people," "There are no vampires," or we have to use "exist" or "real." Priest (2014, 432) weirdly claims these locutions are perfectly grammatical "but sound rather stretched and precious in English."

"No bears eat people" or "Most bears eat people" imposes a particular relationship on the extensions of "bear" and "eat people." It's not to directly indicate ontological commitment—or anything about the relationship of the extension of "bear" or that of "eat people" to what exists (to the extension of "exist"). To do that is to impose a particular relationship between the extension of a noun phrase and the extension of the verb phrase "exist" ("exist" here taken ontologically). This can happen *implicitly*—due sometimes to ontological assumptions contextually in place about the discourse domain. But assertions about the relationship of one class of items to another class aren't (directly) assertions about which of these items exist, if any.

So, on the basis of the foregoing, I draw the tentative conclusion that assertions and denials of ontological commitment occur directly by using terms such as "real," "exist," and "there is," and not by using natural-language quantifiers.

There are other things we say that support this suggestion, and support more generally the neutralist interpretation of discourse domains. We often restrict what we're talking about explicitly to what exists. To make sense of these expressions, it looks like the discourse domain must contain more than what exists:

(31) If any vampires exist, they're pretty angry.

This isn't meant to be vacuously true by virtue of an unsatisfied antecedent. It won't be if all and only the vampires that exist (if any) are angry, and some of the other ones (that don't exist) *aren't*.[6] Also consider the following exchange:

"Everything exists."
"That's not true. Hobbits don't exist."

The most straightforward construal of this exchange uses a discourse domain containing nonexistent hobbits.

That nothing in the semantics of quantifiers requires ontology one way or another is compatible with the fact that much of the time speakers make assertions where they intend neither to ontologically commit themselves nor to deny ontological commitments:

(32) Most ways of getting around this are awkward.
(33) A futile attempt is a sad thing to see.

---

[6] Imagine we're watching a film about a happy vampire, and you criticize the film by saying (31). Implied is "*This* vampire, surely, doesn't exist."

I doubt anyone but a philosopher has *ever asked* whether ways or attempts exist. The same is true of numbers, actually, and many other things that nonphilosophers talk about without thinking ontologically *at all*. Whether these things really exist is something some philosophers ask and make decisions about. But that it's not natural to pose ontological questions—except in special circumstances—indicates that nothing about discourse domains should (all by itself) dictate that ontology is involved.

I've been writing as if "exist," "there is," and the like are *always* used to make ontological commitments or denials. They aren't. They naturally occur in sentences speakers use where the ontological commitments (that would arise if these words were always ontologically committing) can be denied by those speakers:

(34) There is a certain imaginary woman that Jane and Heather dream about regularly.
(35) There are many ways of getting around this.
(36) Strategies for circumventing anger exist. Many are found in self-help books.
(37) Although waltzes designed to last more than ten hours exist, people rarely dance unexpurgated versions of them.

Anyone can say these things—regardless of whether they believe that imaginary women, strategies, and waltzes (of any sort) exist, don't exist, or are a matter that they would find bewildering to contemplate as existing one way or the other. On the other hand, in an explicit ontological commitment or denial, "exist" is often coupled with a stressed "really":

(38) Chakras *really* exist. People who think otherwise just aren't enlightened.
(39) Sorry to tell you: Santa Claus doesn't really exist.

Nevertheless, even "really" isn't always so used. Sometimes it's purely a rhetorical stress device and isn't meant to indicate ontological commitment or denial. Imagine this being said by someone who doesn't believe fictional entities exist:

(40) You're just wrong about that. There *really are* good orcs in Tolkien's fiction.

My view—I won't argue for it here—is that all commonly used natural-language expressions are neutral this way. They occur in locutions used for ontological commitment or ontological denial, although those same locutions are elsewhere used by speakers without anything ontological being involved. The ordinary-language "refer" and "about" are, for example, neutral, as natural-sounding sentences indicate, such as "We've been talking about Mickey Mouse and Walt Disney" or "He's referring to Mickey Mouse and the inventor of Mickey Mouse." These are natural things to say, that is, regardless of the speaker's attitude toward the existence or nonexistence of what he's talking about.[7]

"Exist" often plays an ontologically committing or denying role contrastively to a neutral "there is." Consider:

(41) There are hobbits (over there) that I'm hallucinating and that don't exist.
(42) There are many magical beings depicted in works intended to be nonfiction, but nevertheless none of these beings exist.
(43) John is frightened of vampires. There is a specific vampire—Dracula—that he's especially frightened of. I've told him vampires don't exist, but he doesn't believe me.

It can also play a similar ontologically committing role along with a neutral generalized quantifier:

(44) Many creatures of folklore—unicorns and hobbits, for example—only exist because several genetic-design companies are now making them.

It can do this with a noun phrase as well:

(45) Vampires are frightening, but luckily they don't exist.

Here's a case where "real" plays the committing role against a neutral "things":

(46) Vampires, unicorns, fairies—none of these things are real! I'm *so* tired of talking about them. Can't we find something that exists to talk about?

---

[7] See Azzouni (2010a, section 1.7) for further details. I'll generally employ a regimented "refer" that's strictly ontologically committing. See Azzouni (2012b, 368–69) for a full treatment of ontological and non-ontological characterizations of "about" and "refer," both in natural language and in regimentations.

Finally, "objects" can function neutrally against an ontologically committing or denying use of "exist." Consider:

(47) Objects that don't exist puzzle philosophers.

Letting the relevant discourse domain contain more than what exists straightforwardly makes these locutions cogent.[8]

On my view, "there is," "real," and so on are often used in sentences without the speaker or audience intending anything ontological. Speakers can subsequently stress or deny ontological commitments, if called on to do so. One way this happens is that the audience treats the previous utterance of "exist" or "there is" as ontologically committing even though the speaker had no such intentions. (Philosophers, especially, like switching contexts on people in this way.) Consider this exchange:

"You're just wrong about that. There really are good orcs in Tolkien's fiction."
"*You* believe there really are good orcs? How weird."
"I said, *in Tolkien's fiction*. I don't mean that orcs *really* exist."

There are, in principle anyway, several possible views about sentences (1)–(47) and the dialogues I've exhibited. One is my view. The words "exist," "there is," and so on are ontologically neutral. Ontological commitment is a pragmatic matter—not one of public meaning—and speakers impose an ontological understanding of their sentences (in ontological debates) by a battery of tools, including rhetorical stress and contextual clues of various sorts. Sometimes an ontological understanding is imposed because of the topic being discussed. "Does God exist?" is a question invariably understood as ontological. The neutrality of these words means, however, that the extension of a noun or verb phrase can be understood by speakers to "contain" only what exists, both what exists and what doesn't, or to have entirely unreal contents. Most often, ontology ("existence"—ontologically understood) isn't

---

[8] Whether "exist" or "real" functions ontologically in a sentence, in contrast to a neutral phrase "there is," a quantifier, or a noun phrase, depends on word order and other factors. Schaffer (2009, 358) writes: "The neutralist seems committed to the following unfathomable conjunction: 'Numbers do not exist, and there are numbers.'" In Schaffer's example, "exist" can't play an ontologically contrastive role to a neutral use of "there is" because "and" connects two apparently independent assertions. Notice, further, that (42) reads very naturally, but "Magical beings depicted in works intended to be nonfiction don't exist, but nevertheless there are many of them" doesn't. It doesn't read naturally, that is, even though I've replaced Schaffer's "and" with a contrastive "but."

relevant one way or the other. The same thing happens in the semantics: the background discourse domain of noun and verb phrases "contains objects" appropriately understood as existing, not existing, or indeterminate.

A far more popular view than mine (among philosophers) is that ontological language—"exist," in particular, or "there is"—is ambiguous/polysemous. These words have different readings or meanings.[9] On one version of this view, they have a "heavyweight" ontologically committing or denying reading; on another, they have a "lightweight" reading.[10] A related view is that "exist" has a single, ontologically committing reading, although it has nonliteral uses. Yet another view is that "exist" has only a lightweight ontological usage; there is no genuine way to interpret use of the word *seriously* as ontological or metaphysical.[11] Despite the popularity of these views, they are all wrong, as I show in section 3.4.

3.4 "Exist" Isn't Metaphorical or Ambiguous/Polysemous

I mentioned in section 3.2 that there are acceptable uses of noun and verb phrases with extensions that speakers treat indifferently as containing items they think exist and don't exist. There are also uses of "there is," "exist," "real," and so on that involve both reference to items the speaker can be ontologically committed to and otherwise. This raises a general problem with ambiguity/polysemy/nonliteral interpretations of ontological language, specifically of "there is" and "exist." Usage seems to reveal no symptoms of ambiguity, polysemy, or metaphor.

Consider this example:

(48) Before he got home he got some beer to get drunk.[12]

---

[9] Ambiguity, e.g., lexical ambiguity, is a matter of different words written and spoken the same way. "Bank" is the typical example. Polysemy is when a single word has closely related but distinct readings, for example, "get," as in "get home" and "get beer."

[10] For differing versions of this kind of view, see Chalmers (2009), Fine (2009), and Hofweber (2007a). In all these cases, the lightweight/heavyweight view is extended from "exist" to "there is," and to the quantifiers, generally, because all of these philosophers model natural language along the lines of the first-order predicate calculus—or generalizations of it; and the natural-language meanings of "exist" and "there is" are taken as captured by the first-order "($\exists x$)." This is true, generally, of all the views (expressed by philosophers) that I describe in the paragraph this footnote belongs to.

[11] I criticized a version of this view—held by Thomasson—in section 2.3. The thought that *only* ontological "lightweight" uses of the words (apparently used for ontological commitment) are available in English can motivate fleeing the vernacular for "Ontologese," as in Sider (2009).

[12] I borrow this example from Hofweber (2007a, 27).

One symptom that "get" is being used in three *different* ways is the infelicity of:

(49) He got home, some beer, and drunk.

Infelicity is the result of differences in meaning, differences in perceived usage, and differences in literality. Although distinct occurrences of the same written/spoken expression in the same sentence can function differently with respect to perceived meaning or literality, *one* such occurrence can't support these distinctive functions *simultaneously*.

Consider, however:

(50) There are cartoon characters and ordinary people who look like one another.

The contrast between (49) and (50) shows that *a single use* of "there ..." can *simultaneously* govern what a speaker can regard herself as committed to and what she doesn't regard herself as committed to (and more generally, what there is and what there isn't).

A defender of the polysemy/ambiguity view for "there ... ," however, might claim that (50) has two *readings*, a lightweight one and a heavyweight one.[13] *More* than two readings are possible if lightweight/heavyweight differences induce different readings—and in a way that puts pressure on the idea that the alternative purported lightweight/heavyweight readings can be due to different readings of "*there is* ..." There is certainly the foot-stamping reading of (50) on which someone ontologically commits herself to *both* cartoon characters and ordinary people. There is also the lightweight reading of (50)—one can imagine—by a person who thinks neither cartoon characters nor ordinary people exist. Interestingly, *neither* of these is popular. The most popular reading is a *third* one on which cartoon characters don't exist and ordinary people do. Yet a *fourth* reading—quite rare (I imagine) but possible—is that cartoon characters exist and ordinary people don't. That's *four* readings, not just the two that Hofweber's view requires there—at most—to be.

This shouldn't be surprising. After all, the central figures for ontological commitment or denial are the noun and verb phrases. If speakers can differ

---

[13] Suggested by Thomas Hofweber, December 2013, and in later emails. He isn't responsible for my presentation.

on what they think exists, then these differences manifest as differences in attitudes toward noun and verb phrases rather than toward uses of "there . . ."

There are cases where speakers can be explicit about thinking that some but not all of the items exist that are picked out by a noun phrase. These cases create problems for those tempted to say that "mice," for example, is metaphorical, or has a different reading, when used to refer to nonexistent mice. Recall the earlier (44):

> Many creatures of folklore—unicorns and hobbits, for example—only exist because several genetic-design companies are now making them.

Required here is that the extensions of "creatures of folklore," as well as "unicorn" and "hobbit," contain things that exist *and* things that don't. Here's another nice example:

(51) Nearly all of the frightening bears we hear about in the news media, luckily, don't exist.

Debates about whether "exist" has more than one "sense" go back well into the last century. Arguing that "exist" has different senses, just as "rising" has different senses in "the tide is rising," "hopes are rising," and "the average age of death is rising," Ryle writes (1949, 23):

> A man would be thought to be making a poor joke who said that three things are now rising, namely the tide, hopes, and the average age of death. It would be just as good or bad a joke to say that there exist prime numbers and Wednesdays and public opinions and navies; or that there exist both minds and bodies.

Ryle is right that it sounds weird or off-key to say:

(52) There exist prime numbers and Wednesdays.

or

(53) There exist cows, Wednesdays, public opinions, and navies.

But *why* do these things sound weird or off-key? Not because different senses of "exist" are betrayed by (52) and (53) but because of an interaction of factors having nothing to do with different senses of "exist." It's hard to think of any context in which it's natural to say (52) or (53). What would someone be trying to indicate by these statements? Without a background story for why someone might say these things, the listener tries to interpret the phrase "there exist" as asserting a bald ontological commitment; but this interpretation is flummoxed because a bald ontological commitment to Wednesdays or (for that matter) public opinions sound weird.

On the other hand, notice what happens when a background story *is* presented. Imagine, for example, that someone—a philosopher—has just made a case that ontological commitments to certain objects arise because of an indispensability argument that has been applied to ordinary physical objects, days, and relations such as beliefs about others. It would certainly be natural, *in that context*, to conclude with "Therefore, there exist cows, Wednesdays, and public opinion." Those philosophers who would downplay the significance of this example because they mistakenly think "the philosophy room" is an artificial and specialized context can instead contemplate this wonderful example that van Inwagen (2009, 487) quotes from Venclova (1983, 34), a non-philosopher:

> In the U.S.S.R. ... as we know, there is a prohibition on certain words and terms, on certain phrases and on entire ... parts of reality. It is considered not only impermissible but simply indecent to print certain combinations of graphemes, words, or ideas. And what is not published somehow ceases to exist. ... There is much that is improper and does not exist: religion and homosexuality, bribe-taking and hunger, Jews and nude girls, dissidents and emigrants, earthquakes and volcanic eruptions, diseases and genitalia.

What's striking about the evidential value of intuitive inappropriateness claims, such as Ryle's, is how comparatively weak they are. This is because the impression of inappropriateness that statements can induce—when they appear numbered on a page without suitable cues to a background story—often *immediately dissipates* when a background story is given.

3.5 The Cogency of Ontological Debate

A lot of the results in this chapter and chapters 1 and 2 are supported by my ongoing assumption that ontological debate makes sense not just to philosophers but to everyone else as well. I've already discussed some challenges to this. My disagreements with philosophers about this sometimes turn on disagreements about language (as the disagreement with Thomasson over sortals does); but it turns as much or more on a disagreement about debating practices among non-philosophers. This deserves further discussion.

There are several ways that contemporary philosophers try to undermine how non-philosophers take ontology seriously. One has already appeared. I'll call it *the Way of Carnap*. The Way of Carnap denies the cogency of natural-language debates altogether: cogent discourse takes place only within a formalized language. Such languages differ in their quantifier domains; as a result, ontological debates are demoted to "internal" descriptions of what's in those quantifier domains, or "external" pragmatic choices of which such languages to speak.

There are (at least) two other ways of attempting to undercut the cogency of ordinary ontological disagreements—even if one accepts ordinary language as a suitable medium for intelligent debate. A second is *the Way of the Existence Pluralist*. This is to claim that there are many different uses of "exist"—all equally good and none of which has a firmer claim to ontological significance than any other. On one version of this kind of view, the non-philosopher is confused about his own usage. He says "Numbers exist" in one context, "Cartoon mice exist" in another context, and "Tables exist" in a third. When he denies that cartoon mice exist, what's actually going on is that he's denying (say) that cartoon mice exist in that sense of "exist" suitable for tables, but not in that sense of "exist" suitable for cartoon mice.

The most straightforward versions of this view are undercut by examples like the ones I used in earlier sections to undermine ambiguity/polysemy/metaphor interpretations (of some of our talk) of what exists, what's real, and so on. Consider (in addition to (50)):

(54) Numbers and people exist who are equally famous—π and Einstein are two examples.
(55) There are dumb ways of doing things and people who are trying to do them that have similar annoying properties.

It's easy, with a bit of inventiveness, to design sentences using "exist" and "there is," like the above, that confound attempts to categorize what "exists" pluralistically.

This motivates the third way of denying the cogency of ontological debates: *the Way of the Existence Deflationist*.[14] The existence deflationist accepts there being one notion of "existence" but argues not only that it applies indiscriminately to all the many kinds of things we describe as existing in various contexts but also (and much more importantly) that no other significant ontological notion can be extracted from natural-language usage.

The Way of the Existence Deflationist founders, however, on the important datum that non-philosophers completely understand ontological disagreements when they take them seriously: this *is* evidence of a significant ontological notion that non-philosophers share with philosophers. The non-philosopher's understanding of this notion manifests in three ways. First, non-philosophers understand when they're having ontological disagreements and when they're not—for example, over God, extraterrestrials, ghosts, angels, Bigfoot, and so on. Second, as mentioned, they take themselves to understand what their opponents are claiming—they understand what it is they are arguing over the existence of. And third, they understand when they want to be committed to something and when they don't.

Notice further a point I made in section 2.1. Non-philosophers understand the distinction between an ontological attribution that seems reasonable to them to argue over and one that instead strikes them as absurd or bewildering—that is, (i) it makes sense to them to argue about the existence of God and extraterrestrials, but (ii) it's bizarre and strange to them to seriously argue about the existence of *ways* of skinning cats or *ways* of being smart, and (iii) it's off-putting to them to argue about the existence of numbers or universals.

This is the data—especially that non-philosophers take extremely seriously the ontological debates they care about—that forces the attribution of a "heavyweight" notion of ontological commitment to non-philosophers that's not in effect every time "there is" or "exist" is actually used. Trained contemporary philosophers forget something Kant never forgot—that there is a great deal of strange metaphysics out there among non-philosophers.

---

[14] See Price (2009). McDaniel (2009, 300) attributes a "generic" deflated sense of "there is" to Heidegger to enable Heidegger to avoid Matthews's (1972) Sense-Kind confusion. Schaffer (2009) is also an existence deflationist: his "permissivism" draws the conclusion from the widespread applicability of the *word* "existence" that existence claims are "obvious." He would dislike the label "existence deflationist" because he claims that the existence so widely attributed is robust. Nevertheless, the description of existence deflationism (and more importantly) the objection to it, both forthcoming, apply to his position. This objection also applies to Thomasson's view on ontology, discussed in section 2.3.

Almost every non-philosopher has heard of various mystical claims about "negative and positive energy"—this talk is popular in New Age circles—as well as reincarnation, levels of enlightenment (accompanied by various kinds of "recognition" about what "reality" is really like), and similar stuff. Ontological disagreements about this are definitely heavyweight; philosophers shouldn't confuse a non-philosopher's disinterest in the ontological topics that professional philosophers study with a disinterest in ontology altogether.

It's true, of course, that professional philosophical debates (over universals or abstracta—even statue/clay concerns) leave non-philosophers pretty cold. It takes most people unfamiliar with real philosophy at least a year or so of intensive study to even get *excited* about such issues. But that's a point about the accessibility of a *subject area*, not about the non-philosopher's understanding of ontology and ontological issues *in general*. Non-philosophers immediately wake up when ontological debate touches on matters that concern them—almost always religious topics, traditional or otherwise (God, angels, chakras, levels of enlightenment, and so on).

Philosophers often condescend to non-philosophers not just by ignoring the (weird) stuff non-philosophers are interested in but also by denying the reality of their ontological concerns altogether or by changing the contours of those concerns in ways non-philosophers would find misleading—for example, that the concerns aren't about whether things exist or not but instead about whether they're "fundamental" or not. The latter is a concern that isn't the same as whether something (a kind of thing) *exists or not*.

Notice that the Way of the Existence Deflationist (and the other ways, for that matter) can be refuted not by denying what its proponents claim about language but by indicating the seriousness that non-philosophers bring to the ontological issues they care about—even though (most) trained *philosophers* refuse to take those topics seriously.

3.6 Regimenting Ontological Discourse: "Existence" Predicates

I've suggested here (and argued elsewhere) that no ordinary terms force sentences to have ontological implications just by their literally used presence in those sentences. Even so, it's possible to coin always ontologically significant words in (slightly) regimented English. "Exist," because of its contrastive role, described in section 3.3, is *very often* used to ontologically commit or deny. Recall (42) and (44) from earlier in this chapter:

> There are many magical beings depicted in works intended to be nonfiction, but nevertheless none of these beings exist.
>
> Many creatures of folklore—unicorns and hobbits, for example—only exist because several genetic-design companies are now making them,

Consider a freshly minted word, "exist$^$$$", that's *always* ontologically committing. In terms of *it*, one can non-contextually (explicitly) introduce ontological commitments despite the other terms of the language it now belongs to being neutral. For example, suppose the regimented predicate is introduced into a first-order language with neutral existential quantifiers, and suppose, in that language, one wants to ontologically commit oneself to at least one dog. This works:

(56) $(\exists x)(Dogx \ \& \ Exist^\$ x)$.

A commitment to the existence of all dogs is managed by:

(57) $(\forall x)(Dogx \rightarrow Exist^\$ x)$.[15]

Capturing ontologically committing statements in the vernacular (ones expressed contextually with otherwise neutral idioms) by means of an artificial existence predicate is, of course, only one of many ways to regiment. Using neutral quantifiers along with an always ontological "exist$^\$$" predicate,

---

[15] See Azzouni (2004a, chapter 3). Fine (2009, 167, and n. 4), using the same approach, alludes to my earlier discussion. He claims, however, that my understanding of the "meaning and role of the predicate appears to be very different" from his. It seems he misdescribes our disagreements. My understanding of the "existence predicate" is that it may be used regardless of one's antecedent metaphysical beliefs about what "real existence" comes to. It's a purely logical tool to be used contrastively in a context where other terms, especially quantifiers, *don't* convey onticity (whatever "onticity" comes to). Fine's use of his existence predicate doesn't differ on this point. (See Raley and Burnor 2011 for a good discussion of how usefully broad—with respect to different metaphysical assumptions—uses of the existence predicate can be.) It seems that my differences with Fine largely come to what the best interpretation for the ontically weighty use of the existence predicate is—what I've elsewhere described as the best criterion for what exists. He pushes "real," writing (Fine 2009, 168): "I myself would prefer not to use the term 'exists' to express the thick sense given its customary association with the thin sense. A better term would be 'real.'" This route is closed to *me*, however, because (as I indicated in section 3.3) I acknowledge that "real," just like "exist," is neutral in natural language. I instead have argued for a criterion of "mind-independence" and "language-independence" as the interpretation of the regimented existence predicate. See Azzouni (2012c), or section 8.7 of this book, for discussion.

however, is very natural because of the already present contrastive use of this word in natural languages.

3.7 A Very Short Conclusion

Quantifier onticity traditionally comes packaged with several other doctrines—ones about truth and logic. It's therefore not enough to establish, as I take myself to have done, that semantic formalisms are compatible with neutralism, and that natural-language usage invites an application of semantic formalisms that respects a neutral interpretation of natural language. What also has to be shown is that incompatibilities don't arise with other doctrines about truth and logic that we want to retain. I turn to this in chapter 4.

4 | Truth and Bivalence

4.1 Introduction

In chapter 3, it was illustrated that sentences with noun phrases or verb phrases that don't refer can nevertheless have truth values.[1] The standard view takes sentences to have truth values because of correspondences between how objects referred to by the terms in the sentence are and how sentences say they are. Neutralism—true to its name—doesn't reject this for every sentence; if all the terms in a sentence refer, then the truth or falsity of that sentence can be due to how the objects are that are referred to by its terms. If some of the terms in a sentence don't refer, its truth value is determined (if it is determined) in a different way, by one or another mechanism of "top-down" coherentist principles and practices that induce a truth value.

A neutralist approach to semantics—especially truth-conditional semantics—nicely combines with a neutral deflationist view of truth (one I've described in other work). In sections 4.2 and 4.3, I sketch how the neutralist approach preserves the description of the compositional properties of language and how (similarly) the deflationary view of truth preserves the needed role of "true." In section 4.4, I explain how, on deflationary views, the language-world relationship isn't determined by semantics or by truth. I also

---

[1] In what follows, I'll often describe noun and verb phrases as "terms." If we view natural language through a first-order lens, "terms" are namelike. Predicates "have extensions" in domains, names "refer to" items in the domain, and quantifiers "range over" the domains. If we view natural language through a generalized-quantifier lens, noun and verb phrases "have extensions" in the domain, and quantifiers (proper names are included among these) are operators "on the extensions" of noun and verb phrases. All the issues I raise and resolve can be described indifferently using either lens. I'll sometimes use one terminological approach and sometimes the other, as I've done in previous chapters.

contrast what I call "fundamentalist metaphysical approaches" with the view being taken here: that the intermediary connective tissue between the truth values of ontologically empty discourse and how the world is isn't determined by grounding relations of some sort, but instead is determined by coherence conditions that impose truth values on sentences. Language-world relations aren't handled exclusively by the logic of "true," nor are they fully described by the deflationary theory of "true"; similarly, the truth conditions supplied by semantic theories don't impose truth values on all sentences. Truth values happen upon sentences in a variety of different ways. Sometimes this is through a straightforward correspondence relation; more often, truth values are induced by coherence conditions (that are parasitic on our ways of discovering correspondence relations). I illustrate this in some detail in sections 4.6 and 4.7 with three examples of sets of truth-inducing coherence principles: axiomatics, the fiction model, and the perception model.

Among the truth-inducing coherence conditions that apply to any discourse—empty or otherwise—is the norm of bivalence. Section 4.5 considers a challenge to this norm. Bivalence, so the challenge goes, can't be attributed to a discourse with truth value gaps. I respond to this challenge by describing the role of ignorance claims that we use to navigate truth value gaps. In section 4.8 I make a few general observations about the coherence model of inducing truth on ontically empty discourse (which I've been illustrating), and section 4.9 is a brief conclusion.

4.2 The Neutral Interpretation of Quantifier Domains and Truth-Conditional Semantic Clauses

Some terminological conventions: Call those uses of sentences "ontically saturated" where all the terms in those sentences, as used, refer only to what exists (where the extensions of noun and verb phrases are restricted to what exists). Contrast these uses of sentences with "ontically unsaturated" ones.

Most of us think that the sentences "Mickey Mouse was invented by Walt Disney," "All the orcs in *The Lord of the Rings* are evil," and "I dream of angels regularly" are ontically unsaturated. Most of us think "Most tables are made of wood," "All people die," and "*Word and Object* is a book" are ontically saturated. (There can be disagreements about this—especially among philosophers.) My current purpose is to illustrate how the neutralist approach to semantics handles truth conditions, truth, and logical principles when ontically unsaturated sentences are involved. So I *assume* that certain sorts of things *don't exist*: fictional objects, dream figures, and so on. (I'll be clear in what follows about what I think *doesn't* exist.) Some (maybe many) philosophers will disagree with me. That disagreement is beside the point during the course of this chapter.

I'll continue my convention of almost always restricting "refer" to terms (names, kind-terms ...) that correspond to things that exist. According to this convention, "Barack Obama" refers and "Mickey Mouse" doesn't; "vampire" doesn't refer either. I'll sometimes describe non-referring names, such as "Hercules," as "empty." (Occasionally, however, I slip into the natural-language neutral way of speaking of reference—one that's shared with neutral interpretations of semantics, as I discuss below.)

One other terminological point. There are well-known issues about whether *sentences* are asserted to be true or false, or if instead it's *uses* of sentences, or utterances, that are asserted to be true or false, or speech acts, or something else. Furthermore, the truth-apt item may change depending on whether the language in question is artificial or natural, and relative to the views of the particular practitioner applying a kind of semantics. I circumvent this complexity with "statement." Statements are to be whatever relevant truth-apt item is the central topic of semantics. None of the issues I'm concerned with are affected by the cluster of issues about sentences, speech acts, propositions, and the like.

Philosophers specializing in semantics have almost universally thought that if standard semantic theories are extended to ontically unsaturated statements, then something new is called for. The appendix to the general introduction shows this isn't true. Philosophers who take seriously a semantics in which truth conditions play a significant role, however, may be worried because they may think that the truth notion involved must be a "correspondence" one. This isn't the case because the linkages between object languages and metalanguages don't require *reference achievement*. In particular, if object-language statements are ontically unsaturated, then the metalanguage statements describing their truth conditions are ontically unsaturated as well. Consider this simple truth-conditional clause:

(1) "Hercules is strong" is true iff Hercules is strong.

This is a perfectly acceptable (although fairly trivial) truth condition, in a metalanguage, of an object-language statement containing the empty name "Hercules"; the metalanguage contains the homonyms "Hercules" and "is strong"—these are "homonyms" of the corresponding object-language words "Hercules" and "is strong" because they are in a different language.

A second illustration will help. Consider the statement "Some talking mice are in Disney cartoons," and consider this truth condition:

(2) "Some talking mice are in Disney cartoons" is true iff {talking mice} ∩ {being in Disney cartoons} ≠ ∅.

This truth condition requires a bit of standard interpreted set theory—in particular, one with urelements[a]—that allows mappings, subsets, intersections, power sets, and so on. Let's assume, for illustrative purposes, that the set theory in question is a first-order interpreted one. (The argument to follow goes through even if this is false—as the discussion in the appendix to the general introduction makes clear.)

Some will be worried. {talking mice} = ∅, they'll complain; and therefore the truth conditions don't turn out as required. "Some talking mice are in Disney cartoons" is false, not true. This presupposes an illicit constraint on the quantifiers of the metalanguage set theory: that the quantifiers aren't ontologically neutral, so that $(x)\neg$Talkingmice$x$. On the contrary: this particular application of set theory (with urelements) has quantifiers that "range over" items like talking mice, and so, in this particular application of set theory, we have: $(\exists x)$Talkingmice$x$.

"But wait," someone may protest, "isn't it *really* the case that {talking mice} = ∅? After all, talking mice *don't* exist (last *I* heard, anyway)." I agree. What's true is that there are no talking mice. But we don't capture that claim (in this neutral set theory) by $\neg(\exists x)$Talkingmice$x$. If we must capture this metaphysical truth, we introduce (as in section 3.6) an existence predicate, "Exist$^\$$", say, and capture the metaphysical claim this way: $\neg(\exists x)$(Talkingmice$x$ &Exist$^\$x$). The quantifiers of the applied set theory are neutral: they "range over" both the nonexistent and the existent, and all such "objects" are the urelements that the sets (and thus the extensions of the noun and verb phrases of the object language) are defined in terms of.

I've mentioned more than once that semantic theories are unchanged by whether language-world relations are had by metalanguage terms or not. In particular, the subsentential compositional properties of statements are describable in either case. Neutral notions of "reference," "extension," and so on are part of the semantic package describing an object language; for

---

[a] Urelements are the non-sets—for example, ordinary physical objects—contained in some sets. For the purposes of this example, Disney cartoons are urelements: patterned celluloid strips, past, present, and future. (Actually, things are more complicated now since cartoons are digitized too.)

example, "'Hercules' refers to Hercules," and "The extension of 'Greek gods' is included in the extension of 'gods.'"

This makes salient a different issue: how do the truth conditions such theories provide, "{talking mice} ∩ {being in Disney cartoons} ≠ ∅" for "Some talking mice are in Disney cartoons," connect to the actual truth of "Some talking mice are in Disney cartoons"? How do they indicate language-world relations? In particular, how can such truth conditions (together with how the world is) *determine* that the statement within quotation marks in (2) is true?

They can't. "Truth conditions" is unfortunate terminology originally coined for a certain Tarskian semantic theory because of the false impression that such semantic theories must yield (that is, *determine*)—together with how the world is—the truth values of the statements to which these semantic theories are applied. On the ontologically neutral view of semantics, a "truth-conditional" semantics can be given to a set of expressions exactly as it's done in various semantic traditions. These truth conditions, furthermore, are *compatible* with the truth values that these expressions actually have. For example, on the generalized-quantifier approach to "Some talking mice are in Disney cartoons," this statement is correlated with the truth of a metalanguage statement, "{talking mice} ∩ {being in Disney cartoons} ≠ ∅," which itself involves various descriptions and (if it's first-order set theory, for example) neutral quantifiers. These semantic theories, thus, although they give necessary and sufficient conditions on when these statements are true, nevertheless don't (together with the world) *determine* the truth values of those expressions. Something else has to. I turn to this in sections 4.3 and 4.4.

4.3 Deflationary Truth: Some Brief Remarks

Most philosophers will recognize the "deflationary feel" to the description of truth conditions given in the last section. I'll now get explicit about certain aspects of "truth" as I understand it.[3] The first point to make is to repeat something I've said. Ontically saturated statements can have truth values on the basis of a correspondence relation between the subsentential parts of those statements (e.g., names) and things in the world; how those things are determines the truth values of statements about those things. Ontically unsaturated statements are different. Although the same subsentential compositional principles are applied by semantic theories to both of these kinds

---

[3] I summarize bits of part 1 of Azzouni (2006) and Azzouni (forthcoming) in what follows.

of statements, these principles yield truth values for ontically unsaturated statements not on the basis of a correspondence relation to non-empty extensions (for example) but on the basis of coherence principles.

Am I therefore offering a pluralist truth position, according to which a correspondence theory of truth applies to some statements and a coherentist theory of truth applies to the rest? I'm not, as I'll explain in the next couple of paragraphs. "True" is a logical device needed for "blind truth ascriptions"—statements of the form "Everything Einstein said on January 2, 1943, is true," or "(1) is false"—statements from which the word "true" is expressively ineliminable. (By contrast, "true" is eliminable from sentences like "'Snow is white' is true."). Given a broad range of conditions,[4] a truth predicate can play this role if the truth predicate obeys Tarski's constraint (T):[5]

(T) For all statements S, "S" is true iff S.

This purely logical constraint on the truth predicate is metaphysically neutral. It guarantees only that statements on both sides of the "Tarski biconditional" have the same truth values. This is enough to enable "semantic ascent" and the other desirable properties of the truth predicate, but it doesn't further demand of statements that they "correspond" to reality in any way at all.

I stress the metaphysical neutrality of the truth deflationism I'm offering: the statements that "true" and "false" apply to may correspond in the traditional sense to how the world is, or they may not. On this form of truth deflationism, the role of the truth predicate is taken as exhausted by its blind ascription role. It can thus be described as a theory of "true"—a theory of the truth *predicate*. It needs supplementation by a theory of "truths"—a theory about how statements in our discourse are *truth-valued*. The traditional theories of truth—correspondence theories, coherence theories, and so on—are theories of *truths*, not theories about the predicate "true." This is why the deflationary theory of "true" is compatible with what I'll describe as "correspondence theories of truths," "coherence theories of truths," and so on.[6]

It's here that these (very brief) remarks about deflationary truth line up with the remarks in the last section about semantic theories. I claimed that,

---

[4] Among them that "true" is a predicate that grammatically applies to all the statements in a discourse, and that something to the effect of quantification within the scope of the truth predicate is managed.

[5] One or another convention, Quine's quasi-quotes, or something else, is in force in (T).

[6] There is more complexity to the categorizing of theories of "true" and theories of truths than what I've indicated here—but nothing that falsifies the points stated. See Azzouni (forthcoming) for the details.

in general, the study of language-world relations separates from the science of semantics. In the same way, theories about *truths*—how statements become truth-valued—separate from deflationary theories about the predicate "true." I turn now to that topic.

4.4 Determining Truth

We still have this question that arose at the end of section 4.2: What determines the truth values of ontically unsaturated statements? We can put the question another way. Many philosophers understand "providing truth conditions" as the project of supplying language-world relations for statements. Apart from the compositional properties of a language described by a semantic theory (which are, importantly, preserved on the neutral view of semantics), "truth conditions" are also given—the conditions under which these statements are true—because these semantic theories are taken to connect statements to the world in such a way as to indicate various worldly circumstances in which those statements will be true or false.

But semantic theories only do this in a special case. Only when a statement is ontically saturated do the extensions of its terms determine whether the statement falsely or truly attributes properties and relations to these things.[7]

By contrast, when a statement is ontically unsaturated, then what induces a truth value for that statement (if anything does) can't be described in this way. As I explain in later sections, describing how truth values are forced on ontically unsaturated statements is complicated—no simple story applies to all cases. Here are two brief initial descriptions of how it can happen. First consider "Mickey Mouse is depicted as a mouse." What determines the truth value of this statement (and what explains *why* it's true) can't be *Mickey Mouse* (because there is no Mickey Mouse). This truth-value determining is

---

[7] In earlier work (e.g., 2010a, 2012a), I borrowed talk of "truth makers": the how-it-is with the things referred to when quantifier domains contain all and only what's real. I contrasted this talk with "truth-value inducers"—what I described as the things in the world that force truth values on ontically unsaturated statements. I've found this language misleads philosophers (e.g., Effingham (2012)) into taking my position as similar to metaphysical fundamentalist positions—ones, for example, that take grounding seriously. Worse, other philosophers see the talk of "truth-value inducers" as indicating a promissory note that a *theory* of truth-value inducers is required; thus my not doing this invites adjectives such as "obscure." See, for example, Priest (2011, 361): "The notion of truth-induction needs to be articulated and explained in much more detail." Required, he thinks, is "a systematic account of the notion [of truth-value inducers] (including how it functions with respect to empty discourse in general, and not just [with respect to specific cases])." So in this section and in sections 4.5 and 4.6, I'll explain how truth values are imposed on ontically unsaturated statements; I'll also explain why the demand for a "general systematic account" is unwarranted, and I'll compare and contrast my view with metaphysical fundamentalism.

done, rather, by certain cartoons and by certain social practices (including verbal ones) associated with those cartoons.

The coherence conditions governing mathematical statements are different. On the deflationary nominalist view (on *my* view), it isn't the nature of the numbers—it isn't the nature of 2 and 4—that determines "2 + 2 = 4" to be true. There aren't any numbers (there isn't any 2 or 4), so there's no relationship between 2 and 4 that can be relevant to the truth value of "2 + 2 = 4." What's forcing the truth value of this statement, rather (and all that *can be* forcing this truth value) is a blend of the (relevant) properties and relations among certain objects that exist—including us, various language events, and our mathematical practices—that jointly yield the truth of "2 + 2 = 4." I'll give more details about these two examples, and others, later in this chapter.

For now, the crucial point is this: although "truth conditions" do supply necessary and sufficient conditions in the technical sense for the truth of statements, the actual truth values of these items are often not *determined* by those truth conditions. This point holds of Tarski's constraint (T) as well as the truth conditions of semantic theories, and for essentially the same reason. Consider (1) and (2) again:

"Hercules is strong," is true iff Hercules is strong.

"There are talking mice in Disney cartoons" is true iff {talking mice} ∩ {being in Disney cartoons} ≠ ∅.

These supply necessary and sufficient conditions for truth in the technical sense that a condition on when statements are true is stated by an "iff" clause. But, as I noted before, these conditions don't determine language-world relations because the statements within quotation marks and the statements on the right wings of the biconditionals are ontically unsaturated. This is why neither the Tarski condition (T) nor the special science of semantics *are whole stories about language-world relations*. At best, semantic conditions are used to tell us how language-world relations respect compositional facts about statements and their semantically significant parts. These compositional facts, however, are operative regardless of whether there are language-world relations or not. Semantics must be supplemented by a direct study of those relations themselves and how they operate. In the case of ontically unsaturated statements, those relations are intricate and complex, and they can't be characterized by the simple laying out of correspondence truth conditions as it's done in semantic traditions that involve truth conditions.[8]

---

[8] This is controversial, of course. But some linguists and philosophers have views similar to mine on this matter. See, e.g., Chomsky (1986), Collins (2011), and Pietroski (2005). Chomsky

Long ago, some philosophers of science who took "unity of science" doctrines seriously attempted to work out reductions of statements about various macro-objects (tables, chairs, zebras, cells ...) to statements about micro-entities (atoms, molecules ...) in a (more or less) *statement-by-statement manner* that would transmit the truth of micro-statements to the truth of macro-statements.[9] The latest incarnation (metaphysical fundamentalism) of this old approach is similarly engaged in trying to show how facts about various "fundamental" entities suffice for making statements that are derivatively true or false about non-fundamental entities.[10] The success of any such ambitious truth-reducing philosophical project, however, requires a certain kind of logical tractability in the relationship between the language (the truths and falsehoods) of what's to be reduced—statements about the non-fundamental—and how the fundamental is.

It seems that contemporary metaphysical fundamentalism is compatible with pretty much any view of the ontology of non-fundamental objects. One can think of non-fundamental objects as either not existing or existing, or one can even think of them in the twisted way Meinongians do. When Cameron (2010) talks of non-fundamental things as "not really" existing, it seems he *really* means it. They don't *exist*, he thinks, and we may apply the word "exist" to them as we ordinarily speak—but that doesn't mean (metaphysically) that they *really do* exist. When Schaffer (2009), on the other hand, talks of fundamental and non-fundamental entities as *all* existing, it seems he means it too—metaphysically speaking. The important relationship for him is the grounding relation between these two kinds of entities—both of which exist in the same sense and to the same degree.[11] Crucial to all fundamentalist views, it seems, is a shared demand—shared in turn with the old philosophy-of-science reductionist proponents—about the *grounds* for truth. When it comes to statements with quantifier domains that contain only fundamental entities (perhaps statements of the fabled language Ontologese), then a simple correspondence-truth picture can work: "*a* is P" is true iff *a* has the property P. If, however, statements have quantifier domains with entities

---

and Pietroski suggest further that there is nothing to be gained—theoretically—by a study of natural-language-world relations; Pietroski (2005) specifically describes such relations as involving a "massive interaction effect," and suggests they are theoretically intractable. I'm hoping they *aren't* theoretically intractable despite involving a massive interaction effect.

[9] Problems with various forms of reductionism were discussed in some detail in Nagel (1960). A giant supervenience literature soon emerged. I discuss this in Azzouni (2010a).

[10] See, e.g., Cameron (2010), Schaffer (2009), and articles in Correia and Schnieder (2012).

[11] I'm not sure there currently are any fundamentalists who sound like Meinongians—but surely that will change. It's a philosophical law that every *niche* in logical space is occupied eventually.

that aren't fundamental, one is required to explain the truth or falsity of these statements in terms of what's true or false about fundamental entities.

Regardless of how this grounding demand is motivated by various fundamentalists, it seems that deflationary nominalists who claim that ontically unsaturated statements have truth values are similarly required to explain how truth values are forced on these statements by what's real. And it's quite natural to presume that at least as far as this aspect of deflationary nominalism is concerned, meeting the demand requires something in the neighborhood of what fundamentalists are searching for.[12]

The presumption, however, is wrong. To start to illustrate this, let's return to the project of working out a specific truth-grounding relationship between statements with terms that refer to objects that don't exist (according to deflationary nominalists) or aren't fundamental (on other views) and statements with terms that refer to objects that do exist or are fundamental. I doubt such a project can work outside applications to a narrow set of cases. Given statements about the nature and number of holes in a piece of cheese (and assuming that holes don't exist or aren't fundamental), for example, we can say for sure that how it is with that piece of cheese (something taken to be fundamental or to exist, for the sake of the example) induces the truth values of the various statements about the nature and number of holes in that cheese. But this only works (more or less) with things like *cheese*. In general, the factors that make certain ways of talking about what doesn't exist true or false are holistic ones based broadly on various linguistic practices (ways of speaking) and corresponding epistemic practices (ways of finding out things about what we're talking about). They needn't be determined by specific objects of the world and how it is with those objects (although sometimes they are). I'll have more to say about this in the sections 4.5 and 4.6. Once that discussion is in place, it will be clear why I'm here expressing pessimism about truth-making-style projects—of any sort, actually. Such projects take their original inspiration from correspondence views of truth, but what's needed to explain the truth-aptness of ontically unsaturated discourse are projects that take their inspiration, instead, from coherence views of truth.

---

[12] Effingham (2012, 339), when describing the project of determining the truth-makers for statements about fictional entities that fundamentalists regard as non-fundamental and that deflationary nominalists regard as nonexistent, writes, "It's a project [both] will find themselves united in answering in more or less exactly the same way." He (2012, 336–39) describes the project this way: For each non-fundamental sentence A (the quantifiers of which range over non-fundamental entities), provide a fundamental sentence B (the quantifiers of which range over fundamental entities). Despite the weakness of this condition (no definition of non-fundamental entities in terms of fundamental entities is required), I argue in what follows that it still can't be satisfied.

4.5 The Apparent Challenge of Bivalence to Ontically Unsaturated Discourse

Here are a couple of worries sections 4.2 through 4.4 may have engendered. Let's consider the set of ontically unsaturated statements about the (nonexistent) elephant that I have as a pet.[13] It seems that statements about my nonexistent pet are free-floating: there is nothing that determines most of them either being false or being true. Maybe that it's an *elephant* and that it's my *pet* have been made truth-determinate by how I introduced the example, but that's at most (along with the implications of these few statements) what's been made determinate. The worry, therefore, is this: why should other kinds of talk about the nonexistent not be equally truth-value-indeterminate?

The second worry: what precludes the truths and falsities of an ontically unsaturated discourse from logical incoherence? Consider an ontically saturated discourse. These statements have truth values *because of* the properties of the objects in the extensions of their noun and verb phrases. It's this (according to certain views) that *makes* an ontically saturated discourse bivalent, and indeed what makes that discourse obey classical logical principles. For example, if a property $P*$ is codified by a predicate P, then for an object $o*$, named by o, "Po" is true if and only if $P*$ holds of $o*$. For the same reasons, the terms of a referring discourse exhibit coherent identity relations. A statement containing an identity sign flanked by two names is true (or, respectively, false) if the objects referred to by these two names are the same (or not). Finally, we have a natural way of speaking of our ignorance of the truth values of statements—p, say—when we don't know what they are. We say: "We don't know whether p is true or false" (or: "We don't know whether p"). What's meant, of course, is that how objects are in the world *forces* one or the other truth value on p, but we don't know which particular truth value is so forced.

How is this managed when noun and verb phrases are empty? What grounds the logical principles governing the statements of an ontically unsaturated discourse? Let's describe a discourse as *coherent* if the distribution of the truth values to its statements obeys (classical) logical principles—including ones about identity. Let's describe a discourse as *truth-value-induced* if our practices with that discourse force it to have truth values. I'll also speak of individual statements in a discourse as being truth-value-induced if they are forced to have truth values by our practices. On a correspondence view, *all* the statements of a discourse are forced to have truth values, and the

---

[13] I owe this way of putting the forthcoming concern to David Laprade.

discourse is coherent. Our questions, therefore, are: what practices do we have that make ontically unsaturated discourse truth-value-induced, and do those practices make the discourses coherent?

Two preliminary points. The pet elephant example shows that we can imagine (or stipulate) ontically unsaturated discourses many or most of the statements of which *aren't* truth-value-induced. Coherence (and the consequent truth-inducing of some statements) is achieved by consistently including enough other truths and falsehoods along with the initial elephant truths (e.g., "A (nonexistent) elephant is my pet") to satisfy the requirements of classical logic. For example, for any statement B, "A (nonexistent) elephant is my pet or B" are among the truths. This isn't an interesting case. To be established in the next few sections is that *there are* interesting cases.

The second preliminary point to make, as I've already indicated in section 4.4, is that it's a mistake to think that the truth values of statements of a coherent ontically unsaturated discourse are derived statement by statement from "fundamental" statements all of the terms of which are ontically saturated. One reason for this is that coherence is induced in an ontically unsaturated discourse "top-down" by verbal practices applied *to* that discourse, not "bottom-up" because of real objects with specific properties. I'll illustrate this concretely in the next few sections.

But first, notice what's required: a discourse is truth-value-induced and coherent if the distribution of its truth values obeys classical logical principles (including ones about identity). This *doesn't* force *every* statement in the discourse to have a "determinate" truth value.[14] This is easy to see, because consistent discourses (in general) aren't complete. Our practices with respect to vagueness in ordinary language illustrate our method of handling a discourse we can describe as governed by a classical (bivalent) logic, although we don't have access to the truth values of every statement. What we do is *speak of* every statement being either true or false, although we also say about most statements that we "don't know" of each one whether it's true or it's false. We can speak of "not knowing" whether a statement is true or whether it's false even when there seems to be no way—in principle—of determining whether it's true or whether it's false, and even when it seems (metaphysically speaking) that the statement is "neither true nor false." Quine (1995, 56–57) is good on this:

> We know from Gödel's incompleteness theorem that every consistent proof procedure is bound to leave infinitely many closed sentences of classical

---

[14] I'm scare-quoting "determinate" to flag an issue I'll raise later in this section: how do we speak of statements "not having truth values" in a discourse that's simultaneously treated as bivalent?

> mathematics indemonstrable and irrefutable. A stronger proof procedure will catch more of them, but never all. Nor can we banish the outliers, even by acquiescing in a heroically complex gerrymandering of grammar; for there is no way in general of knowing which ones they are. Should we declare them meaningful but neither true nor false? This only puts a name to the predicament while complicating the logic. . . . I see nothing for it but to make our peace with the situation. We may simply concede that every statement in our language is true or false, but recognize that in these cases the choice between truth and falsity is indifferent both to our working conceptual apparatus and to nature. . . . It is like Kant's thing in itself, but seen as a matter of human usage rather than cosmic mystery. . . . There is a parallel in our accommodation of vagueness. . . . What I call my desk could be equated indifferently with countless almost coextensive aggregates of molecules, but I refer to it as a unique one of them, and I do not and cannot care which. Our standard logic takes this also in stride, imposing a tacit fiction of unique though unspecifiable reference.

Key is the idea that "I do not and cannot care which."[15] Imposing classical logic on a discourse isn't compatible with truth-value gluts (assignments of both values to a statement), but it *is* compatible with truth-value gaps. The residual issue is how we're to talk about those gaps in a way that's consistent with simultaneously stating classical logical principles such as $A \vee \neg A$.

Some philosophers, nevertheless, think this way of speaking needs correction when it comes to *certain* truth-value gaps. They argue that the actual logical principles—that we express ourselves as taking to be true—should respect metaphysical facts about when statements "really" have truth values and when they don't. So, in this case, permanent truth-value gaps should be explicitly accounted for, not buried in a claim of ignorance. But why? *Officially* deserting classical bivalent logic is costly—not least because that logic best accords with our implicit inference practices.[16] Complementing our acceptance of classical logical principles are admissible expressions of ignorance that handle both kinds of truth-value gaps. "We don't know," we say, both when we don't know enough to determine whether someone is bald and when it's the case that nothing in our (collective) understanding of how the word "bald" applies to heads determines whether "bald" applies or not

---

[15] Also see Quine (1981) and Azzouni and Bueno (2008).
[16] I can't pursue this further now, but it's not that our implicit inference practices actually exemplify one or another instantiation of classical logic. It's rather that our implicit inference practices are best regimented by classical logic (best treated as obeying those principles as a norm). See Azzouni (2009b). Also see the conclusion to part I for a discussion related to this.

to a particular head.[17] Furthermore, as many cases of vagueness in ordinary language make clear, there is often no "bright yellow line" marking out those statements that "metaphysically" lack truth values from those that we've only so far failed to determine truth values for. One reason is that revisions in our methods for determining the truth values of statements or in how we take our terms to apply may change the class of "determinable" statements.

Some philosophers argue that our ways of describing ourselves as ignorant *require* there be a something (a "fact of the matter") of which we are ignorant. If there is no fact of the matter whether the word "bald" applies or doesn't apply to a particular head, then we aren't ignorant of whether or not it applies—so these philosophers argue. But everyone *does* speak of being ignorant in exactly these kinds of cases ("I don't know whether he's bald or not—no one *can* know this"). Notice: this *isn't* the claim that (unknown to us) there actually *is* a fact of the matter about whether "bald," say, applies or doesn't apply to an indeterminate case. *That's* Williamson's view (1994). It's this weaker view: "bald" *can* apply or not apply. Flip a coin to determine this (if you're too neurotic, that is, to leave the situation unresolved).

It *is* quite natural, apparently, to think that if not every statement is "determined" as true or false, then we aren't "entitled to assert that the principle of bivalence is true," as Walker (1989, 33) writes. To say—straight out—that *there are* statements that are neither true nor false is, of course, to *officially* embrace a denial of bivalence. It's—at least—to use "true" in a way that disallows semantic ascent (and thus to unfit "true" for the logical role we need it for). That's why I informally employed the weasel word "determinately." But to say that there are statements that *we don't know* to be true or false isn't to do either of these things. To say, further, that there are statements that (most likely) we will never know to be true or false isn't to say this either—because we're making a prediction about what we're never going to "know," and in particular, we aren't (on pain of contradiction) connecting the permanent and principled unknowability of a statement with its "lacking a truth value." Indeed—bringing in the coin-flipping option—we can say that we're never going to know because we aren't going to bother to (or we can't) assign the statement a truth value with a coin flip. So to say that there is "no fact of the matter" about whether a statement is true or not is *not* to say that it isn't the case that the statement is either true or false. (For to say the latter *is* to desert bivalence.)

---

[17] That we can use "don't know" in cases we recognize to be metaphysically indeterminate I call "the broad ignorance thesis." See Azzouni (2010a, 91–93). I first offered it to handle truth-value gaps in Azzouni (2000, part IV, § 6).

Suppose a (stubborn) opponent complains: "An ontically unsaturated statement, in certain cases, won't have a truth value because, in these cases, we will never *assign* it a truth value (so far as we know), and that means *it hasn't got one.*" (A parenthetical response: What a slender basis on which to deny us the right to adopt bivalence!)

The official response: We're tussling over our talk about *truth values* in exactly the same way that proponents of neutral quantifier domains and *their* opponents tussle over talk about *property attributions to what doesn't exist.* B says: "Mickey Mouse was created by Walt Disney." C responds: "You can't say that because there is no Mickey Mouse." In this case, and in the truth value case, the opponent is insisting either that (a) ontically unsaturated discourse isn't acceptable or, more mildly, that (b) ontically unsaturated discourse must be marked out—semantically—in some way. The response, as always, is that it certainly *is* acceptable (and needn't be marked out semantically) because (i) we employ ontically unsaturated discourse in the vernacular, (ii) doing so isn't to engage in an inconsistent practice, and (iii) the practice can be formalized (proof-theoretically and semantically) in a way identical to ontically saturated discourse.

We can thus speak of a statement having the property of being true or not true (even if it's neither—even if there are no statements) just as we can speak of a nonexistent object having a property or as not having a property (even if it doesn't exist). Alternative ways of speaking, of course, desert standard bivalent discourse (by introducing additional or "determinate" truth values). The suggestion I'm offering is to instead embed this complexity into the epistemic idioms and thus leave untouched our talk of truth and falsity, and the related talk of truth values. I claim further that this is already our practice in natural language.

Two last bits about this. Some philosophers may be tempted to say that we are giving up on a kind of explanation that's required. *Why*—some might ask—is it that we won't ever know whether certain statements are true or false? Answer: Because those statements *don't have* truth values. ("See?" these philosophers might exclaim. "Something has been explained that we didn't understand before.") Response: This isn't a genuine explanation. It's merely the imposition of a semantic-sounding convention instead of an epistemic-sounding one on a verbal practice that we antecedently engage in. The verbal practice leaves—in a discourse—the truth values of a number of statements unaccounted for. We can neither assert nor deny them, and we recognize this to be (with respect to certain statements) a position we are likely to remain in for the indeterminate future. The *explanation* for this is in our verbal practice itself: what we do (or fail to do) to induce truth values on particular statements. This can be conventionally codified either as a matter of statements "lacking truth values" or as a matter of our "ignorance of the truth values of such statements." We can go either way in our description of the situation, but (so I've argued) the former way leads to complications—without corresponding payoffs—that the latter way doesn't incur.

This absence of an "explanation," which some philosophers feel the pressure of, is something that will show up later in this book in other philosophical contexts. (See, in particular, section 9.4.) Without going into a lot of detail about this now, notice that "an inference to the best explanation via positing a set of entities" is an explanatory practice we engage in *a lot*: we posit the existence of entities to provide explanations for the machinations of certain "phenomena." By no means am I denying the value of this method of explanation. I *am* arguing, however, that in the neighborhood of this useful method of explanation is the temptation to commit an ontological fallacy, and an inappropriate shifting of argumentative burdens: the invocation of made-up entities and the charge (against those who would deny the existence of such entities) that without them a certain explanation is lacking.

In this case, specifically, "truth values" are a formal tool—codified mathematically—for characterizing the semantics underlying our logical practices. Even if such a semantics is explanatorily valuable for characterizing our logic, it doesn't follow that we must reify "truth values" the presence or absence of which then forces us to certain choices—in this case to denying we can couple expressions of ignorance with adherence to the norm of bivalence.

The last bit: Philosophers may be tempted to suggest that all this is treating bivalence "as though" it's true, or "as if" it's true—rather than as genuinely true.[18] No—at least as far as our verbal practices are concerned. To repeat: The view I'm offering denies that there are any semantic signals or operators needed to indicate that the application of "true" to ontically unsaturated discourse is unusual or differs in any way from its application to ontically unsaturated discourse. Even the use of the idiom "don't know" can be the same in both cases. It *can* be said, as Quine says, that a "tacit fiction" or a "pretense" is involved. This is a harmless way of conveying the position as long as it's recognized that a pretense- or fiction-operator is *not* involved or required—that's the point of Quine's word "tacit." The aim is to keep the

---

[18] A version of this position can be found in Blackburn (1984).

language as straightforward and simple as possible. I think, however, this isn't just a virtue of a good regimentation of natural language. We speak this way naturally—as I've indicated.

I've offered two arguments against the idea that any approach to discourse that allows truth-value gaps must officially desert bivalence. First, I deny that an acceptance of bivalent logical patterns requires the logical connectives (e.g., "or") to be read as implying that the same truth-value determining practices apply to every statement. The second is that the view being held about bivalence is a companion to the view being held about neutrality, more generally. A statement like "Hercules is strong" needn't be read as attributing to an object—Hercules—the property of being strong. For there needn't be any such object and yet the statement can still be true. Similarly, a statement like "Hercules is strong or it isn't the case that Hercules is strong," needn't be read as attributing to a statement, "Hercules is strong," that it has one or the other property, truth or falsity, because this needn't be the case; and yet the statement ("Hercules is strong or it isn't the case that Hercules is strong") can still be true.

It's time to introduce specific examples of valuable ontically unsaturated discourses. I do that in sections 4.6 and 4.7.

4.6 Coherently Truth-Inducing Ontically Unsaturated Discourse: The Axiom Model

Imagine we assent to a set of statements (in a language) that we call "the axioms" and describe as "true"; we also give ourselves a set of rules that allows us to augment any set of statements we describe as true by applying syntactic transformation rules to them. We describe any statement that "follows from" a set of true statements (using the syntactic transformation rules) as true as well. Imagine that the axioms are first-order theories of various sorts (e.g., Peano arithmetic) and that the transformation rules are some version of first-order logic.

There is no general decision procedure for determining when a set of axioms is consistent. We can only provisionally establish the consistency of a set of axioms by deriving statements from those axioms, and seeing that the transformation rules (as far as we can tell) don't yield contradiction. If this practice successfully goes on long enough, we preliminarily regard the axioms as consistent. Furthermore (think of this as a stipulation), we *regard* every statement in the language of the axioms as either true or false, but not both.

The transformation rules and base set of statements, nevertheless, clearly *threefold categorize* the statements of the language of the axioms. There are those we know to be true because we have proven them, those we know to be false because we have derived their negations, and the remaining ones—those that (we say) we *don't know* to be either true or false. As a result of these (top-down) stipulations—including the one about when we don't know statements to be true or false—such a discourse is *truth-value-induced* and *coherent*. It's also—given certain sets of axioms—a rich and interesting collection of truths.

Axiom systems are often incomplete, as Quine indicates above. So not every statement is truth-value-induced. A version of Gödel's theorem, for example, *proves* that the axioms of Peano arithmetic are incomplete (if, of course, they are consistent). Why should we talk about "not knowing" whether a statement is true or false if we know that neither the statement in question nor its negation is provable? Well, first, nothing *prevents* us from talking this way.[19] Second, it's really convenient, especially if our axiomatic practice includes *augmenting* axiom sets with new axioms. This is an example of what I earlier described as "revisions in our methods for determining the truth values of statements." Once we introduce additional axioms that aren't conservative, methods of proof will (in principle) yield truth values for statements that the earlier axiom system didn't yield.

Let's say we do regularly augment axiom sets, when we can. If an axiom set is syntactically incomplete, we can always add new axioms to it. We can do so via Gödel's theorem, by introducing new statements that we've shown aren't decided even in principle by the axioms and the transformation rules. We can talk of such added statements being "discovered" to be true, or as ones we "now know" to be true.

Let's say we replace an earlier axiom system with a successor one in this way. But we can still identify some of the terms in the new system with terms in the old system.[20] A necessary requirement on this practice is that

---

[19] Priest (2011, 361) claims that when truth outstrips proof, "it will often be the case that we can establish neither A nor $\neg A$. So it would seem that we have truth-value gaps of some kind. How, then, can we justify using classical logic? ... Classical practice establishes everything of the form $A \vee \neg A$. So the classical account of disjunction would seem to go." The argument, as Priest gives it, is enthymematic. I've argued against various candidates for suppressed premises in earlier sections of this chapter.

[20] In some cases, we identify all the terms of the new system with terms already occurring in the old system. Other cases involve new "objects" that aren't to be identified with any of the "objects" already talked about in the old system. Two examples: we stick with what we take to be the standard model of arithmetic—and we interpret our new axiomatization to be about the same objects (numbers) the old one was about. Or we augment an axiomatization of the real numbers with new objects: complex numbers.

we endeavor to make the new resulting system consistent—if, of course, the original is. There is usually a lot of arbitrary latitude in how an axiom system can be augmented.

On my view, the above description can be refined so that it models perfectly our current practices in *pure mathematics*.[21] The point here isn't to make *that* case but only to illustrate that making a discourse truth-value-induced and coherent doesn't require that its terms refer or that its quantifiers range over anything real. For notice: no aspect of this practice *requires* taking the quantifiers as ranging over real objects; nothing in this practice *requires* taking the constants to refer to anything. Nevertheless, we can talk about the "numbers" (or other objects) that the statements of this discourse are about.

That a truth-value-induced ontically unsaturated discourse can be valuable is indicated by the small number of families of axiom sets that can be empirically *applied*. Consider an ontically saturated empirical discourse,[22] and assume further that (as a result) its logical principles are classical (and bivalent) and that we self-attribute ignorance when we can't determine the truth values of empirical statements. Our pure mathematical statements can now be utilized *along with* statements from the empirical discourse in inferences without causing trouble. We can, that is, apply mathematics by adopting a quantifier domain that contains both empirical items and mathematical items. We can also, indifferent to the ontological status of what we're talking about, describe ourselves as not knowing whether an "object" has a property or not. Coherent truth-induced discourses can be joined together with correspondence-truth discourse in just this way because the logical principles are the same, the role of "true" is the same, and the semantics is the same.

---

[21] See Azzouni (1994). I've introduced substantial idealizations, however. One important idealization is that the language of mathematics has been stipulated to be artificial. See Azzouni (2009b) for discussion. Another important idealization is that I've made mathematical practice sound like it's a product of explicit stipulations. That's false—especially with respect to proof methods. But for current purposes these idealizations don't matter: it's relatively unimportant for the illustration of an ontically unsaturated discourse practice if the properties that render it truth-value-induced arise naturally or by artificial stipulations, or if that discourse is itself one that arises in a natural language or in an artificial one.

[22] This is idealization too. Scientific discourse often employs empirical terms that don't refer. *Indispensable* scientific discourse is often like this. See Azzouni (2010a, chapter 4). I'll give some straightforward examples in chapter 5 of this book.

4.7 Coherent Truth-Induced Ontically Unsaturated Discourse: The Fiction Model and the Perception Model

Let's consider a different way that a truth-induced ontically unsaturated discourse can be constructed. Imagine we already have in place a practice of naming and describing *real* objects. We now introduce a game where we name and describe objects that we recognize not to exist. Furthermore, we institute a rule about ascribing properties to those nonexistent objects: game players must do so in a way that's logically consistent with all the ascriptions of properties to those nonexistent objects that have already been stated. Imagine that everyone playing the game has a good memory and is very good at following out the implications of what has been stated to be true so far. Consistency, here as in the earlier axiom model, is something that the players can discover that they have failed to adhere to, because (say) they've failed to recognize an inconsistency in the statements that have so far been stated.

As in the previous case, talk of knowledge and ignorance of the truth values of statements about what doesn't exist nevertheless makes sense. Game players can ask: "Does Sherlock Holmes have hair?" Someone can respond: "No one knows." (This can be true because what's been stated to be true of Sherlock Holmes *so far* doesn't imply anything about this.) And then someone can say: "I know. He does." (The statement "Sherlock Holmes has hair" can now be added to the statements the players know about Sherlock Holmes.)

We can be a lot more sophisticated about this "game." We can *write stories* about fictional beings and allow that contextually given factors about the stories play roles in assigning truth values to statements about the characters in those stories. For example, Sherlock Holmes can be taken to be depicted in a story as a human (even if nothing in that story states that he's human) because that he's human is a tacit presupposition of the "genre" the Sherlock Holmes story belongs to. The claim isn't that *the statements in the stories themselves* have truth values. *Those* statements are (largely) only pretended to have truth values. Rather, truth-valued statements with non-referring terms arise when we talk *about* the stories (and their *contents*). We can talk about Sherlock Holmes *across* stories; we can compare how Sherlock Holmes is depicted in stories with how real people are depicted in anecdotes about those people. In short, just as in the mathematical case, a coherent truth-induced ontically unsaturated discourse about fictional beings (beings that don't exist) can be seamlessly joined together with a referring discourse—one that talks about real objects, such as stories, people who write them, and so on. This is because the logic, the truth predicate, the semantics, and the ways we have of describing ourselves as ignorant are the same.

Notice there are *several* coherence principles our practice uses to impose truth values on statements in this discourse. (In the last example there were just axiomatic derivations and stipulated premises.) There are, first, initial-stipulation conventions: an author making up a character has (more or less) complete latitude in what properties can be attributed to that character. Second, in writing a story, there are additional conventions that determine properties of the characters even if the author never states them—the point about Sherlock Holmes being human is an illustration. These additional conventions parasitically rely on various truths that are adopted by virtue of the kind of story this is. Humans need to eat, for example; they (mostly) live in houses. Houses have such-and-such properties. And so on. A great deal of the implicit detail in a Sherlock Holmes story arises from importing these truths pretendedly into the story, and thus *actually* into the truth-valued discourse *about* the characters and events in that story. Lastly, there is a parasitic reliance on public-attribution practices already in place. Others can talk about the characters in a story and get their properties right or wrong. We can read about a character and be misinformed. In this case, the social tools we normally use to share knowledge when that knowledge is of objects that exist are applied in cases where the objects don't exist.

A child can point at a cartoon character and ask, "Who is that?" "Mickey Mouse" can be the correct response. In saying that "Mickey Mouse" is whom the child is pointing at, an extension of an understood practice of deferred reference has occurred. We can "point at" someone by pointing instead at her representation. In ontically saturated cases, both the representation and what is represented exist. This isn't so with Mickey Mouse, but we allow that the child has nevertheless deferredly pointed to the nonexistent fictional character, and that the child can be informed or misinformed about who that is.

This case illustrates a common method for finding coherentist principles for determining the truth values of ontically unsaturated statements of a discourse: borrow them from our epistemic practices of determining the truth values of ontically saturated statements. Here's yet a third example where the borrowing of coherentist principles is pretty obvious. When it comes to objects of a certain size, we use observation to determine their properties. If I want to describe the color and shape of a table, I can look at it; if I want to determine the texture of part of its surface, I touch it. The properties I attribute to objects on this basis are (defeasibly) the properties these objects have; the methods we use to discover those properties are methods of observation.

Suppose people recognize that there are things they *see* (holes, shadows, afterimages) that aren't real. In describing these as things people *see*, I'm using ordinary language: "Do you see that shadow over there?" "Watch out for that hole, it looks big." We use the same observational practices to attribute properties to holes and shadows that we use to attribute properties to objects that exist. We can determine the shape of a hole by looking at it, or by measuring its depth. And these practices are defeasible in exactly the same way our methods of attributing properties to real objects (that we see) are: we may not have looked closely enough, or something about the way the object appears may fool us.

The last paragraph brought up a point about defeasibility that deserves amplification. An important aspect of referring to (and talking about) real objects is that we can make mistakes about *them*—the objects are different from what we took them to be. Defeasibility arises with the nonexistent as well: making a mistake doesn't require an *object* that we've gotten details wrong about. Each discourse case, however, brings in defeasibility in *different* ways. When perception is involved (as with holes), the defeasibility arises, as just indicated, by our not looking carefully enough. When proof is involved, we can (of course) make mistakes in the *proof*—think that something has been proved (or refuted) when it hasn't. Even in cases of fiction, finally, mistakes are possible, depending on the nature of the deference practice: one can ignorantly think Hamlet is the prince of Latvia, or that Lear has five daughters. An author in the throes of writing a novel can make mistakes—momentarily describe a character's eyes as blue when they're *not*.

This raises a point that needs stressing. To speak of "fictional discourse" and to distinguish that "discourse" from real-entity discourse is to engage in an evident artificiality with respect to our actual-discourse practices. Notice, again (because this came up in sections 3.4 and 3.5), how we regularly speak of what we know (and don't know) about the real and the unreal simultaneously, like so:

We know as little about Shakespeare's early life as we do about Hamlet's.

I think that Mickey Mouse was invented by Walt Disney, but I'm not sure.

Sherlock Holmes is more famous than any real detective, but π is even more famous!

Furthermore, we reason naturally with *groups* of statements that are like these. More generally, the foregoing discussion shows that our ordinary language practices reveal no (linguistic, semantic, inferential, or referential) rifts between statements containing vacuous terms and ones that don't, at least when it comes to making claims about how things are, or when making inferences, or when expressing ignorance of some fact or other, or when talking about what conversants are referring to or talking about; they show no rifts across ontological borders, at least with respect to the semantics of ordinary discourse, its logic, and the epistemology governing that discourse.

I've engaged in an artificiality, therefore, in describing various discourses about nothing (in particular, mathematics, storytelling, and discourse about holes and shadows) as if practices of referring to (and knowing about) nonexistent objects that we see arise when people (i) deliberately introduce terms to "refer to" these nonexistent things and quantifiers that "range over" these things, (ii) introduce a practice of attributing properties to these things that are parasitic on their ways of attributing properties to things that do exist, and, finally, (iii) ensure that these practices are truth-value-inducing by being consistent about their property attributions and by describing themselves as not knowing certain things that can be asked about these nonexistent objects. These toy illustrations, which I've used to make clear to *philosophers* the unproblematical nature of referring to what isn't, shouldn't allow an impression that such discourses are isolated in a way that enables them to be treated (semantically, for example) as special cases.

So the exposition of these three examples of ontically unsaturated discourses has been deliberately simplified in various ways. Nevertheless, the added complications—I claim—are just that: added complications. They change nothing essential to the cases.

4.8 Some General Points About Coherence As a Model for Truth-Induced Ontically Unsaturated Discourses

I've recommended we conceptualize the process of truth-inducing ontically unsaturated statements along the lines of the coherence theory of truth. Recall how this old view went:[23] Statements are true if they cohere with other truths. What I've done is treat coherence as part of the package of understanding how truth values are imposed on statements (along with correspondence for ontically saturated statements) under a general deflationist understanding of the logic of the truth predicate. In particular, the coherentist principles I'm offering are non-global impositions of truth values on ontically

---

[23] See, e.g., Lynch (2001, 99–102) and citations; also see Walker (1989).

unsaturated statements. The suggestion *isn't* the offer of self-contained discourses governed by coherentist truth-imposing principles. Ontically unsaturated discourses (about fictions, about mathematical entities, about hallucinated entities) aren't independent of other self-contained discourses, ones governed (say) by correspondence truth. This is because referring and non-referring terms can occur together in the same statements.

Instead (but only to the extent that different kinds of discourse are distinguishable), discourses can be coherentist in different ways. All coherentist principles involve augmenting truths (and falsehoods) against a background of already-in-place truths—although this isn't (strictly speaking) necessary. But the methods of augmenting the truths (and falsehoods) differ in each case. What motivates the choice of methods can be described as: what we're trying to say in each case. In the case of holes, we're using language to describe different aspects of the contours of actual objects (or what we take to be actual objects) in ways difficult or impossible to do otherwise. We have pieces of cheese, for example, that are perforated in all sorts of ways. We want to describe and compare these perforations. To do so involves talking about holes and attributing properties to them, even though there aren't any.[24] And many cases are like this. The coherence principles used to induce truths about the holes are a parasitical application of the perceptual methods used to recognize truths about hillocks.

It might be thought that talk of afterimages, appearances, or even hallucinations are similar: we're trying to describe brain states but haven't the language to do this directly. This isn't what I think is going on: we're trying to describe how things *seem* to others and ourselves. This invariably involves talking about what isn't real, but the coherence methods for inducing truths are different. In this case, for example, there are a lot of inferences from the behavior of others to how we would describe things were we behaving similarly. Sometimes we use perception; but a lot of what we call "introspection" doesn't fall under that category.

Practicing mathematics, lastly, has *many* motivations. Like fiction, one of these motivations is entertainment. But proof-governed discourse about imaginary objects has proven indispensable to science—and so another motivation for mathematical practice is to generate proof-tractable ways of teasing out the implications of scientific theories. Here we use reasoning methods of proof that are widely applicable, but we apply them in this case to stipulated truths.

---

[24] See Lewis and Lewis (1983).

Fiction—being motivated almost entirely by sheer entertainment—often has (as a practice) the weakest grip on coherence: we can create contradictory characters. But discourse *about* fictional characters—a discourse that must be ontically unsaturated[25]—must be coherent to mesh with ontically saturated discourse. Its aim, of course, is to capture as accurately as possible our fictional practices. So the way its ontically unsaturated statements are given truth values tracks as closely as possible those practices. As I mentioned earlier, the coherentist truth-inducing methods are, in part, conventions of genre and, in part, parasitic on how we would describe situations if they were real. Hearsay and what we witness are both relevant.

The old coherentist view faced a famously major philosophical quandary because the coherentist characterization of truth was to apply to *every* statement in our discourse. Coherence can't be beefed up into a tight enough constraint to avoid arbitrariness.[26] Mere consistency plus logical principles, for example, yields numerous equally good maximal collections of statements. The localized version of the application of coherence constraints on ontically unsaturated discourse on offer here doesn't face this problem. Pure mathematics escapes the concern altogether because it can embrace the arbitrariness. Alternative set theories, alternative mathematics based on different logics—all these can coexist comfortably within mathematical practice. Applied mathematics meets the constraint because applied mathematics must fit with the empirical doctrine it's applied to, and empirical discourse isn't (generally) coherentist. In the fictional case, something different (yet again) is at work: the ontically unsaturated discourse is keyed to specific fictional works. Characters can be made up at any time, and later stories can change the traits of characters. But when talking about those characters we must generally index which stories our claims about the characters apply to, and then the constraints on what we can say are tightened up. Hallucinations, finally, are involuntary experiences (they usually are, anyway) and we are trying to describe those experiences. We can't, therefore, say anything we want because we use the ordinary epistemic methods of perception to determine (defeasibly) the properties of nonexistent hallucinated objects.

The old truth coherentist faced a second quandary that's not as famous as the arbitrariness charge, but is as important. This was the issue of what *coherence* means. Coherentists pointed vaguely in the direction of logic or meaning. But none of this is particularly rich in content, and it looks quite a bit thinner than it did perhaps a century or so ago, when coherentist truth

---

[25] See Azzouni (2010a, chapter 3), Azzouni (2012b, 375–77). I discuss this further in chapter 5.
[26] See Russell (1912, 122).

was more in vogue. Logic doesn't supply enough connective tissue to even yield the observational consequences of scientific theories. The vocabulary of scientific theories—especially in physics—is different from observational vocabulary, and pure logic can't bridge vocabulary differences. Definitions of theoretical nomenclature in terms of observational vocabulary would suffice, but the various failures of definitional reductions of scientific theories to one another, or to the language of observation, rules this out.[27] Meaning relations won't help, especially in scientific settings, where they are at best temporary heuristics, deserted as soon as things get difficult. But even in natural languages they're pretty useless because we've since learned just how rare they actually are.[28]

My invocation of "coherentist" truth-inducing principles is deliberate. For these principles that I've described are a rich source of alternatives to the thin and abstractly described offerings of traditional truth coherentists. Our discourse about hallucinations, for example, is—at least in principle—as detailed as anything we might learn by ordinary perception. I may be able to say a great deal—that's true—about particular hallucinated figures. These truths are induced by treating our knowledge of hallucinated objects as perceptually accessed in the same way that our knowledge of middle-sized objects that we perceive is accessed.

I'll close this section with a last point. By no means have I exhausted the ways that we can cleverly introduce coherentist truth-attributing practices to ontically unsaturated statements. There are many ways to do this, and that is why I'm not offering a *theory* (despite Priest's demand) of how ontically unsaturated discourse is truth-induced. My aim has been to illustrate some central examples of this kind of discourse and sketch how they operate. There are other cases as well; I intend to talk about them in later work.

4.9 A Short Conclusion

Here and in chapter 3, I've endeavored to present the neutrality approach in some detail—more detail than I've given previously. In particular, I've responded to a number of objections raised recently by philosophers critical of my approach. More broadly, I've indicated why the scope of semantic theories shouldn't be bloated to the point that they are required to explain language-world relations. Pressing the requirement that semantic theories

---

[27] See Azzouni (2000, part I) and Azzouni (2010a, chapter 4) for further discussion.
[28] See, e.g., Fodor (1981) for a nice discussion of this point.

characterize language-world relations is equivalent to a quantifier-domain onticity requirement—something ruled out by the evidence of ordinary usage. Language-world relationships, instead, are more subtle: coherentist factors play as much of a role as correspondence relations between terms and the world—perhaps even more of a role.

In chapter 5, I turn to providing additional evidence for the neutralist construal of ordinary language—by exhibiting some applications of the approach to mathematics, to ordinary life, and to the sciences.

5 | Applications of Neutrality

5.1 Introduction

Broadly speaking, there are two ways that the neutrality interpretation of quantifier domains can be applied. The first is to use it to make sense of how we speak in natural languages, ways of speaking that are distorted by quantifier-onticity interpretations of that talk. The primary collection of examples, seen in previous chapters, were of how we normally talk about what we simultaneously take not to exist. I revisit the topic in more depth in this chapter, focusing on the role of talk of nonexistents in ordinary life, the sciences, and mathematics. The other kind of application is more officially philosophical—although it's intimately related to the first. There are many cases where, in order to engage in a practice (mathematics, science, characterizations of one or another common-sense situation), statements of the form $(\exists x)Px$, where P characterizes a kind of object, seem indispensable. During an ontological debate over Ps, and without the neutrality option, the proponents of Ps (numbers, space-time regions, furniture ...) have the debating advantage because of the apparent ontological commitments undertaken by having to assert certain statements. Given the neutrality option, how we speak won't force commitments on that basis alone. I illustrate the form of these debates if the neutrality option is admitted.

5.2 Ontological Debates

Imagine that the debate between Platonists and nominalists has reached this stage. Both parties recognize that mathematical talk (i) is indispensable and (ii) can't be replaced with talk that has quantifier domains that *don't* contain mathematical objects. By describing mathematical talk as indispensable,

I mean there is a practice in place with mathematical statements S, empirical results E, and an (open-ended and indeterminate) class of empirical results R, where the statements of R can be deduced using statements of S and E but can't be deduced from the statements of E alone. Furthermore, among the needed statements of S are ones of the form $(\exists x)Px$. Finally, near as we can tell, there is no replacement class of statements S* that can be used instead of S and that don't imply statements of the form $(\exists x)Px$.[1]

If neutralism wasn't an option, this indispensability argument would enable Platonists to score an initial win against nominalists on the grounds that statements of the form $(\exists x)Px$, where P designates a kind of mathematical object, are indispensable in the above sense. Given the neutrality option, both parties can agree that a class of mathematical statements is indispensable to empirical science, but can disagree over whether the objects that appear in the quantifier domains of these statements exist.

Given neutralism, the ontological disagreement can be treated as a disagreement about *ontology* and nothing else. Introduce the regimented existence predicate "Exist$^\$$" from section 3.6, and consider the number-theoretic claim $(x)(y)(\exists z)(x + y = z)$. If addition is indispensable in the above sense, then this is a statement that both parties to the dispute agree with. Their disagreement is over this: $(x)(y)(\exists z)(x + y = z\ \&\ \text{Exist}^\$ z)$. Let N hold of numbers. The nominalist claims $(x)(Nx \rightarrow \neg\ \text{Exist}^\$ x)$; the Platonist claims $(x)(Nx \rightarrow \text{Exist}^\$ x)$.

Notice the intuitively satisfying flavor of this dispute. The nominalist understands the various Platonist claims, and agrees with most of them. (The only statements he *must* disagree with are the existence claims.)

As we saw in chapter 1, however, the cogency of this dispute is undercut by quantifier variance (or quantifier immanence) doctrines. In order for nominalists and Platonists to have a dispute, they must share an existence predicate, "Exist$^\$$," that they disagree about the extension of. Thus the Platonist can disagree with the nominalist by asserting something the nominalist denies: "There are many prime numbers, and they all exist." This shared existence predicate must be *transcendent*; it can't have different meanings as each disputant uses it so that they talk past one another.

---

[1] Both parties to this debate agree, that is, that Field-style nominalist-paraphrase strategies, and others like it, have failed. As they have. See Bueno (2014) for a survey of many of these approaches and their technical drawbacks. See Azzouni (2015) for why nominalist approaches detouring through non-first-order logics fail. See Azzouni and Bueno (forthcoming) for discussion of various technical (and philosophical) drawbacks of Field's approach and for discussion of similar drawbacks of the recent descendant approach of Arntzenius and Dorr.

A similar debate occurs between proponents of commonsense metaphysics and metaphysical nihilists—where "metaphysical nihilists" are understood only to be ontologically committed to metaphysical simples of some sort that aren't composed of smaller items the way that furniture and other macro-objects are.[2] Assume we have a theory of some sort, or (more vaguely and uncontroversially) a way of describing ordinary objects, such as furniture. We talk about chairs, and describe some of their properties—they're artifacts, for example; most of them have four legs; they're composed of atoms; and so on. Call this (indeterminately large) set of statements D^v. We speak in natural languages about these things, but find that—as in the mathematical case—statements like "There aren't enough chairs in this room" and "Some tables have chairs designed for them" are indispensable to our furniture discourse. That is, we seem to have ontological commitments to middle-sized macro-objects of the sort metaphysical nihilists want to deny. As before, both parties recognize that furniture talk (i) is indispensable and (ii) can't be replaced with talk that has quantifier domains that *don't* contain items of furniture.[3]

If neutralism wasn't possible, this indispensability argument would enable commonsense metaphysicians to score an initial win against metaphysical nihilists because statements of the form $(\exists x)Px$, where P designates a kind of furniture, are indispensable. Given neutralism, both parties can agree that a class of furniture statements is indispensable to commonsense discourse but disagree about whether the objects exist that those statements quantify over.

As before, the ontological dispute can be precisely focused as a disagreement about *ontology* and not about anything else. Consider the furniture-theoretic claim $(x)(Tx \rightarrow (\exists z)(Cz \ \& \ xFz))$ ("For each table, there is a chair that fits with it"). Suppose that this claim (or some other claim like it) is one both parties want to preserve agreement on. With neutrality, they can. Their disagreement can be focused on $(x)(Tx \rightarrow (\exists z)(Cz \ \& \ xFz \ \& \ \text{Exist}^s z))$. Indeed, given that F holds of all items of furniture, the metaphysical nihilist

---

[2] I draw material from van Inwagen (1990, 2001) and from some of the subsequent literature on this topic, e.g., Bennett (2009), Hudson (2001), Sider (2011), and Wasserman (2015). I'm also borrowing some of my own discussion from Azzouni (2015).

[3] Similar to the mathematical case, many metaphysical nihilists think they escape ontological commitments to chairs by the use of, in this case, plural quantifiers: "There are chairs" can be replaced by (they think) "There are simples arranged chairlike." As in the mathematical case, however, detours through formalisms are no escape from indispensability arguments. See Azzouni (2015).

claims $(x)(Fx \rightarrow \neg \text{Exist}^\$ x)$; the commonsense metaphysician claims $(x)(Fx \rightarrow \text{Exist}^\$ x)$.

The upshot is that Platonist and nominalist, commonsense metaphysician and metaphysical nihilist, can possess the same vocabulary and share the same quantifier domains. The disagreement is over whether the extension of the existence predicate includes mathematical entities or items of furniture.

Let's turn to the car/incar-outcar debate between two communities that are otherwise nominalists. This is somewhat different. Here too, though, both groups can talk about incars, outcars, and cars; both groups can accept truths about incars, outcars, and cars that enable mutual understanding. What they disagree over is only whether cars (respectively, outcars and incars) *exist*. There is no danger, therefore, of these opponents talking past one another because they don't have an existence concept in common. The nub of their debate (as with nominalists, Platonists, and furniture disputants) turns only on the extension of the transcendent, ontologically significant existence predicate.

Vehicle disputants have another option, however. They could say instead: *If there were* incars and outcars (*if there were* cars), they would have such-and-such properties; but there aren't. This way of characterizing the dispute, however, forces it to be over more than the extension of the existence predicate. Statements, instead, must be listed that each opponent holds—as I described their debate in section 1.3.6. Each opponent "understands" the other opponent's position by virtue of the statements they disagree over. The car-believer, for example, will list the entire set of sentences about incars and outcars that the incar/outcar-believer accepts, and understand the incar/outcar-believer's position that way. There is nothing that rules this out, as there is in cases (as with the Platonist/nominalist and furniture disputes) where indispensability issues intrude. But it does seem to slightly distort the dispute, which otherwise is a clean matter of ontology: whether something exists that both parties describe the same way.

Regardless, it seems that vehicle disputants will prefer understanding each other in one of the above two ways rather than by Hirsch's sentence-to-sentence mappings (discussed in section 1.3). They won't like this construal of their debate: "Well, using such-and-such a sentence-to-sentence mapping, it's obvious that the person who talks about incars and outcars is *really* just talking about cars (and vice versa)." Given that both parties have the same vocabulary items, "car," "incar," and "outcar," their disagreement is over what it *seems* to be over: whether things like incars and outcars *exist*. The disputants can agree that their ways of talking can be mapped to one another, but they'll also agree that sentence-to-sentence mappings obscure what they're disagreeing *about*: what sorts of ontological boundaries carlike objects *have*, and how many there *are*. Their ontological disagreement, thus, is mishandled by Hirsch's quantifier variantist in two ways: first, by eliminating a mutual tool needed for debate, the shared transcendent existence predicate, and second, by treating disputants as agreeing when they don't.

It *can* be argued, of course, that their disagreement is metaphysically insignificant (because, say, it's a disagreement over where to draw ontological borders, and that isn't metaphysically important—contrary to the views of *both* disputants). This, however, needs to be *established* (if it's true), and it's very different from taking away the disputants' tools for arguing with one another and then claiming that they agree on the basis of some other tool that obscures the source of their disagreement.

It's striking how *intuitive* the neutralist's analysis of ontological debate is: how close to the ordinary understanding of ontological debates is a characterization in terms of a shared neutral quantifier domain coupled with an ontologically significant transcendent existence predicate. This is additional evidence that the neutrality picture correctly captures natural-language debates. It's, in particular, an application to ontological debates of the contrastive role of the ordinary-language word "exist" (section 3.3). It also supports the idea that "exist," when used this way, is transcendent.

The Platonist/nominalist debate and the furniture debate (and others like these) are special cases because of the substantial numbers of truths (and falsities) that both opponents must accept—because of indispensability issues. This means that they understand one other very well—well enough, for example, that a nominalist can be a successful mathematician if she wants without giving up on her nominalism. (And well enough for metaphysical nihilists to nevertheless design furniture.) These are cases where a disagreement over ontology takes place against a background of *many* truths held in common. The vehicle debate needn't be characterized in terms of truths held in common—but the recognized disputed truths are equally available to both parties. Cogent ontological disagreements are possible, however, even when there aren't many background truths for the two parties to rely on to understand one another.

The paradigmatic case of an ontological debate—over God—often has this quality; it needn't be at all like the ontological debate between Platonists and nominalists. "God exists," says one or another kind of theist; "God doesn't exist," says one or another kind of atheist. Non-philosophical opponents of this sort typically see themselves as completely understanding one another, and as disagreeing only over whether God exists.

What's needed, to get the argument going, is a contested statement, "God exists," assented to by the theist and denied by the atheist. But forms of this particular debate needn't turn on specific characterizations of "God" that the atheist and theist are implicitly working with. The atheist and the theist may not have definitions for their respective notions of "God." They may not be confident about what truths they take to hold of God. This is a point—first stressed by Kripke (1980)—about non-philosophers with respect to most proper names. So we can imagine that the disputants both have a proper name, "God," in their vocabulary, and that they correctly presume that they more or less agree on how they would apply that word—to the same being—if they agreed on the ontological status of God.

They also agree, independently of their particular views about whether God *exists* or not, that what they think about God could be wrong: it could be he's not quite omnipotent, say, but only nearly so, or that he's omniscient but this is compatible (or not) with the future being open-ended in various ways that go beyond his knowledge, and so on. It's hard to supply definitions for most of our names—but it feels especially hard to do this for "God" because of these kinds of complications over what believers take themselves to be *sure about* with respect to God.

This means that, although this theological debate can be characterized ontologically in terms of a disagreement over the existence of something, there aren't clearly stated further claims about that being that the opponents need agree (or disagree) about. Nevertheless, both speakers can describe their disagreement easily if they have access to a neutral quantifier domain (and empty names) as well as to the transcendent existence predicate "$\text{Exist}^\$$." They can disagree over the sentence "$(\exists x)(x = g\ \&\ \text{Exist}^\$ x)$," or, equivalently, "$\text{Exist}^\$ g$." They take themselves to understand one another, and as able to state their disagreement even though they can't be specific concerning the truths about God that they agree or disagree about. The name "God," along with their access to an ontological transcendent existence predicate, suffices.[4]

Interpreting quantifier domains neutrally coupled with an ontologically significant existence predicate makes ontological disputes as easy to represent in natural languages (and in formal languages) as disagreements over the properties of objects that both parties agree exist. If A and B disagree over whether a certain object o is red (R), their disagreement amounts to a disagreement over the statement $(\exists x)(x = o\ \&\ Rx)$, or, equivalently, Ro. It's

---

[4] Most opponents of neutralism don't have a problem with this case. The most difficult cases for the traditional Quinean—notoriously—are the first two, where indispensability issues intrude. Of course, the quantifier variantist can't handle *any* of these cases—not as "disputes," anyway.

clear, in ontological debates, that both disputants place the item in question in their respective quantifier domains; the disagreement is over whether the existence predicate applies to the item so placed or whether it doesn't apply.

The expressive resources had by neutralists (and that occur in natural languages) allow discussions of the nonexistent in ways that even non-philosophers, however, can get confused about. Saying that Sherlock Holmes doesn't exist and that he's a fictional being who was addicted to cocaine can be made to sound inconsistent because, after all, if Sherlock Holmes doesn't exist, then *he* can't have been addicted to cocaine (nor not addicted to cocaine, for that matter). Again, the point to be clear about is that consistency in our discourse is the only requirement (nothing metaphysical is involved); and that often we demote a nonexistent character's properties to the safer ones of being *depicted in such-and-such work*, to avoid the apparent inconsistency with our own claim (say) that no one (with Holmes's particular attributed set of properties) was ever addicted to cocaine.

It isn't *always* necessary to invoke the "depicted as" or "presented as" phrases when talking about nonexistent fictional entities.[5] Write $(\exists x)$ $(\ldots x \ldots \& \text{Exist}^\$ x)$ as $(\exists x_E)(\ldots x \ldots)$, and notice that $(\exists x_E)(\ldots x \ldots) \vdash (\exists x)$ $(\ldots x \ldots)$, but not vice versa. Similar principles hold with respect to when and how we instantiate empty and non-empty constants.[6] So we can comfortably claim that Sherlock Holmes himself lived at Baker Street and not worry about a conflict with nobody (fitting such and such a description) living at Baker Street. The latter claim (about nobody ..., etc.) is restricted to existing things. The first statement is of the form Bh, where h is vacuous; the second statement is of the form $\neg(\exists x_E)Bx_E$. These don't contradict each other.

Some of us want to say: Sherlock Holmes *didn't* live at Baker Street. Doing *this* is to challenge the very idea that there can be (true or false) statements containing vacuous singular terms. The right response, therefore, is to say that the challenger is trying to undercut one ordinary—and perfectly acceptable—way of speaking by replacing it with another ordinary way we have of speaking. This second way of speaking occurs when we try to restrict ourselves to talk that must be characterized by a quantifier domain containing *only* what exists. When someone does this in a debate over what's true or false about, say, Sherlock Holmes, the right response is that the term

---

[5] I more or less overstated the need to invoke such phrases in Azzouni (2010a, e.g., 83–84).
[6] Not in ways that go beyond ordinary logic to any of the varieties of "free logic"—the principles involved are simply the classical-logic ones involving constants and restricted quantifiers. If Sherlock Holmes doesn't exist, you can't infer $(\exists x_E)(\ldots x \ldots)$ from $\ldots h \ldots$; only $(\exists x)(\ldots x \ldots)$ may be inferred.

"Sherlock Holmes" doesn't pick anything out, and so there is *nothing* to say (in this *second way* of speaking) using it.

We never have a problem using vacuous terms, of course—that's been one burden of this chapter and previous chapters. But if we know a term is vacuous *and* we assert truths using it (such as "Sherlock Holmes is depicted as living at Baker Street") *and* we simultaneously attempt to honor onticity constraints on the quantifier domain—*that* results in incoherence.[7]

It's important to state (not for the first time and not for the last time) that a *metaphysics* of nonexistents (*nontology*, one might call it, if one were kind of witty) is *not* on offer here. The presumption is that there are no such objects and so they have no properties. What's primarily of concern is how vacuously termed statements can be true or false in ways that satisfy the demands of indispensability without landing in contradiction.

Given the foregoing, a valuable supplementary notion for the characterization of truth-value-inducing—described in sections 4.6 and 4.7—is the distinction between *object-based property attributions* and *truth-based property attributions*.[8] Object-based property attributions are statements of noun-phrase/predicate form that are true or false in virtue of whether the predicate applies to the (existing) object the noun phrase refers to. We can thus correctly attribute the predicate "gray" to the table because the table *is* gray. By contrast, the property attribution "Mickey Mouse has black ears" is true not because there exists an object (Mickey Mouse) that *has* black ears, but only because the *sentence* "Mickey Mouse has black ears" is true.

5.3 Scientific Quantifier Domains

A great deal of scientific language indispensably involves what many practitioners in the field will describe as things that don't exist. Consider this example from Melia (1995, 227):

(1) The average star has 2.4 planets.

No one (pretty much) believes there *are* average stars that have 2.4 planets. And yet a statement like this is indispensable because we can't paraphrase it into something without the vacuous term "average star." Even if we

---

[7] Honoring onticity constraints, in any case, can't be managed systematically and consistently—because of the widespread indispensability of vacuous terms.
[8] See Azzouni (2012a).

knew the exact number of stars and planets, we'd be unable to write down the extremely long statement that this one is standing for. "Average things" ("average men," "average cars," "average zebras," and so on) are extremely common in the sciences. Scientific laws, or what amount to laws in certain sciences—biology, sociology, economics—are often stated in terms of average Ps, or in terms of other "calculated nonentities"—things that practitioners don't take to exist.

As in philosophy of mathematics, there are heroic attempts (by philosophers) to either paraphrase statements like (1) away, treat them as a kind of metaphor, or design a kind of operator—fictional, pretense, or otherwise—that protects us from what are otherwise apparent ontological commitments to average things. I have argued against these approaches in previous work.[9] To a very large extent, the problem they face is "the external discourse demand" (Azzouni 2010a) that such statements have to function compatibly with the rest of our statements.[10] They can't be isolated from the rest of our discourse logically or semantically or confirmationally. This is a very strong constraint, and most approaches fail to meet it. I'm not fully rehearsing these considerations again. My aim in this section is, first, to indicate how prima facie empty terminology shows up in the sciences, and, second, to illustrate that the neutralist approach is equipped to handle such terminology straightforwardly.

Speaking of "calculated nonentities," as I did two paragraphs back, indicates how ubiquitous vacuous terminology in the sciences is. I wouldn't have faulted the reader of that paragraph for thinking that statements with vacuous terms are restricted to "soft sciences." This isn't so. What often induces the introduction of calculated nonentities into the quantifier domain of a scientific discipline is that no other tractable application of scientific doctrine to a phenomenon is possible. Melia notices average entities, Maddy (1997, specifically 143–57) notices infinitely deep oceans, continuous energy, continuous charge, continuous angular momentum, and frictionless planes; and numerous philosophers of science have noticed many other idealized entities, among them point masses, isolated populations, and so on.[11] A nice illustration of how

---

[9] See Azzouni (2004a, 2010a, 2011, 2012b, and 2013b).
[10] Although the focus here is on ontology, this is also an issue for pluralist positions on truth (and logic), and for the same reasons.
[11] The literature is *huge*. For a tiny taste, with some references, see Frigg and Hartmann (2012). Some of the "models" they describe must be treated as false science from which we deduce true consequences. (See Azzouni 2009a, section 2, for analysis of this kind of case.) But there are cases where the science is treated by practitioners as true *despite* the presence of nonexistents in the quantifier domain. I go on to discuss how cases like this can arise and how neutralism handles them.

vacuous terms work their way indispensably into the science—this is a *specific* example of how it often happens in *physics*—is the introduction of calculated nonentities in order to solve a pair of differential equations.[12]

Imagine two nearly spherical and nearly homogeneous masses m_1 and m_2 that are connected by a strong spring; the assemblage is tossed up into a gravitational field.[13] We can imagine the objects involved here in a perfectly natural way (a way that, in fact, the description of the situation presupposes): what's involved are (for example) machine-tooled smooth spherical metallic balls welded together with a strong spring.

Because the gravitational field is acting on each mass, and because the masses (via the spring) are also acting on each other, the separate motions of the masses in this field are actually very complicated to calculate directly.[14] But if we rewrite the system in terms of the movement of two *fictitious* point masses—namely, what's called the center of mass (which has mass $m_1 + m_2$), and what's called the reduced mass (which has mass $m_1 m_2/(m_1 + m_2)$—it then breaks up into the motion of two *non-interacting* point masses.

This *calculational* maneuver corresponds to the uncoupling of two differential equations (which makes them *easy to solve*). I'll go over the details of this briefly. Let $\mathbf{a}_1, \mathbf{a}_2$ be the positions of the two particles, let $\mathbf{F}_1 = m_1 \mathbf{g}$, $\mathbf{F}_2 = m_2 \mathbf{g}$ be the gravitational forces on the respective particles, and finally, represent the interaction forces by $\mathbf{F}(\mathbf{a}_1 - \mathbf{a}_2)$. These obey the following coupled equations of motion:

$$\mathbf{F}_1 + \mathbf{F}(\mathbf{a}_1 - \mathbf{a}_2) = m_1 \ddot{\mathbf{a}}$$

$$\mathbf{F}_2 - \mathbf{F}(\mathbf{a}_1 - \mathbf{a}_2) = m_2 \ddot{\mathbf{a}}.$$

If we "change the coordinates," as it's put, by setting $(m_1 + m_2)\mathbf{A} = m_1 \mathbf{a}_1 + m_2 \mathbf{a}_2$, where $\mathbf{A}$ is to be the center-of-mass coordinate, and $\mathbf{a} = \mathbf{a}_1 - \mathbf{a}_2$, where $\mathbf{a}$ is to be the relative coordinate, then adding the two equations gives us:

$$\mathbf{F}_{sum} = (m_1 + m_2)\ddot{\mathbf{A}},$$

---

[12] I draw this example explicitly from Mattuck (1976); I borrow some of my discussion of it from Azzouni (1997).
[13] In what follows, the terminology "m_1" and "m_2" is used both to designate the objects possessing masses m_1 and m_2 as well as the quantities of mass that the objects m_1 and m_2 possess.
[14] And this is apart from the fact that we are ignoring the massive complications introduced because the objects in question aren't perfectly spherical, the materials they are made from aren't perfectly homogeneous, and other forces besides the gravitational field (e.g., from the air) are affecting them. (These are "massive" complications because the way they must be introduced into the differential equations yields formulas extremely difficult or impossible to mathematically manipulate for desired implications.)

while multiplying the two equations by m_2 and m_1, respectively, and subtracting gives us:

$$\mathbf{F}(\mathbf{a}) = m_1 m_2 \ddot{\mathbf{a}} / (m_1 + m_2),$$

a pair of differential equations much easier to solve.

Three sorts of "object" have come up in this example. First are the spherical masses I started the description of the example with (as well as the spring); second, there are the physically significant calculated entities, the center of mass and the reduced mass, that no one takes to be anything that exists; and lastly, there are various mathematical quantities that naturally arise when we transform the first set of equations into the second set—but which don't correspond to anything physically significant in the example (e.g., $m_1 m_2$).

The laws of motion—applied to this particular case—become tractable when we replace the objects (that we ordinarily take to be in play) with what can otherwise naturally be described as entirely *imaginary* objects. (Instead of two spheres moving in the complicated way that they are moving in relation to one another, we instead have two *points*—the center of mass and the reduced mass—moving *entirely independently* of each other.)

As I mentioned, this illustrates something that's fairly common in the sciences. Centers of mass, for example, are often among the items that appropriate laws describing a system of objects must have in the quantifier domain. In particular, the point masses—which are ubiquitously present in Newtonian physics—sometimes aren't even "in" the objects we started with. We may, for example, describe the motion of a galaxy of objects partially in terms of its center of mass, where that center resides in none of those objects.[15] Not only will there be items—that practitioners don't think exist—in the quantifier domain, but further, nothing in the design of optimal scientific laws requires that the objects we start with (and that we want to design laws *for*) be in the quantifier domain of the laws that result.

Of course, as I mentioned, the original pair of differential equations are already idealized in that important causal factors are left out. But this needn't be. Even if the original mathematical characterization is accurate, the needed transformation of it to secure mathematical tractability often involves the importation of nonexistent entities. More generally, nothing about the empirical laws that we may discover to govern our world requires that the quantifier domain of those laws must contain all and only what exists.

---

[15] See the discussion of conservation laws in Landau and Lifshitz (1976). The point can be easily seen if you imagine a homogeneous metal disc with a hole in its center: the center of mass isn't contained in the disc.

The second example I'll give makes the respective sciences *possible*. Consider the rather rich and important branches of fluid dynamics and rational continuum mechanics.[16] Here, too, substantial (but known to be false) geometric and topological assumptions are made about various materials—specifically, about the topological, metrical, and geometrical properties of their posited parts. These assumptions are indispensable for a family of empirical sciences: the needed physical concepts deployed (arising from various physical continuity and differentiability conditions) presuppose that the substances studied are smooth—apart from additional approximation assumptions. The resulting physical theory must be applied to the phenomena in an autonomous way, relatively independent of more fundamental sciences (for example, quantum mechanics) because of the mathematical intractability of the latter sciences, and because the specialized concepts of these branches of micro-physics are wedded so thoroughly to particular applications of the mathematics of analysis and topology. Notice, crucially, that it's exactly the supposed structural postulations of these materials—that they contain such-and-such kinds of entities as *parts*—that are falsely mathematicized this way.

The result is that the (nonexistent) mathematical entities that appear in the quantifier domains in these cases aren't standard Platonic "nowhere and nowhen" entities—like numbers. Instead, they are characterized parts of the substances under study—pieces of wood, bodies of water, steel beams undergoing stress, and so on. Causal predictions about what happens to these things under various circumstances are enabled by structural postulations known to be false about these materials—in other words, the fictitious entities postulated as within these materials are known by the physicists not to exist.

The neutralist approach to this is straightforward and neat. The truths (and "approximate" truths) indispensably needed in these sciences are semantically characterized in terms of quantifier domains containing things that don't exist.

Notice something that the neutralist takes account of easily. Many items indispensably appear in quantifier domains contoured to handle scientific talk. As in the commonsense case, practitioners debate the existence of some of these; most assert the existence of some, and most deny the existence of some. The neutralist approach allows us to easily capture ontological debates among scientists who disagree about theoretically indispensable entities.[17]

---

[16] See, for example, Malvern (1969), Truesdell (1991), Truesdell and Rajagopal (2000).
[17] It's important to realize that it's not just philosophers of science who argue (and have argued) about the existence of theoretical entities; scientists argue (and have argued) about this *too*.

5.4 Quantifier Domains for Talk about Fiction

Unlike the case of the sciences, where many entities that seem indispensable are nevertheless ones that we argue about the existence of, fictional entities seem pretty uniformly to be disbelieved in except by certain philosophers. Despite this, talk of them is indispensable.[18] Philosophers have adopted several positions about this—one of the more prominent ones is that such objects exist, and indispensable talk about them is why.[19] This faces the problem that most people don't want to be committed to fictional entities—and yet their talk seems cogent nevertheless. This is especially the case because it's entirely natural to say "There are no fictional entities" or "Fictional entities don't exist."[20]

Notice two very important properties of this statement. First, it doesn't sound tautological. This means that "fictional" can be used in a way that doesn't foreclose on the existence of what's "fictional." Similarly, "Fictional beings have come into *existence*—I saw *hobbits* running around at the mall yesterday" doesn't sound *contradictory*. (This is important to observe because *many* philosophers attempt to always read "fictional" or "mythological" ontologically, despite these terms clearly having non-ontological readings.) Second, this is exactly what the non-philosopher who is explaining to his or her child that these things don't exist will

---

See Azzouni and Bueno (forthcoming) for discussion of one important case: the ontological debate that occurred at the turn of the last century over atoms. A more recent debate concerns the status of the wave induced by, e.g., Schrödinger's wave equation. Despite indispensability, it is *not* taken for granted by practitioners in this area that such waves (living in complex infinite-dimensional spaces) exist.

[18] For exactly the same reasons, talk of hallucinated entities is indispensable both in ordinary life and in vision science, and related branches of psychology. See Azzouni (2010a, chapter 2). I'm focusing on fiction for reasons of concision, but the issues are the same. (Namely: the external discourse demand.)

[19] See van Inwagen (1983, 2001), who runs an indispensability argument for fictional entities.

[20] Schaffer, Voltolini, and Thomasson have all suggested that domain-restriction phenomena can explain away these sorts of remarks. Just as when speakers who assert "There's no beer" mean "There's no beer in the refrigerator" rather than "There's no beer at all," speakers who say "Sherlock Holmes does not exist" are similarly restricting the domain of discourse to entities that are mind-independent or that aren't fictional. Walton (2003, 240–41) and Everett (2013, 147–52) notice this strategy won't work. "There are *F*s" is subject to quantifier domain restriction, but "*F*s exist" or "*N* exists" isn't. As Daly and Liggins (2014, 473) put it: "Suppose I inspect the contents of my garage and discover there is no bicycle there. Then it is appropriate to say 'There is no bicycle,' but inappropriate to say 'Bicycles do not exist.' ... The same goes for names: if N exists outside the domain of quantification, it is inappropriate to say 'N does not exist.'"

say: "Mickey Mouse doesn't exist," "Santa Claus doesn't exist," and so on. Among the least satisfying aspects of running an indispensability argument for fictional entities (the way van Inwagen does) is that it makes this talk incoherent.

Others have hoped to handle the talk by means of a pretense operator (or depiction operator) or by reconstruing the talk metaphorically. These kinds of solutions are "scope restriction" solutions: they require vacuous-termed statements to occur *within* the scope of a sentential pretense operator (or of a depiction operator, or—more generally—an intensional operator). Equivalently, for our purposes, vacuous terms must appear "de dicto," not "de re"; they must take "narrow scope" in relation to intensional terms.[21] When they do so, they are subject to the constraints imposed by the intensional terms taking wide scope with respect to them. Call the syntactic pattern of these statements, in which all empty terms are interpreted as within the scope of one or another such operator, *predicative intensional form*.

The literature in this area is complex because the semantic properties of intensional terms are (empirically) complex. In what follows, though, two very simple points are being made and illustrated. First, there are things we need to say, or uses that we need to put our statements to, that *can't* be satisfied by statements restricted to predicative intensional form. (This is a corollary of the external discourse demand.) Instead, in these indispensable statements, vacuous terms (noun phrases, quantifiers, and so on) must be interpreted as taking wide scope. This directly puts pressure on quantifier-onticity approaches because the intensional-term constraints (on what falls within the scope of those terms) won't nullify the ontological commitments induced by quantifier domains (according to those quantifier-onticity interpretations). I'll illustrate this problem in the rest of this section, and then in later sections I'll examine a related version of the problem originally due to Geach.[22]

---

[21] Classic papers, of course, are Quine (1956) and Kaplan (1969). The literature is huge. See especially Heim (1992). Some of the terminology I'm invoking here is misleading from the neutralist point of view—I'm speaking specifically of "de re."

[22] The discussion in the rest of this section relies on Azzouni (2010a), Azzouni (2012b), and Contessa (2012). I focus specifically on pretense (or depiction), construed as intensional operators, because they fit the fiction cases best (and because one proponent of this approach—Contessa—advocates pretense). But the challenges I raise are easily seen to generalize to all intensional approaches.

Statements often have both readings. Consider this example from Heim:

John thought that *the person who was going to kill him* had come to read the gas meter.

Heim (1992, 207) writes:

> In the salient reading [of the above], this [italicized] definite is interpreted *de re*. Analyses of this phenomenon vary, but somehow or other they all imply that it is the speaker [of the above], not John, who is "responsible" for the definite description.

That is, on this de re reading, what John thinks (or doesn't think) has no impact on the ontological commitments (if any) induced by "the person who was going to kill him."

There are issues about when de re readings are forced or not. But one way they are forced is when anaphoric relations occur across the scopes of more than one intensional operator. They are also forced by certain kinds of comparisons.

Consider, for example, this:

(2) Sherlock Holmes, as he is depicted in the Conan Doyle stories, is smarter than Mickey Mouse, as he is depicted in (such-and-such) Disney cartoons.

We may want to similarly compare real and fictional characters:

(3) Sherlock Holmes, as he is depicted in the Conan Doyle stories, is smarter than Trump actually is.

(3) can't be reconstrued as:

(4) As depicted in the Conan Doyle stories, Sherlock Holmes is smarter than Trump actually is.

This is because Trump doesn't appear in any Conan Doyle stories.[23] In general, these comparisons require an interpretation of fictional names as

---

[23] Notice that the use of an actuality operator within the scope of a fiction operator—which would indicate that the comparison is to be with Trump's intelligence as it actually is (and not as it's depicted in the fiction)—won't do. Trump doesn't appear in the fiction.

outside the scope of fictional operators or pretense operators, such as "It is pretended that —A—," or "In such and such stories, A is depicted as —." They also require treating *being-depicted-as-intelligent-in-Conan-Doyle-stories*, *being-depicted-in-such-and-such-Disney-cartoons-as-a-talking-mouse*, and so on, as predicates applicable in principle to both real and fictional creatures.

I turn now to the indispensability of such statements, interpreted de re. Uses of empty terms in statements not in predicative intensional form can be used confirmationally to show (for example) sociological generalizations. Here's an example. Assume there is a (bad) movie called *The Hound of Brooklyn Heights*, and that:

(5) In the movie *The Hound of Brooklyn Heights*, it is depicted like so: Sherlock Holmes lives in New York City.

A comparison can be made:

(6) Sherlock Holmes is depicted in Conan Doyle's fiction as living in London; but he is depicted in the movie *The Hound of Brooklyn Heights* as living in New York.

There could also be a generalization of (6) that's true, such as:

(7) During the 1930s, any movie based on a short story in which the characters are depicted as living in London depicted them as living in New York instead.

(7) involves "quantification into" such depiction contexts and "quantification over" fictional entities. That is, "the characters" is taking wide scope with respect to "depictions in the movies" and "depictions in short stories." We may find that (7) helps confirm a sociological fact:

(8) Film producers in the 1930s were sensitive to the demographic fact that New Yorkers watched more movies than Londoners.

This may, in turn, provide evidence for:

(9) During the 1930s, New Yorkers had more discretionary income than Londoners.

A couple of important points should be made about this imaginary case.[24] It might be hoped that statements interpretable as in predicative intensional forms could be used instead. For example:

> (10) American movie producers in the 1930s predominantly produced movies that engaged their viewers in the pretense that the movie's characters lived in New York,

or

> (11) Some American movie producer in the 1930s produced a movie, *The Hound of Brooklyn Heights*, which engaged its viewers in the pretense that Sherlock Holmes lived in New York City.

Unfortunately, although statements of these sorts can be used confirmationally, comparatives that force wide scope on vacuous terms may be more valuable. For example, (10) may *itself* be confirmed on the basis of (7)—because sociologists don't have direct access to (10). Furthermore, it may be that a comparative *across* pretenses is precisely what's needed. The important point being confirmed above is a comparative between actual New Yorkers and actual Londoners on the basis of a shift in depictions of characters living in London and New York. This is what motivates confirmation by the use of a vacuous term taking wide scope in relation to more than one depiction or pretense context.

Contessa (2012, 364), in defense of predicative pretense forms, writes:

> What contributes to confirming [an] empirical hypothesis is not the proposition that forms the content of the pretence—the proposition *that such and such is the case*—but the proposition *that the individuals in question pretend that such and such is the case*.

This isn't the bone of contention between me and any proponent of predicative intensional forms. The debate, rather, is over whether we can *express* the appropriate empirical hypotheses in predicative form in this

---

[24] Here's a point about a real thesis, however. Braudel (1986) describes the city-centered economy as the appropriate unit of analysis at a certain sociological/economic level. He further suggests that London supplanted Amsterdam, and (eventually) that New York supplanted London as the central city of the Western economy. Evidence of the above sort—if it existed—could certainly contribute to confirming a thesis like this; evidence that takes the comparative form of (6) and (7) *is* used to establish claims of just this sort.

case: "Individual(s) such-and-such are pretending so-and-so." However intuitive it may seem to be that of course we ought to be able to do this—after all, what's *really* going on is a bunch of individuals pretending different things—the tractable forms that empirical hypotheses may have to take needn't result in predicative forms.[25]

This gets to the real issue between me and Contessa's pretense theorist. If pretenses are significant to fictionalizing practices (and I entirely agree that they are), then references both *to* the pretenses and *within* those pretenses matter to our empirical claims: (6) illustrates this because it's the *difference* between Sherlock Holmes as *he* is pretended to be in the two fictions that confirms the sociological claim.[26]

Contessa's particular form of pretense theory is a "multi-level" one: there are levels of pretense.[27] In particular, there is the (primary) meta-fictional level where

> readers of the Sherlock Holmes stories pretend that ... Conan Doyle created something (i.e., a fictional character). They also pretend that the name "Sherlock Holmes" refers to that character and that the character appears along with other characters in a number of novels and short stories written by Conan Doyle. Finally, they also pretend that this character is depicted in a certain way in those stories and that the character also appears in a number of other works of fiction by other authors. (Contessa 2012, 362)

This invites a possible defense of predicate intensional forms (pretense ones in particular). The requisite sentence, in predicative pretense form, that confirms (8) isn't (7) but instead:

(7P) It is pretended (by us) that: During the 1930s, any movie based on a short story in which the characters are depicted as living in London depicted them as living in New York instead.

It's hard to see, however, how to construe (7P) in a way that allows it to confirm (8), or anything, really. The problem is that we need to get the content following "It is pretended (by us)" *out from under* the scope of the pretense operator, since it's that content that's doing the work; but (7P) allows

---

[25] That this is so, I hypothesize, is one of the reasons natural language exhibits neutral quantifier domains.
[26] In this very statement, notice, "Sherlock Holmes" must be interpreted as taking wide scope.
[27] Contessa's particular multi-level pretense approach generalizes to any intensional approach—and so do the objections I raise.

no implications that make the needed aspects of that content *truth-apt*. The burden, therefore, is very much on proponents of such predicative forms to explain how this challenge is supposed to be met.[28]

5.5 How Hob and Nob Thinking About the Same Witch is Evidence for the Neutralist Interpretation of Ordinary Language

A prima facie evidential requirement on ways of interpreting ordinary-language quantifier domains is that our ordinary ways of understanding truth conditions are respected. Relevant points—as discussed in this and previous chapters—are (i) that we are willing to assert truly statements that we simultaneously recognize to be about things we don't think exist, and (ii) our ways of debating one another ontologically. A relatively famous example of a conflict between quantifier onticity and our ordinary ways of speaking about what we don't think exists (where vacuous terms take wide scope) relies on an example due to Geach (1967): his Hob-Nob statements.

Consider the sentences

(12) Hob thinks that a witch has blighted Bob's mare, and Nob wonders whether she (the same witch) killed Cob's sow,

and

(13) Hob thinks that a witch has blighted Bob's mare, and Nob wonders whether she killed Cob's sow.

Sentences like these (*Geach sentences*) have been the focus of an intensive study in philosophy of language.[29] This is no surprise given their semantic complexity—they involve intentional contexts, vacuous descriptions, and empty categories. Many philosophers (myself included) have, in Braun's terminology, Geachian intuitions about Geach sentences, about (12) and (13) in particular. These intuitions aren't metaphysical intuitions—rather, they are

---

[28] One solution is *global* pretense or metaphor. Extend *pretense* to all our statements, and to our supposed inference patterns. I should think we'd prefer quantifier domain neutrality to *this*.

[29] They first occur, to my knowledge, in Geach (1967). See Braun (2012) for references to previous discussions of them, and for a thorough discussion of the intractable issues Geach sentences pose for non-neutralist approaches. Some of the discussion to follow is drawn from Azzouni (2013b).

indicators of a straightforwardly ordinary way of using such sentences, and consequently of what the truth conditions for such statements are taken to be. These readings (interpretations) of (12) and (13) allow that (12) and (13)

(a) can be uttered correctly by speakers who don't believe in witches, and in circumstances in which witches don't exist;
(b) can be uttered correctly in circumstances where Hob and Nob aren't thinking of the witch in question in the same way;
(c) can be uttered correctly in circumstances where Nob isn't aware of Hob or of Hob's thoughts about witches;

and yet,

(d) Hob and Nob are, nevertheless, understood to be thinking of the same witch.

Some elucidations:

About (a): The speaker may be applying the word "witch" to certain supernaturally innocent older women, and Hob and Nob may be thinking of a particular one of those. It's possible, however, for the speaker to be instead thinking of witches as sheer fantasy, so that the word "witch" applies to nothing at all whatsoever. In this case the speaker will correctly deny that the particular witch that Hob and Nob are thinking of is *anything at all*.[30]

About (b) and (c): Hob and Nob may have independently read about Meg the witch in a local newspaper, and this reading experience may have triggered their respective thoughts (ones that are being reported by the utterances of (12) and (13)). They needn't even know each other. Furthermore, utterances of (12) and (13) are compatible with Nob recollecting the newspaper article a week later and misremembering the witch's name (if a name occurred in the newspaper article). An utterance of (13)—but not (12), it seems to me—is further compatible with Nob mistakenly recollecting the article as being about a troll (and not a witch). Hob, however, has to be thinking of a witch—so (13) implies. My ear indicates that (12), because of the phrase "the same witch," requires Nob to also be thinking of a witch. Apart from these constraints, the two men needn't be thinking of the witch in the same way at all (because, say,

---

[30] I draw much of my discussion of this issue, and much of the terminology, from Braun (2012). There are important differences, however, and this is one of them: that it's a crucial part of our Geachian intuitions that the speaker may be *correctly* thinking of witches as nothing at all isn't recognized by Braun.

they recollect the newspaper article in different ways, or because they reacted to that article in different ways).

About (d): If the speaker doesn't think that there are any witches at all, a natural reading of both (12) and (13) is that Nob and Hob are nevertheless thinking of the same *witch*. This natural reading is allowed even in circumstances where Hob is now thinking that what he read in the newspaper was an article about Meg the troll. But this natural reading is independent of the speaker's belief that (and circumstances in which) witches aren't anything at all because even if the speaker thinks of witches as actual people who were (historically) mistreated, this reading is still correct. Hob and Nob are both thinking of an (imaginary) *witch*, even if Nob is under a misapprehension about this.

Together, these conditions make impossible any construal of the Geachian readings of (12) and (13) in terms of ontically committing quantifiers that quantify into "Hob thinks" and "Nob wonders" contexts, such as:

(14) A witch x is such that: (i) Hob thinks the witch x has blighted Bob's mare, and (ii) Nob wonders whether x killed Cob's sow,

or

(15) Something x is such that: (i) Hob thinks the witch x has blighted Bob's mare, and (ii) Nob wonders whether x killed Cob's sow.

These readings of (12) and (13) work if the speaker is committed to the existence of mythical witches (*whatever* those are, exactly, metaphysically speaking), or to something (mistreated women, say) that the word "witch" applies to—as the speaker uses it—but they are unacceptable readings if witches are nothing at all.[31]

On the other hand, none of the candidate ways of handling Hob and Nob sentences where all the quantifiers are internal to "Hob thinks" and "Nob wonders" contexts preserve *all* the aspects (a)–(d) of the Geachian readings. This is (in general) because what's needed is a way of connecting the (imaginary) object that Hob is thinking of to the (imaginary) object that Nob is thinking of from within the respective "Hob thinks" and "Nob wonders"

---

[31] It's open to a philosopher, of course, to try to force the speaker (against her will, as it were) to be committed by her use of (12) or (13)—construed as in (14) or (15), where the quantifiers are ontically committing—to *some* sort of metaphysical object, fleeting ephemeral abstracta, for example. (See, e.g., Salmon forthcoming.) But maneuvers like these violate our Geachian intuitions about the sentences in question.

contexts. In particular, one general strategy (that doesn't work) is to look for similarities between Hob's thought and Nob's wondering, and place conditions on the similarities between their mental states that can be described as their "thinking of the same thing." Unfortunately, (b) and (c) mean that such conditions invariably violate Geachian intuitions.

Braun (2012, 171–72) draws the following conclusion:

> There is no semantic disambiguation of [12] that is (a) true at some worlds in which there are no witches and Nob is unaware of Hob and Bob, and yet (b) is true at a world only if Hob and Nob are (in some robust sense) focused on the same thing.

A significant presupposition that Braun needs in order to draw this dramatic conclusion, however, is that a neutralist construal of these statements isn't available.[32] Given the neutralist option, a characterization of (12) and (13) that captures all of (a)–(d) is enabled:

(16) Something x is such that: (i) Hob thinks x is a witch that has blighted Bob's mare, and (ii) Nob wonders whether x killed Cob's sow,

where (unlike in (15)) the phrase "Something x" is neutrally construed.

The naturalness of the Geachian readings of (12) and (13) is evidence, therefore, for the neutralist approach to natural language.

Braun is flummoxed by this option because it strikes him—as it strikes *many* philosophers—that (a) and (d) are flatly contradictory. Braun (2005, 612) describes the series of statements "There is no Sherlock Holmes. Sherlock Holmes does not exist. Sherlock Holmes is just a fictional character" as inconsistent *precisely because* after denying the existence of Sherlock Holmes the speaker goes on to attribute the property of being a fictional character to that nonexistent being. So too, Austin (1962, 96 n. 1) writes: "For how could one possibly say, in the same breath, 'It must really have the qualities

---

[32] Michael Glanzberg protests: "I am deeply suspicious of the Braun claim that is being endorsed here. ... Given the huge amount of work that has gone into anaphora in intensional contexts, the claim that nothing can do the required work is very, very strong." I'm with Braun on *this one*. I don't know of any work that solves the Geach problem to my satisfaction (and, apparently, Braun doesn't either). More importantly, I don't see how it *could* because these statements must be interpreted so that "a witch" takes wide scope, and because of (a) and (b) above. Notice the same problem arises regardless of the attitude term, as long as the de re interpretation is forced by anaphora: "Hob hopes that a witch has blighted Bob's mare, and Nob wants her (the same witch) to kill Cob's sow." The ball is very much in Glanzberg's court as far as this claim (of his) is concerned.

it seems to have,' and 'It may not exist'? *What* must have the qualities it seems to have?" And (to quote yet one more philosopher among many who have made this point) Salmon (forthcoming) writes: "How can Nob wonder about a witch, and a particular witch at that—the very one Hob suspects—when there is no witch and, therefore, no particular witch about whom he is wondering?"

I turn to discussing this issue in some detail in section 5.6.

5.6 Identifying and Distinguishing Nonentities

In describing certain objects as nonexistent, as I've been doing, recall that what's been meant is that there is no metaphysical dimension to such objects whatsoever. To say (correctly) that something—that doesn't exist—has certain properties (for example, that Mickey Mouse has black ears) is therefore:

> (a) not to refer to something specific and claim that *it* doesn't exist, although *it* has certain properties. For if something doesn't exist, then "it" can't be referred to because there isn't anything *to* refer to,

and it's therefore:

> (b) not to attribute a property to a thing. For if there is no such thing, then it can't have properties. (There's nothing in question that can *have* such properties.) To say that the nonexistent can't have properties, notably, is to exclude *all* properties, even philosophically tricky ones—for example, lightweight properties, pleonastic properties, subject-dependent properties, et cetera. For if something doesn't exist, it isn't possible for it to have properties *of any sort*. (There's nothing there *to* have such properties.)

Together, (a) and (b) elucidate what I mean to say by there being no metaphysics involved when vacuous terms occur in truths and falsehoods. And precisely here is where a denier of one or another kind of entity (when, that is, describing something that's neutrally quantified over as not existing "in any sense") breaks with the standard Meinongian. The standard Meinongian, even when agreeing with the letter of ontological denial—that some objects don't exist (and don't exist in any way at all)—still understands these nonexistent objects (having particular properties and not others) as contributing to the truth values of statements *about* those nonexistent beings. To genuinely assert the nonexistence of a certain class of objects requires a very different (non-metaphysical) story about what's going on when statements "about" such beings have truth values.

Here's a way of making salient the difference involved. Stalnaker (2011, 120–21) writes:

> For Carnap (and here I think Quine would agree), if you accept a framework that involves the full apparatus of standard first-order quantification and thereby commit yourself to the intelligibility of questions about the extent of the domain, about which predicates of one's language are correctly predicated of which members of the domain, and about questions of identity and distinctness of what is picked out by various specifications of members of the domain, then that is all there is to ontological commitment to the domain.

"Thereby" indicates Stalnaker's assertion that accepting "a framework that involves the full apparatus of standard first-order quantification" forces acceptance of the "intelligibility" of various questions. The intelligibility of these various questions, notice, amounts *purely* to a demand about how *bivalence* is to be imposed on the framework. Any question of the form F*o*, for predicate F and member of the domain *o*, is to be rendered "intelligible"; so too corresponding questions are to be rendered intelligible when equality is involved. Stalnaker, of course, makes this a condition for ontological commitment *across the board* ("that is all there is to ontological commitment to the domain"). Meinongians disagree: ontological distinctions can be drawn in other ways even if the bivalence imposition is extended to what Meinongians describe as nonexistent objects. Meinongians, historically, have agreed that the bivalence intelligibility demand places a prima facie metaphysical condition on their descriptions of nonexistent beings. As a result, they respond to the demand in one of two ways: either they treat their nonexistent objects as "incomplete," and in this way explain the unintelligibility (in certain cases) of bivalence-induced questions, or they show how this demand is satisfied by their otherwise nonexistent objects.

Neither of these responses is available for those who refuse to attribute a metaphysical status (of any sort) to what doesn't exist. Instead, recall from section 4.5 how describing ourselves as ignorant allows the compatibility of a "top-down" commitment to bivalence with the denial that we have (or can ever have) answers to F*o* questions, for a specific F and a specific *o*.

Let's now consider identity statements, which raise (so I claim) no *new* issues. This may strike many philosophers as wrong because they're worried about what possible identity conditions there could be for nonexistent beings. More dramatically, they may think identity claims make no sense if objects aren't involved. They don't understand, that is, what an identity claim *is* when there is nothing there to stand in the identity relation.[33]

I said that identity statements raise no *new* issues, and I meant it. We've been here before: What can a statement of the form "Mickey Mouse has black ears"—the attribution of a property to Mickey Mouse—mean if there is no Mickey Mouse? What is a property attribution claim when there is nothing there to which a property can be attributed? (Recall the discussion in the general introduction of the "I don't understand" objection.) The response is: We can (and do) talk this way. With the full belief that fictional characters don't exist, we can nevertheless argue over whether we're talking about the same character (King Lear) or not. *Imposing* a semantics in which identity statements require references to real objects begs the question against the neutralist, and rules out of court a priori any attempts to show that the ways we speak in mathematics (where identity statements are rampant), in the sciences and in ordinary life, support that neutralism.

According to the neutralist, therefore, the cogency of identity statements isn't a metaphysical worry: it's a worry about how identity statements involving vacuous terms (for example, statements like (12) and (13)) are to be rendered true or false *coherently*. "No entity without identity" is the famous Quinean slogan. For Quine, and I suspect for many other philosophers (e.g., Stalnaker), this wasn't (and isn't) merely a cogency condition on something existing—so that things that don't exist don't have to satisfy it. Instead, most philosophers who invoke the Quinean dictum think that identity conditions are a cogency requirement on *any* use of terms and the identity predicate. The worry that, for example, if there is nothing that Hob and Nob are (actually) thinking about, then there can't be one (unique) thing that they're thinking about is (ultimately)—according to the neutralist—a worry about how cogent identity conditions can govern vacuous terms.

It always helps to consider related subject areas—in *this* case, areas where talking about nothing is routine, and where characterizations nevertheless involve successful identifications and distinctions among what's being talked about. So notice that when reading a novel and thinking about the characters in that novel in successive episodes, and when thinking about characters that appear in more than one novel, we routinely—*automatically*—identify characters and distinguish them. Furthermore, there is a process of correcting initial impressions that's built into our distinguishing and identifying characters. We may discover late in a novel, for example, that a character that

---

[33] My thanks to Michael Glanzberg for putting the objection this way.

we thought was one person is actually twins; and if the novel has been done well, we can go back over the previous episodes and convince ourselves that it was *this* twin and not *that* twin that appeared in such-and-such scenes. So too, we often identify characters *across* novels—that she has these traits in that novel but these other traits in this novel. Rather than just assuming that what renders this practice cogent—to the extent that it *is* cogent[34]—is that there must be fictional characters that *exist* and that speakers are referring to, let's instead notice that our methods for establishing the identity statements about characters and other fictional entities (taking ourselves, for example, as reading about the same imaginary characters in subsequent chapters of a book) are very similar to how we manage this for identity statements that refer to real objects.

Speaking of real objects, it should be obvious that we don't establish these identifications and distinctions by means of necessary and sufficient identity conditions that we all have ready at hand to apply to all and any circumstances where such questions can come up. The evidence for this should be relatively obvious to philosophers because they know better than anyone that they've *failed* to find any candidate necessary and sufficiency conditions for pretty much *anything*.[35] Notice what's required of such necessary and sufficient conditions: they are supposed to handle *all* possible cases. Part of the problem, of course, is that sometimes we're perplexed: we don't know what to say about whether (in such and such circumstances) we have the same object, person, and so on that we had in earlier circumstances.[36] That we are so stymied (intuitively) by such cases shows that however we identify and distinguish objects across circumstances, it isn't by necessary and sufficient conditions on these things that *we* grasp.

Our competence in distinguishing objects involves, at best, some necessary conditions, some sufficient conditions, but no necessary and sufficient conditions. Our competence, therefore, works quite well up to a point in ordinary life, but is revealed to be quite limited when only mildly inventive

---

[34] Because, after all, the practice of identifying or distinguishing characters doesn't *have* to be cogent. The novelist may slip into inconsistency or pursue it deliberately, e.g., as Calvino does in *Cosmicomics* (1968).

[35] Kripke writes (1980, 43): "Really, adequate necessary and sufficient conditions for identity which do not beg the question are very rare in any case. Mathematics is the only case I really know of where they are given even *within* a possible world, to tell the truth. I don't know of such conditions for identity of material objects over time, or for people" (italics his). See the discussion of this passage in Azzouni (2010a, chapter 2), which suggests Kripke overstates his claim with respect to mathematical entities.

[36] See, e.g., the problem cases described in the articles in Perry (1975) and Rorty (1976); think about the gigantic literature on ship-of-Theseus-style problems. These issues will be revisited in some detail in part II of this book.

cases are presented. It's important to add, of course, that these necessary conditions and sufficient conditions must not be overintellectualized: we have various, more or less automatic and involuntary, responses to situations where we identify items as the same or different, or (more significantly) where we're willing to describe items as the same (or different) and then, in the light of new information about the circumstances, revise those descriptions.

Our methods of determining fictional identifications and distinctions, therefore, are largely parasitic on our methods we use with real objects; this is because *all* of our epistemic methods are largely so parasitical (as noted in chapter 4). This is most transparently so in plays and movies, where the same visual and auditory cues (that we use in ordinary life) are used to identify objects and persons as the same or different. Notice, as well, how *defeasibility* is involved—that built into fictional practices are possibilities of revisions of what we thought were true identifications of characters. Just as in real life we can discover that someone we're acquainted with is actually twins (or vice versa), so too—and more often than in real life—the same things can happen in movies and plays.

Literature (but not film) differs only in that the cues that trigger our impressions of sameness and difference are restricted to what can be conveyed by words—in particular, the use of names and descriptions. Indeed, an important aspect of how objects are identified and distinguished in literature is by sheer acts of *stipulation* by authors that readers *automatically* react to: for example, two characters are distinguished by their being given different names, or by virtue of being described as different. Thirteen dogs in a room can be distinguished as thirteen *different* dogs by sheer virtue of the phrase "There were thirteen dogs in the room," *even if nothing more is ever said about those dogs* in the rest of the fiction. This ubiquitous practice—one that goes well beyond *fiction*—will be used to illuminate Nob and Hob sentences in the next section.

5.7 Hob and Nob Again

I apply the point just made—that how we take ourselves to establish the truth or falsity of identity statements about entities we take not to exist is quite similar to the ordinary ways that we establish the truth or falsity of identity statements about real objects—to the Hob and Nob case. Imagine that Hob and Nob have independently read about Meg the witch in the local newspaper. This suffices to induce *in us* the propensity to describe the witch (that Hob and Nob are respectively thinking about) as the *same* witch. Similarly, if you and I think about King Lear because we've both (at different times) read Shakespeare's play, that alone induces the identification of the nonexistent characters we're thinking of as the same one. If instead I've recently read a new play about a lecherous alcoholic that his friends sarcastically call "King Lear" and I'm thinking about *him*, then I'm not thinking about the same character that you are even if the thoughts have exactly the same descriptive content (for example, "That guy sure is deluded about his daughters").

What's true and false about the (nonexistent) witch that Hob and Nob are thinking about is due to factors that lie outside the individual thinkings that Hob and Nob are engaged in. In this respect, the external factors that play such an important role in fixing what's true about the real objects that our names name, and that the quantifier domain contains, are equally at work when it comes to the nonexistent. It can be said, in particular, that "it's because of that newspaper article that both Nob and Hob are thinking about Meg"; it can be said that "that newspaper article is what made Meg the witch famous"; and so on.

Here's a helpful way to describe about what's going on. We can *think about* many people and objects only because of various public representations of them that are available to us. I'm able to think of George Washington, in large measure, because there are stories circulating about him in which the words "George Washington" occur, as well as various pictorial representations (on money I use, for example). The same is true of Plato and Aristotle. In making this point, I'm *not* disputing the views of many philosophers that the truth conditions for these statements and other representations turn on their having the right "causal" relationship to the objects represented, for example, George Washington, Plato, and Aristotle. The point is a different one. It's that it's psychologically automatic for us to identify a set of representations as about one particular thing based on their publicly being *treated* as about that one thing. But exactly the same practices are in place for objects that we know to be unreal, such as Santa Claus and Mickey Mouse. And what enables these practices to work in cases where we know the objects in question don't exist is that we psychologically respond to the public treatment of a set of representations as "about" the same object even when we know that no such object exists.

It can be asked, of course, why these psychological propensities to identify and distinguish characters should be taken seriously when the characters don't exist. The answer to this is that the ways of talking about identities and differences among nonexistent entities that we've hit upon are *indispensable*. We've no other way of doing it, no other way of describing what people are thinking about when what they're thinking about isn't real. Part of the evidence for this indispensability is the impossibility of finding alternative ways of managing our discourse about the nonexistent—in a word, paraphrasing that discourse into predicative intensional forms.

5.8 Some Conclusions

This chapter has attempted to marshal further evidence for the neutralist perspective on quantifier domains—both for natural languages and formal ones. I've focused, first, on how neutrality allows ontological debates to take place. This is because an ontologically significant existence predicate coupled with a neutrally interpreted quantifier domain allows us to simultaneously describe entities while denying they exist. That we find this such an effortless practice in natural languages strongly suggests that natural languages should be interpreted neutrally.

The Hob-Nob case illustrates the same point, and more: our natural ways of speaking about how more than one individual can believe in the same nonexistent entity are intractable on a quantifier-onticity approach. This raises, of course, more concerns than ones of representation. There is also the question of how truth values are assigned to sentences that don't describe what's real. I've applied the general points about truth-value-inducing (described in chapter 4) to this particular case.

It should be noted that this discussion provides evidence not only for my claims about natural languages but also for my claims about how natural languages should be regimented. The logical point is that formal languages with neutral quantifier domains have additional expressive power not possessed by languages with non-neutral quantifier domains. This is valuable in many ways, as I've illustrated so far and will continue to illustrate throughout the course of this book. One thing it makes possible is the description of metaphysical positions that should be taken seriously but are ruled out because they're inexpressible in languages non-neutrally interpreted. Giving details about that is the aim of part II.

Conclusion to Part I

I've suggested that regimentations of ontological pronouncements in the vernacular officially transform something purely contextual/intentional into an explicit bit of formalism—for example, a neutrally interpreted quantifier domain coupled with an ontically significant predicate.[1]

One common misapprehension, however, about regimentations—the formal reconstruals of natural-language discourses—is that they should respect the (natural-language) semantic properties of sentences but not (say) pragmatic enrichments. That is, it's often (implicitly) thought that the pragmatic/semantic divide, whatever it turns out to be, should be replicated in formal regimentations. But there is no motivation for this constraint. Whether intuitively apparent properties of sentences are a matter of semantics, pragmatics, or something else is an empirical question about natural languages. Issues about what should be characterized in formalizations and what should be treated instead "contextually" with respect to those formalizations are entirely different; they don't generate empirical questions (about natural languages). They should, thus, be driven by independent considerations of what formalizations—as they're structured—can handle.

Chomsky has argued—very persuasively, in my view—that any attempt to read ontology directly out of the syntax/semantics of natural language is hopeless.[2] Ontology and ontological commitments—if they show up in

---

[1] See, e.g., Azzouni (2004a, chapter 6). I *don't* recommend, by the way, that this be managed by a definition that's regarded as available in the vernacular. See Parent (2014) for why this is an impossible demand.

[2] See, e.g., Chomsky (2000). Collins (2011, section 6.5) is extremely valuable—both for a clear interpretation of Chomsky's views on "internalism vs. externalism" as well as for a discussion of the surrounding literature on this topic. A number of linguists have long made similar claims, including E. Bach, R. Jackendoff, M. Krifka and many others. Indeed, it's not unreasonable to describe ontologically deflated views about syntactic/semantic theories as *widespread* among linguists.

natural-language discourses at all—show up in some other way entirely. All by itself, this doesn't require that regimentations not formally represent ontological commitments. I've instead argued against onticity constraints on quantifier domains because the resulting formalisms are too expressively impoverished to handle the things we need to say. This doesn't, of course, prevent the introduction of another formal apparatus—a predicate, for example—that's to unequivocally carry ontological significance.

Philosophers are sometimes explicit about adopting, for philosophical purposes, the vantage point of an artificial language of some sort. They often imagine, for example, *toy languages* or *pretend languages* that they presume are possible. Ontologese is an example of a (usually first-order) language where the quantifiers and singular expressions are taken to only range over, and to refer to, what exists, or what "fundamentally" exists. Let's imagine such a language is possible.

Several linked questions arise. The first is whether a version of Ontologese that's sufficiently like natural languages is possible. Relatedly: Are there reasons (e.g., "practicality constraints," like: don't change the language so much that *humans* can't use it) that rule such a language out for a general population of speakers? Even if there aren't, can such languages still be used by metaphysicians in restricted but philosophically significant ways? If so, what sorts of roles can they play in metaphysics?

Finally, one can ask this: Given that Ontologese is understood as a language in which all the "parts of speech" correspond to fundamental worldly structures, do we *need* such a language in order to successfully practice metaphysics? The answer to this last question is *no*. What should already be clear, and will become clearer in part II, is that a focus on Ontologese by metaphysicians is misguided. One (bad) motivation behind it is one we've seen at work already: the thought that quantifier domains—natural or formal—can't be interpreted neutrally.

I've suggested (in chapter 2) that, in any case, the terms of natural languages conceptually hang together in such a way that makes it naive to just assume that it's *easy* to change the properties of words in fundamental ways: to make predicates such as "exist"—when understood ontologically—criterion-immanent.[3]

---

[3] Austin (1962, 63) once wrote:

> Certainly, when we have discovered how a word is in fact used, that may not be the end of the matter; there is certainly no reason why, in general, things should be left exactly as we find them ... [but] ... tampering with words in what we take to be one little corner of the field is always *liable* to have unforeseen repercussions in the adjoining territory. Tampering, in fact, is not so easy as is often supposed, and is often thought to be necessary just because what we've got already has been misrepresented.

A *case* has to be made that this is possible: that it doesn't have really bad side effects (like making ontological debate incoherent).

This point aside, I've indicated in earlier chapters how many contemporary ontological debates—in particular, metametaphysical debates about whether ontological debates are genuine—arise within a philosophical framework where quantifier domains are interpreted immanently and ontically. It's a natural question to ask to what extent these issues mutate if this framework is rejected (as I've been urging us to do) for one in which quantifier domains are understood instead neutrally and the existence predicate is understood transcendentally. My thought about this (and this will serve as a transition to part II of this book) is that remarkably little about substantial ontological issues is affected.

I've already indicated some of the reasons for this in section 1.2.1, where I argued that the immanent and transcendent interpretations of the quantifiers are independent of realism/irrealism issues. But there is more to say. Consider the position, urged by Hirsch (2011a), of quantifier variance—that there is no best quantifier meaning.[4] Recasting that position within a framework where quantifier domains are neutral and there is a transcendent existence predicate leaves its cogency intact. More interestingly, it also leaves intact the kinds of examples ("intuition pumps") that Hirsch (2011a) uses to argue for his position.

Consider—following Hirsch's lead—two groups of individuals, one that takes shrees (and not trees) to exist, and the other that's like us and thinks there are no shrees but only trees. There are no issues of translation, nor any problems with the two groups understanding each other; that's been established already. There is no problem with the two groups engaging in an ontological debate; that's been established too. Each group takes their quantifier domain to contain the same things—shrees *and* trees. What they disagree over is the extension of the existence predicate. We can now ask, quite simply and straightforwardly: is anyone *right* about this? We can ask, more pointedly, what is it about the *world* that dictates that one group is right and the other one is wrong? We *could* agree with Hirsch (broadly speaking, I mean, since the quantifier-variance apparatus that he couches this issue in has been rejected) in thinking there is *nothing* about the world that dictates

---

[4] Accepting quantifier variance doesn't force Hirsch, on his view, to a kind of quantifier-meaning relativism. For he thinks the particular quantifier meaning exemplified by *our* quantifiers—natural-language quantifiers—defeats other possible quantifier meanings for reasons independent of those that establish quantifier variance.

an answer to this question—other than, of course, the fact that one group (and not the other) agrees with *us*, agrees with us English-speakers.

On the other hand, we *could* agree with Sider (2011) instead (again, broadly speaking), in thinking that there is something in the world—*ontological borders*, I call them, though *fundamental structure* is probably the term he would prefer—that dictates one answer or the other as right.

This question is a genuine metaphysical one: notice how the neutrality interpretation along with a transcendent existence predicate allows it to be neatly stated. And once red-herring issues about indispensability are eliminated, we're dealing with a *relatively straightforward* metaphysical question: what is it about the *world* that dictates one answer or another about what there is? What is it about the *world* that dictates one answer or another about what *things* there are, and how those things begin and end (in space and time, for example, but also along any other dimensions that might be relevant to the "individuation conditions" of objects)? Notice: these questions look to be in principle answerable. An answer, for example, that there is *nothing* about the world that does this *is* an answer. It's an answer that would make certain metaphysical debates pointless; it's an answer that some philosophers might try to use to motivate a kind of ontological relativism; but that doesn't stop it from being an *answer* nevertheless.

I turn now (in part II) away from metametaphysics—the topic of part I—to metaphysics itself.

II | What There Is

But what there is is another question.

—W. V. Quine (1953, 16)

Introduction to Part II

Object projectivism is the position that all "this is here"/"that is there *too*" identifications (across space and time) on *anything* are not worldly but projections onto the world by us—by our (largely subpersonal) psychological mechanisms (sensory ones, for example) and by linguistic reification practices. More specifically, there are two components to our understanding of objects, neither of which are worldly. First, there are no worldly ontological edges that border purported objects. Less metaphorically (although I'll regularly use the phrase "ontological boundaries"): there are no properties, no relations—no aspects of anything *in the world*—that metaphysically underwrite (or provide the metaphysical support for) the individuation conditions for objects. Nor are there ontological boundaries that are "brute"—out there in the world prior to (or independent of) the properties and relations of the objects they are the purported boundaries of. "Individuation conditions" are supposed to characterize when presentations or descriptions of purported objects are presentations or descriptions of the *same* object and when they aren't. The claim, therefore, is that individuation conditions for objects are—in a sense to be specified—*projections* we impose on the world.

The second aspect of objects is what I'll call their "location conditions." These are logically independent of the ontological borders of objects; they are seen by us as operative even when we don't see objects at play in a situation. For example, we can describe the flow of a liquid—LIQ, say—in such a way that we can claim that some LIQ that was here then is there now. The cogency of this reidentification needn't presuppose that LIQ is composed of molecules, nor that the individuation conditions for each molecule underwrite the epiphenomenal (or supervening) fact that some LIQ that was here then is there now. Perhaps LIQ is a continuously deformable substance that can expand (or shrink) and the LIQ that was here then, although there now, has expanded spatially (or the opposite), or has deformed in such a way that it now occupies two discontinuous locations; or perhaps two portions of LIQ have continuously but thoroughly mixed together, and so on. Location conditions require tracking of parcels of stuff over time, but they don't require that the contours and volumes of those parcels remain fixed; they don't even require the spatial contiguity over time of those parcels (parcels can flow apart into distinct parcels of arbitrarily different volumes and contours). Location conditions are logically implied by the individuation conditions of objects—when the latter are available—but they're understood as present in situations where applications of individuation conditions aren't cogent. Certain fluids are understood in just this way.

Location conditions require a background against which objects and stuffs change position over time—against which the *same* stuff or the *same* objects have changed positions. Object projectivism describes location shifts of the same object or stuff to be projections too. There is nothing in the world that determines that something perceived later is the same as what was perceived earlier. Object projectivism denies the worldly presence of anything that metaphysically underwrites individuation conditions and the looser location conditions: over time and space, and along other dimensions as well (viz., modal ones).

Object projectivism is rather close to—if not identical to—what some call "ontological nihilism" (O'Leary-Hawthorne and Cortens 1995, Turner 2011). It's anticipated by Strawson (1953–54, 1959), when he discusses feature-placing languages. O'Leary-Hawthorne and Cortens (1995, 146–47) suggest that Bradley held something in the ballpark of this position. I'm sceptical that Bradley's position is genuine ontological nihilism rather than a confused amalgam of stuff metaphysics and monism; and Strawson's (1953–54, 1959) discussions of feature-placing languages similarly confuse stuff metaphysics with ontological nihilism. To my knowledge, O'Leary-Hawthorne and Cortens (1995) are the first to make the right distinctions here. Regardless, the *metaphysics* of ontological nihilism remains unexplored even by the later philosophers who instead focus on the question of what *language* such a doctrine can be successfully couched in rather than on the substantially minimal metaphysics itself along with its implications. (They are grappling with the consequences of an indispensability argument of the sort refuted in part I.)

As far as labeling goes, I prefer "ontological projectivism" to "ontological nihilism" because "ontological nihilism" suggests the position "repudiates ontology altogether" (O'Leary-Hawthorne and Cortens 1995, 145) or that the position is that "there is nothing at all" (Turner 2011, 3). Neither formulation is quite right. The real denial isn't about what's real or not real: the importance of *that* distinction survives the demise of worldly individuation and location conditions. To deny the worldliness of individuation and location conditions isn't to assert that "there is nothing at all." If "ontology" is wedded to "objects"—in the very strict sense that objects *require* worldly location and individuation conditions—then ontology, so called, *is* rejected. Features remain worldly on the object-projectivist picture, however. Arguably, that's sufficient for "ontology" to survive as a subject matter.

I prefer "ontological projectivism" for a second reason. This is that any discussion of the nonexistence of worldly location and individuation conditions needs to be accompanied by an analysis of how (nevertheless) such conditions are spoken of, or perceived to be in the world. This isn't because ontological borders are "Moorean facts" that one must accommodate one's philosophizing to (that suggestion will be undermined in chapter 6). It also isn't because an error theory has to be introduced to handle the irreality of there being such borders (despite the folk believing in them).[1] Rather, it's because crucial to metaphysics is an understanding of how our experience of the world is made up of separate contributions from us and from the world—and these should be teased apart ("factored") if possible.[2]

Here's a brief overview of the chapters of part II. Chapter 6 gives what I call the master argument for object projectivism. Here's a bit of setup for that. As I've noted earlier, the universal style of argument against ordinary conceptions of objects (specifically, how they're bordered) is to exploit the apparent metaphysical variability we intuitively seem to allow for those borders. We can strip objects of some of their bits (or add to them), while the objects remain the same or remain the same kind of object (sorites arguments). We can slowly put the parts of an object together to create it without a clearly perceived event of the emergence of that object (snap-together tool parts); we can worry about the relationship of an object to what it's made of, whether it is the same or different (statues and clay); we can worry about whether the object amounts to nothing more than its parts because what it does amounts to nothing more than what its parts do (causal overdetermination).[3] These concerns, as I've mentioned before, drive philosophers to certain metaphysical stability positions because the object(s) posited according to those positions are immune to these destructive strategies: monism, universalism, and nihilism.

---

[1] E.g., as Korman (2009) deploys the "challenge from folk belief" against revisionary metaphysical positions.
[2] My thanks to Anthony Adrian, Nat Carter, Corey Dethier, Dave Gottlieb, Justis Koon, David Laprade, and Isaac Wilhelm for careful discussion about my terminological choices.
[3] See Korman (2016) for a survey of these metaphysical strategies.

Interestingly, there is an apparently overlooked possibility—a diagnostic one. This is that all these argument-puzzles that can be brought to bear against ordinary objects are compelling because there is no metaphysical echo to our conception of an ontological boundary. The intuitive looseness of our notion of object, and that such looseness isn't just "intuition" but is exhibited in our practices of describing what we describe as objects, results from our having no idea what a worldly ontological border (of any sort) *could be*. This is a symptom that the notion of the borders of an object is a projection onto the world rather than something we find in the world. We certainly *do* understand that what's in the world shifts over space and time; but we have no metaphysical characterization of which of those shifts (that we see, or that we can imagine) constitute a change from one object to another or a change from where an object ends to something else. We have no idea which shifts across space and time (or modally) are ontologically special and which aren't, nor why they would be. Other than the brute impressions that *objects*, in fact, end here and begin there, we have no idea what the metaphysical facts could be that determine changes from objects *to* other objects, as opposed to mere changes *of* (or *in*) an object.

Hirsch (2004, 138) writes:

> Our common-sense selection function [a function that determines what, according to common sense, is an object and what isn't], as far as one can make it out, seems to be an amorphous and intractably complex mess, containing in all likelihood disjunctive conditions and grue-like exceptions.

This indicates that there are no metaphysical bright lines that we are recognizing in the world that mark out what the objects are. If we could sense such things, we'd have a sharp sense for when we were using "object" metaphorically to describe something as an object and when we weren't. We'd have a sense of necessary and sufficient conditions for "object" that *really* described what objects *are*.

The stability positions, which many philosophers are drawn to, indicate these facts. Universalism, for example, allows every possible ontological border. Any way of contouring an object (any possible physical or modal profile) is real, and determines a real object. But this is like a child who, suddenly realizing that she can draw a line anywhere she wants on a piece of paper, says: *Every line is already there.* The monist and the nihilist similarly press their respective views that the borders (metaphysically) are where *they* say they are because in this way various puzzle-arguments can't be brought against their positions. But they can't say, any more than anyone else can, what exactly is found *in the world* that shows that the border around *everything* is the only *ontological* border there is or that the borders around the simplest bits that the world can be broken into are the only ontological borders there are. We are never told by these philosophers what it is *in the world* that makes these things (but not the other conglomerations) *objects*. We're never told what the magical ontological flavor is that we can notice as present in the world that determines such-and-such items as objects and not the other purported objects we might instead break the world up into. Notice the point: it's not that philosophers propounding these positions don't give (various) necessary and sufficient conditions for something being an object—it's that they don't tell us (*can't* tell us) what in the world especially reflects ontology other than that their conditions (and not other conditions) avoid argument-puzzles. In fact, philosophers who owe allegiance to certain stability positions and not others engage in various methodological maneuvers (Occam's razor, etc.) to argue for their own stability positions over opponent ones—but these maneuvers even more obviously are imposed on the world. Occam's razor, in its various forms, for example, isn't something we see that the world obeys; it's one or another simplicity constraint on the design of theories.

I can put the point of the above two paragraphs in a more formal way—this is what I call "the master argument." It's different, as I said earlier, from the puzzle-arguments philosophers offer against various conceptions of objects (and it hasn't appeared in the literature until now, to my knowledge). There are two and only two metaphysical possibilities for the relationship between ontological boundary conditions and the relations and properties exemplified by the purported objects governed by those boundary conditions.[4] Either ontological boundary conditions are *sui generis*—something in the world that's apart from and additional to the relations and properties exemplified by the purported objects (they're "brute")—or those ontological boundary conditions come to nothing more than (possibly a distinguished subset of) the relations and properties exemplified by those purported objects. Metaphysical primitivism,[5] the first possibility, is false. The second option,

---

[4] I'll speak of "relations" and "properties" in this introduction and in chapter 6, even while the metaphysical position that there are objects—in the sense of items with ontological borders and location conditions—is being undermined, as it is throughout chapter 6. In chapter 7 and thereafter, however, I'll largely (although not entirely) switch to speaking generically of "features"—both one-place and relational—that are exhibited by the world.

[5] Metaphysical primitivism hasn't emerged explicitly in the literature in the general form presented here. It shows up—specifically with regard to composition—in the Lewis-Sider argument from vagueness (Lewis 1986, 212–13; Sider 2001, §4.9.1), specifically when Sider (2001, 122) writes: "But perhaps the special composition question has no informative answer because

however, vindicates object projectivism because we cannot make sense of the metaphysical presence of objects over and above changes across space and time (and across possibilities of changes in space and time). In the course of giving this argument, a number of subsidiary but important theses are argued for. Among these are (i) that predication needn't be presupposed in a language that's otherwise as fully expressive as first-order (and more powerful) languages, (ii) that scientific theorizing (along with the crucial and ubiquitous imposition of coordinate schemes) never *requires* worldly objects, (iii) that arguments from explanatory success don't establish *metaphysical* object boundaries, (iv) that our sensory recognition of the location and borders of objects—despite being involuntary—simultaneously involves a capacity to be aware of the projective nature of these perceived locations and borders of objects, and (v) a number of other important and interesting theses. Later chapters revisit and amplify these various theses, treating them as significant topics to be explored for their own intrinsic interest, and not merely as steps in the general argument for object projectivism, as in chapter 6. In the process of doing this, of course, my hope is that the various subsidiary theses employed in chapter 6 to establish object projectivism—and object projectivism itself—are made more convincing.

Chapter 7 takes up one of these theses, and at the same time supplies a response to what some opponents of the master argument might regard as a lacuna. This lacuna is what I call the "package-deal objection"—that objects, predicates and relations that hold of those objects, and predication stand or fall together; and if they fall, the resulting metaphysics becomes inexpressible. In response I introduce a feature-placing language that's adequate to our saying what we need to say about the world (given the truth of object projectivism), and I show that such a feature-placing language is notationally equivalent to a first-order language with neutral quantifiers. The purpose of doing this is *not* to solve a paraphrase problem: create a language that doesn't involve object commitments over and beyond what the object projectivist is committed to. (The need to do this has already been ruled out in part I.) The purpose, rather, is to help make sense of the position itself: what exactly is the object projectivist claiming about what the world is like? Relatedly, the purpose is to blunt various challenges of the form *We can't understand this*

---

whether composition takes place in a given case is a 'brute fact' incapable of informative analysis." Sider (2001, 122) describes bruteness in the strong sense (of not even supervening on "causal and qualitative factors") as extremely implausible, but allows a weak supervenient sense of it. See chapter 6, where I distinguish metaphysical primitivism and definitional primitivism. See Korman (2010) for a survey of responses to the argument from vagueness.

metaphysical position. Feature-placing languages dispense with objects, properties, relations, and predication, without any cost to expressive strength.

Chapter 8 addresses various aspects of the metaphysics of object projectivism. The nature of coordinate systems is one important topic; a specialization of this question is the nature of "empty space." Why, by (indispensably) invoking space and time, and specific properties attributed to space and time, are we not simultaneously taking on ontological commitments of one sort or another? Also introduced and analyzed is one aspect of the relationship between the various ways we view the world—in what sense our differing perspectives on the world involve implicit levels of focusing (e.g., microscopic or macroscopic).

The first half of chapter 9 takes a closer look at certain scientific tools that philosophers have been especially concerned with: laws and induction. Philosophers have thought that such tools establish (or justify) particular individuation conditions for specific sorts of objects—scientifically established micro-ones, for example. At the same time, scientific discoveries are taken to have undermined there being other sorts of objects, and these undermined objects are often understood to be the macro-objects of ordinary common sense.[6] I show in this chapter that no particular *worldly* ontological boundaries are favored by science.

The second half of chapter 9 deepens the understanding of the projectivist part of object projectivism. One sort of project earlier philosophers engaged in (see, e.g., Chisholm on "logical constructions") was various forms of reductionism: showing that objects of such-and-such types can be constructed out of objects of more fundamental types. This isn't the topic of chapter 9. The issue, rather, is that we have many ways of talking about objects: we have—perhaps this is the way to put it—many sorts of noun phrases. The question is how the various sorts of ways that we talk induce various sorts of object boundaries. A related question is responded to: What sorts of relations (if any) do these boundaries have to what's real? Along the way the role of Leibniz's law in our thinking is explored, various object-overlap puzzles are tamed, and a "conventionalist" view of our modal thinking about objects is tentatively offered.

The way I structure the presentation of object projectivism in part II yields, I hope, a lucid and first-time detailed description of this extremely radical metaphysical picture—a position that's been anticipated by only a quite small number of earlier philosophers but until now never spelled out so that its powerful challenge to traditional metaphysics can be seen clearly. One important dialectical fact is that the position—largely by virtue of never

---

[6] Famously encapsulated in Eddington's "two tables"—see Eddington (1929, ix).

being seen clearly—has almost never been directly opposed.[7] Most arguments in metaphysics—about ontological boundaries in particular—tacitly assume that object projectivism isn't available in logical space. This is why even drastic forms of eliminativist metaphysical positions (monism, nihilism, certain foundationalist positions) continue to presuppose the metaphysical presence of ontological borders. Crucial to the success of object projectivism is the ruling out of an indispensability argument that requires objects for a cogent quantification language. That work was done in part I.

One last point. To show that ontological boundary and location conditions are projections *isn't* to show something revisionary about our ordinary commonsense and scientific practices. One reason for this—with the notable exception of psychology (and sciences relying to some extent on psychology, e.g., linguistics)—is that the distinction between (i) projections of object boundary conditions and/or location conditions and (ii) the features that aren't projected is irrelevant. This will be illustrated, in particular, in chapter 9. But what I'm suggesting here isn't the commonly expressed shibboleth that philosophical positions are irrelevant to practical concerns. Any study of the human mind—in particular, any study of the mechanisms of cognition—requires an antecedent recognition of what's really out there and what isn't. A distinction, that is, between what is surely cognitively projected onto the world and what needn't be. This is a distinction, therefore, that's hardly irrelevant to practical or scientific concerns.

---

[7] It may be that the *only* argument that's ever been directly offered against the position (to date) has the same structure as most contemporary arguments against nominalism: *language indispensability*. In this case, the argument takes of the form of the indispensability of language forms that philosophers fallaciously take to presuppose object commitments.

6 | The Master Argument Against Ontological Borders

6.1 Introduction

This chapter establishes two main theses of *object projectivism*: (i) there are no worldly ontological borders between purported objects; there are no properties, no relations—no aspects of *anything* in the world—that constitute or amount to worldly individuation conditions for objects, and (ii) we project object boundaries onto the world.

The argument for these theses is straightforward—and independent of issues about bivalence or epistemology. There are two metaphysical possibilities for relationships between the ontological boundaries of objects and their properties and relations. Either their ontological boundaries are *brute*—something worldly, but additional to their properties and relations—or their ontological boundaries are just (a possibly distinguished subset of) their properties and relations. We can't make metaphysical sense of there being something in the world above and beyond the properties and relations of objects that distinguishes objects from one another—an extra metaphysical something that *is* an object's boundaries. The second option is also metaphysically puzzling: we can't make sense of what it is about properties and relations (or a subset of them) that makes them—apart from being changes in properties or relations (over space and time)—ontological borders or shifts *between* objects.[1]

---

[1] This, perhaps, isn't a *new* argument (or metaphysical insight), although how I'm structuring it *is* new—and independent of irrelevant epistemic and other metaphysical presuppositions it's been historically associated with. I detect it in Hume (1961), when he writes about substance and the self—although his concern with whether we have *ideas* of substance or the self isn't the same. I also sense acceptance of the metaphysical-primitivism limb of the master-argument by

It might be thought the conclusion of this argument should be: either object projectivism *or* mereological universalism is right.[2] No; mereological universalists still have to indicate the additional worldly element that's *why* every possible object border is an actual border of an object. What's the metaphysical "special sauce" that makes (any possible) ontological border mind-independent and real? *Stipulating* that every possible border of an object is an actual border *doesn't* answer this question; it just concedes that mereological universalism is indistinguishable from object projectivism. The mereological universalist *can* take the additional metaphysical element that induces the mind-independence of every possible ontological border as a mysterious something beyond human comprehension. This confers no advantages over object projectivism, especially since mereological universalism tells the same story about projecting borders—in terms of psychological mechanisms, language, or whatnot—but labels it "selecting borders" instead of "projecting borders." How this is different from object projectivism hasn't been explained.

One partially terminological point. In the course of giving the master argument in this chapter I'll sometimes speak of "properties and relations" and sometimes of "features." For the purposes of *this* chapter, what's being established *is* a disjunctive thesis: either the world is a spread of properties and relations, as philosophers such as Dasgupta (2009), Paul (2012, 2013), and Simons (1994, 1998) think, or it's a spread of *features*, as I think. The package-deal argument (discussed later in this chapter and in chapter 7) puts pressure on property/relation metaphysics but not on feature metaphysics. Apart from that, there are identity issues (accompanied by underdetermination issues) also faced by property/relation views that aren't faced by feature metaphysics. I discuss these in chapter 7 as well.

---

certain contemporary metaphysicians; see, for example, footnote 5 of the introduction to part II, on Lewis and Sider on composition. Proponents of what Korman (2016) calls "arguments from strange kinds" (Hirsch 2011a and Sosa 1999, among others) run examples of possible objects (e.g., shrees) that support the conclusion of the master argument dilemma. Compositional nihilists (see van Inwagen 1990, Rosen and Dorr 2002) are perplexed over what composition can be; if we can characterize composition metaphysically, we can derive a characterization of ontological borders (the borders of composed objects, if any, plus the borders of metaphysical simples). Object projectivists take these various forms of perplexity as evidence that we can't make sense of worldly ontological borders *at all*. Mereological universalists face this problem too, as I indicate in the next paragraph above.

[2] Here's a description of mereological universalism to motivate this disjunctive conclusion for the master argument: Our actual experiences select some of the objects out of all the ones there are available to be selected. All exist. All have mind-independent ontological borders. The only thing that's mind-dependent is which particular borders we're disposed to experience and so take an interest in. I thank an anonymous referee for posing the issue this way.

6.2 Metaphysical Primitivism

I start with the first limb of the master argument, metaphysical primitivism. This *isn't* the impossibility of characterizing ontological borders in terms of properties and relations. That's a cousin doctrine, *definitional primitivism*: there is no (finite) set of properties and relations in terms of which all ontological borders can be *defined*. Definitional failures aren't sufficient to establish metaphysical primitivism because objects may be distinguished from one another by properties or relations, but ones that uncharacterizably differ from object to object. Metaphysical primitivism is about what's in the world, and what it's like—it's not about language.

The issue is: how do we make sense of metaphysical primitivism, *metaphysically speaking*? What could borders between (and of) objects *be* in the world, above and beyond certain properties and/or relations that distinguish those objects from one another? What could such borders be if they *aren't* the specific ways the world's landscape changes across time and space? Adding to this perplexity is that *all* our impressions about when and where objects begin and end—more generally, *all* our object-boundary impressions—are cued by specific properties and/or relations that what's out there seems to have.

Here are illustrations. To imagine two items in space are different objects rather than different parts of the same object, we imagine them separated by empty *space*, or a physical border (a crack or colored line). It's imaginatively crude impressions like these that are behind a priori principles such as *No two objects at the same time and place*. If the objects are presumed not to be in space (e.g., numbers), we instead distinguish them by (non-spatial) properties. Puzzlement results if we're told: "Two objects at the same time and place can have the same properties and relations *too*."[3] We really can't *imagine* an infinite number of angels, with identical properties, all simultaneously dancing indistinguishably on the head of a pin. (If I try to imagine this, I get angels with slightly different dancing contours; that's *not* the idea.) We're similarly perplexed by an infinite set of numbers all with the same properties that zero has: infinitely many numbers all identical to zero in their properties?![4] I'll stress (although this won't help the primitivist) that these

---

[3] The "identity of indiscernibles" isn't conceptually required by *identity*. It isn't *a priori* that identity supervenes on relations and properties: identity can be brute. (Philosophers may not *like* that, but the suggestion *doesn't* render the notion of identity incoherent—or some *other* relation—as, arguably, denying that it's an equivalence relation does.)

[4] Do numerous zeros cause problems for the use of equality in arithmetic? No. "=," in arithmetic, is demoted to an equivalence relation distinguishing classes of numbers, each member of which has the same properties and relations. I thank Michael Glanzberg for raising this question.

suggestions don't *contradict* our notion of an "object." We may think God can create things like *this* (if we think we understand "omnipotence").

"Seems to have"—the phrase ending the paragraph before last—is crucial. These cues—especially the visual ones—are powerful: they affect us (as certain optical illusions show) even when we know no objects are involved, or that object contours aren't where we experience them to be.[5] All by itself, this doesn't show there aren't primitive worldly ontological borders. It *does* show that all *our* ways of marking differences between objects supervene on (some of the) properties and relations attributed to the objects in question; it shows (for example) that involuntary visual experiences of the contours of objects are driven by perceived shifts in (some of the) properties and relations visually had by those objects.

I just said that nothing in our practices of distinguishing and identifying objects or in our experiences of objects indicates the existence of brute worldly ontological borders. Here's a "transcendental argument" for brute worldly ontological borders that tries to sidestep this. The indispensability of object/predicate languages shows ontological divisions (i) are worldly and (ii) are (metaphysically) prior to property and relation attributions. The opponent position to metaphysical primitivism is incoherent, therefore, because it asserts that ontological borders supervene on or are constituted by (or whatever) "other property and/or relational aspects of *what's in the world*," or that they supervene on or are constituted by (or whatever) "properties and relations *exhibited in the world.*" But these are *euphemisms*. "What's in the world" are *objects*; properties and relations "exhibited" in the world are properties and relations *had* by objects.

To counter, I temporarily grant the opponent's presupposition that's nevertheless not obvious: the object/predicate structures of natural languages (and similar formal languages) indicate that objects have a logical/conceptual priority over their properties and relations. This concession is about *language* (or about *thought*); it doesn't show anything about the world. Asserting otherwise is unjustifiably inferring metaphysics from language properties or properties of thought. Additionally, this doesn't meet the primary objection to metaphysical primitivism: we can't make sense of it. Granting a priority claim (about objects over properties) in language (or thought) tells us nothing about *what in the world* ontological borders can be.

One more point. There is an argument in the neighborhood, not for metaphysical primitivism, but against object projectivism. This is that language

---

[5] Contour illusions nicely illustrate the phenomenon. See Gregory (2009, 211) and Pylyshyn (2003, 117–18) for Kaniza figures. These illusions are also widely available on the web.

and logic come with a package deal: predication, objects, *and* properties and relations. To excise objects (leaving properties and relations) is incoherent—our entire way of thinking collapses. I'll return to this argument at the end of this chapter to prepare for chapter 7, where the argument will be responded to by an analysis of feature-placing languages.

Summary: Metaphysical primitivism *isn't* ruled out by our concept of an *object* or because *identity* requires the identity of indiscernibles. It's ruled out by there being no *metaphysical* characterization of ontological borders if they *aren't* specifications of (some of) the properties or relations of objects.[6] Labeling borders "brute" makes them worldly "I know not whats"; this reveals a conceptual trap in our notion of *predication*. There is force to the thought that objects are *presupposed* by properties and relations—properties and relations must be properties and relations *of* something. This doesn't fit, however, with some or all of those properties and relations being what an object amounts to. The alternative is brute object boundaries—something that makes no metaphysical sense. This tension is a symptom of the object/property/predication package not being real but a projection.[7]

6.3 Criterion Transcendence Again

Let's turn to the second limb of the master argument: object projectivism is vindicated if ontological boundary conditions are certain properties and relations of purported objects.

Consider, first, the possibility of an inference from criterion transcendence to object projectivism. Certain words and phrases, recall, when used ontologically—"there is," "exists," "real," and so on—lack necessary and sufficient conditions (being in space and time, being a mereological sum ...). This is established by usage facts, for example, that speakers understand strange metaphysical possibilities about what there is (even if they think they're "crazy"), and that extreme views entertained by philosophers about

---

[6] This strikes at mereological universalism directly because that view takes borders to be real regardless of an object's properties or relations: any arbitrary object slice may be joined to any other arbitrary object slice to make a real object. All possible object borders *whether or not they supervene on properties or relations* are actual (real) object borders.

[7] Puzzles about predication are ancient and modern; see, for example, Plato (1963), Davidson (2005), and Collins (2011). (Collins 2011 provides a good discussion of the puzzles for Frege, Russell, and Wittgenstein.) The puzzles are intricate and hard to characterize (they're sensitive to background metaphysical/logical assumptions). I won't dwell much on them, but it will be clear by the end of chapter 7 that object projectivism doesn't face them because of the successor notion to predication in feature-placing languages.

what there is (it's all water, it's all one, it's all stuff...) nobody experiences as violating the public meanings of these words.

An implication of *the absence* of necessary and sufficient conditions on these ontologically used phrases: any way of individuating objects (of chunking what's in the world into objects) is compatible with how we understand the public meanings of "exist," "there is," and so on. It's a trivial corollary, therefore, that the perceived meanings of these words generate no conditions on ontological borders. The hope that necessary and sufficient conditions arise from our understanding of *specific* words, such as "zebra," "microbe," "electron," "raspberry," and so on, is also dashed by their criterion transcendence.

This looks sufficient to establish object projectivism because (so the argument goes) if there *are* worldly ontological borders, they're reflected in the (perceived) meanings of the appropriate ontologically used words, or of the more specific sortal expressions applied to objects with these borders. Another way to put the suggested refutation of worldly ontological borders: nothing worldly need satisfy the "application conditions" of these words because they have no "application conditions" in the needed sense—they're not *those kinds* of words.

This, however, *illicitly* moves from language properties to metaphysics. It isn't words (or their public meanings), it can be countered, that single out appropriate properties and relations that constitute (or are supervened on by) ontological boundaries. The *world* does that.

Even without a direct argument from criterion transcendence to object projectivism, there is still a problem: language is no guide to object boundaries. We must look elsewhere.

6.4 Arguments for Ontically Relevant Properties and Relations

Hope for *metaphysical connections* between privileged properties and relations and ontological boundaries hasn't *yet* been dashed, although the language route is gone. Another option is a *philosophical argument* that singles out specific properties and relations. There are two ways to go, and this chapter explores them. *The argument from phenomenology* focuses on our (involuntary) experience of *objects*. The sensory cues that induce *object-experiences* also imply a role for certain properties and/or relations. This set of properties and relations are the privileged properties and relations that constitute ontological boundaries. *The argument from optimal theorizing* instead tries to establish the specific properties and/or relations exemplified in the world as constituting ontological boundaries by the best-theory-of-the-world maneuver. There is a best (scientific) theory, and the ideology of this best theory—the ways that this best theory individuates objects—corresponds to worldly ontological boundaries.

Arguments from optimal theorizing differ from fundamentalist language projects (e.g., Cameron 2010 or Sider 2011) that characterize "fundamental" languages—ones utilizing only ideology that "carves the world at its joints" (and, sometimes, quantifier domains only containing "what really exists"). These projects *presuppose* the existence—and cogency—of ontological boundaries *to begin with*. That metaphysical assumption is *subsequently* confirmed by providing certain needed explanations, or sometimes it's presumed established by other metaphysical arguments. *The argument from optimal theorizing* is different. There *is* a parallel hope that optimality constraints on scientific theories induce optimality constraints on the many options for ontologically contouring the world's insides. *But*, the further requirement is that these constraints have metaphysical implications: they give reasons for thinking we don't impose ontological contours on the world but instead *discover* them there.

6.5 The Argument from Phenomenology

Philosophers have treated human experience—visual experience in particular, but not just visual experience—quite shoddily during the centuries they've talked about it. They've claimed until recently that we don't *see* objects, and that we don't *see* depth either. We *infer* depth, and *infer* where objects begin and leave off too. We infer these things from what we *do* see: a (flat) manifold of raw feels (e.g., colors and tones). Philosophers know better now. Most contemporary philosophers claim we *do* see objects and depth. They also admit that we can't help seeing objects and depth; the experiences are involuntary.[8] Even better (because of insights from vision science), we are *beginning* to discover the cognitive mechanisms that cause these involuntary

---

[8] I'm unconvinced we "see" objects the way that we obviously "see" depth; I think we *don't*. This is why I use "experience" to describe our sensory relationship to "objects." (Nevertheless, our "experience" of objects is involuntary—that's important to what follows.) Pylyshyn (2003, 51 n. 2) distinguishes between the ordinary use of "vision," which describes the result of several processes including various kinds of higher-level cognition, and what he calls "early vision," which is encapsulated. (He often describes the second as "vision" and the first as "seeing.") I'm

aspects of our experience. We are beginning to understand the mechanisms that build *objects* (as it were) into our experience of the world.

These *object-experiences*—these involuntary experiences of where objects begin and end—are coded into "object-intuitions" that we also have (usually involuntarily) about whether we're facing two presentations of the same object (at different times or under different descriptions) or two different objects. Object-intuitions have two sources: (i) sensory and other sorts of experience, and (ii) uses of noun phrases and other related linguistic devices (whereby object-intuitions are prompted by the understanding of words).

A *naturalistic* viewpoint toward object-intuitions is required—not an *a prioristic* one. It can't be assumed that object-intuitions, just because they're *involuntary*, correspond to objects *as they really are*. This follows only if (i) these intuitions are generated by psychological mechanisms coordinating them with worldly objects, *or* (ii) our object-intuitions *determine* worldly objects. For reasons already given, (i) is problematic. Object borders are supposed to be metaphysically real. So we need a metaphysical characterization of them to which we can compare our involuntarily experienced object borders.[9] On the other hand, (ii) collapses into object projectivism. If how we experience object borders determines those borders, then worldly facts aren't relevant. The sense in which we can be wrong about object borders (which is crucial to them being worldly—to them being mind-independent) is gone.

The requirement on ontological borders being worldly: Ontological borders must be something beyond mere experience of them. Mereological universalism, I've noted, doesn't meet this requirement unless it explains what *makes* every possible border worldly. A psychological story about how our experience of ontological borders arises *does* meet this requirement—provided an explanation of a correspondence to worldly borders is also given.

---

sympathetic to his distinction (versions of which other psychologists embrace—see footnote 10), although I won't dwell much on its importance outside this chapter.

There are important issues to adjudicate about sensory (and cognitive) content, ones that have been raised in philosophy of perception and in discussions of visual (and auditory) phenomenology. See Pitt (2004), Siegal (2010), Strawson (1994), articles in Bayne and Montague (2011) and Hawley and MacPherson (2011), as well as Azzouni (2013a). This isn't the place to get into debates about thick and thin sensory views and cognitive phenomenology. A book-length discussion is needed—in a *different* book.

[9] Objection: "*Do* I need a metaphysical characterization? The world hands me a virus. I have little or no idea what makes a virus a virus, but I know there is one, it is a thing, and it is unpleasant." I *don't* know these things. What I've been handed I call a "virus" just as I speak of "genes." What I have in both cases is a functional characterization of an "I know not what" based on its "powers." What this "thing" *is* (one or many, or even stuff) is up for grabs, as the gene case (or the heat case) makes clear. (See Griffiths and Stoltz 2007 for an accessible history and characterizations of evolving gene concepts.) I thank Michael Glanzberg for raising this issue.

This, as I mentioned, presupposes a characterization of ontological borders apart from something we experience (and apart from the brute characterization that they can be anything at all).[10]

There's a style of argument in epistemology, however, that's recently popular, and looks like it undercuts this conclusion. This is the G. E. Moore–style proposition that if we perceive something, then we're (defeasibly) entitled to believe in it.[11] The application in this context is: *Given* we experience objects—we *perceive* objects—we're defeasibly entitled to believe in them. That we perceive objects with such-and-such specific ontological boundaries defeasibly entitles us to believe in those objects (and not in objects we don't perceive).

Suppose a language is *possible* that refers to shrees, as Hirsch imagines; and suppose its speakers *perceive* shrees. Nevertheless, *we're* defeasibly entitled to beliefs in trees (and disbeliefs in shrees) because of what *we* perceive. We can say we're right and they're wrong. This response treats Hirsch's

---

[10] Compare psychological studies of the experience of objects with psychological studies of the experience of depth. A rich literature exists on the visual elements that cue depth perception. Included is the study of optical illusions—mismatches between impressions of depth and what's out there. A (geometrical) characterization of three dimensions is metaphysically presupposed in these studies. (We *are* in three-space—*that's* presupposed by those studying depth perception.) There is also a rich psychological literature developing on object perception; it *avoids* relying on a metaphysical characterization of objects. Marr (1982, 270) writes:

> Is a nose an object? Is a head one? Is it still one if it is attached to a body? What about a man on horseback? . . . These questions show that the difficulties in trying to formulate what should be recovered as a region from an image are so great as to amount almost to philosophical problems. There is really no answer to them—all these things can be an object if you want to think of them that way, or they can be part of a larger object.

Scholl (2002, 31) echoes Marr:

> Marr's pessimism is certainly appropriate when considering the mind as a whole; certainly, for instance, we can *conceive* of almost anything as an object. . . . With regard to what mental processes such as visual attention *treat* as objects, however, there may be well-defined answers to such questions.

Indeed, a number of psychological theories of how object representations are maintained over time (during tracking-object tasks) treat the adult mind as possessing two representational systems for individuating objects. Carey and Xu (2001) posit an attention-based tracking system concerned not with features but with spatiotemporal continuity or parallel movements, and a kind-based system that's fully conceptual. Kahneman, Treisman, and Gibbs (1992) have a similar view. Objects are perceived and tracked by the attention-based tracking system even if their features are misidentified or change drastically ("frog into prince"); this system (operating primarily on spatiotemporal factors) is complemented with "object files" that store information about the properties of objects. Pylyshyn (2003) also distinguishes between encapsulated "early vision" and broader cognizing. These distinctions are behind Scholl's optimism that a study of the factors involved in attending (and tracking) objects can succeed (as it is succeeding) without presupposing a metaphysical characterization of objects, or even the possibility of a metaphysical characterization.

[11] See, e.g., Pollock (1974), Pryor (2000). The primary application is to breaking a widely perceived philosophical standoff between the sceptic and the Moorean hand-waver.

possibilities as being like the sceptical possibilities Moore challenges. It puts pressure on what's otherwise a metaphysical standoff between we-believers in trees and those-believers in shrees because of *our* defeasible entitlement to our belief in our own objects—because that's what *we* see.[12]

An interesting aspect of our experience of objects—revealed by introspection—is largely unrecognized by philosophers,[13] and undercuts this argument. Experience of objects isn't as simple in its epistemic layering as this argument presumes. Although we *do* involuntarily experience objects as *worldly*, we also simultaneously experience them as projections *onto* the world. This phenomenon is striking enough to deserve a section of its own.

6.6 Recognizing Object Boundaries are Projections

My claim is this: We *experience* that object boundaries aren't *only* certain perceived features (shape, color, perceived depth, occlusions, etc.). We recognize the ontological boundaries of objects are feature-independent. This, perhaps, isn't done by staring at a cup (or a couple of zebras) and just *noticing* we could experience the cup (instead) as a plantlike outgrowth of the table, or the zebras as two parts of a single object (a single-minded zebra with two bodies). We realize this, perhaps, because we could watch a carpenter carve a sculpture of a cup on a table where the cup-and-table is one unit, or because we could recognize that the cup-on-the-table is a hologram and therefore is either one object or numerous ones (depending on exactly how we think holograms are individuated). We could also see an (extraterrestrial) plant grow rapidly from a seed into the odd shape of a table with cups on it, where the "cups" loosen and drop off because they're seeds. (We've all seen movies like this.)

We also recognize that, depending on the artifact, it can be broken apart (a printer can be disassembled, and certain parts replaced), and the object is seen as the same both during and after the process; although if it's broken into too many small parts (its molecules, say) or if too many of its parts are replaced, we don't experience it as still there or even as the same object

---

[12] Hirsch (2011a) breaks the tie in a different (although related) way: resolution in favor of trees because *we* speak English and not a language with a quantifier domain containing shrees. Notice, contrary to my view (see footnote 8), I'm allowing my Moorean opponent to say we "see" objects in her sense of the word "see"—whatever that is.

[13] It's revealed by introspection, but it's just about *predicted* by two-representation psychological theories of object perception—where, on these theories, our concept of an object isn't due to early vision or the attention-based tracking system but is a background-belief-permeable "full-mind," or "objects-file" concept. See footnotes 8 and 10.

when put back together. We also recognize that we experience some objects (a stereo with wireless components, a galaxy, a doorbell, a deck of cards, or an electronic or paper manuscript) that have parts that aren't contiguous, or even close together. If a creature could continue to ("wirelessly") control limbs, tentacles, arms, or eyes that it could detach from its body, we would nevertheless think of those detachable limbs as *its* parts.

This makes it easy to conceive of someone who experiences different object boundaries: who can't experience a creature with detachable limbs as *one thing*, who *can* experience a stereo as one object *only if* its components are wired together but not if they're wirelessly attached, or who can experience a deck of cards or a manuscript not as one object but only as *groups* of objects.

We can recognize that our own experiences of several objects or instead of several attached parts of one object are asystematic. For example, if two gloves are stitched together along the thumbs, we continue to experience them as two objects; but if two pieces of fabric are stitched together into a shirt, we experience one object. If two people are stitched together along their thumbs, we don't experience *them* as one object—we don't think this even about Siamese twins. But two black filled-in squares, just touching along their sides, are experienced instead as a rectangle; this is true even if the squares are different colors but there is no black-lined border between them. It's not hard to imagine, therefore, people who experience objects differently from us, people who experience gloves stitched together along their thumbs as one object or people who experience Siamese twins as one object (despite having two minds).[14]

To recognize this asystematic variability in our experience of worldly ontological borders is to recognize the projective nature of object boundaries. We can recognize how our *experience* of specific object boundaries is nevertheless compatible with an experience (that we're *not* having) of different object boundaries. *This* is to recognize the independence of our experience of object boundaries from our experience of the other features of objects that we perceive.

Because of this recognition of the projective nature of the experience of object boundaries, a number of dramatic thought experiments are accessible to non-philosophers as well as philosophers. We *easily* recognize what

---

[14] I'm giving examples here that are raised by philosophers who puzzle over the special composition question (e.g., van Inwagen 1990). Rather than using these examples to motivate compositional nihilism, however, I'm using the intuitive availability of these examples to show that the projective nature of object-experience is easily grasped. This bit of metaphysics—puzzles about the special composition question—is as accessible to intro philosophy students as scepticism is; I make something of this momentarily.

it would be like for people to experience object boundaries differently from how we actually experience them—although (it needs stressing) we can't simultaneously make ourselves *actually experience* things this way.

Imagine, for example, you're sitting in a garden at dusk when your experience suddenly shifts. Now ... there are shrees all around! Or consider this: Suddenly ... *the object boundaries you normally experience are gone*; you're not experiencing object boundaries anymore. And when you try to explain what this experience is like, you say, "I was experiencing everything as *One*." You might say (as if you've had a sudden mystical insight), "Everything *is* One." And—in some circles, anyway—people would classify this as a mystical experience of the genuine metaphysical *Oneness* of everything.

You might say, trying to describe the Oneness experience, "It was like everything was water." Or "Everything I used to see as distinct objects I now see as patterns in the One." But neither description is right because you're not mentioning how *everything continues to look the same*. The properties and relations look the same. In particular, the depth experience is entirely untouched (the world isn't flat). "Seeing patterns in the One" isn't the vanishing of object-experiences; it's instead an experience of something else that we'd describe as only "looking like" objects, in the sense that patterns in something sometimes "remind us of objects." The same is true of formations of clouds that occasionally "look like" camels or faces, or patterns in sand, and so on. That's not a Oneness experience because those experiences involve flows or ripples across the objects—the properties and relations are perceived differently. Approach the no-object-border (Oneness) experience this way: Imagine everything is the body of a powerful being (who is everywhere). In this way, the experience of everything being One is like experiencing a person who controls his own limbs, even when he detaches them from his body. I call these different (or vanishing) object border experiences *Hirsch visions*: experiences of the objects around us having different object boundaries (or no object boundaries).[15]

---

[15] That such experiences are *actually* neurophysiologically possible *isn't* needed to respond to the Moorean entitlement argument. That we experience object borders as independent of other object features doesn't imply that the experiences I'm describing can be had (if, say, various brain mechanisms that generate object-experience are damaged). This isn't true even if—as implied by the psychological theories mentioned in footnote 10—object-tracking mechanisms are subpersonally separate from feature-attributing mechanisms. It may be, for example, that depth cues inextricably involve certain object boundary projections. What's important is that it's not part of our *experience* of object boundaries that they're inextricably connected with depth experiences. This is what allows us to *conceive* of certain experiences. The Moorean argument isn't about subpersonal constraints on what's imaginatively possible; it's about defeasible entitlement on the basis of what we *experience*.

Consider two-dimensional Hirsch visions. Imagine a flat polka-dotted plane, with each polka dot identically sized and the polka dots uniformly spaced out in infinite rows and columns. We (because of color shifts along the boundaries of the polka dots) *in these cases* experience polka-dot-shaped colors as distinct objects against a background (perceived as *nothing*): just polka dots. The experience of objects is more robust in three dimensions with spherical polka dots. One Hirsch vision is to experience the same distribution of colors as we do, but to experience "objects" instead as tiny arrayed pixels, each one colored, or instead (more weirdly) to experience objects as polka-dot halves—even without color change cues across the invisible vertical middle dividing each polka dot half from the other one it's joined to. Or: *to experience* any of numerous arbitrary ways of imposing objecthood onto this color distribution pattern.[16]

Consider the experience of an object in two places at the same time on a two-dimensional polka-dotted plane. O is the entire polka dot here *and* there. This isn't O having two non-contiguous polka-dot-shaped parts. (That's an object-experience *too*, but not this one.)

"*Not possible*," some philosopher will say. "These purported objects violate Leibniz's law" (an object can't have different spatiotemporal locations; only its parts can). No, the suggestion doesn't violate Leibniz's law.[17] An object has such-and-such spatiotemporal locations *as well as* such-and-such spatiotemporal locations. The object C—that A and B each is—has two sets of properties, A-relative properties and B-relative properties. It isn't singly located in space and time; it's A-located and B-located. We don't experience this, of course. (Not in *this* setting, anyway.) We simply recognize that the independence of the experience of object borders from the experience of other features of objects *allows* an experience of objects bordered this way while still experiencing the other properties and relations the same way. And so someone experiencing this could say: "No, it's not that part of the object is here and now, and the other part is then and there. *That's something different.*"

A philosopher might stubbornly retort: "Objects have boring and trivial relations to themselves like self-identity. They have interesting relations to

---

[16] Consider moving polka dots. Movement cues impel *us* to experience the shifting colors as individual moving objects. Those gripped by Hirsch visions needn't have that experience: they might experience the polka dots as pairs of objects moving in *lockstep*—or as something else entirely. As I've noted, depending on background assumptions about the kinds of objects we're seeing (gloves, planets, stereos), we can also experience objects with boundaries like these.

[17] Adams (1979, 113, 120 n. 18) describes the violated principle as "the same thing cannot be in two places at once—that is, cannot be spatially distant from itself"—and notes that Occam denies it's a necessary truth.

their parts, and their parts have interesting relations to one another. But these so-called objects have interesting relations to themselves (like being two feet away from themselves). I don't like that." *So? This is a contradiction?*[18]

This *isn't* an experience of everything as "One." *That's* losing a sense of object boundaries entirely. *This* is experiencing as one object what *we* experience as distinct objects—John and Sarah, say, who never meet, as John lives in London and Sarah in Melbourne. If we extend this experience to every object, we get a different way in which someone could have the mystical experience that "everything is One."[19]

What about *identity* in these cases? How does it work? Along the lines of endurantism: A is wholly present at each moment—A at t_1 = A at t_2. (Not: there are two temporal parts of A, one at t_1 and the other at t_2—that's "perdurantism.")[20] Similarly, "Jarah" is wholly present at Sarah and at John. We can say Jarah is "incarnated" simultaneously at Sarah and John. We can distinguish the incarnations of Jarah (and others), and introduce an equivalence relation on incarnations, "same incarnation of A as," which is valuable for comparing people at different incarnations. We can thus say that Sarah and John are identical; we also can say that Jarah's Sarah-incarnation is such-and-so, although Jarah's John-incarnation is so-and-such.[21]

6.7 The Argument from Phenomenology (Again)

I return to the Moore-style argument for the existence of objects as *we* experience them, and additionally take up Korman's "challenge from folk belief." Recall that our object-experiences are supposed to defeasibly entitle us to certain beliefs. These beliefs aren't that these are just ways of seeing objects among many other equally metaphysically acceptable ways of seeing objects. No, the hope is to undercut object projectivism. So our defeasible entitlement has to be that these perceived objects are actually found in the world,

---

[18] Consider sci-fi scenarios in bad movies, stories, and comic books, where someone meets himself because "universes collide." Incoherent? Not according to our concept of objects.
[19] Someone could experience numbers this way. "All the numbers are the same object." Oh, we say, *you mean all the numbers are aspects of the One (or something like that)?* "No," the person responds, "in talking about aspects you're really just talking about one thing having parts (but speaking euphemistically). I mean they're all the same object. That's what an abstract object *is*: numbers. All of them." Does this make equality problematic in arithmetic? No. See footnote 21.
[20] See, e.g., Lewis (1986, chapter 4.2).
[21] If all the numbers are the same object (footnote 19), identity (where every number is identical to every other) is distinguished from "=" (not genuine identity), which applies to incarnations of numbers, and is used in arithmetic.

and (accompanying this) that other possible ways of experiencing objects in the world are wrong about how they *actually are*. Our experience of objects—so I've argued—doesn't allow this entitlement. We recognize (if only because of the asystematicity of our object-experiences) that object boundaries are "subjective" (as non-philosophers might put it).

Somewhat related to a Moore-style argument is Korman's (2009) "challenge from folk belief." This attacks "eliminativist" views—denials that objects are as the folk think of them. Korman's "eliminativist" category needs division into "replacement" views—compositional nihilism, monism, and so on—which replace the folk objects (and object borders) with different ones, and "pure eliminativist" views, which deny object borders altogether.

Korman correctly identifies the weakness of replacement views. They need principles to establish the object borders they want, while simultaneously rejecting principles that posit object borders they deny. Thus they're vulnerable to two forms of self-undermining. First, they can be "globally self-defeating": they can fail to explain why the folk find it "reasonable to believe in the objects they do" (Korman 2009, 243). They can also be "locally self-defeating" (Korman 2009, 244): while undercutting folk claims that certain objects exist, they may simultaneously undercut their own claims that other objects exist. More broadly, the evidential basis (in intuitions, say) for principles that support a position can't involve "cherry-picking": rejecting some intuitions and accepting others, without good reasons for the choices made.

I forgo evaluating Korman's attacks on replacement views. Important here is that object projectivism—being a pure eliminativist position—doesn't face local self-defeat: it doesn't need principles to support object borders. Global self-defeat is another matter. Object projectivism *does* have to explain why the folk are wrong about there being object borders. It can't attribute an error to the folk that's "so thoroughgoing [that] the most likely source would seem to be idiocy or else a general inability to form true beliefs about the world" (Korman 2009, 244).

Object projectivism doesn't attribute *that* kind of error to the folk because it helps itself to the cognitive psychological mechanisms of object projection currently being discovered (see footnotes 8 and 10 for references). These (largely subpersonal) mechanisms explain why the folk find it "reasonable to believe in the objects they do." Simultaneously, because they are object *projection* mechanisms—not ones that simply "see" what's out there—metaphysical considerations that establish there are no worldly object boundaries don't endanger scientific descriptions of these mechanisms. Lastly, what establishes object projectivism—as I've indicated in this chapter—*aren't* principles based on object intuitions (such as "no two objects can be in the same place at the same time"). What establishes it, instead, is that what worldly object-boundaries *could be* can't metaphysically be made sense of (and furthermore, worldly object boundaries play no role in the science that studies how we come to believe in objects).[22]

Preliminary conclusion: We can't justify an inference from the experience of objects (with particular boundaries) to objects as they are independently in the world. This result *does allow*, of course, the cogency of our experiencing the world as chopped up—or chunked—in the very way we do it (or choosing to talk as if this is so). Object projectivism allows that we can give (at least in principle) good evolutionary reasons for why we experience and talk about objects as we do, and not elsewise. An evolutionary story can explain why the particular visual cues that our perception of objecthood is sensitive to have been selected to induce experiences of ontological borders; it can even explain the context-sensitivity of our perceptions of objecthood—why we are aware of *these* contextual factors (in *this* class of cases).

Object projectivism, finally, is compatible with *actually discovering* necessary and sufficient conditions—in terms of specified properties and relations exemplified in the world—that match how we automatically chunk the world into objects. (Object projectivism, I stress, is *compatible* with this possibility even though there are reasons for thinking it's unlikely there are such necessary and sufficient conditions.) What it doesn't allow is sense to ontological boundaries *being in the world*. In the strongest way this can be understood, we *discover* the properties and relations exhibited *in* the world; we don't discover object boundaries there.

6.8 The Argument from Optimal Theorizing

I turn now to the other strategy against object projectivism: *science* reveals worldly ontological boundaries. The fatal problem *here* is we need a metaphysical principle to conclude that an optimal language structure, with a specific quantifier domain, is reflected in the metaphysics of the world. That only question-begging maneuvers are available for this is shown in what follows.

This argument has traditionally drawn its strength from indispensability considerations. Just formulating a particular indispensable scientific theory and showing (as far as we can tell) that there must be certain items in its quantifier domain is taken to force an *ontological* commitment to such

---

[22] The quotations from Marr and Scholl in footnote 10 are especially relevant to this point.

things. This family of argument strategies has been ruled out by the neutrality interpretation of quantifier domains established in part I. We need, therefore, to see if there are other reasons—independent of arguments based on the indispensability of sheer language forms—for why an optimally formulated scientific theory forces commitments to worldly object boundaries.

I'll start with a crucial scientific tool: coordinate systems. In this section, I'll evaluate ways of forcing ontological commitments to metaphysically real objects on the basis of such systems. Then, in section 6.9, I'll consider a different idealized example to probe other ways of attempting—in the name of science—to impose metaphysically real objects on the world.

Imagine an infinite two-dimensional plane that's arbitrarily colored. One can recognize—metaphysically speaking—that the *landscape* in question "exemplifies" different colors (different color properties) over its extent. And it exemplifies different relations too: a color is over here and the same color is over there. We desire, let's say, to describe this exemplification of color properties more precisely. We want to say *where* in the landscape such-and-such colors are exemplified, and we want to say *where* the landscape changes from one color to another. To do this, we impose a *coordinate system* onto the landscape—a uniform grid of boxes of some fixed dimension or other, for example—to enable us to speak of two colored places being adjacent to each other, or two colored places being certain distances from each other (the blue box is seven boxes away from the red box). Or perhaps we impose something a lot more fine-grained—the familiar Cartesian coordinate system of *points*.

Let's describe the imposition of point talk (or region talk) on something (on "space") as a *coordinatization*. There are many different kinds of coordinatizations: one kind will fit certain spaces well but not others. For example, Cartesian coordinatizations won't fit nicely onto a finite sphere. Polar coordinatizations do far better. We can imagine spaces with all sorts of properties (e.g., curvature-differing spatial regions of various dimensions, with holes), and it can be correspondingly easy or hard to supply specific coordinatizations that fit such spaces. Often, more than one kind of coordinatization is optimal, although there are always suboptimal ones. Required (usually) of an optimal coordinatization is that it enables sharp mathematical results. What we can say about what the coordinatizations are applied to is inferentially tractable: theorems can be shown.

I'll assume (for purposes of evaluating the argument from optimal theorizing) that a particular coordinatization is optimal—one that describes regions, points, or spatial whatnot.[23] Equally useful for a foil position is an optimal *family* of coordinatizations, with quantifier domains that share certain items (spatial regions, say).

Given the above assumptions, and given that this is an indispensable way of speaking about the colors in the plane—points being purple-colored or green, or a region being partially blue and partially red, and so on—*must* we in addition take the needed contents of the quantifier domain, boxes or points or regions or whatnot, to exist *in the plane*? Suppose the distribution of colors over the plane is so fine-grained that how one part of the landscape differs from another turns on making ever-finer distinctions in space—so that we *need* to speak not of boxes (of such-and-such fixed dimensions) but instead of points (or of ever arbitrarily smaller boxes or regions of some sort). Does our *need* to speak this way, in order to describe how colors change, force us to take such points or arbitrarily small regions to *exist*? Once indispensability arguments are short-circuited, what remains to force *there being* such things as patches or points or regions or anything of this sort—even if talk of such things is unavoidable to describe how the landscape changes over the extent of a spatial region?

Here's an argument (call it "the argument from the description of the setup"). The description *I've* given is committed to objects of some sort, apart from what's required in the quantifier domain of the optimal theory. After all, *words* in the description of the setup refer to a *plane*—or, more generally, to a *space*—the *regions* of which are colored. How are we supposed to understand what I'm describing the coordinatizations to be applied to without thinking of colored *regions* in a *plane*? Response: This is *not* required. As I'll show in chapter 7, all that's being described here is a *distribution of features*; objects aren't in the setup, nor are references to objects required. Furthermore, in saying "objects aren't required," I'm including "absolute space" in any form. A distribution of features isn't "in" anything. To speak of "infinite planes," "curved space," and so on is only to speak in a picturesque manner to characterize *how* features are distributed. Further, notice that the argument from the description of the setup is one of those indispensability arguments already ruled out in part I. The difference is that instead of it being directly applied to the quantifier domain of the theory providing the coordinatization of the plane, it's being applied to the informal description *I* gave.

---

[23] In many cases, a coordinatization is given axiomatically that characterizes certain items primitively, and other useful ones are constructed from the primitives: two-dimensional figures from points, say, or points from nested two-dimensional figures. (See, e.g., Tarski 1983b.) The quantifier domain, of course, contains *both* the primitive items *and* the constructed items.

There is a second argument; call it "the argument from the need to explain optimality." The optimality of the coordinatization is *explained by* what in its quantifier domain corresponds to metaphysical realities (or those metaphysical realities *being in* the quantifier domain). That is, an *explanation* is required for why such talk (of points, of regions, of whatever) is needed. In particular, a quite specific explanation is needed for why some coordinate systems (of points, say, with such-and-such a metric, etc.) are superior to other coordinate systems—relative (of course) to what the coordinate system is being applied to. And the explanation that's clearly needed (so it's claimed) is that the things spoken of in the coordinatization *exist*, and exist *in* what the coordinatization is (successfully) applied to. There's a matchup between the coordinate-system talk and what's exemplified in the spatial region the coordinate system has been successfully applied to. What's said in the mathematical theory underwriting the coordinatization—about the points and their properties, for example—*is true of* the points in the region itself: *they* have those properties.

No—this is wrong too. The example (all by itself) makes clear *why* coordinatizations are needed—talk of boxes or points or regions—if we want to describe the color distribution. That is, merely that color features shift the way they do requires a fine-tuned coordinatization of such-and-such a type; the various ways colors can distribute explains why one or another coordinatization—possessing various capacities for *resolution*—is more or less optimal. It's also clear that certain global properties of how colors distribute (e.g., as like on a plane, a sphere, a saddle, etc.) affect whether and which coordinatizations are optimal. In all these cases, notice, the explanation *does* turn on there being such-and-such (complex) *features*—certain color distributions manifesting certain global curvature and size properties—and there not being other complex features manifested.

Therefore, nothing in these sorts of explanations *requires* a further inference to there being things. These sorts of explanations don't require there being *somethings* that exist *in* (or *on*) the surface (or space) that enable the *application* of a coordinatization or that induce the superiority of certain coordinate systems over other coordinate systems. Nothing in these sorts of explanations requires a further inference to the existence of the space itself either.

Notice the response being made to *the argument to explain optimality*. Either the description of the color features presupposes objects (e.g., points or regions) or it doesn't. If it does, *the argument from the description of the setup* is being presupposed; no new considerations arise. If it doesn't, then the need to capture the distribution of color features itself explains the optimality of a particular coordinatization; bringing in points or regions tells us nothing further about the optimality of the coordinatization.

These examples of coordinatizations are spatial, but the notion easily extends further. The way to think about a coordinatization is as an application of a node/property/relation structure in order to talk about aspects of something. A coordinatization structure is a notation that imposes topic-"objects" with certain properties and relations onto what it's applied to. Understood this way, standard ways of talking about fictional texts, for example, also involve coordinatizations: the topic-"objects" are the various fictional characters (and other fictional props in a story), and the properties and relations are the various events and character traits attributed to those characters.

The application to fiction looks like mere metaphor, but it's not. As I mentioned earlier, spatial coordinatizations allow sharp mathematical results. The language of characters and their traits (and what happens to them), in contrast, isn't very inferentially tractable. But otherwise the coordinatization imposition is the same—in particular because of the imposition of talk of objects and their properties. This point is generally relevant to any explanation of the success of scientific theories: various language-internal needs are satisfied by good scientific theories, most notably the already mentioned tractability of inference. But this has nothing to do with ontology, although it's central to the value of formal quantification. Indeed, the imposition of quantification "on the world" directly enables such inferential tractability, and yet this tractability-inducing role of quantification is fully independent of ontological considerations.

These are toy examples. But they clearly illustrate differences in viewpoint that can be (and have been) taken in this metaphysical vicinity; more importantly, they expose the need for additional argument to draw ontological conclusions from indispensability/explanatory considerations. In particular, granting the indispensability of some language or other with a quantifier domain containing spatial objects—points, regions, or whatever—doesn't result (all by itself) in such things *being where* what that language is applied to. Even granting there may be a *best choice* of item to be quantified over—points, say, because changes in landscape are arbitrarily fine-grained—doesn't force the result that such things *exist*.

The two points established here are (i) that a presupposition of a worldly kind of object (points, regions, whatever—on the grounds that a quantifier domain containing them is indispensable to the mathematics of coordinatizations) isn't *required* to explain the success of the application of that mathematics to a distribution of features, because (ii) the actual distribution of the features themselves is enough to explain the optimality of a choice of coordinate system.

6.9 The Argument from Optimal Theorizing: An Idealized Theory

This second illustration is a best case for anyone pushing the argument from optimal theorizing. The illustration involves false assumptions about scientific theories, but ones beneficial to the argument. Nevertheless (I'll show), the argument fails even in a context designed to satisfy it as much as possible.

Call this example *the metaphysician's dream come true*. Suppose we finalize science, and the result—satisfyingly—is *one* scientific theory that explains *everything*.[24] Suppose this theory is first-order, and that its quantifier domain contains a certain set of small dense spherical items. There are various laws characterizing the properties and relations of these items over time, laws that explain (enable the prediction of) every event in the universe. Call these items "simples."[25] Suppose that *nothing more* is quantified over. No abstracta, no numbers, no functions, and so on. (Those who know some science know that three falsehoods about, or deviations from, actual science have just been described: that a final unified theory can exist, that it's first-order, and that it has a quantifier domain without abstracta.)

Let's assume additionally that a certain set of properties and relations are simultaneously singled out as marking the ontological boundary conditions for these objects—for example, these objects have certain borders in space and time, the composition of these objects is characterized by certain properties had by them and not by the space contiguous to their borders or between them, and so on. So, *how* does any of this theoretical optimality establish *worldly* ontological borders? The reasons it doesn't echo considerations raised in the last section.

Here's the problem. The proponent of worldly ontological boundaries has to successfully oppose the following position: *Everything* about the relationship of this theory to the world *is still explained* even if we treat singled-out worldly ontological borders as metaphysical *projections*. That is, if we treat metaphysical facts about the world as *exhausted by* the descriptions of the properties and relations exemplified in the world (and singled out by the

---

[24] Never mind what this means, exactly, or if it's even possible. The point is that this is a popular desire not just among philosophers but among some physicists too.
[25] These are metaphysical simples only insofar as nothing more is quantified over besides them: they are the quantifier commitments of an optimal scientific theory.

theory), there is nothing more needed to explain how this theory fits the world so well (both descriptively and explanatorily).

Here's why the "burden of proof" isn't on the object projectivist but on the proponent of worldly ontological boundaries. It's not because an Occam's razor principle is being deployed: *All things being equal, we should posit the least amount of metaphysical structure in the world that we can.*[26] The point is that the strategy in play uses an explanation for the optimality of a scientific theory to *force* that ontological borders (of such-and-such a sort) exist. But instead, we find that the fit between theory and this world is fully explained by describing the distribution of features. In particular, the specialized grip that *the quantifier domain* has on chunks of world is explained *entirely* by theoretical sensitivity to certain exhibited features (and not others). That the quantifiers, as a result, chop the world into these bits and not those bits is explained entirely by sensitivity to *these* features and not *those* features. There is no additional explanatory burden left that the positing of ontological borders *in the world* needs to shoulder.

The falsehood of metaphysical primitivism is playing an (until now) tacit role in this argument. The role of the quantifier domain, in distinguishing the chunks of world that it distinguishes, goes *beyond* a sensitivity to features if in fact the individuation of objects goes beyond the features that distinguish them. In that case, the theoretical explanation for the aptness of this choice of quantifier domain will correspondingly extend beyond its sensitivity to features to include a recognition of brute (primitive) ontological borders.

Consider the following objection. The laws of motion (let's say) are optimally presented in terms of a quantifier domain containing spherical balls of such-and-such dimensions with such-and-such properties. Why isn't this to be *explained* by there being objects of such-and-such kinds in the world? Answer: The best theory contours what's in the quantifier domain in terms of such-and-such properties and relations. Let's say, for example, that an object is stipulated to extend only so far as mass is contiguously exemplified in the world. And the laws are optimally predictive if the quantifier domain of the laws contains (and only contains) such "objects."

But what in this description tells us something *about the world* that we didn't already know after we were told how features are exhibited in that world? We already know that quantifier domains require chunking the *feature presentation*[27] into parts *in one way or another*. And we already know that

---
[26] O'Leary-Hawthorne and Cortens (1995) offer this on behalf of "ontological nihilists."
[27] My thanks to Anthony Adrian for this suggested phrase.

fact doesn't tell us anything additional about the world. If a philosopher takes it to, that's because the philosopher is presuming something like Quine's criterion, or some sort of structure-in-the-world-matching-truths premise. We must avoid importing these considerations into the argument *now*, since they've already been shown to be toothless. We already know that some ways of chunking the world into parts produce better descriptive instruments than other ways of doing it—precisely because those ways nicely contour the world along certain property/relational lines, and other ways don't; but this all by itself isn't sufficient to posit the metaphysical presence of object borders.

So opponents of object projectivism seem to be in an awkward situation if they want to use an optimal theory to impose metaphysical structure on the world: they need to presuppose that the chunking mechanism built into quantifier domains gives a reason for thinking the objects that the quantifier domains of the resulting truths carve out of the world—carve out of what's *real*—are themselves additional worldly phenomena those truths are about. And we haven't found any reasons to presuppose this.

We *do* know that the laws of this universe are clearly sensitive to how properties and relations distribute in that universe. We also know that this singles out certain properties and relations, and (presumably) not others. It's *these* properties and relations (and not others) that end up being exemplified in the laws. That certainly makes these properties and relations special—but their specialness isn't relevant to establishing the existence of objects in the world. They are relevant to what the quantifier domains (of a theory) are to contain. But that's a fact about theories, not one about the world (unless, again, opponents of object projectivism simply impose language facts about quantifiers onto the world without justification).

Ontological divisions aren't part of the world. This means that everything we need to explain about why the quantifiers (of a theory) treat *this* as dividing off from *that* is explained in terms of the optimality of a theory (for certain purposes) and—as far as the world is concerned—solely in terms of the properties and relations singled out by that theory. In chapter 9, I'll sketch out some of the many ways that actual scientific theorizing takes advantage of this freedom from ontological borders. Once we're no longer blinded by the false assumption that the quantifier domains of true scientific theories need connections to ontological boundary conditions (as they supposedly are exemplified in the world), we can see how—almost always—successful scientific theorizing ignores considerations of ontological borders.

6.10 Some Concluding Remarks

My strategy in this chapter for undercutting opposition to object projectivism—that is, my strategy for undercutting *any* position asserting that there are object boundaries in the world—hasn't been to oppose object-border proponents on a case-by-case basis for each particular set of objects, and (in each case) undercutting the principles used to support this. I've gone to the sources of these principles—which can only be (i) how we experience objects to be in the world (that is, how we experience them to be distinguished and identified, or how we talk about them being distinguished and identified) or (ii) how various accepted bodies of knowledge (e.g., science) so distinguish and identify objects. I've shown that these sources have insufficient resources to oppose object projectivism.

An important element of my approach is to separate the factors that contribute so strongly to the impression of there being a world around us that's composed of objects above and beyond the presence of features. This is because various factors psychologically operate together to impel an impression that's hard to see past. When we, for example, recognize that the perceptual cues that impel the impression of objects are "subjective," we easily fall back into one or another view that (of course) well-designed scientific theories are independent of these intuitions and can establish the metaphysical reality of objects all on their own. When, on the other hand, we see the fallacy of thinking that quantifier domains somehow require a metaphysical echo (we recognize it's a mistake (i) to think exemplifications of features require an antecedent positing of objects or (ii) to think optimal theorizing about the world requires there be something more for quantifier domains to latch onto other than a privileged set of features), we are nevertheless apt to be blinded by those very object-directed intuitions in our own thinking that impel us to see quantifier domains as containing "objects."

Sider's remarks about this are illuminating. He considers the nature of a "fundamental language," one without any idioms (or "ideology") that impute false structure to the world—structure that isn't metaphysically present (2011, 183). If one doesn't think objects aren't a part of the structure of the world, then—Sider claims—the logic of any such language can't involve first-order quantifiers because the result will be ontological commitments to *objects*. He first describes a foil position, attributed to the quantifier variantist, who says (according to Sider):

> I have no need for objects in my fundamental description of the world. The world fundamentally consists of the distribution of properties over spacetime. One can then introduce the ordinary notion of an object in various ways atop this foundation.

Sider writes (2011, 183):

> This is just confusion. Far from renouncing quantifiers in his fundamental language, this variantist helps himself to quantification over points and regions of spacetime.

Suppose the variantist *has* done this.[28] *So what?* The neutrality established in part I shows that the indispensability of a particular quantifier domain does *not* require a metaphysical echo—real things (with those properties) in that domain or correspondingly in the world. On the other hand, it's also clear why the philosophical recognition that (something in the neighborhood of) object projectivism is true is so often accompanied with the view that *radical changes are in the offing* (new kinds of languages are called for, ones that don't have quantifiers, or new kinds of perceptual capacities are needed, such as being able to *see* the Oneness of everything) or—generally—with some view or other that this is a profound metaphysical discovery as a result of which a radical kind of fallout must ensue. The next few chapters show that almost nothing in language need change as a result of object projectivism. This should be no surprise. If there are no ontological boundaries in the world—if object boundaries really are projections in the sense that I've argued for in this chapter—then nothing changes. Our theorizing and language practices, how we perceive the world, and so on *already accommodate* this metaphysical fact.

I've interchangeably used the ideas of "properties and relations exhibited in the world" and "feature distributions." Several recent metaphysicians have argued for the former idea (see footnote 15 of the general introduction for references); it has a long pedigree as well. A feature metaphysics, by contrast—that all there is are features—is different in two respects. First, there is the logical point that, unlike properties and relations, features have no residual association with objects. Whatever features are, they don't require inherence in, or any relationship to, objects. The second difference is more important, however. This is that the various metaphysical views about properties and relations—that they are universals multiply instantiated, that they are tropes that bear resemblances to other tropes but aren't multiply instantiated—require arguments for one or another set of *individuation conditions* on these

---

[28] Why would the variantist *have to* do this? Precisely because an adequate description of how properties and relations distribute across space-time indispensably requires talk of space-time points or regions (of some sort), as we saw in section 6.8.

things. Features have no individuation conditions. I'll develop this point in chapter 7.

Any language, some may argue, even a feature-presentation language (whatever that looks like), requires predication; and so there is still one argument against object projectivism to be dealt with. This is that predication is a package deal that inextricably involves objects as well as what *holds of* those objects. This is addressed in chapter 7.

Notice, though, something interesting about the package-deal argument. Suppose it was sustained. Nevertheless, it would give us no advantages in dealing with the master argument of this chapter. For (in the style of all transcendental arguments, actually) it establishes worldly objects without telling us anything about them other than they're required by the logic of predication. They must be posited so that properties and relations have something to inhere in. But this tells us nothing about how to make sense of metaphysical primitivism, or what that special ontological something is that makes certain properties and relations *in addition* ontological borders. It leaves intact the evidence—discussed in this chapter—that the object boundaries we're prone to believe in because of our experiences or our theories are projections. This suggests there is something wrong with the package-deal argument and not that the master argument has somehow overlooked a way that worldly ontological boundaries are justified.

One last point. The central "can't make metaphysical sense" move of the master argument shouldn't be confused with other methodological moves philosophers use in metaphysics. There is what might be called "simple-minded Occam": an ontology of no objects is better than an ontology of some objects, where "better than" means "simpler," in some sense. This approach is diametrically opposed to the spirit of the master argument. The master argument is focused on the independence from us of ontological borders—if there are any. Simple-minded Occam is an attempt to impose on the world human-all-too-human standards of simplicity.

The same point applies to a move that looks closer to what I've argued for, what I'll call "explanatory Occam." This is that objects are "explanatory danglers"—they offer no advantages to explanation that we don't have otherwise, *therefore* we shouldn't accept them.

My argument is different. To begin with, objects provide nothing explanatory that a description of shifts in properties and relations don't already provide. Because of this, scientific theories don't provide an inference to the best explanation of the form: *there are* ontological borders in addition to mere shifts in properties and relations that we already recognize as metaphysically present. This "inference to a best explanation," if it had succeeded, would have been similar to a transcendental argument for objects based on predication. It would have established ontological borders despite our inability to make metaphysical sense of them. As it stands, since everything about the success of a scientific theory can be explained without such borders—including how items in the quantifier domains of those theories are contoured—no such transcendental argument gets off the ground.

Dasgupta (2009) runs an underdetermination argument against "primitive" individuals. Just as a Galilean geometry of space and time (in the Newtonian setting) should be adopted instead of the standard Euclidean geometry because in that way empirically inaccessible absolute velocities are eliminated from metaphysics,[29] so too, individuals should be eliminated from metaphysics because they are similarly empirically inaccessible. This is a version of explanatory Occam: nothing should be introduced into metaphysics that our scientific theories don't need. This isn't the master argument. We can certainly make sense of a geometrical setting in which absolute velocity makes sense; we can make sense of why creatures in such a universe would find absolute velocities intrinsically undetectable—despite their presence. Whether it's therefore *rational* for such creatures to deny a metaphysics in which absolute velocities occur (but are inaccessible to them) is something I've not tried to evaluate in this book.[30] The master argument, to repeat, is that we can't *make sense* of ontological borders as *additional* bits of metaphysical landscape, above and beyond feature distributions. There are also subsidiary supporting considerations for the master argument. This is that transcendental arguments—that we must posit such ontological borders despite an inability to make sense of them—don't work. One such argument is the package-deal argument that I evaluate in chapter 7. A second arises in the context of scientific theories: that an explanation for scientific success requires positing such borders, regardless of whether we can make sense of them or not. This argument has been undercut in this chapter.

Consider a primitive "thisness" property held by each individual: the property of being identical to oneself (Adams 1979). It's reasonable to treat these things as explanatory danglers—they certainly have no presence in scientific theories. Dasgupta (2009) will rule them out on these grounds.

---

[29] See Stein (1967), Friedman (1983), and DiSalle (2016) on this.
[30] For the record, I don't think *any* inference from underdetermination (epistemic limitations) to metaphysics is licensed. One thing that I find very appealing about object projectivism is that a host of metaphysical underdetermination cases—due to our inability, in general, to determine how many objects there are (e.g., in Max Black universes, statue-clay cases, and so on)—vanish along with object boundaries. What's appealing, to be explicit, is that the vanishing of such cases is a corollary of the view—not an argument *for* it. See chapter 9 on this.

My approach rules them out on the grounds that we can't make metaphysical sense of them.[31] My approach, notice, reverses the verificationist theory of meaning: no empirical fallout for a scientific/metaphysical hypothesis implies it makes no sense. I say: if a hypothesis makes no metaphysical sense to us and, further, a transcendental argument for it fails, it's to be rejected.

---

[31] We can make *linguistic* sense of thisnesses, presumably, if we can name individuals: Jack has the property of being identical to Jack. But that doesn't meet the challenge of saying what it is in the world that this so-called property *is*. (Adams seems to try to ground them in the first-person perspective—I'll pass over this by dogmatically saying that a perspectival move doesn't meet the metaphysical "what exactly is this?" challenge either.)

7 | Feature-Characterization Languages

7.1 Introduction

Imagine a philosopher who is sympathetic to neutral quantifiers and the distinction (from section 5.2) between object-based and truth-based property attributions. "All this makes sense," this philosopher says, "because genuine predication only occurs when a sentence that's true is about real objects. Real things are referred to and properties are attributed to *them*. What makes sentences about real objects true is that the predications they describe correspond to metaphysical states those objects are in. (Things in the world *are* certain ways and they aren't other ways.) Falsity, in these cases, is understood similarly: a property is incorrectly attributed to something real. (Things *aren't* the way the sentence presents them as being.)

"Truth-based property attributions are different: predication *isn't* involved," the philosopher goes on. "Consider the true sentence 'Sherlock Holmes is a good detective.' There is no object Sherlock Holmes, and so there is nothing to predicate anything of. 'Good detective' is attributed truly to 'Sherlock Holmes' not because Sherlock Holmes *is* one but because the *whole truth* in question (the true sentence) is induced by background facts.

"All this I understand (or at least, I accept it for the sake of argument)," this philosopher adds. "But things got strange in chapter 6. You described a plane as exhibiting certain colors, and using a coordinate grid you allowed us to say, for example, that 'c_4 is red' or 'd_{18} is green.' You claimed, in addition, that no ontological commitments to grid items arise by doing this; you claimed this to be true even if a genuine coordinate system is introduced—one that involves (for example) quantification over points.

"The neutrality interpretation of quantifier domains defended in part I, I presume, is supposed to help us grasp these claims," this philosopher continues. "We're supposed to think quantifier domains provide 'topics of conversation' instead of objects. They're 'demarcating *targets*' for predicates and relations. And it's true that talking this way about 'demarcation' fits nicely with the arbitrariness involved in choices of coordinate systems (or grids). Your plane examples in turn are compelling because we can see how, by choosing a different coordinate system, we can arbitrarily contour what's in the quantifier domain.

"Nevertheless, I'm having trouble fitting the lessons of section 6.8 together with your earlier distinction between object-based and truth-based property attributions. It seems obvious that the truths determined by the use of coordinate systems *aren't* like fictional truths such as 'Sherlock Holmes is a good detective.' The reason is that it looks like predication is still metaphysically in play. Something *is* colored thus-and-so, and that this something is so colored makes 'c_4 is red' or 'd_{18} is green' true. By contrast, nothing being good-detective-like makes 'Sherlock Holmes is a good detective' true. So your coordinate plane cases are like 'John is running' rather than your Sherlockish non-ontological fictional examples."

This philosopher continues: "You can *claim* we aren't ontologically committed to spatial neighborhoods (or points or whatnot); you can obviously invoke the neutral-quantifier apparatus as a tool for this. Nevertheless, *this* application of the neutrality apparatus isn't convincing because it doesn't look like other uses of neutral quantifiers. You can argue that my claim, in the last paragraph, that 'something *is* colored thus-and-so' is a misdescription. Instead, you say, it's better to talk about properties and/or relations being 'exhibited.' Here also, you can choose your rhetoric carefully and use terminology that sounds more neutral. You can call them 'features,' and you can say things like, 'Features are exhibited by the plane; they are exhibited by parts of the plane.' Still, nothing like *features* is involved with Sherlock Holmes being a good detective. There isn't anything to feature Good-detectiveness the way that a plane or its parts feature Red.

"So it seems to me," this philosopher concludes, "that the complaint in section 6.2 is still forceful despite what you say in the rest of chapter 6—despite your so-called 'master argument.'"

I'll repeat the objection with slight modifications:

> [Talk of features or what's in the world] are *euphemisms*. "What's in the world" can only be *objects*; anything "exhibited" in the world has to be some blend of those properties and relations had by objects in the world. What else could they be?

7.2 Feature Metaphysics

To adequately respond to this challenge, I must give more details about feature metaphysics. Only then will it be clear why predication is really being set aside, and along with it objects, properties, and relations; only then will it be clear that space and time aren't metaphysically distinguished the way that the examples I gave in chapter 6 seemed to indicate. I'll start by recollecting and refining claims I made in the general introduction about the individuation conditions of features.

Recall that I claimed that accepting the worldliness of features *isn't* to make the additional metaphysical assumption that features are themselves objects. I denied that features are tropes, immanent universals, or anything like this. What I took this denial to mean was that I could refuse the legitimacy of questions like "Do features multiply occur in various places and times or only uniquely?" I called these illegitimate identity questions, and I denied it makes sense to ask whether it's the same Red (a universal) that's instantiated and bears the identity relation to itself or two different Reds (tropes) that bear the "exact resemblance" relation to each other. Either move, I said, treats Redness as an object, and tries to provide object-boundary contours for *it*.

Let's revisit these claims in more depth. The master argument of chapter 6 denied metaphysical sense to ontological borders, and the same lack-of-sense objection applies to the relata of predicates. Consider a Max Black universe containing only two identical red spheres. There are (at least) two apparent metaphysical positions possible about the Redness. One is that the spheres share the *same* Redness, a "universal." Another is that the spheres have *two* properties (tropes) exactly similar to each other, but otherwise possessed uniquely by the spheres. These metaphysical positions individuate *what's* possessed by the spheres differently.

Now consider two presumably metaphysically distinct universes. In one, the two spheres share the Redness universal; in the other, they have *two* identical but distinct Redness tropes. One is hard-pressed (to put it mildly) to see what these supposed *differences* come to. What metaphysical distinction corresponds to this difference between there being two trope Rednesses, or only one universal Redness? How are these two universes actually *different*? It isn't just that the respective positions on Redness look underdetermined by these Max Black universes; it's that we *can't understand* what this metaphysical difference can possibly amount to.[1]

---

[1] Lewis (1983, 10–11) distinguishes between Armstrong's universals, which are fully located at each item that instantiates them, and his own properties, which are spread out—located

Irrelevant is that individuating relata of *predicates* differently may lead to languages with different virtues. And, just as in the case of object boundaries, stipulating that the difference is "brute" helps no more now than it did in chapter 6. The trope theorist and the universal theorist individuate predicational metaphysics differently; the feature metaphysician rejects these individuation claims altogether because they lack metaphysical sense.

Here's a way to contest the "can't make sense" claim to attack feature-theorists. There are features placed when—to speak informally—red is here *and* there. There are two metaphysically distinct ways of describing these placed features: SAME-COLOR-ASxy, or EXACTLY-RESEMBLING-DIFFERENT-COLORSxy. The first applies to the same features, whereas the second applies to distinct features that resemble each other perfectly. This metaphysical difference is real, the contester claims. Depending on which feature-placing term, SAME-COLOR-AS or EXACTLY-RESEMBLING-DIFFERENT-COLORS, correctly applies, features are either trope-like or universal-like (*universalia in re*).

The difference, that is, turns on what relations the features bear to one another. Similarly, for the identical spheres, the difference turns on what the predicational structure *is*. In one Max Black universe, there are two Redness tropes, with an "exact similarity" relation between them. In the other Max Black universe, there is one universal shared by the spheres, and a "same universal as" relation that the universal has to itself. Response: One *must* say these things because of the initial assumption that it's one or two Reds that the spheres exemplify, or the initial assumption that one (or another) relation is exemplified by the red-feature-presentation. If the reds are instantiations of the same universal, then the relevant relation has to be identity; if not, then the relevant relation has to be similarity. Why this makes the initial stipulation about the individuation conditions of Redness understandable is murky.[2]

There *is* a metaphysical fact, one we can loosely describe as "indistinguishable feature-swaths here now and there then." But this doesn't mean that a

---

distributively at all their instantiations. This too is an individuation condition among predicational items that we can't make metaphysical sense of. In this case the two universes of red spheres are ones where, in the first case, the redness property occurs distributively at both spheres, but in the second it appears fully at each. Again: exactly *how* do these universes metaphysically differ?

[2] The feature metaphysician *isn't* rejecting the cogency of *identity*. Everything (whatever it is) is identical to itself: that's not in dispute. In dispute is the cogency of identity across space and time, or across instantiations. More generally put, what's in dispute is identity across *coordinates*—as I'll explain shortly.

thing—a feature—appears here and there, and that we can ask for its identity conditions. The contester thinks: "We can chop up space-time and ask: 'Is it the *same feature* here as there, or are they different features that resemble each other?'" This *sounds* like a genuine question with genuine answers—one sensibly posed to a feature metaphysician. The possible *answers* appear to generate a genuine *metaphysical* distinction because answering no or yes yields (respectively) something like trope theory (features occur uniquely and are exactly similarly to one another) or something like immanent property theory (the same feature occurs more than once)—*universalia in re*, or *immanent* universals. But this supposed metaphysical distinction isn't reflected in the world. It's a distinction of language.

Diagnosis: The problem is English—certain aspects of English, anyway, and of other natural languages too. We reify colors—more generally, we reify features, and so we can impose the logic of identity on the terms (designating features) that we've introduced to enable that reification. But this language apparatus doesn't echo metaphysically, because we can't make metaphysical sense of the distinction: *exactly resembling features* here and there versus *the same feature* here and there. So we've found that, just as we can't make sense of object boundaries in the world, so too we can't make sense of the various ways philosophers have sought to individuate what's attributed to objects.

The reasons look slightly different for why attempts fail to make metaphysical sense of identity conditions for objects, properties/relations, and features, but they amount to the same point pressed three times over. For objects, I've presented the puzzle primarily in terms of spatial and temporal boundaries, but the problem generalizes to whatever kinds of coordinates the individuation conditions of purported objects are given in terms of. There is a lesson here: coordinates are central to the issue in all three cases. Different individuation conditions for predicational items—treating them as tropes or as universals—turn on treating objects as coordinates at which properties (and relations) occur, and worrying about the ontological boundaries those predicational items have. The issue dangles in the air for predicational items just as it does for objects; nothing metaphysical adjudicates it. Finally, given feature-presentation metaphysics, the issue is—again—whether features exhibited here and there are the same feature twice or two features exactly resembling each other. If features are the ground floor—if there is *nothing else* but features—then nothing remains to answer this question about identity conditions. As I illustrate next, the issue of identity conditions can be posed for features only after we import some features to function as coordinates for other features.

I promised, at the beginning of this section, to show that space and time aren't metaphysically distinguished—that they are features too. In order to facilitate discussion of this, I'll first introduce a small terminological modification. "Feature," as I've been using it (and as it's normally used in English), is a count noun. And for certain purposes, that's desirable—when, for example, I describe color as a feature and curvature as a different feature. But I'll sometimes use "feature" as a mass noun: a feature presentation is a presentation of *feature*. I'll thus sometimes speak of "feature" instead of "features" and also speak of "portions of feature," especially when I'm speaking of the arbitrary contouring of the feature presentation into the boundaried items belonging to quantifier domains.

When in chapter 6 I described features as exhibited on surfaces, and evaluated the optimality of various coordinate systems placed on surfaces, I implicitly allowed a view of features as *themselves* distributed in space and time, and consequently I allowed (in some readers' minds) a natural assimilation of this relationship to the predication of features to space/time entities of some sort. But that's—metaphysically—*wrong*. The feature presentation is itself metaphysically central. And central to feature presentation—here's a way of putting it—is *co-featuring*. Spatial features (dimension, curvature, continuity, extension) can co-feature with color and other features. It isn't *mandatory*, therefore, to assimilate feature characterization to predication. Describing some feature as placed somewhere isn't to obviously predicate anything *of* the spatiotemporal region where it is; nor is it to obviously predicate a spatiotemporal property of that feature. Rather, spatial features are co-occurring *with* other features.

"Co-occurrence" is misleading, for it may sound like "co-occurrence" must involve space and time—that is, co-occurrence is at a place and time. This isn't the idea, if only because spatial and temporal features are features too. Instead, think of a portion of feature presentation itself as "where" the co-occurrence of the features is.

7.3 The Language of Feature Metaphysics

Some philosophers will hear the last section echoing bundle theories of objects: objects are sets of properties (or tropes, or . . .), along with a co-occurrence relation.[3] Such views start with properties, build objects out of

---

[3] See, e.g., Van Cleve (1985), Casullo (1988), as well as the more recent philosophical work mentioned in the general introduction, footnote 15. Bundle theories have a long pedigree.

sets of those properties, and then, on some bundle views, handles there being distinct bundles that contain the same properties with a primitive instantiation relation. Feature metaphysics is different. The feature presentation comes first. And a feature presentation is—as it were—a landscape of features we "portion" in order to talk about it. That is, we demarcate segments of the feature presentation and allow those segments to appear within a quantifier domain. This is a metaphysically arbitrary act of distinguishing ontological borders in the feature presentation. We label the portions "F," "G," and so on, and describe them as "at" themselves. Language that describes feature metaphysics looks like this: "F@f," where "F" denotes the feature presentation *at* the portion of the feature presentation designated by "f"; "R@ef," where "R" denotes the feature presentation at the portions denoted by "e" and "f."

So far, this is pretty uninteresting. "F@f" just involves two labels for the same portion of feature, where we describe it as at itself. But there are alternative ways of describing portions of the feature presentation that are interesting. We can divide the features between the right and left sides of the @-relation; we can also nominalize certain features while leaving the remaining features in what amounts to predicate positions. So, for example, we can nominalize some of the space-time features. This requires a bit more explaining.

In scientific practice, space and time play two easily confounded roles. One, of course, is as properties and relations of objects. Objects themselves are taken to have temporal and spatial properties, and these properties and relations of objects are often treated as derived from the spatiotemporal properties of the manifold they appear in; but this isn't mandatory. Important, though, is their other role—as devices of coordinatization. Coordinates are a means of manipulating talk about the world by providing language pegs for what we talk about. When doing this, we stipulate answers to certain (puzzling) identity questions we can otherwise ask, and which arise from the introduction of coordinates. Although for a two-sphere Max Black universe we can ask if the spheres are actually the same or if the color instantiated by those spheres is the same, we don't usually ask if the distinguished moments of time or spatial locations of the two spheres are *themselves* the same or not. Once a coordinate system is in place and the identity conditions of its "pegs" are fixed, we can use it as a background against which to raise identity questions about whatever we're placing in the coordinate system. (Or we can use it as a background against which to *stipulate* answers to identity questions—to stipulate ontological boundaries in a metaphysically arbitrary way.) In thinking about whether the moments of time at which two objects are located are the same or different, we're instead treating the objects as a coordinate system for temporal moments and raising "identity across objects" questions for moments of time instead of "identity across time" questions for objects.

Used this way, a coordinate system is purely imposed language—there is no sense to asking if certain coordinates are the same as other ones, for they're stipulated not to be. But in practice, we bundle in certain features *as* coordinates. If features exhibit certain patterns, they make very natural coordinates—in the sense that they make it easy to *describe* the feature presentation in detail in ways that inducing other features as coordinates fails to do.

To illustrate this, start with a particular feature presentation f. For concreteness, allow it to be a two-dimensional color presentation. Imagine (this is how we might put it) it's a distribution of two colors over two-space: red and green. One possible language for describing the feature presentation is a coordinate system of spatial points, p, q, r, . . . , and two one-place feature characterizations R and G that apply to each point, depending on whether, respectively, the red or green feature is at that point. In this language, the spatial feature of two-dimensionality is bundled into the coordinate system by having ordered pairs of numbers be the coordinate points; spatial features of density, continuity, and infinity are similarly bundled into the coordinate system by the choice of the numbers admissible in the ordered pairs (all the real numbers, say, or all the complex numbers, or only the rationals, or a finite field, and so on). Other spatial features (no curvature) aren't bundled into the coordinatization, but are instead captured by characterizations of functional relations among these points (the way a metric is characterized, for example).

Other choices for spatial coordinates are possible too. The plane could be divided into an infinite number of square tiles of some finite size, for example. Doing this would make it harder (or impossible) to capture certain spatial features. Correspondingly, depending on what sorts of patterns of red and green appear within these tiles, a larger number of color feature characterizations (different patterns of green and red) are needed to capture distinctions in the feature presentation at such tiles—perhaps an infinite number of such characterizations.

Another possible language uses terms a, b, c, . . . that apply to maximally complete feature presentations, and feature characterizations F, T, P, G that hold of classes of maximally complete feature presentations. Ta is true if and only if a refers to f and T holds of a class of feature presentations that includes f; Fa, Pa, and Ga are false if F, P, and G hold only of classes of feature presentations that don't include f. This language choice, notice, treats maximally complete feature presentations as its coordinates. (And notice it's pretty useless at describing details of feature presentations as a result.)

Here's yet a third kind of language. Introduce r and g as coordinates (let the red and green features be coordinates), and introduce the feature characterizations S_{NM} (where N and M are subsets of the real numbers) as features. $S_{NM}r$ is true if and only if S_{NM} is at r—that is, if and only if every ordered pair of real numbers (n, m), where n is in N and m is in M, is red. Notice that it's stipulated that all the red featuring and all the green featuring are the same by choosing them as coordinates. Other (more refined) choices could be made instead. If color features are numerous enough and structured in some interesting way, this language could be useful, although the one I've given clearly isn't.

The feature metaphysician argues that *none* of these alternative languages involve genuine metaphysical differences—metaphysical differences that we can make sense of, anyway. The only real metaphysical fact is the feature presentation itself. There are numerous arbitrary choices, however, in what coordinates may be chosen, and, correspondingly, in what feature characterizations may be chosen to be at them. Imagine the feature presentation is an infinite spatial spread of red and green. *That*, the feature metaphysician claims, is all that's real. *That*, the feature metaphysician claims, isn't "colors in two-space"—to describe the feature presentation this way is already to engage in additional metaphysical positing because there is no real metaphysical distinction between there being colored two-spaces and there being two-spaced colors. There is no genuine distinction to be made, therefore, between the decision to treat spatial points (or spatial regions) as the "objects" that color features are at and the decision instead to take color features as the "objects" that spatial features are at.

It might be thought that, despite all this, the @-device (the "at-relation") really is predication. The feature metaphysician will demur. Predication requires objects and properties of some sort. Properties are attributed to objects. But the @-device isn't doing this because it's not presupposing either objects *or* properties as present in the feature presentation. Rather, these languages offer a family of ways of describing how the feature presentation is. This involves (at least as far as the feature presentations I've been describing are like) colors *and* spaces. It can be described as colors at spatial locations; but it can be described equally well (from the metaphysical point of view) as spaces at colors. To stipulate that one of these approaches is metaphysically significant, the feature metaphysician argues, is to illicitly impose a chosen language structure onto a metaphysics that doesn't support it.

Let's return to the imagined philosopher of section 7.1. Two issues were raised: first, whether feature characterization is different from predication, and second, if feature characterization *is* different from predication, whether it involves ontological commitment or not, either to features or to coordinate items (e.g., temporal/spatial regions), or to the space itself that features are distributed in. I've argued, based on feature metaphysics and the free play available in constructing languages for feature presentations, that it doesn't involve predication, and that it doesn't involve ontological commitment either. The feature presentation *is* real, however, and the truth conditions I sketched for the languages I described are sensitive to its reality.

Although this is controversial, one interpretation of weather reports in natural languages is that they exemplify feature characterization without predication (and with spatial/temporal coordinates of some kind):

> It's raining.
> It's snowing.
> It's raining here but not there.
> It was raining in the northeast but it's now no longer raining anywhere.
> It's raining in Chicago.
> It's snowing everywhere.
> It's raining more in Chicago than it is in New York.
> Soon it's going to rain *a lot*.

It's been thought by a number of philosophers that these idioms can be broadened beyond the weather idioms they're usually restricted to:

> It's catting here.
> It's angrily personing over there.
> It's treeing everywhere.

We can also say, with only a shadowy hint of metaphor:

> It's Euclidean over here.
> It's curvier here than it is over there.
> It's Riemannian everywhere.

I admit a kind of science fiction scenario has to be introduced to make sense of "geometrical weather reports," but it's not hard to understand.[4]

---

[4] Imagine that differences in space-time curvature travel across regions of space and time, rather like weather does. We (or parts of ourselves) are far curvier on certain days, for certain periods of time and in certain places, than at other times and in other places.

First: Predication—at least in English—uses "is"; placement operates with "in" or "on," as in "It's sunny *in* Chicago" or "It's snowing *on* Mount Sir Wilfrid Laurier."[5] Philosophers (and logicians) distinguish the "is" of predication from the "is" of equality. In turn, the latter "is" is often treated as a specific (although unusual, according to some) two-place predicate. Feature placement, at least as far as natural-language (English) grammar is concerned, is neither. Notice we can say "That's flat," or "That's purple," or "That's John." We can't say "That's raining" or "That's sunny." And if we *can* say "It's catting," it doesn't follow that we can say "That's catting."

Second: On my interpretation of weather reports, the coordinates are spatiotemporal. That still leaves a lot of room for play in how sophisticated these coordinates are. They can range from the simple "here" and "there" (and a couple of other terms) to the pointwise detail of standard mathematical coordinates.

Third: To claim that the above lists of example locutions involve feature characterizations but not predications isn't to exclude quantification or the other apparatus that we're familiar with from formalizations of predication languages—not on those grounds, anyway. At the very least, it must be explained why feature placement but not predication is forced to operate without quantifiers.[6] One common reason for thinking this is because of a failure to acknowledge the neutrality interpretation for quantifier domains: quantification is seen as introducing ontology in just in the way that feature characterization is supposed to exclude it.

Fourth: As I've shown earlier in this section, when we impose a coordinate system, we can describe it as the imposition of an @-relation. This use of "relation" isn't meant to describe "relations" in the sense that they arise in formalisms, as for example the non-logical two-place relation "next to," but instead describes relations in the quite different sense that predication can be described as a relation. And this notion of relation is neutral: a "relation" in this sense doesn't require that what are being related by the @-relation (or the predication relation) exist. We can imagine that we are by means of the @-relation characterizing real features exhibited in the world, for example, or we can imagine instead that we're locating hallucinations (hallucinated features) against a background of real features. Coordinatizing things

---

[5] Other phrases can be used as well: "It's snowing *all over* Cincinnati."
[6] Sometimes I use "feature placement," especially when the coordinates are spatiotemporal; otherwise I use "feature characterization." Nothing deep turns on these shifts in terminology.

doesn't presuppose that those things exist. There's no obvious reason, anyway, for why this has to be. Some of us (alas) have hallucinations. Some of us have hallucinations situated in reality: the hallucinated elf wearing red shoes is sitting on a real chair. In the same way, we can simply deny that the features that are @-related to coordinate-definable regions exist. We can express sentences that truly place features without incurring "reality commitments" to them. A neutral interpretation for quantifier domains for @-languages is available just as it is for the quantifier domains of first-order languages.

This is why a distinction between "reality" and "irreality" is needed, is metaphysically significant, and survives the denial of objects, properties, and relations. This distinction underwrites the difference the thoughtful philosopher of section 7.1 noted between cases where something like truth-making is occurring: the distribution of features is relevant to the truth or falsity of how feature-placement statements describe it. But "reality" doesn't need to be fleshed out into a metaphysically real notion of an "object"—one with border and location conditions.

7.4 @-ication

I'll now get a *little* more formal about @-languages. Instead of using the standard predication operation (conventionally represented in formal languages by concatenation: "Pa"), I'll use the earlier introduced symbol @. The rest of the language is familiar: individual names, a, b, c, for coordinate posits, and individual variables, x, y, z. The formation rules are indistinguishable from standard formation rules, except for the substitution of @ for the concatenated predication relation. Instead of predicates and n-place relations, there are @-icates and n-place @-tions, P, Q, R, that appear in formulas on @'s left side, and the corresponding n variables or coordinate names that appear on its right side, like so: P@b, R@xy, or R@ax. Quantification looks as expected, for example: $(\exists x)(\exists y)$R@xy.[7]

We can understand the @-icates to correspond to various one-place features, such as SUNNYx, RAINYy, TREEINGz, HAVING-RADIUS-16x, and the @-tions to stand for various relational features, such as SUNNIER-THANxy, the four-place SAME-COLOR-AS$xyzw$, FOUR-MILES-FROMxy, FOUR-HOURS-LATER-THANxy, and so on.

---

[7] The annoying intrusion of "@" notation is restricted to this chapter, for reasons that are momentarily emerging.

What do the individual constants name? What do the individual variables stand in for? In general, whatever are functioning as coordinates. In the case of weather reports, we can imagine that the quantifiers are ranging over some given set of spatiotemporal items: grid boxes of some grade, for example, or arbitrary sets of space-time points, or a designated set of space-time regions, and so on. I'll call "coordinate posits" whatever set of these items is deemed to be in the quantifier domain. The individual constants, a, b, c, in turn, correspond to individual coordinate posits. We can thus (given the appropriate @-icates) describe certain coordinate posits, c_{15} or f_{31}, as "sunny in" or "rainy at," or we can say that "c_{15} is sunnier than f_{31}," and so on.

Despite @-languages lacking predication, their notational equivalence to standard first-order languages is trivial: map an @-language sentence to a corresponding first-order-language sentence by erasing all occurrences of @ and closing up the white space. Correspondingly, replace talk of @-icates, @-tions, et cetera, with the familiar talk of predicates, relations, et cetera.

The resulting language family, therefore, has resources far beyond what previous philosophers have allowed for "feature placing." Neither Turner (2011), O'Leary-Hawthorne and Cortens (1995) nor Strawson (1953–54, 1959) allow quantification in the nakedly obvious way I do. Their reason for avoiding it is obvious: they presume the ontological significance of the standard first-order quantifiers, and so they take it that introducing quantifiers defeats the purpose of providing a language compatible with "ontological nihilism."

Turner (2011, 33 n. 26) writes:

> The semantics of "is raining" may make it a predicate of places. Even though the "it" must be semantically empty ... "is raining" may nonetheless include a location "slot" at the semantic level, filled in by context in a bare assertion of "It is raining" but explicitly filled in constructions such as "It is raining in Austin" or bound as in constructions such as "Wherever Joe went, it rained." ... Out of charity towards the Nihilist, though, we ignore these complications here.

The linguistic literature is rich and complicated. For our purposes it's best to regard Turner's concern as a linguistic question about natural languages[8]

---

[8] See Collins (forthcoming) for an up-to-date discussion of weather reports. Many think natural-language verbs are predicates of events, and if that's right, then even weather reports in natural languages can be treated as predicational despite "an unusual lack of real subjects (or objects, for that matter)." As I mentioned, I'm leaving aside the question of natural language. It can easily be that object/property metaphysics is so embedded in the semantics of natural languages that even when it seems to have gone missing, as in weather reports, this isn't so. Regardless, weather reports have inspired philosophers into thinking a feature-placing language is possible; and a feature-placing language (in any case) suits feature metaphysics. (My thanks to Michael Glanzberg for the quoted phrase.)

that's orthogonal to feature metaphysics and the languages suitable for that metaphysics: on offer is a regimentation. Crucial is Turner's assumption that quantification is ontology-inducing. Part I gave us reasons to reject this.

Like the rest of the literature I'm citing on this, Turner gives no *argument* for his presupposition that quantification in feature-placing languages is unfriendly toward ontological nihilists. Because of this presupposition, O'Leary-Hawthorne and Cortens (1995) try to increase the expressive strength of feature-placing languages by instead allowing predicate operators; they express optimism that the resulting expressive strength is compatible with the ontological-nihilist metaphysics of sheer feature placement. Turner (2011) instead argues that increasing the expressive strength of the language with predicate operators that yield sufficient expressive strength leads to one or another version of predicate functorese—and this he claims is notationally equivalent to the introduction of standard quantification.[9]

Turner offers a thought experiment that can be drafted to suggest that the notational isomorphism of @-languages to standard first-order languages with quantifiers shows that feature placement (at least in these languages) *really is* ordinary predication. Imagine Eustace speaks a language indistinguishable from ours except that wherever we use "blue" he uses "eulb." Turner (2011, 17) writes:

> Eustace and I seem to mean the same thing by all of our terms *other* than "blue" and "eulb," and he uses "eulb" in exactly the same way that I use "blue." But, since our words get to mean what they mean thanks to the way we use them, "blue" in my mouth and "eulb" in his should have the same meaning. Since "blue" in my mouth means *blue*, "eulb" in his mouth must mean that, too.

These plausible-sounding considerations lead to (Turner 2011, 17):

> (*) If every term (other than α and β) is interpreted the same way in L_1 as it is in L_2, and if the speakers of L_1 utter φ_α in all and only the circumstances in which speakers of L_2 utter φ_β, then α and β have the same interpretation also.

---

[9] Quine's (1960a, 1976) interest in predicate functorese was never more than sheerly terminological: an exemplification of his typical love of logical detail. Escape from ontology *wasn't* on the table for him. Since a translation of any theory in this formalism to one in first-order logic is straightforwardly available, Quine presumes quantificational commitments arise in it as well. (See Azzouni 2015 on Quine's translation criterion for ontological commitment.) Turner's (2011) style of establishing an ontology-committing claim about predicate functorese is different from Quine's approach. Turner instead endeavors to show that a particular operator in predicate functorese plays a role indistinguishable from the first-order existential quantifier. I turn to the principle he uses for this in the next paragraph above.

This principle doesn't *obviously* apply to the case of @-placement languages and their first-order siblings, if only because the antecedent ("If every other term ...") lapses because *every* term—excepting, perhaps, the various connectives—is treated by the proponent of @-ication as different from its first-order correspondent. Not only are the individual constants and individual variables different (in the ontologically interpreted first-order case, presumably, they respectively *refer* to or *range over* spatiotemporal objects; in the @-ication case they don't), but relations and predicates only correspond to the (presumably quite different) @-tions and @-icates, items that don't "hold" of objects but instead are only placed features.

Nevertheless, the clause "since our words get to mean what they mean thanks to the way we use them" suggests this is mere notational relabeling. It's hard to see how these two languages *could be* differently used by speakers. Speakers will, presumably, point at the same swaths of reality and make what look like isomorphic claims about them.

Perhaps this shows too much. It seems to show that the neutral interpretation of the first-order quantifiers isn't distinguishable from the standard ontological interpretation of the first-order quantifiers. For there is an easy isomorphic mapping of a neutral formal language with quantifiers plus an existence predicate to a standard ontologically interpreted first-order language. This, however, isn't a genuine application of Turner's principle (*) because the discussion of the specific cases in chapter 5 indicates that the respective populations won't assent to the *same* sentences, such as in the Hob-Nob case.

This defense of the distinction between neutral and non-neutral interpretations of quantifier domains is the key to responding to Turner's principle (*) in the case of @-ication languages. If we simply restrict ourselves to languages as I've described them in this section, we won't detect disagreements in usage between the two populations. But this is because those differences are metaphysical: the speakers can agree—given the isomorphism—that $R@c_{15}f_{31}$ and $Rc_{15}f_{31}$ apply under the same circumstances. What they don't agree on is what the applications of these sentences *mean*. They don't agree, that is, about what c_{15} and f_{31} (or R, for that matter) *are*. More fundamentally, they also don't agree about what "@" and the concatenation of a predicate symbol with a name or variable means either. These disagreements aren't expressible in the languages as I've so far described them: they have to be supplemented.

Several metaphysical positions were described in section 7.2 that individuate predicational items differently, or reject the cogency of such differences altogether. We can supplement feature-placing languages and ordinary predication-languages to enable expression of this disagreement. We can describe the properties and relations themselves predicated of objects, and provide various identity conditions for them, along with statements of identities and differences (or similarity relations). Feature theorists reject these additional claims about features altogether. Languages thus supplemented allow the expression of the metaphysical differences I've been describing in this section; this responds to the objection I derived from Turner's discussion. In section 7.5, I'll describe in more detail a disagreement between feature metaphysicians and object-believers, and offer regimented languages that enable expression of it.

7.5 Refining the Regimentation of Ontological Independence

In previous work, and in part I of this book, I've represented ontological disagreement as handled by ontologically contrasting idioms—neutral quantifiers and an ontologically understood existence predicate. This isn't the full story, however. To fully represent the debate between ontological projectivists and their opponents—those who think objects have worldly ontological borders—additional (non-logical) apparatus is needed.

I've stressed, in the introduction to part II, that the projectivist/border-realist debate *shouldn't be* characterized as the projectivist "repudiating ontology altogether," or as claiming "there is nothing at all." That this won't do is already clear from the brief discussion, in section 7.3, of the distinction between "reality" and "irreality"—a distinction object projectivists want between when features *really are* exhibited and when they're *not*.

What needs to be captured, therefore, is that object projectivists think that any way of portioning the feature presentation in quantifier domains is—metaphysically—as good as any other; border realists deny this. But simultaneously with characterizing this debate, a distinction must be respected between real and unreal features.

An ontologically understood existence predicate along with a neutrally interpreted quantifier domain is insufficient for this because we have only unsatisfactory choices. On the one hand, we might interpret the existence predicate as demanding that *both* features *and* borders be real. Then object projectivists must deny the existence of features because commitment to them is bundled together with a commitment to borders. On the other hand, if the existence predicate requires only that the features be real within a demarcated something that the existence predicate is applied to, then we can't distinguish the border realist's metaphysical claims from the object projectivist's metaphysical claims.

It looks as though ontologically committing uses of "exist" and "there is" by non-philosophers require the reality of both features and borders of objects. Recall from section 2.2.3 that Hirsch (2011a) forcefully argues that everyone—except for certain philosophers—denies the existence of shrees and incars, and believes in trees and cars. These ontological differences turn not on the reality or irreality of shree or incar *features* but only on the real ontological borders of ordinary objects.

What's needed is an additional non-logical predicate with a specific ontological interpretation. A regimented one-place predicate term **B** (standing for "border") suffices. Given any t among the items determined by a division of the feature-presentation into units, **B**t is true if and only if the borders of t are worldly. For a given language, if some of its quantifiers range over objects that the border realist takes to be real borders (in the world), then **B** holds of those objects. For the object projectivist, **B** holds of nothing. We can, thus, treat the object projectivist's positive claim that such-and-such features exhibited in a certain portion of space-time s are real (although the portion s *doesn't* demarcate an object) as the claim (**E**s & ¬**B**s).

There are additional subtleties in debates between ontological projectivists and their opponents that this simple language expedient also captures. Stuff metaphysicians think everything is stuff (one stuff or many stuffs) and that stuff flows. Talk of the same stuff being here then and being there now makes sense to stuff metaphysicians. The ontological borders that stuff metaphysicians are committed to are spatiotemporal ones—spatial borders that shift continuously across time. The object projectivist denies the reality of these borders as well.[10]

We normally understand temporal (and spatial) ontological borders as indicating when we are dealing with a change *of* the *same* object from one moment to another, as opposed to a change *from* one object to a *different* object from one moment to another. (This is how we understand the flow of the "same stuff" over time, as well.) The object projectivist denies that there is metaphysical sense to the distinction between a case where there is one apple that subsists over time (and perhaps changes in its spatial contours or other properties) and a case of a series of nearly identical apples

---

[10] I'm skipping over details, but the same irresolvable identity questions arise for stuff metaphysicians that arise for object realists and universal (or trope) realists. What's the *metaphysical* difference between there being the same stuff here (and there) as opposed to there being different stuff that resembles other stuff? What, in other words, is the metaphysical difference between an endurantist position about stuffs and a perdurantist one? I say more momentarily.

replacing one another from moment to moment. To use familiar language, the object projectivist rejects a worldly distinction between endurantism and perdurantism.

In doing so, the object projectivist *doesn't* reject the idea of motion or change.[11] The issue, rather, is whether motion or change is one thing changing in position, or the change being many things (as it were) replacing one another over time and in (overlapping) position. Although there is a logical analogy with the famous McTaggert B-series and A-series,[12] the problem complex raised by McTaggert's discussion—and taken up by many philosophers—is different. The nature of time—strictly speaking—isn't at issue here. Denied as metaphysically cogent is only the distinction between "identity across time" and "difference across time." Motion survives: what it's motion *of* is all that goes.

The object projectivist also disagrees with what we might call fundamental border realists. These philosophers think that although there are possible languages with quantifier domains that contain items with real borders, there are "fundamental" languages where quantifier domains contain something if and only if its ontological borders are real. The object projectivist denies this too. This debate is captured not *within* one or another formalism of the sorts I've described but instead by an examination (as it were) of *all* of them.

The non-logical predicate **B** enables a clear distinction between object projectivists and their border realist opponents—at least when debates are couched in a neutral-quantifier formalism. They won't agree on some of the same sentences that contain this predicate—at least they won't if the quantifier domain contains items that the border realist thinks have real ontological borders. Furthermore, if the border realist thinks that a condition on objecthood (and thus on the cogency of predication) turns on there being real ontological borders, then we've also circumvented a challenge via Turner's principle (*): **B** is an additional idiom by means of which disagreements about metaphysical realities can be expressed.

Here's another advantage of **B**. When introducing the idea of a "radical cluster of metaphysical pictures," including ontological nihilism, O'Leary-Hawthorne and Cortens (1995, 143) write that these views "seem to suggest that just about everything we say is false. They seem to gesture at a noumenal reality that human language is unable to describe." The object projectivist claims much less: *borders* don't exist. This doesn't lead to a stampede of

---

[11] My thanks to an anonymous referee for pressing me to discuss this further.
[12] McTaggert (1908, 1921).

falsehoods attributed to the folk when they say things like (*) "There are only three chairs in this room." When someone says this, taking herself to be ontologically committed to chairs, object projectivists *accept* most of what's claimed. Object projectivists can allow their quantifier domain to contain what the quantifier domain corresponding to (*) is understood to contain. Further, they can even take the existence predicate **E** to apply to the items in the domain. The disagreement is over the application of the predicate **B**. **B** holds of each of the three chairs, according to the utterer of (*); it doesn't hold of each of them, according to object projectivists. This disagreement hardly shows that object projectivists think everything we say is false; neither is the borderless state of affairs that object projectivists are committed to particularly indescribable.

One last issue. How, exactly, is object projectivism different from "ontological conceptualism" or "relativism"? Sosa's (1999, 33) "existential relativism" is that "what ... exists relative to one conceptual scheme may not do so relative to another." As the distinction between borders and real features indicates (and as it's codified by the use of the specialized predicates **B** and **E**), this is *not* object projectivism. What's real isn't relative to one or another conceptual scheme—it's a matter of the metaphysics of the world. What's projected, of course, is relative to one or another conceptual scheme. But, of course, what's projected *isn't* a matter of the metaphysics of the world.

7.6 Real Features and Unreal Features

The object projectivist needs a distinction between real and unreal features. This distinction resembles a currently popular metaphysical view about natural kinds. I'll briefly describe points of agreement and disagreement. Lewis (1983, 1984) influentially invokes a picture where the world manifests "natural" kinds and relations. Feature metaphysicians can be seen as accepting something like this picture when they treat as cogent, as I have above, the question of what features (both predicational and relational) are *truly* exhibited by the world. This doctrine, however, in Lewis's hands, comes with additional and substantial epistemic assumptions that in one form or another have been very influential but which feature metaphysicians reject. The Lewisian idea is that languages—with such-and-such properties (scientifically ideal languages, fundamental ones, etc.)—have predicates and relation terms that correspond to these metaphysically natural properties and relations. A number of epistemic strategies have been introduced to enable the claim that there is an appropriate fit between the predicates and relation terms of such languages and the metaphysically natural properties and relations in the world, among them a priori constraints on the reference of terms, methodological presuppositions of one sort or another on semantics, or explanatory requirements on scientific theories.

Much of this falls under what has come to be called "reference magnetism." This is a term, subsequent to Lewis's work, that labels one or another of the above epistemic strategies for explaining how the world's own natural-kind structure contributes (somehow) to our predicate terms successfully picking out that natural-kind structure. I reject all this *magical epistemology*, and provide instead an entirely different (and naturalistic) explanation of how we invest our predicates and relation terms with open-ended extensions, and ones that (if the world is kind enough to us, or at least accessible enough) succeed in capturing some of what the world actually exhibits. This, however, isn't the place to rehearse my objections to the various reference magnetism views, or to argue (again) for my alternative.[13]

To include "natural" features as part of feature metaphysics, however, doesn't require an additional positing of object structure. In my discussion of scientific theories and scientific explanation in chapter 9, therefore, I separate the role (if any) of features from the role (if any) of object boundaries.

This should be stressed, especially because some philosophers (e.g., Elder 2011, Sidelle 1989 and Sider 2011) implicitly or explicitly imply that metaphysical structure—in particular, worldly objects *and* natural kinds—is a package deal where the philosopher is either stuck with all of it or can have none of it. Nothing in this book so far undermines the thought that there is a way that features really are exhibited in the world; nothing to come will undermine this thought either. And I'll do nothing to undercut the further thought that a scientific theory (or a fundamental theory) might depict the features of the world as they really are exhibited. There will be serious questions—as it turns out—about whether the success or

---

[13] Lewis invokes natural properties and relations against Putnam's "paradox"—see the citations in Lewis (1984, 56 n. 1)—and against Kripke's (1982) Wittgensteinian rule-following puzzle as well. See Azzouni (2000) for discussion of the Lewis/Putnam debate, and for further references. See Sider (2011, section 3.2) for discussion of it as well, and Williams (2007, especially section 2) for an attempt at a justification of the doctrine in terms of "theoretical virtue." See Azzouni (2017) for criticisms of reference magnetism, as well as a characterization of how reference practices are possible without adopting a metaphysics of reference magnetism—in *any* form.

the explanatory value of actual scientific theories requires those theories to truly depict features as they are exhibited in the world; but that isn't the primary focus of this book, and in any case, none of this opposes the suggestion that, metaphysically speaking, the world really does exhibit feature.

What's crucial, instead, is the complete irrelevance of worldly object boundaries to scientific practice, scientific explanation, and scientific success—as already indicated in chapter 6, and to be illustrated further, specifically in chapter 9.

7.7 Short Conclusion

I mean this chapter to provide enough details about feature metaphysics and feature-characterization languages to convince philosophers that quantification in this context—despite having truth-makers—doesn't induce object boundary commitments. In doing so, I extended the master argument given in chapter 6 to predicational structure, stuff identity claims, and features.

I've engaged in a complex dialectic. Perhaps predication requires objects *and* properties. The neutral interpretation denies this: standard predicational language can lack referents. Instead, whole sentences are given truth values relative to background practices. Feature metaphysics and languages describing features, as illustrated initially in chapter 6, don't look like this. There seems to be truth-conditional sensitivity to properties or relations in a space-time. I deny this, arguing that features aren't properties or objects. Instead, coordinate systems enabling descriptions of feature presentations use some features as coordinates and describe other features as "at" those coordinates. Truth-conditional sensitivity is to the co-occurrence of features. Thus, the truth-based v.s. object-based distinction survives—but is mislabeled in this context. It's better described as a truth-based versus feature-based distinction. The neutrality interpretation of quantifier domains thus continues to echo in feature-characterizing languages.

Feature-characterizing languages are isomorphic to first-order languages. There are different ways to interpret this result, but feature metaphysicians can accept any of them. Suppose, for example, a philosopher thinks "predication," understood generally enough (or abstractly enough), operates in @-languages—the @-relation *is* predication. Then the isomorphism *really is* trivial. But "predication," so described, doesn't need objects and universals of any kind—because, metaphysically speaking, features aren't either.[14] Suppose, contrarily, a philosopher denies that concatenation (in first-order languages) has to be interpreted as predication; it could be feature characterization. In this case, the metaphysical distinction between features and properties is sustained—but predicate/term concatenation has been shown (by the isomorphism) to be open to more than one interpretation. That works too.

Regardless, a takeaway of this chapter that I'll tacitly employ here on is this: the easy translation between feature-placing languages (with quantifiers) and standard (ontically neutral) first-order languages—both with **B**—allows me to approach metaphysics with all the resources supplied by first-order formalisms. In particular, I'll shift back and forth between talk of features (when I'm being explicit about the metaphysics of what there is) and talk of properties and relations being exhibited by objects (relative to a contouring of the real by quantifiers). In the latter case, I'll often be describing how things strike us intuitively; but it's important to realize that the apparent talk of predication of properties and relations to objects can always be dropped for a feature-characterizing language with corresponding quantifiers.

In what follows I'll often talk about particular ways we project object boundaries onto the world—"contour a portion of the real" is a way of putting the matter. Object boundary projection can be treated as how a quantifier domain portions the real. It's important to realize, as well, that along with the projection of object boundaries onto the world, there is also a projection of a predication relation and a corresponding set of properties and relations that various features are transformed into. Thus, in chapters 8 and 9, when I'm speaking of how we are thinking about a portion of the real, I'll naturally speak not only about the object boundaries we project there but also about the properties and relations the corresponding objects are taken to possess.

It's worth noting (again) that there is a family of problems about the predication relation; they appeared philosophically early—in Plato and Aristotle, and, much later, in Frege, Russell, and Wittgenstein. Davidson, in his last

---

[14] It's not beyond a philosopher, of course, to argue that "objects" or "properties" don't require the individuation conditions I denied are available. Fine; now the issue of whether "features" are objects (or properties) or not is just terminological. My substantial claims have been conceded by this imagined philosopher.

book (2005), also worried about this problem.[15] The problem comes in both language-based and metaphysically based versions. The metaphysical version is something like: What *is* the relationship of a property to the object it's a property of? Object projectivism offers a clean solution: since object boundaries, properties, and predication are a package projection onto the world, there is no metaphysical issue left.

---

[15] See Davidson (2005) for some discussion of how extensive philosophical discussion of the problem has been over the ages. See Collins (2011) for an interesting attempt to approach a version of the problem via contemporary linguistics.

8 | Focusing in on (Some of) the Real

8.1 Introduction

The views I've earlier quoted about "ontological nihilism" make clear that it's easy to think that object projectivism costs us the distinction between what's real and what's not. Crucial (many think) to anything being real are its real ontological boundaries. That's not true, however, because what remains, as we've seen in section 7.5, is a distinction between what's sketched on the real (tables, chairs, molecules, black holes ...) and what's conjured up out of nothing (Sherlock Holmes, the elf with red shoes that I'm currently hallucinating ...).

Another way of elucidating this distinction in an ontological-boundary-free way is to distinguish between describing a "piece of the real" *accurately*—that is, taking features to co-occur when they indeed co-occur—and not doing this. Even without worldly ontological boundaries or stuff (flowing or otherwise), it still makes sense to think what's real is "out there"—it's independent of us (it's mind- and language-independent). It still makes sense to say we *discover* the world's features. This shows, furthermore, that when it comes to the real, a correspondence between what we say about it and what it's like makes sense.[1]

Nominalism, thus, survives the adoption of object projectivism—although it needs reformulation. It's the view that all there is *is* the *feature presentation*. The *bit-sized targets* of the quantifiers are real if they contour (a part of) the feature presentation; otherwise not. There is nothing more to nominalist

---

[1] If we could restrict the quantifiers of scientific (or commonsense) discourse only to items sketched on the real—if our discourses, mathematical, fictional, empirical, and so on, could be isolated from one another—we could introduce a *correspondence notion of truth* for discourses restricted only to the real. But discourses can't be isolated from one another this way. See Azzouni (2010a), specifically the discussion of the external-discourse demand.

metaphysics; nothing else exists, not abstracta, not numbers, not universals, and so on. Despite this ontological minimality, object projectivism nevertheless makes substantial metaphysical assumptions. It posits a simple feature/co-occurrence structure that could be wrong.[2] (There is nothing a priori about feature metaphysics.)

This chapter further explores the ontological distinction between what's real and what isn't. I investigate the apparent changes in ontological focus when we shift our concern from macro-objects to the micro-objects that we take to compose those macro-objects. These shifts in focus reveal how we commonly think of differing scientific domains of discourse as related to one another. We understand certain domains (e.g., the various domains of biology) as quantifying over objects that other domains either analyze into parts (e.g., other branches of biology, chemistry or physics) or chunk together into larger items (e.g., the sociology of institutions). I also explore certain puzzles that arise in the vicinity of space and time because a feature metaphysics analysis illuminates them.

Our interaction with the real—features genuinely co-occurring—is more intricate than I've so far indicated. In this chapter and in chapter 9, I will offer details about the many cases of things we talk about in the various sciences but that seem to comfortably fit neither "being sketched on the real" or "being conjured up out of nothing"; I'll further discuss why we sketch such-and-such things out of the real (and not other things).

On the basis of chapter 7, a coordinate system is presupposed hereon—a classical space-time one. "Objects" are portions of the feature presentation appearing in quantifier domains, and the co-occurring features are impounded as "relations" and "properties" for those objects.

8.2 Focus, Grain, and Quantifier-Relative Objects

Each science—roughly speaking—seems to be *about* a collection of objects. The same is true of ordinary discourse at particular times. Although ordinary discourse undergoes (continuous) change both in vocabulary items and in implicit quantifier domains, there often seems to be a relatively fixed collection of objects that we can speak about (at least for relatively long periods of time). This implicit "separate discourses" model of the sciences, however, badly fits the way evidence works in those sciences.[3] In addition, scientific

---

[2] It *is* more complex, on my view, than I present it here. Co-occurrence needs a "quantum reconfiguration" to handle Heisenberg "uncertainty." I can't, unfortunately, get into this now.
[3] See Azzouni (2010a) on the external discourse demand.

discourse (like mathematical discourse) takes place in natural language.[4] The separate-domains characterization, nevertheless, can be temporarily adopted as an expository convenience—along with the first-order language assumption—the falsity of which doesn't affect the points I'm after in this chapter. I'll add caveats, though, when it's important to see how they distort our picture of scientific practice.

So we understand the quantifier domains of particular sciences—roughly—as either relativized to or specialized upon specific kinds of objects; and we understand those sciences as engaged in the discovery of the properties of those objects. For illustrative purposes (and for ease of exposition), let's think of the language of a particular science as Carnap would have: a quantifier domain is given (a kind of variable is given), and properties and relations are attributed to its objects by the truths expressible in this language.

Truths about the entities of the quantifier domain of a scientific language isomorphically survive shifts of *ontological scale*. This is one lesson of Hirschian examples (incars, outcars, and shrees): the quantifier domain of a language can be changed so that parts of the objects in the original domain, or the mereological sums of those objects, or some irregular combination of these, are instead in the domain; and the predicates and relations of the new language are appropriately modified from the old one so that what's true or false of the objects in the original domain is correspondingly true or false of the objects in the new domain. We could, for example, replace the original objects of the domain with space-time points, and correspondingly replace the macro-properties and micro-relations exhibited in the original domain with appropriately defined point-applicable micro-properties and micro-relations. This induces a *minimal* ontological scale for all objects. Or, we can have the domain contain a single large object (with all the original objects as its parts) and we can correspondingly treat the various properties and relations of the objects of the original domain as one complex mottle-property of the one big object. Here we introduce a single object with a *maximal* ontological scale. And, of course, we can generate arbitrary domains containing objects of differing ontological scales between these two limits, as well as including objects of differing ontological scales within the same domain.

As long as the predicates and relations are correlated appropriately, these various languages—specifically, the truths couched in these languages—differ only in corresponding to what I'm calling the "ontological scales" of

---

[4] See Azzouni (2014a) for why it philosophically matters that natural language is the language vehicle of science.

the objects in their quantifier domains. The truths are clearly equivalent in a metaphysical sense, although this equivalence usually can't be characterized by definitions (or definitional reductions) of the truths in one language in terms of (or to) the truths of the other language. Rather, the equivalences are truth-conditional ones induced by objects and parts-of-objects mappings of the quantifier domains (with corresponding mappings of the relations and properties).

The sense in which these interpreted languages are equivalent, because they differ only in how widely or narrowly quantificational contours are drawn, is coded by these mappings, and can't be represented in any more specific language-relative definitional way (except in special cases). Recollecting that all this can be described without remainder in feature-metaphysical terms, a useful way of characterizing the corresponding feature presentation relative to a domain is to describe it as the *grain* of the world that the objects in that domain contour.[5] The relatively trivial point being made (in these terms) is that grain is insensitive to changes in *ontological scale*. What can be said about the feature presentation is unaffected by how we chop it up into "objects" and corresponding "properties" and "relations." Call this *grain invariance*.

8.3 Varying Amounts of Reality in Various Scientific Domains

It would be nice if the "domains" of all the various sciences exhibited grain invariance in their relations to one another. Even though, as I indicated above, some versions of scientific reductionism (e.g., ones based on the definitions of predicates in one language in terms of the predicates of another language) would still fail, there would remain a satisfyingly nice metaphysical relationship between the domains of these sciences that we could indicate by describing the appropriate objects-parts mappings and properties and relations mappings. We can say, more abstractly, that a grain-invariant set of domains, among which the appropriate mappings exist, *agree on what's real*, and *agree on what grain the real has*.

The domains of the various sciences, however, don't exhibit grain invariance. They *don't* agree on the real. The immediate effect is that there are no objects-parts mappings between the domains of these various sciences.

---

[5] I considered introducing the technical term "tattoo," as in "the feature presentation is the world's *tattoo*." But I assume that's too cute for anyone who's reading me to *tolerate*.

Mappings can fail to exist, of course, because one domain contains items absent from the other—quantifier neutralism allows this. That is, a quantifier domain can contain items that don't contour *any* of the real—*abstracta*, for example. But more interesting kinds of failures occur because—here's how it can be put—two quantifier domains can characterize the grain of the real differently.[6]

Examples are called for, and here's an ancient one. One domain S contours the real into small spherical objects: *tiny simples*. The second domain O contours the real into large standard macro-objects (zebras, tables): *ordinary objects*. The two quantifier domains are related, however. Ordinary objects are made up ("composed") of tiny simples; they have tiny simples for *parts*. So the desired objects-parts mapping—if it existed—would map ordinary objects to the sets of tiny simples composing them. The linked problems are these:

> *There are tiny simples that aren't the parts of any ordinary objects.*
>
> *Ordinary objects can be indifferently described as including or excluding different tiny simples as parts.*

The ordinary-object domain O, naturally, has objects that don't correspond to the real at all. This is because we don't *just* talk about grasshoppers, rocks, and clouds. We talk about holes and shadows, hobbits and elves, borders and credit. *Some* of this stuff isn't *real*; and those things aren't composed of tiny simples. We don't want to swell our domain of tiny simples M to accommodate hobbits and elves—although we may want (in some way) to accommodate credit.

The disagreement goes both ways. It does, anyway, if we treat "tiny-simples talk" as metaphorical for actual contemporary micro-theories. In those cases, there's quite a bit else in the quantifier domain S of micro-theory talk: numbers, functions and spaces of various sorts, and so on. There are things in both domains we deny the reality of. This isn't a disagreement about *objects* because the reality of ontological contours is denied, regardless. It's a disagreement over the correspondence of the objects in these domains to the feature presentation. In practice, scientists pick and choose in fairly

---

[6] In section 8.4, I'll discuss another way that grain invariance fails for domains of scientific theories: there are features that seem to "emerge" at larger ontological dimensions, although they're apparently absent at smaller ones.

principled ways just as it seems they do: this (in this domain) is real, they say, and that isn't ("Magnetic monopoles aren't real").

But apart from issues about what's real, there are the mismatches I italicized above. These mismatches tempt philosophers to argue about which object borders are genuine—those around simples or those around larger items. The master argument short-circuits this temptation.

There are also, of course, powerful object intuitions that motivate metaphysical nihilism,[7] although these usually emerge only indirectly in philosophical argument: they give a priori metaphysical principles a feel of plausibility.[8] These intuitions arise from the sensitivity of our object-experiences to metaphysical focusing—in particular, they're *exclusionary*. That is, changes in metaphysical focus replace experiences of objects of such-and-such a sort with experiences of other objects entirely: how we experience objects doesn't allow that the objects we see "close up" and the objects we see "more at a distance" nevertheless both exist. So, for example, magnifying the surface of an object enough so that we see its particle-like bits jiggling about obliterates the impression of that surface being a part of *one* thing.[9] The recognition that these intuitions originate from psychological mechanisms of projecting object borders clarifies their irrelevance to metaphysics.

The second linked problem noted earlier, namely that ordinary objects can be indifferently described as including or excluding different tiny simples, poses a different problem. There should be one unique way objects of O are composed of objects (the simples) of S. We've discovered, however, that our characterizations of the objects of O are indifferent (within certain parameters) to which items of S they contain. Notice: we're worried both about how the world is and how we're to talk about it. Object projectivism eliminates the first worry because that worry illicitly presupposes *worldly*

---

[7] Based on its meaning, "metaphysical nihilism" should apply to the position that there are no worldly objects *at all*—what I call object projectivism, and what others have called ontological nihilism. The term has instead been co-opted to label the only-metaphysical-simples position (originally by van Inwagen 1990, I think) because the former position (due to not recognizing quantifier neutralism as a live option) seemed *impossible*: it seemed to require a language without quantifiers. Once quantifier neutralism is vindicated, however, and we introduce terminology to distinguish borders from features (as in section 7.5), object projectivism becomes a describable possibility unhampered by metaphysically irrelevant issues of language indispensability.

[8] Principles like *Two objects can't be in the same place at the same time* (Wiggins 1967, 90), or *a composite thing must have causal powers beyond the causal powers of its parts* (Van Inwagen 1990, 122, Merricks 2001), etc. Not everyone feels the intuitive force of these principles, of course. Mereological universalists don't.

[9] A cognitive-evolutionary speculation for why this exclusionary aspect of object-experience is so ubiquitous: One role of cognitively grasping such-and-such as *objects* is preparing the perceiver to react to or act on the *objects* individually (apart from the rest of the context). This also explains why causal intuitions link to object-experiences the way they do.

boundaries for ordinary objects, and also describes those boundaries (at least partially) in terms of which tiny simples belong, and don't belong, to ordinary objects. Denying worldly ontological boundaries leaves nothing to explain—*metaphysically*. There is still the sloppiness of the boundaries we project for ordinary objects: they don't allow systematic answers to questions about which tiny simples—exactly—belong to those objects. There may be something left to explain—about our practices and our ways of talking—but this isn't something about the *world*.

What *about* how we're to talk? There's a problem, but we've already seen it in part I: bivalence. When we recognize that the language of ordinary objects isn't isolated from the language of tiny simples, we realize we're saddled with numerous substantial questions about how *this* is composed of *those*, substantial questions we can't answer.

There is still no problem (recall section 4.5): we express ignorance about answers to these questions, and address questions we *can* answer. Heap problems, special (and general) composition questions, et cetera—all prove illusory concerns once object projectivism is in place.[10]

When do some objects compose another object? If the question is *metaphysical*, the answer is "never," because there are no object boundaries. If we recalibrate the question in terms of contouring so much feature (and not more), then the answer is "always": a portion of feature presentation can always be expanded to include more feature presentation. There are still empirical questions to answer, but these take a non-metaphysical cast: When do we talk about an object in addition to the objects that compose it? Relatedly, when do we experience some objects to be (in addition) an object that's composed of those objects? The metaphysical cousins of these questions are complex and intractable. Easy moves fail because of obvious counterexamples.[11] Complex moves require sophisticated and ontologically rich (neo-Aristotelian) theories.[12] I say this not to fault such theories on intrinsic grounds of complexity; rather, these theories are non-starters, in any case, if the master argument is successful.

---

[10] Some philosophers know that positions in the neighborhood of object projectivism have this advantage. Van Inwagen (1990, 111–12) writes: "If there are no artifacts then ... there are no problems about the persistence of artifacts." O'Leary-Hawthorne and Cortens (1995, 158) write, "[Ontological nihilism] has the consequence that many metaphysical disputes—concerning, *inter alia*, identity, composition or alternate ontologies—are somehow perverse."

[11] See van Inwagen (1990). For discussions covering some of the same territory but using other terminology, see Hirsch (1982, 1993, especially chapter 4).

[12] See Koslicki (2008), which seems to require commitments to Platonic/Aristotelian structures of various sorts *in* objects—the *forms* of those objects, as it were.

The point here is different. It's that the psychological and linguistic facts (as well as user-friendly facts about different possible scientific theories) behind why we describe the world in terms of one or another kind of object are, although quite complex, far more tractable than the metaphysically construed puzzles. In particular, the various factors cueing object-experience (and object-talk) can be teased apart, and how they separately induce quantification over objects can be described. These factors needn't be consistent with one another—whether they are is an empirical matter—and they needn't (in any case) provide necessary and sufficient conditions for the individuation of objects. As I've stated, I'm *not* saying this to argue that object projectivism is superior to worldly metaphysical approaches to object-experience; I'm only pointing out that the empirical study of the various mechanisms behind object projection is potentially more tractable then the metaphysics of objects is. This is indicated by the ancient history (and contemporary status) of the latter endeavor.

Recall, though, the discussion in section 5.7 that we, individually and collectively, don't grasp necessary and sufficient conditions for object identifications. Our practices for determining when a person "stage" at one time and place is the same as a person "stage" at another time and place are only partially systematic. Those philosophers who think that there are fully determinate conditions must explain why we don't grasp them, and why we find problem cases problematic enough to generate interminable philosophical literatures. The object projectivist, of course, doesn't believe in a purported gap between the "complete" individuation conditions actually had by objects and the more fragmentary ones we're aware of.

This point aside, maybe object projectivists still face the requirement of explaining the mismatch between language and world (one long noticed by philosophers). Why does vagueness, in this sense, arise? What bits of language (or aspects of the world) are to blame?[13] There is nothing to explain about this either. When projecting ontological borders onto the feature presentation, for one purpose or another (or just because we experience certain objects as *there*), we overlook (or are simply ignorant of) some of the feature presentation. This usually, however, makes no difference to how we attribute properties and relations to the objects we speak of, and it usually makes no difference for the purposes for which we use a language that quantifies over such objects. (We stipulate answers if it does make a difference.) The reason for vagueness (a reason I'll do more with in section 8.4) is that in

---

[13] See, e.g., van Inwagen (1990), Lewis (1986), Sider (2001), for different (controversial) answers.

characterizing objects as being such-and-so, we've left out some real; but as far as those characterizations are concerned, *it doesn't matter*.

Some challenges seem to remain. Here's an easy one. Perhaps one discourse is superior to another because bivalence problems are present in one discourse relative to the other but not vice versa. There are no sharp answers to questions about how many, and which, tiny simples make up a zebra. This isn't true for tiny simples—unless, of course, tiny simples (contrary to their name) are composed of smaller bits.

This claim *isn't* about metaphysics; it's that a bivalent discourse is superior in some way to one that isn't. Even if true, this won't give tiny-simple-sized ontological boundaries a metaphysical presence larger ones don't have. But in fact the choice isn't about the superiority of a bivalent discourse over one that isn't; it's between two bivalent discourses, where one uses expressions of ignorance more widely than the other. It's hard to see why a narrower use of ignorance is better than a wider one, except in cases where the ignorance really is of something (and something that matters). This is especially the case if, generally, quantification over nonexistents occurs in both discourses, for those always give rise to bivalence failures that require expressions of ignorance.

Here's a second challenge that looks harder. Although composition problems about objects are eliminated by object projectivism, a related problem arises—a feature-placing boundary problem. We presumably impose boundaries on ordinary objects according to certain features we identify; this is to reject metaphysical primitivism. But, so it seems, those features must bear peculiar relations to the properties and relations we treat as possessed by tiny simples. Otherwise, the misfit problem between the two domains wouldn't arise. So what's going on, metaphysically speaking, with the underlying features to induce issues about composition and the accompanying problem with bivalence failures?

An example of this purported problem: How far does a particular instantiation of the property of catness extend in space and time? (How far does the catness feature extend?) This problem looks only terminologically different from the vagueness problem: Which molecules are or aren't parts of a cat? Instead, we're asking what spatial points the cat feature is at. But forcing a problem here misdescribes the metaphysics. There is no vagueness—presumably—in co-occurrence. Features either co-occur or they don't.[14] There may be an issue about whether we want to include the cat feature

---

[14] Subject to whatever qualifications are needed to accommodate Heisenberg uncertainty.

among certain co-occurring features (including spatiotemporal ones)—but that's a labeling question (a question of language), not one of metaphysics. Relative to a spatiotemporal-point coordinate system, there is a sharp answer to what features are at each point; the remaining question is only the labeling issue whether those features are (or co-occur with) the catness feature.

8.4 The Different Properties and Relations Attributed to the Objects in the Domains of Different Sciences

There is a sense in which the differing relations and properties—the differing grain—attributed to objects in domains of different sciences seems to reinstate metaphysical primitivism. This is because if these properties and relations don't straightforwardly correspond to featural shifts in space and time, perhaps the purported features used to impose object boundaries (relative to a discourse domain) are themselves only *apparent*. The result can be this, it seems: practically speaking, metaphysical primitivism is true. We think we're using actual features to determine the boundaries of certain objects (as contours for what's in our quantifier domains), but we aren't because those features aren't real but only *seem to be*. We're not only projecting object boundaries; we're also projecting the features these boundaries depend on. This isn't—of course—to undercut the master argument because a projection of borders on the basis of a projection of features isn't to capture anything *metaphysically real*.

We need an example. Here's one.[15] (I'm going to discuss this example at some length.) Imagine a plane on which circular discs are moving.[16] These discs, let's say, exhibit regularities. They seem to cohere rigidly, and move as units. When they collide, they recoil without deforming or shifting in size. We can describe their movements over time by laws; these laws predict Newtonian patterns of movement along with the results of collisions that transfer momentum strictly according to the size of the discs. (Further, these circular discs are trapped within a square, and the same laws also describe how discs recoil from the sides of squares.)

Suppose, however, a shift to a smaller ontological scale reveals something different. The boundaries of the large discs are only apparent because the circular discs are composed of much smaller ("microscopic") circular discs that

---

[15] I'm sort of borrowing this example from Dennett (1991a).
[16] For no significant reason, I often focus on planes. Spheres moving about in three-space work just as well. And, for testing object-intuitions, the three-dimensional case should always be examined because many object-cued intuitions differ from those cued in two dimensions.

constantly jostle one another. The macro-discs, that is, are actually crowds of numerous rapidly moving micro-discs. When we impose a smaller ontological scale on the world, we discover that, over time, the macro-discs change in their composition of micro-discs. Freely moving micro-discs are pulled into the crowds of micro-discs, while other micro-discs near the boundaries of those crowds break free and wander off.

"Pulled in" and "break free" are informal descriptions of the apparent operation of a force law (somewhat like the residual strong force)[17] governing the micro-discs. Together these laws explain why—more accurately, enable us to *predict that*—the micro-discs form clumps (which look like macro-discs, given the imposition of larger ontological scales). They explain why (more accurately, enable the prediction that) particular micro-discs will acquire a certain amount of kinetic energy before they can escape from a clump of micro-discs they're among. The laws that the micro-discs can be described as obeying, in addition, fully explain (fully predict) the movements of the macro-discs; they predict, that is, the laws that the macro-discs apparently obey. When it appears that two macro-discs are rigidly bouncing away from each other after a collision, the reality is that numerous micro-discs in two crowds of micro-discs are rigidly bouncing away from one another after collisions in such a way that the *appearance* of macro-discs doing what they're doing is preserved.

I've used language nearly everyone will be tempted to use. First, I've talked of certain kinds of objects—micro- and macro-discs—doing certain things. Second, I've talked of what's happening among the macro-discs as being (almost involuntarily) seen as unreal; what's real are micro-disc movements that give rise to the appearance of collisions among apparently rigid macro-discs. The laws of macro-discs, similarly, are phenomenal and derivative; the real laws govern micro-discs. These intuitions naturally arise from the example as well. The micro-discs (micro-particles) have *causal effects* on one another: they *really* push and pull one another around. The macro-discs *appear* to causally affect one another, but this is phenomenal: the real causation is micro-level causation. Finally, as I explicitly flagged in the language above, we see what's going on with the micro-discs as *explaining* the appearances among the macro-discs.

The intuitions invoked by this example of certain objects really existing, and other ones only appearing to exist, is generated by our visualizing the situation, and experiencing the described items as objects because of induced

---

[17] I choose this force deliberately: it shifts from attraction to repulsion, depending on distance.

object-experience cues. Here's a way to short-circuit these object-intuitions. Imagine instead that we're watching the movement of slowly deforming patterns of color percolating through a watery medium—what looks like discs looks this way only temporarily, eventually deforming (Dali-esquely) into elongated shapes and then diffusing altogether into other colored shapes, perhaps in combination with other previously separated ones. We may find, as with the discs, a set of laws governing how these patterns change over time. And, as with the discs, we may find that a closer focus reveals these macro-patterns of color composed of quite different micro-patterns of color to be changing much more rapidly, and according to a different set of laws.

What's valuable about this second example is that everyone has seen (or can visualize) how colors can percolate or disseminate through fluids in quite distinctive ways; they've also experienced how watching patterns of colors in liquid *doesn't* trigger object-experiences. Nevertheless, the relationships between the patterns "seen" at different ontological scales that I described in the case of micro- and macro-discs can be replicated in a fluid example—especially how color motions can be different at different scales of focus. Mathematically speaking, the complexity can scale down strikingly, as it does in fractal patterns. Fluid examples show how the resolution of a changing pattern in terms of other underlying patterns—of motions, of colors, and so on—doesn't need to be characterized in terms of different *objects* exhibited at different scales of focus, or different "magnification degrees." Just as sufficient "melting into" one another of the patterns of colors short-circuits object-experiences, it similarly short-circuits causal intuitions. We see these different changing patterns of grain, macro- and micro-, *even if they are mathematically linked*, as nevertheless not bearing causal relations to one another.[18]

Equally important, we don't experience the patterns at one ontological scale as *explained* by ones at another ontological scale. This reveals that intuitions of causation and explanation are closely linked to object-experiences. We spontaneously see collisions of discrete objects as causal events: we experience subsequent behavior and properties of the objects as causally related to their previous behaviors and properties. This kind of experience often doesn't arise when we don't experience a phenomenon as involving objects.[19] Similar facts hold of our experiences of when an explanation is

---

[18] Intuitions change immediately, however, if the micro-structure is instead micro-atomic: small spheres, for example, rather than just a more intricate fluid pattern. Then we experience the macro-fluidity as just an *appearance*.

[19] Michotte (1963) is still valuable to read. Also see Carey (2009). It seems these intuitions linking contact causation to object-experiences emerge when we're very young. It also seems the behaviors that objects are expected to manifest during causal interactions aren't open to empirical correction: children simply expect certain resulting behavior on the basis of previous

provided of macro-events in terms of micro-events, as opposed to compatible (even mathematically linked) *descriptions* of a phenomenon at different levels of grain.

Even if object-intuitions can be set aside, however, as I've just attempted (by giving a pure-fluid example), perhaps the relationships between the micro- and macro-laws that occur in both examples—and, linked to this, the relationship of the respective patterns (grains) exhibited by the world when these different ontological scales are imposed—indicates that only the patterns revealed at the smaller ontological scales are *real*. The other grains are merely apparent. If so, then to return to the considerations raised at the beginning of this section, we project object borders onto unreal features. We project the borders of the macro-objects not on the basis of actual features (which are, presumably, accurately depicted by the machinations of the micro-objects) but on the basis of an appearance of how worldly features (inaccurately) appear to us.

I argue against this suggestion in what follows. It will take a while, and the work will only be finished by section 8.8. One thing needed is to replace the metaphor of closer and more distant "focus" built into how we visualize these cases of ordinary objects and tiny simples, or moving patterns of colors in fluid. After all, the world doesn't require a particular "point of view," a focus from which we're automatically given what's (objectively) genuinely seen, whereas any other focus from any other point of view is misleading. What exactly is involved in this so-called ontological focus, and what shifts when the focus changes?

One thing that's involved is easy to see, and I've explicitly indicated it: boundaries of different sizes around portions of the feature presentation. But this isn't the whole story of what's different in seeing the world macro-disc-ally as opposed to seeing the world micro-disc-ally. (I'm *so* sorry for these awful coinages. I'll only do it once, *here*.)

---

behavior. The intuitions in question, therefore, are cognitively deep and rigid. Of course, I should add that some causation intuitions don't require object-experiences to be concomitant. We experience someone as dying because he's drowning—this is because of the *water*. We can also experience an avalanche causing changes in the distribution of snow in a landscape.

There is a lot of interesting stuff I'm passing over about the interconnections between intuitions about causation and intuitions about objects. In particular, there are strong locality intuitions about causation that explain why we don't naturally take the oxygen in the room to be a cause for why the match lights, or why (again, intuitively) we don't treat omissions as causes. In both cases, locality intuitions are violated. There is definitely the following linkage between object-experiences and causation-experiences: specific objects affect other objects. I can't get further into this now, as it's—strictly speaking—a digression.

What else? To get at this, think of the macro-/micro-disc example, as I suggested in the last section, as involving a difference in how much *real* is included. Quite a bit of what's real (of what we take to be real) is *missing* from the macro-disc story that's being included in the micro-disc story. Indeed, the grain exhibited by the micro-disc story isn't visible (or needn't be visible) in the macro-disc picture simply because there are all these additional objects (all these additional micro-discs) swirling around but nevertheless ignored.

Here's a helpful visual tool to grasp the point. Imagine that every micro-disc is either red or green, and that as they move about the plane they occasionally change from red to green or from green to red. Imagine further that we notice that the red micro-discs seem to come in clusters and that we see a way to draw the borders around the clusters of red micro-discs so that the changes in color are correlated with the micro-discs crossing those borders. They change from green to red as they get close enough to a cluster to cross one of our imagined borders, and from red to green as they get far enough away from a cluster to cross a border in the other direction.[20]

We're not there yet because there are still (varying) distances between the micro-discs within a macro-disc boundary that can be seen: this means the macro-disc patterns I've just induced on the plane are spotty red. (The micro-discs within the macro-disc boundaries can still be distinguished.) So treat the empty space between the micro-discs as *missing*. Here's a tempting way to put it: we discard some of the *unreal*. When there is a certain density of micro-discs within a macro-disc boundary, the entire macro-boundary is painted red.[21] Discarding some of the "unreal"—the "empty space," the "white space"—is, as I said, an extremely tempting way to put the matter. And because of its intuitive appeal, I'll use it in the rest of this section. But it really won't do, and I'll correct it in section 8.5.

In the meantime, and apart from the issue of "white space," it may be feared that I haven't characterized ontological focus free of visual metaphors; I've substituted one visual metaphor for another. No, I haven't. The color metaphor dispensably codes a way of fully capturing how the macro-grain and the micro-grain are correspondingly exhibited that doesn't invoke any visual metaphors *at all*; it doesn't invoke the metaphor of one's focus

---

[20] I should give up trying to convey this sort of thing in words and become a professional animator—a philosophical cartoonist, as it were. (Sigh.)

[21] Illuminating, I think, is the phenomenon of perceptual "filling in." See, e.g., Dennett (1991b) on this (see "Filling in" in his index).

zooming closer or farther away. Here's how a particular *ontological focus* can instead be characterized:

(i) We only allow ontological boundaries of certain scales (and we can include other conditions here as well, e.g., that the ontological boundaries are operative only at specific space-time locations, or only when a required density of the real occurs within those boundaries, etc.).
(ii) We ignore the real *outside* those boundaries.
(iii) We ignore the unreal *within* those boundaries. (We ignore the "white space" within the macro-ontological boundaries.)
(iv) We characterize the world's features (its grain) in terms of the remaining real included within the boundaries.

It's worth pointing out that what particular swaths of the real (and what I've called "the unreal") are being included or left out of the description of the world at any given ontological focus is relative to time. This is dispensably indicated—imagistically indicated—by how micro-discs shift in color over time as they cross boundaries. It's also indicated by how certain geometric relations between micro-discs are either ignored or registered when micro-discs cross boundaries (I discuss this in section 8.5). What's *excluded* changes over time.

I've characterized "ontological focus," first, to capture what's involved in our intuitive experience of changing focus. Second, I've redescribed the phenomenon (while retaining everything essential to it) to make clear how "focus" talk is genuinely metaphorical: the characterization doesn't involve point of view. This is crucial to showing that none of the different patterns seen at different "ontological focuses" are legitimately described as "only appearances of how the world is" (depictions of feature that "actually isn't there"). This is the first step in doing this.

8.5 How Real is Empty Space?

I've indicated three factors involved in ontological focus that can be used to calibrate any characterization of the grain of the world at a particular ontological focus, and relative to a quantifier domain for a language. The first are scale differences of the ontological borders. The second is that portions of the real can be left out of what the quantifier posits encompass (these portions of the real aren't contoured within any of those posits). This can be done in space- or time-relative ways, so that the systematic ways that (some of) the real that's left out can change over space and time. But, third—and

I deliberately chose this misleading way of speaking—portions of the *unreal* can be left out as well.

The point of this section is to analyze the mistakes involved in this way of talking about particular ontological focuses, and to replace my characterization of particular ontological focuses with a better one that doesn't use the (strange) talk of ignoring the "unreal."

Let's return to the moving discs. Important to notice is that object-experiences cued by the example involve the classification of what we see into objects and a background (or a "landscape") that the objects are moving in. This makes picturesquely explicit the contrast between features impounded as a coordinate system and features (treated as properties and relations) that they co-occur with. As I indicated in section 7.3, this separation into foreground and background (coordinates and what's at those coordinates) is more general than cases of objects. It's required for flowing stuffs.[22]

Given a spatiotemporal coordination (implicit in our experience of objects), the intuitions elicited from us (by our involuntary experience of objects) in the discs-on-planes example is that the discs are moving in "empty space." If the visual depiction is manipulated to make the plane instead seem to be a body of water,[23] we'll experience the discs as moving through *a medium*. We very naturally have intuitions of various media—"liquid stuffs" that objects may or may not be moving through—but we can't simultaneously experience a medium as (itself composed of) objects. This is, again, because of exclusionary sets of completing intuitions induced by certain visual cues (or by changing those cues). If the experience of the medium is gradually changed—if we "zoom in" so that we eventually experience it as composed of atomic spheres—we'll lose the impression it's a medium.

Even a visualization of a dense crowd of small flying spheres that someone is trying to walk through—shielding his face from the onslaught, let's say—won't be experienced by the viewer instead as a medium he's trying to walk through. (We can't experience someone as *swimming through* a sea of marbles, or distinguishable *particles* of any sort, really.)

Here's another way of transforming an experience of a medium into one of an object that also illustrates the exclusionary nature of the cues affecting intuition in these cases. Imagine a cartoon where a smiling fish is swimming along rapidly, and suddenly encounters a disturbing change in viscosity: the fish is

---

[22] A foreground/background experience, for example, takes place when viewing patterns of colors percolating through a transparent watery medium—this is a case where no object-experiences whatsoever (as I've indicated) need be cued.

[23] Again, a visualization of what I'm describing here—a kind of waviness that seems to distort how we see the objects moving about—will make the point transparently clear.

now having problems making progress in its *swimming*. (And imagine the fish's expression correspondingly changes to one of *concern*.) The point of view of the cartoon then pulls back—this experience of pulling back is essential—and we realize the fish has wandered into the interior of a giant *jellyfish*.

Apart from the cued experience of a medium (of a stuff) that objects are moving through, we also can intuit "empty space"—a spatial "nothing." This impression is strongest in three-space, and it's an intuition that treats the nothingness "mere" three-space is experienced to be as (nevertheless!) Euclidean. How slow (historically speaking) we were to reach the mathematical generalizations of manifolds shows this. Mathematized "spaces," we realized only after eons, could be endowed with all sorts of properties (curvature, dimension, etc.) that are, strictly speaking, deviations from the Euclidean properties that we previously imposed on what we experienced as empty space.[24]

But my characterization of ontological focus indicates—as it were—a genuine "taking hold" of the space between objects, and (crudely put) discarding some of it. This literally means that, just as entire features contained within macro-discs are ignored, spatial and temporal features are ignored as well. This therefore seems to require the description of what was called empty space with objects moving through it as instead something that *itself* exhibits feature. It seems there can be more or less of it between discs; there can be (absolutely speaking) more or less of *all* of it (if the universe is finite); it can be infinite, and, independently of this, it can apparently be curved in various ways. It seems capable of even more intricate properties: for example, it can be composed of geometric items of a more or less rich structure, not just collections of points of various cardinalities, but—say—of threads of various sorts that determine the possible trajectories of objects moving through it; it can have holes, themselves possessing various intricate geometric properties; and so on. This invites treating space, if not as involving "objects," at least as involving *real structural features* of some sort.

Therefore: It seems the reality of space (and time), *at least in principle*, should be embraced by object projectivists in the only sense in which they embrace the reality of anything. A way to see this is to return to the language of weather reports and notice that feature-placing language works nicely

---

[24] The same considerations explain why characterizations of zero—characterizations of what was also seen as "nothing"—emerged so slowly. Notice two things needed: first, acceptance that zero is a number, and concomitantly, a willingness to attribute *distinctive* properties to it, for example, that it's *even* and not odd. In the case of space, although it's easy (intuitively) to experience media—e.g., the flow of water—as inducing curvature in the movement of objects through those media, it's quite hard to experience "empty" space doing anything similar.

for global geometric properties and relations. Imagine a three-dimensional world with moving globules of color; imagine that the geometry of this world involves varying curvatures and varying changes in metric. (One can stick a hand into a spatial region, and that hand will "distort" because of the local geometry.) In this case, we can easily claim things like this:

It's Euclidean over here.
It's curvier here than it is over there.
It's Riemannian everywhere.

Various geometric (relational) features are reasonably attributed to what we otherwise intuitively describe as "empty space." There is no reason, therefore, speaking metaphysically, to regard even the default Euclidean space as "featureless."[25]

I illustrated a conceptual looseness in section 7.3 between placed features and what—broadly speaking—they're placed at. As readers even modestly familiar with the relevant physics know, what's described as space, as time, as space-time, and more generally as event spaces, quantum-foam, et cetera, can be characterized as features of various sorts. In particular, and remarkably, significant aspects of the physics—what we might otherwise think as features—can be encapsulated in what physicists call space-time, for example, mass-energy. *Mathematically speaking*, anyway, every feature can be so encapsulated.

Nevertheless, a principled distinction between features and the placement apparatus can, and should, be drawn. As far as the placement side of feature placement is concerned, there is an absolutely minimal requirement driven by the logic of feature placement: there must be distinct coordinates for the features to be at. (Recall section 7.3.) *That's it*. Everything else that can be (and usually is) included on the placement side in mathematical and physical practice—including geometrical assumptions, continuity assumptions, and nearness relations, as well as all the richer mathematical structural assumptions studied in topology, measure theory, and so on—belongs, strictly speaking, on the feature side of the relationship.

Consider Turner's (2011) "pegboard model" of quantification to contrast his "minimal role" of quantifiers with the minimal role they have in feature-placing contexts. According to Turner, noun phrases are pegs (placed on the

---

[25] I'll refine this point in section 8.6. That Euclidean geometry isn't featureless doesn't mean that all the features we attribute to Euclidean space are *real* features, as opposed to unreal features imposed by our choice of Euclidean *mathematics*.

pegboard) and rubber bands are either hung from those pegs (corresponding to predicates) or stretched across one or more pegs (corresponding to relation terms). We are in a position, at this stage, to recognize that this model—by sheer imagery alone—begs all the really important questions against feature metaphysics. Certainly this is true if the model is meant, as Turner means it, to capture the *minimal* structural demands that quantifiers make on the world to enable their application *to* the world.

To begin with, recall from section 7.3 that placing features *in the world* isn't to necessarily place them in a specific place (e.g., in specific holes in a pegboard located thus-and-so *on* the pegboard). For there needn't be any cogent "places" for features. Features co-occur, so relative placement is the best we can get—but it's sufficient for the quantifiers of feature-placing languages. Second, there is no need to agree to genuine pegs being found in the world: we may conveniently contour pegs out of antecedently given feature, or out of nothing at all. And we can "hang" predicational rubber bands on them nevertheless. The pegboard imagery is about as misleading as imagery in metaphysics ever gets.

Given the minimal characterization of placement, the placed features (both what I've been describing as geometrical features and the others) are treated in one of two ways. They can be *real* features. But they can also be non-worldly impositions of the coordinate systems we use (and included among these impositions, of course, are also quantifier-contouring assumptions). More generally—and this is something to receive more detailed discussion later in this chapter and in chapter 9—we often project features on the world that *aren't* there.

Intuitively speaking, of course, we put all the Euclidean properties of space and time on the placement side of the relationship, and scientifically speaking, we may put a great deal else there as well. But, as a matter of the pure logic of feature placing, this isn't mandatory. This should be kept in mind to prevent philosophical worries about what *isn't* metaphysics but only the imposition of coordinates. The question of what space and time are like, for example, is from the object projectivist's point of view a question about *real* features. It shouldn't be confused with the fact that the logic of feature characterizing requires distinct coordinates.

These points aside, there is still an important distinction to be made, with respect to scientific theories, between those aspects of theories that reflect—or should be taken to reflect—the actual feature presentation and those aspects of theories that are non-worldly impositions of pure mathematics. It's nontrivial, for example, whether an aspect of what's treated (empirically) as part of space-time is an imposition of pure mathematics or reflects genuine feature. To explore this further, but still in an illustrative way, I need what I've elsewhere called a criterion for what exists. I turn to this in section 8.6.

Before that, I'll rewrite the characterization of *ontological focusing* to avoid talk of the nonexistent. Needed is a rough-and-ready distinction between placed features and other features that I'll call "geometrical." The latter features are exhibited as "white space" in the imagistic thought experiments that I above described. The resulting characterization of ontological focusing, precisely because it doesn't utilize the minimal notion of coordinate placement, may seem less general than it should be. It suits the examples, however, that I'm crafting it to handle, because intuitions of "zooming in" and "zooming out" so crucial to ontological focus are ones where we experience objects in space and time, and specifically in a space and time with the topological properties that make sense of "zooming in" and "zooming out." Thus the examples clearly require the cogency of notions such as "interior" and "boundary," as well as the further requirement of a metric. We establish an ontological focus when:

(i) We only allow ontological boundaries of certain scales (and we can include other conditions here as well, for example, that the ontological boundaries are operative only relative to particular features, e.g., when a required density of the real is located within those boundaries, and so on).
(ii) We ignore the feature *outside* those boundaries.
(iii) We ignore purely geometric feature *within* those boundaries.
(iv) We characterize the feature exhibition (its grain) in terms of the remaining feature within the boundaries.

There are two additional points to make about "purely geometric" features. The first is that at least some of these features are metaphysically present, and playing a genuine truth-maker role for optimal and less optimal choices in what coordinate posits best fit the world. This was implicit as early as in chapter 6, when I mentioned that some coordinates would work and others would be less appealing, based on exactly how the world is. But second, and this is a point I'll develop a bit more in section 8.7, the geometric features exhibited by the world dramatically underdetermine the nature of the posits that we project onto the world when we empirically decide upon one or another coordinate system for our physics (e.g., curved space-time or a thirteen-dimensional space for string theory). This point is intimately related to my earlier observation about the question of what aspects of the mathematics of space-time, for example, indicate actual features exhibited in the world and which instead are un-worldly impositions.

8.6 Mind- and Language-Independence

In order to make the further points I need to make about coordinate posits, and more generally about the application of mathematical formalisms, I need to revisit my earlier work on the mind and language criterion for what exists, and apply that criterion to various coordinate-posits systems in order to cement the case that a commitment to the real isn't induced by the sheer scientific (and informal) uses of coordinates.[26]

I'll start by revisiting the criterion for what exists that's widely though implicitly accepted by non-philosophers, and that's, in addition, metaphysically natural because the dichotomy it induces is central to our concerns. In this section I'll present the criterion as I have before—in terms of "objects" and their properties. In section 8.7, I'll recalibrate its application in feature-characterizing terms, and apply the recalibrated criterion to some illustrative cases.

It's necessary and sufficient for the existence of something (understood in an ontically weighty manner) that it's mind- and language-independent. (Hereafter, I'll call this the "M&L-independence criterion," and talk about things being "M&L-dependent" or "M&L-independent.") Dream figures, fictional characters, and hallucinated objects are all, in the sense meant, M&L-dependent. Dinosaurs, protons, microbes, other people, chairs, buildings, stars, and so on are examples of M&L-independent objects.

---

[26] I first discussed coordinate posits—specifically spatial and temporal ones—in Azzouni (1997, especially section IV). I revisited the issue in Azzouni (2004a, chapter 9),—applying the neutral-quantification apparatus in the Newtonian context to the famous bucket thought experiment. I've revisited the issue three other times, in Azzouni (2009a, section 8), where I addressed more general (relativistic) contexts; Azzouni (2011); and in Azzouni and Bueno (forthcoming). What I say here and in the next section doesn't straightforwardly replicate the points made in earlier and concurrent work because I'm accommodating the concern that shifting from object metaphysics to feature metaphysics requires rethinking mind- and language-independence. Azzouni (2012a), especially, looks like it needs recalibration. Things aren't *so* bad, however. "Feature" in that paper isn't the same as "feature" here—there it's only a label for tropes. Still, given the results in this book about features, I wouldn't now run the arguments the way I do there, especially the ones in section 9.6 of that paper.

An additional (terminological) point: In previous work I've called my mind- and language-independence criterion "ontological independence." Due to a revival of this old terminology by philosophers who use it in a far more ontologically weighty fashion than I do—linking items that they take to robustly exist in "ontological dependence" relations—I'm now deserting this way of speaking.

I exclude a different use of "mind-dependence" or "language-dependence" according to which buildings or chairs are "mind-dependent" (because they wouldn't exist if people hadn't made them). Contrarily, in my sense of "mind-independence" and "language-independence," no one can dictate an M&L-independent object into existence by (merely) thinking it or symbolizing it as so. No one can dictate (all) the properties of such an object by (merely) thinking or stating in language that it has such properties.

It may seem this M&L-independence criterion faces a difficulty if it's understood as a *necessary and sufficient* condition for existence. I'll start this way. An objection to the proposed criterion is that a problem seems to arise because of variations in how something "depending" on a mind or on language can be understood. Must one think of the item in some detail, or name it, for it to be so dependent, or need one merely quantify over it? On the former, more stringent view, unnamed sets are mind-independent (contrary to the result a nominalist like myself would want). On the latter, less stringent view, one can think of numerous fictional characters by thinking, say, of "all the detectives that haven't been written about yet." To invent a fictional character, presumably, is to think of him—but on this less stringent characterization of "mind- and language-dependence" this is too easy.[27]

This objection trades on a Meinongian presupposition that the criterion *is applied to* nonexistent things to determine that they don't exist. No: if something doesn't exist, then there is nothing to apply the criterion *to*; there is nothing to discover about what doesn't exist. If holes exist, therefore, they don't violate the criterion; if they don't exist, they don't violate the criterion either (there's nothing there *to* violate the criterion). So in neither case is the criterion violated.

This solution seems to lead to something worse. If the criterion only applies to what exists (because there isn't anything else), then what real work are the phrases "mind- and language-dependence" and "mind- and language-independence" doing? (What is this supposed necessary *and* sufficient condition doing?) Nothing metaphysical—it can't be (for example) distinguishing what exists from what doesn't. There *isn't* anything else. Response: This is a mistaken concern. Just because a criterion holds of *everything* doesn't mean it isn't metaphysical; it's a metaphysical fact, of course, that it holds of *everything*.

Although the M&L-independence criterion *is* metaphysical, its *value* isn't metaphysical; its value is epistemic. Why, for example, is it informative to

---

[27] I owe this concern to Daniel Nolan.

observe that our community has M&L-independence as its criterion? Because this explains our epistemic practices when we go about trying to discover what exists (and what doesn't). In these explorations we utilize our senses, which we recognize operate in fairly restricted ways, and we use instruments that epistemically generalize on our senses.[28]

It's an *empirical claim* that the only way we have to discover anything about M&L-independent objects involves epistemic processes that include appropriate sensory or instrumental interaction either with those objects, with objects they have affected, or with other suitably theoretically related objects. *Given* this empirical result, we can see how the M&L-independence criterion for what exists classifies an "object" as not existing. It isn't by direct application of the criterion to the purported object—this is impossible. Rather, we discover that the legitimate methods we use to attribute properties to a purported object don't involve the appropriate forms of epistemic access. In the case of fictions, the author stipulates what properties fictional objects have. In the case of holes, properties are attributed on the basis of the actual properties of other real things that we sense (or instrumentally study). Finally, hallucinated items are revealed to be figments of our minds—the hallucinated properties of which are projected onto the world by a process perhaps involving recollections of real objects, or by other aspects of minds.

In all these cases, we thus recognize the "mind-dependence" or "language-dependence" of the items in question from the fact that they don't exist. This latter fact, in turn, is recognized on the basis of epistemic facts about how truths about these objects are established—that the epistemic methods used don't fit the (empirically established) requirements of epistemic access to M&L-independent objects.

Notice that the M&L criterion is valuable epistemically only insofar as it underwrites certain of our epistemic practices for determining that such-and-such exists (or doesn't exist). To repeat: Just because a criterion holds of *everything* doesn't mean it isn't metaphysical; it's a metaphysical fact that it holds of *everything*. And just because it's useful epistemically doesn't mean it isn't a metaphysical criterion that's, in addition, useful epistemically. Consider the criterion "having 79 protons." Suppose this criterion is extensionally equivalent to R—but no one knows about R. That "having 79 protons" is useful epistemically and R isn't is a reason for saying that one but not the other is metaphysical.[29]

---

[28] I omit further discussion of this because it's a digression. See Azzouni (2004b).
[29] I thank Michael Glanzberg, Carrie Jenkins, Daniel Nolan, Benjamin Schnieder, and Ted Sider, for (oral) comments that led to an earlier version of this discussion. My thanks to Thomas Baldwin for raising related issues in email correspondence. My discussion here differs from that in Azzouni (2010a) and Azzouni (2012c). (I like my current response better.)

8.7 Applying the M&L Criterion to Features

So far, I've spoken of objects and the properties predicated of them. But speaking this way involves projecting ontological boundaries. As far as metaphysics is concerned, the criterion doesn't require ontological boundaries. After all, the mind- and language-independence criterion easily applies to features. If features co-occur in the world, then they are real. If, however, we project those features, then they aren't real. In this sense, object projectivists implicitly rely on the M&L criterion when they stress that ontological boundaries are projected: the boundaries aren't real according to the M&L criterion.

This *boundary-free* recalibration of the criterion is straightforward. I'll address, however, two puzzles about our standard *epistemic* identifications of mind- and language-independence. The first is that it seems that our epistemic methods of locating the real (by observing instances of it or by instrumentally interacting with it) are intrinsically bound to characterizations of the real having boundaries. We discover items, and locate *them*. We instrumentally find instances of *things* (viruses, black holes, etc.) and, in this way, verify they exist.

The second puzzle is this. I've often described holes as not existing. But, given the concession in section 8.5 that geometric features are exhibited in the world as much as other features, the result seems to be—straightforwardly—that holes exist, not that they don't. After all, holes have various geometrical features. The difference between the hole in a piece of cheese and the cheese surrounding it is only that the features exhibited in the relevant locales differ, not that there are no features where there are no cheese features.

I'll start with the first puzzle. This puzzle seems to imply that although the metaphysical M&L criterion can be recalibrated purely in terms of feature placing, the operative criterion (that scientists and others use) has ontological boundaries conceptually built into it. It's certainly true that we ordinarily think of real objects as having real ontological boundaries—worldly ontological boundaries. Nevertheless, I'll argue, our epistemic practices for determining what's real (and what isn't) aren't intrinsically connected to ontological boundaries.

It seems straightforward, I want to say to begin with, that epistemic access to the real doesn't require boundaries. When we are (officially) attempting to determine the various properties of something, its mass, its velocity, its color, and so on, this can be redescribed (accurately) as attempts to *localize* features to a greater or to a lesser extent. This shows that even in the case of sensory observation, where it seems ontological borders are crucial to what we see and what we make of it, they aren't. At best, what is relevant are feature distributions.

The second puzzle: What *about* holes? Don't we see them, and so don't we see features *there*? Well, no, we *don't*. Consider holes in ordinary life. Here it's relatively obvious that the Euclidean features of space and time aren't seen; at best, they're inferred from the movements (for example) of things we *do* see. None of the (Euclidean) features that are (let's say) exhibited by sheer space are seen by us. So when we "see" holes, as we often say, we're actually seeing (and we recognize this) something else; we attribute properties to holes (their geometric contours, their ages, etc.) derivatively. Notice—this is important—that none of the properties we attribute to holes are actually featured by the space the hole contours. We don't attribute the properties of the space-time geometry to the interior of the hole.

I'll be brief about this (because I've discussed it so much elsewhere—see the references in footnote 26), but the situation changes very little with respect to the generalizations/deviations to our Euclidean notions of space and time induced by successive physical theories. Certain aspects of the fine structure of the space-time manifold aren't even contemplated as being empirically tested, for example, that its point structure is dense and complete. Other purported features, even the global geometric features we instrumentally verify the presence of (e.g., space-time curvature), are verified in the same indirect way that analogous properties of space and time were previously "verified." *Other things* that we *do* have observational/instrumental access to are measured in various ways.[30] Given the M&L criterion, and specifically our epistemic methods of verifying features to be real, this gives us little reason to think pure geometric features are real in the way a believer in "absolute space" will want to understand them—as an absolute background like Turner's "pegboard."

Of course, it's an empirical matter (as it always is) whether *there are* spatial and temporal features, or generalizations thereof, that we can gain appropriate epistemic access to. So the points I'm making here turn very much on details about our instrumental/observational access to particular features.

One last point I should stress again. This is that the mathematics of what's called space and time (or space-time, etc.) is interestingly layered

---

[30] Again, this point, described in terms of "other objects," can instead be described in terms of localizable features.

in the roles of the applied mathematics it utilizes. First, there are the pure (minimal) coordinate roles that such mathematics has. But second, there are various non-worldly *projections*, both of the quantifier-contouring type and of feature placing, that such mathematics, when applied, imposes on the world. I have in mind, for example, structural details about the space-time posited, such as that it has a continuum-many, continuous, everywhere-dense, et cetera structure. As just mentioned, *none* of this detailed structure is (ever) epistemically accessed, even in the indirect way that space-time curvature is indirectly accessed. These are feature projections—purely mathematical impositions driven by the form that the mathematical theories used in this area have taken. But there are (or can be) other structural details imposed by the mathematics of space-time (or its various generalizations) that *do* correspond to something—sorts of features that the world exhibits—although the characterization of these features is purely mathematical and global. I have in mind, as an example, the role of space-time as itself a repository of mass-energy.[31]

8.8 Is the Exhibition of Grain on the Part of Some But Not All of the Real Only Apparent?

Let's return to the issue raised in section 8.5. Given a characterization of ontological focus as not just scale conditions on ontological boundaries but also a systematic disregarding of some feature, we can return to the question of whether to leave out some feature is to *inaccurately* describe what has been retained. It's not inaccurate. Here's why.

The first point to make is the evident one that there is no requirement on a characterization of a worldly *pattern* of feature that it take account of *every feature* exhibited. A pattern of feature is worldly even if that pattern isn't exhibited by the entire feature presentation. One reason to deny the previous sentence is the thought that a finite array of lit pixels (for example) can exhibit *any* spatial pattern at all if we allow ourselves to say that it exhibits patterns that not *all* the lit pixels have to participate in. *Any* letter, *any* numeral—for example—is exhibited by *some* of the lit pixels in an array. But this is wrong—not *any* pattern can be exhibited. No letters, in particular, beyond a certain size can be exhibited; similarly, numerals that depict numbers beyond a certain magnitude can't be exhibited either. No pattern can

---

[31] See, in particular, my "black box objection," in Azzouni (2006, 144–47), or the discussion of these matters in the other work cited in footnote 26.

be exhibited, furthermore, that requires intricate detail that goes beyond the resolution of the array of lit pixels. *Not anything goes.*

The second point: We aren't just interested in feature patterns exhibited by the world; we're also interested in how the world exhibits these feature patterns over time. More specifically, we're interested in characterizations of patterns over time that can be *predicted* from specified characterizations of patterns-at-a-time. Call these the "lawlike patterns." Lawlike patterns are descriptions of patterns over time that can be characterized by formulations in theories—scientific or otherwise—that, on the basis of the grain exhibited at one moment, dictate the grain exhibited at other moments. It's an empirical question whether, of course, there are *any* lawlike patterns. As it turns out, we've been pretty lucky—or so it seems. We've discovered a great number of lawlike patterns—that's something our *sciences* (specifically the physical sciences) have explicitly done for us.

It needs stressing: lawlike patterns can (at least in principle) exist, or fail to exist, at *any* ontological scale—with respect to any way that ontological borders are drawn, and, correlatively, with respect to whatever ways we include or exclude feature. In particular, there is no reason why there being a lawlike pattern requires *all* the features to exhibit that pattern. And, indeed, although in the micro-/macro-disc example I stated explicitly that the lawlike pattern exhibited at the macro-disc level can itself be predicted on the basis of the lawlike pattern exhibited at the micro-disc level (but not the reverse), there is no reason why this *has* to be their relationship. It could be, instead, that there is no lawlike pattern exhibited no matter how we draw ontological borders if *every* feature is included. That is, it could be that a lawlike pattern is exhibited at the macro-disc focus, but when we insist on including all the features, all that's added (from the point of view of possible predictive laws) is "noise." (Individual micro-discs that are sufficiently isolated from their fellow micro-discs, say, are unpredictable in their motions, so a lawlike pattern emerges only at the macro-disc scale.)

But lawlike patterns, as I initially described the micro-/macro-discs example, are also possible where the pattern at one level can be deduced from (or can otherwise be linked to) a pattern at another level.[32] And some might argue: in a case like *that*, an explanation *has* been given. In the micro-/macro-disc example, in particular, an explanation for the feature pattern at the macro-disc level has been given in terms of the feature pattern exhibited

---

[32] I qualify my description of the relationship this way because, of course, the relationship between two characterizations of feature patterns at two different levels can be rather complex, mathematically speaking.

at the micro-disc level. This explanation, furthermore, takes a particularly neat form: what's going on with the macro–feature pattern *just is* what's going on with the micro–feature pattern.

This kind of explanation may seem to license strong conclusions. It may seem to license (or at least to invite) the thought that real *objects* are involved at the micro-level—that these micro-discs are real *objects*, real objects that have been discovered to be in the world, and it's what these objects are *doing* that explains the pattern exhibited by the world when ontological boundaries are drawn at a larger scale. Furthermore (it can be argued), this has been revealed by our discovery of the laws governing the micro-discs—laws that can be used to explain why "objects" drawn at larger scales behave the way *they* do. The master argument (section 6.8: the argument from optimal theorizing) undercuts this line of thought.

But, object considerations aside, it might seem that we *still* have the resources to describe the micro-grain as real and the macro-grain as only apparent. This is because, still, some of the features are left out at the macro level but (let's say) none of them are left out at the micro-level. We can explain *everything*, we might claim, when we choose our explanations on the basis of what micro–feature patterns are doing; we can't explain everything, we add, when we choose our explanations on the basis of the macro–feature patterns. And in mounting this objection, we might say, we aren't bringing in talk of "objects" at all. Nevertheless, that some of what's real is left out in one case—but not in the other—is what enables us to conclude that one feature pattern is only an appearance, in contrast to the other feature pattern.

We should—I think—dig deeper to see what's behind the suggestion that the feature pattern is real in one case but not in the other. What the claim comes down to is that the features we see exhibited at one level, but not at the other, really are exhibited by the world. What seems to be *all* that's behind the argument is this: in one case the laws governing micro-features are more extensive than the laws governing the macro-features.

When the objection is recast *this way*, it can be seen to be nothing more than the same consideration raised (and rejected) earlier: if a feature pattern isn't exhibited by *all* the real, then the pattern isn't real. Here the variant idea seems to be: if a law isn't about *everything*, then it's not a real law; the features it relies on aren't real features. Furthermore, when object-intuitions are set aside (say, by imagining we're looking at a pattern of colors shifting over time), it becomes clear that the purported explanation being gestured at is bogus: a smaller pattern that changes over time is hardly "explained" by the larger pattern that exhibits it as a part. Indeed, it's possible to think that the order of explanation is the reverse: a larger pattern is "explained" as being the way it is because its portions exhibit certain smaller patterns (that make up the larger pattern). And that a set of laws can be described that predict the larger pattern and a set of laws can be described that predict the smaller pattern, and that from the laws predicting the larger pattern we can deduce the smaller pattern (and/or vice versa), is a mere mathematical fact of no metaphysical significance whatsoever.

There's an important lesson here. This is that something as cognitively deep in us as object-experience will (of course) profoundly affect our intuitions about other fundamental concepts. In particular, our intuitions about when a characterization of a phenomenon "explains" another phenomenon are pervasively infiltrated by background descriptions (or the cueing) of the roles of various "objects." When these resulting object-intuitions are stripped out (by replacing a visual image that induces impressions of objects with one that's otherwise similar but where the scenario is manipulated so that object-intuitions aren't invoked), our sense that an *explanation* has been given (or is required) vanishes. This is important because the philosopher who invokes explanation as a reason to take ontology seriously isn't reaching for an independent piece of intuitive evidence.

Having said this, I should add that it's hard—in practice—to separate object-intuitions from our experience that an explanation of such-and-such a sort is being given. What's hard, in particular, is to separate our intuitions about how the micro-laws provide explanations for the macro-laws, and the genuineness (versus the appearance) of micro-laws in contrast to macro-laws, along with their properties and relations, from the object-intuitions driving this: ones (for example) about how micro-discs or marbles or subatomic particles are real objects, and the macro-discs or ordinary objects composed of these things aren't.

8.9 A Brief Conclusion

Many philosophers are strongly motivated by reductionist ontological programs: the hope that in some way macro-ontologies can be shown to be "nothing more" than micro-ontologies. This chapter undercuts the motivation for such programs. If the world is a feature presentation, then there is no special or privileged perspective or orientation toward the world that's better than any other—metaphysically speaking. Contouring features topically one way rather than another may manifest superior theory virtues, as I'll illustrate in the next chapter, but this hasn't anything to do with metaphysics. Leaving out feature to capture patterns in feature, even if the result is better prediction, hasn't any metaphysical significance except in the purely trivial sense that—of course—some feature has been left out.

Along the way, I've also analyzed in purely featural terms the apparent differences in ontological focus that different sciences seem to have, and I've given more details about how we should think about the role of coordinate systems in our sciences (and in daily life).

9 | Constructing "Objects"

9.1 Introduction

This last chapter discusses aspects of the projection of object boundaries—what might be called the machinery of projection. Crucial to understanding this machinery is the recognition that it's not "anything goes," because the feature presentation induces better and worse choices for the languages we craft to describe it. In the first three sections, I focus specifically on laws, induction, and explanation; in the rest of the chapter, the principle of indiscernibles and Leibniz's law are the topics. Throughout I'm concerned with how we project objects onto the feature presentation, and not (as in current analytic metaphysics) with how to deploy laws, induction, or Leibniz's law in existence arguments for this or that kind of object (this or that kind of ontological boundary).

In the first half of the chapter, I illustrate how laws and induction don't presuppose worldly ontological boundaries (and how features do the job alone). Important to this is the distinction between object projectivism and what I call *quantifier indifference*. That there are no worldly ontological boundaries is a fact about the world. Quantifier indifference, by contrast, is about quantifier *languages*: any way that a quantifier domain contours features into topics for predicates is as good as any other. I show that object projectivism doesn't imply quantifier indifference, and that quantifier indifference is false.

9.2 Induction and Laws

Nelson Goodman (1983) designed a set of influential examples subsequently used by many philosophers (but not by him) to motivate worldly natural kinds to underwrite inductive inference. Define something as grue if and only if it's discovered before 3000 CE and it's green, or it's discovered after 3000 CE and it's blue. Consider the candidate inductions: *All emeralds are green* and *All emeralds are grue*. To infer all emeralds are green after sundry emerald sightings seems legitimate—not so the inference to *All emeralds are grue*.[1] Furthermore, these candidate inferences conflict in their predictions of the color of emeralds found after 3000 CE. Similarly horrific candidate predicates ruin other inductive predictions. One solution to the grueness challenge restricts inductive inference to a selective subset of possible predicates; some philosophers,[2] furthermore, suggest that this suitable subset of predicates should match the natural kinds in the world (so greenness is such a kind, but not grueness).[3]

Some philosophers think specific *object boundaries* (and not others) are also required for successful inductive inference. Consider a rubber ball, a pencil, and the temporally composite object of the ball for a certain number of days and the pencil thereafter. This temporally composite object (and similar ones) seems resistant to inductions and, more generally, to lawlike predictions of every kind. How such objects behave for a time has no lawlike connection to how they behave later.

Elder (2011, 12) gives this example: We flex a piece of copper wire repeatedly and *it* breaks. It certainly seems (so Elder argues) that establishing a generalization on this basis presupposes identifying the later item as *the same piece of* copper wire as the earlier one. If that piece of copper wire is later (and instead) a chair in Istanbul, prediction of its later behavior by its earlier behavior is fruitless. Elder calls this "numerical persistence" and presupposes its importance to successful induction.[4]

---

[1] This example is flawed because emeralds are green *by stipulation*: emeralds are *green* beryls. That is, any beryl that's sufficiently blue is (by stipulation) not an emerald. (I owe this point to Yvonne Raley.) Despite the age of "emerald," its usage and meaning have been *co-opted* by an expert group, unlike, say, "water." (Recall the discussion of this phenomenon in section 2.2.1.) More accurately, the word's meaning is determined by a *special-interest* group—gem dealers. (The same is true of most words for commodities.) I'll continue using this example of an inductively established generalization, despite this, because it's the traditional one—introduced by Nelson Goodman, and used by *everyone* who mentions his riddle of induction.
[2] E.g., influentially, Lewis (1983). Later, Sider (2011), and many others.
[3] It's natural to argue that "grue" and similar predicates are illegitimate because their characterizations use tense and/or parochial considerations of human discovery. But grue items are a collection of things, just like green ones are. Reference to human endeavor and timing is needed to characterize gruish items *in terms of* green and blue ones—but not otherwise (as Goodman (1983) notes).
[4] That is, he *exhibits* inductions like the one about the wire, and *indicates* that *metaphysical* numerical persistence seems required. I'm not objecting to his impressionistic argument-procedure. The burden of proof seems to be on the opponent.

In previous chapters (see section 7.6, especially), I've separated metaphysical considerations about features (and their roles in explanation and in science) from metaphysical considerations about objects (and their roles in explanation and science). So I won't (here) challenge the strategy of characterizing successful inductions in terms of projectable predicates corresponding to actual ("natural") features. Considerations like Elder's, however, seem to show that metaphysical claims about "natural kinds" can't be separated from those about natural ontological boundaries as object projectivism requires—at least when it comes to grounding inductions metaphysically.[5]

To see that object projectivism *isn't* threatened by requirements on the cogency of induction, we must distinguish the ontological-boundary-denying thesis of object projectivism from *quantifier indifference*: all ways that quantifier domains carve up the world (all ways that the feature presentation is topicalized) are equally good, both pragmatically and theoretically.

Many philosophers are concerned with quantifier indifference—Sosa and Hirsch among them. It shows up as "relativism," or "quantifier relativism," and it's sometimes confused with one or another metaphysical claim about the world. It's important, therefore, to realize the doctrine is wrong, and that it is—in any case—irrelevant to metaphysics.

One important point to be established in this chapter, therefore, is that—despite the truth of object projectivism—there are better and worse ways for quantifier domains to single out topics from the world. This is because the resulting formulations of truths can correspondingly be made complicated or simple by different choices of quantifier domains. What prevents this difference in the value—of the "objects" in different quantifier domains—from implying worldly ontological borders is that "better" and "worse," here, *are* due to details about the feature presentation, but aren't due to worldly ontological borders.

To illustrate this, suppose we interact with a small number of macro-objects—copper wires, zebras, and a few other things. Imagine too we've established laws about them by induction. There are a finite number of actions ("shooting zebras," "flexing wires"), and some results ("lying on the ground dead," "breaking") that we've repeatedly seen subsequently. Now introduce objects temporally composed of particular copper-wire-stages at earlier times, but particular zebra-stages later; and exclude the previous

---

[5] The only real argument I can find in the literature, however, is due to Lewis (1983, 48–49) about Bruce, his cat. But the presumption that metaphysical assumptions about natural kinds and naturally contoured objects stand or fall together is found everywhere. Sider (2011) and Elder (2011), for example, presume the two positions to stand together; Sidelle (1989) takes them to both fail for related reasons.

objects from the quantifier domain. Does induction break down? Are these new objects *not* governed by laws? No, these things obey laws *too*. And their laws are precisely related to laws the original objects obey.[6]

A *general* difference between laws about zebras and copper wires and laws about wire-zebras is that zebra and wire laws exhibit *locality* and wire-zebra laws don't. The inductive laws about zebras and wires (that wires flexed repeatedly break; that zebras shot dead fall down and don't move) are ones for which object boundaries (imposed on the world by the quantifier domains) respect the locality conditions that features exhibit over time. We can state in terms of the quantifier domains themselves how they respect locality conditions: the same objects can be referred to in the antecedents and the consequents—laws can take the form $(x)(Px \to Qx)$.[7] Corresponding laws for wire-zebras, however, must take a different form: $(x)(\exists y)(Px \to Qy)$.

This illustrates the relationship between choices of quantifier contourings and expressible truths. What we see here (and this holds generally) is that topic contourings bear *directly* on the complexity of the laws that can be stated, or if they can be stated at all. Although this shows that choices of ontological boundaries affect the simplicity of theories and laws, this doesn't show that theory-superior boundaries are *worldly*.

There are at least two reasons for this. I explore the first in this and the next three paragraphs, and the second thereafter. So, first, we can easily (and fully) explain the superiority or inferiority of a set of ontological boundaries by the locality facts exhibited by the feature presentation *without* additionally invoking worldly objects. Consider the plane again, with its lawlike movement of colors over time. Given a certain designated portion of color pattern, how much of the antecedent color pattern of the rest of the plane is relevant to the prediction of the subsequent behavior of *this portion* of the pattern? Color patterns can exhibit *total locality*: *all* that's relevant to the subsequent

---

[6] I won't develop this point in much detail, but recall the object-parts mappings of chapters 1 and 8. Mappings of objects or object parts in one quantifier domain to those in another, coupled with appropriate mappings of the ideologies of the languages, induce sentence-to-sentence mappings. These sentence-to-sentence mappings contain law-to-law mappings. Of course, how complex these laws are (and whether they can even be stated) will turn directly on the object-parts mappings—in particular, on exactly which pairs of pieces-of-wire-durations and zebra-durations are mapped to wire-zebras.

[7] Some qualifications. First, almost no scientific law looks like *this*. Second, temporal factors are tacitly buried in the predicates (the zebra is shot dead and then doesn't move—but only after twitching for a while in agony). And other qualifications are called for too. Despite this, it's pretty much examples like this that philosophers (who discuss induction) have in mind. The points I make using these examples generalize pretty easily to actual laws. When they don't, it's because object-considerations are set aside by the science in question. I'll illustrate this in section 9.3.

behavior of a portion of pattern is its previous behavior. But the feature presentation may exhibit various degrees of *partial nonlocality*: relevant to predicting the behavior of a portion of feature is feature beyond what's in the portion itself. The relevant extra feature may be adjacent to the portions in question; but it can also be quite far away.

If the feature presentation exhibits partial nonlocality (the antecedent behavior of that portion plus a small penumbra of additional feature around it is all that's needed to predict its future behavior), then it's easy to characterize the laws governing these feature patterns with highly localized portions of feature. This is certainly how the macro-patterns in our world look. Their apparent localized behavior made reasonable the early contact-causation model for physics (one first definitively overthrown, however, by Newton's law of gravitation).

If what's relevant to predicting future behavior of portions of feature pattern are only the antecedent behaviors of other nicely restricted portions of feature (even if they're quite far away), we can still capture this by means of fairly simple laws with quantifier domains containing judiciously chosen feature pattern portions. In these cases, even with drastic nonlocality, the laws remain fairly simple as long as the relevant other bits of feature pattern can be tractably quantified over, and their antecedent machinations neatly described in laws.

Although these laws are best couched in terms of "objects" with such-and-such borders, this doesn't require worldly borders. All that's needed to explain the superiority or inferiority of a particular way of contouring feature into objects is how the feature pattern is—for example, if the feature pattern at a time is locally determined, or if there is, instead, some other kind of tractable relation between portions of earlier and later feature.

The second reason for why different ways of chunking the world inducing better and worse characterizations of laws doesn't falsify object projectivism is that, in any case, a *unique* optimal set of object boundaries (projected by a quantifier domain) isn't determined by fully respecting feature patterns over time. An induction about various purported objects works just as well if we treat those objects not as themselves genuine objects but only as the *parts* of larger objects. Example: Contour zebras and wires as mereological sum-pairs of particular zebras and wires, and appropriately replace properties and relations attributed to, respectively, zebras and wires with "larger" properties and relations that zebra-wires have when their respective parts have the original properties and relations. Laws that hold of zebra-wires can be easily characterized in terms of these new properties and relations.

In *this* case the resulting laws aren't objectionable because the *laws themselves* are less simple or tractable. Indeed, these new laws are as easily stated as the originals. What's been made more complicated—what's become intractable—is the *epistemology*. It's difficult to *discover* these laws by directly studying the objects they hold of. It's also difficult to apply these laws directly to the objects they're about even if we manage to discover the laws to begin with.

Both points are easy to see. Because these new objects are composed of non-contiguous independent parts, laws about *their full behavior at a time* are hard to discover. We must first discover "pre-laws" that govern their separate parts, and only given these pre-laws can we then state a full law. We face an analogous epistemic difficulty if we try to apply these laws to particular zebra-wires. We aren't ever in two places at the same time, and so we never straightforwardly see how *these* objects are behaving.

This, however, is a *pragmatic* drawback—not one of language. It makes evident why it's valuable for us (all things being equal) *not* to chunk the world into objects that *we perceive* to be discontinuous wholes. This is ultimately a consideration about cognitive evolution, since the regularities we evolved to recognize are of items that aren't too big or small, and aren't discontinuous in their behavior (at least as far as our senses can determine).[8] But this is compatible with object projectivism. That laws presupposing certain object boundaries have epistemic drawbacks doesn't bear—one way or the other—on whether there are worldly object boundaries.

A philosopher may be tempted by an inference to objects (with particular ontological boundaries and not other ontological boundaries) as the best explanation for why certain feature patterns are time-linked. Let's help this idea along by assuming, contrary to fact, that a unique characterization of what's in a quantifier domain is induced by how features exhibit over time. So the idea is that what *explains* such-and-such feature patterns—why the laws take the form they take—is that *there are* objects with such-and-such ontological contours. These ontological contours are, in fact, demanded in order to induce the simplest statement of these laws.

But what does this postulation of worldly borders explain that isn't already explained by the brute fact that over time the feature pattern obeys a certain locality condition? What genuine explanatory itch is satisfied by assuming

---

[8] Relevant here are the many vision-science results that show that when we see depictions of items moving around in "lockstep", we experience what we see as "the tip of an iceberg," the visible parts of an object the rest of which is otherwise invisible. More dramatically, we project the (invisible) object to have a particular geometry—one that explains why these visible parts are moving the way we experience them to move.

worldly ontological boundaries? (I'll return to the issue of the role of ontology in explanation in section 9.4.)

9.3 How Perceptual Object-Cueing Intuitions Operate at Cross Purposes with Scientific Object-Positing

One possibility the discussion in section 9.2 is hinting toward is that perceptual (and sensory) cues that involuntarily impel contouring object boundaries can operate at cross purposes with scientific demands for tractable laws. Indeed, this phenomenon occurs widely. Laws in one form, F*, with a quantifier domain that contains such-and-such objects o*, can be intractable—that is, the available mathematics prevents (or impedes) deduction of certain valuable implications of those laws. If, however, they are transformed into another form, F**, with a different quantifier domain containing objects o**, they become tractable—the needed implications are now deductively available.[9]

Recall from section 5.3 two nearly spherical and homogeneous masses m_1 and m_2 connected by a strong spring in a gravitational field. We can imagine these objects in a natural way: they're machine-tooled smooth spherical metallic balls welded together with a strong spring. Some may experience the resulting item as *one* object (the kind of Slinky toy physicists like to play with); some may experience it as three attached objects.[10] These details don't matter: the crucial point is that because we're familiar with these things, we have powerful intuitions about them.

Recall that the separate motions of the masses in this field are very complicated to calculate directly. Rewriting the system as the movement of two point masses, the "center of mass" (with mass $m_1 + m_2$), and "the reduced mass" (with mass $m_1 m_2/(m_1 + m_2)$), breaks it up into the motion of two *noninteracting* point masses. Three sorts of "object" come up in this computation. First, the spherical masses (as well as the spring); second, the physically significant items that aren't perceptually cued as objects (the center of mass, the reduced mass); and lastly, the various mathematical quantities used to transform the first set of equations into the second—but that don't correspond to

---

[9] Strictly speaking, it needn't be that F* and F** are logically equivalent; sometimes a bit of background mathematics M is presupposed so that what's strictly true is that M → (F* ↔ F**).
[10] The number of objects can be cued differently according to how the spring is connected to the spheres—whether, for example, the spheres can be simply detached from the spring (because the spring is latched and fits into designed spaces on the spheres) or whether the result of pulling a sphere off the spring is instead "breaking" the device.

anything physically significant (e.g., $m_1 m_2$). The laws of motion—applied in this particular case—become tractable when we replace the objects (that we ordinarily take to be there) with two point masses moving independently of each other, items that no one normally regards as real objects.

As I mentioned, this illustrates something fairly common in the sciences. Centers of mass, for example, are often among the items that appropriate laws describing a system of objects must quantify over. More generally, nothing requires the so-called objects we want to determine laws for to be in the quantifier domains of those laws. I'm not claiming, of course, that perceptually cued objects *must be* absent from the domain of a physical science. Sometimes (as in continua mechanics) the domain can contain items we antecedently experience as there—metal plates or flowing bodies of water.[11] Nevertheless, when successful scientific laws are formulated (in terms of fields, for example), what we're perceptually cued to see as objects often vanishes, replaced either by other kinds of objects or by something that despite its precise mathematically characterized properties is hard to experience either as an object or as a collection of objects.[12]

We shouldn't be puzzled. As I mentioned earlier, our cognitive evolution developed within a narrow range of ontological focus, variations in which were crudely managed—for example, by moving in for "closer looks." That's why it's natural to characterize ontological focus subjectively, by metaphors of vision. But when ontological focus is drastically changed—both by the science taking account of aspects of reality that we previously had no access to, and by genuine instrumental access to that reality—we can find (we *have* found) that the ontological boundaries we involuntarily experience are irrelevant. Although they are (and continue to be) valuable to characterize gross regularities about macro-objects,[13] we've learned that the more-refined regularities (laws) we've subsequently discovered are best captured by "objects" with different ontological boundaries.

What's important to see, however, is that the *computational difference* between our first set of differential equations (ones with quantifier domains of spheres connected by springs) and our second set of differential equations (domains of centers of mass and reduced masses) isn't in any way metaphysically significant. It isn't, after all, that we have any reason to think that the "explanation" for why the second set of differential equations are easily

---

[11] Although their properties are often drastically changed for theoretical purposes: their boundary properties and their internal topological structure, for example. See Malvern (1969).
[12] E.g., "particle fields."
[13] See Azzouni (2000, part II) and Azzouni (2010a, chapter 4) for discussion of gross regularities and gross correlational regularities.

solved and the first set isn't is because what's "really" going on is that the reduced-mass point and the center-of-mass point are moving independently of each other, and that their (actual!) motions explain the otherwise computationally intractable movements of the spheres connected by a spring.

The previous paragraphs may make it sound like "making up" objects by changing object boundaries emerges only at the cutting edge of science—that ontological boundary shifting only arises when science changes the focus on what's studied. No. What the differential equation example *actually* shows is that we often project objects into the world using descriptions. We imagine, experience, or define objects as "those things"—*whatever they are*—that do such-and-such, or have such-and-such properties; and we individuate them by means of these properties as well. This practice of descriptively projecting objects is—nearly enough—independent of how we're otherwise prone to involuntarily experience objects by our senses. Except for the sketchy discussion in the rest of this chapter, this important aspect of our practice of object projection is a massive topic for future work.

9.4 Real Explanations and Pseudo-Explanations

Some positions—like object projectivism—press the idea that some but not all of the structure (to use a neutral word) that we take the world to have isn't there. Any position like this must provide a general method of *bifurcating* explanatory demands. Some explanatory demands (it must be claimed) are spurious and some aren't. I rush to add that *explanation* is a notoriously murky and difficult subject (I intend—someday—to write a book about it). So what I say about explanation here must be somewhat promissory. In any case, the discussion is restricted to what's directly relevant to the metaphysics of object projectivism.

In section 9.2, I showed that inductively establishing scientific laws doesn't require worldly ontological boundaries to explain (to the extent this *can* be explained) why such laws have certain virtues. Even though certain object borders, and not others, may be optimal (or required) for stating such laws (or for discovering such laws are true), this doesn't show that those borders are worldly.

Other explanatory demands, however, aren't *genuine*. I'm speaking specifically of demands that arise entirely from the presupposition that projected ontological structure is worldly. Unlike the previous explanatory demands (which must be met without invoking the projected ontological structure as real), these should be rejected altogether.

Here's an illustration. Koslicki (2003, 126) criticizes Sider's (2001) ontological "world" for allowing certain objects to exist "in the same sturdy sense of 'existence', even though nothing about them is worth paying attention to." She mentions Lewis's "trout-turkey," a temporally complex object "which fuses the earlier years of a trout with the later years of a turkey." Koslicki (2003, 126–27) writes:

> Now consider the "middle" portions of this worm: there will be a place somewhere in the middle of this worm where the last trout-stage borders directly on the first turkey-stage. But why is it that this trout-stage is followed directly by a turkey-stage? In other words, why is this object, which has been spending its time swimming through rivers and lakes, suddenly, in the matter of a single instant, turning into something which walks on land on two feet and can fly? ... The question is: what are the last trout-stage and the first turkey-stage doing together right next to each other in one and the same worm? This fact has no interesting explanation, causal or otherwise, on Sider's account. They exist right next to each other in the same worm because it is exceedingly easy, in Sider's world, to satisfy the constraints placed on what it means to be an object.... [M]iracles of a certain sort do constantly happen in Sider's world, only the worms which seem to involve generation *ex nihilo* are not the ones to which we normally pay attention. If we consider just the trout-turkey worm in isolation, the last trout-stage in no way "sets the stage" in such a way that, barring supernatural interference and the like, the first turkey-stage cannot help but come into existence.[14]

The only thing that makes this a damning criticism of Sider's world is the worldly realism about ontological borders Sider and Koslicki share. Koslicki's point is that if ontological borders are real, then there must be good reasons for where they occur. How she presses this point presupposes a denial of metaphysical primitivism: she presupposes that facts about causation and the like are needed to explain the locations of worldly ontological borders. But the object projectivist needn't disagree with this.

Instead, the object projectivist can reject Koslicki's explanatory demand because it presupposes worldly ontological borders to begin with.[15] If ontological

---

[14] A small point can be papered over that won't affect Koslicki's objection: there needn't be a *last* trout-stage preceding the first turkey-stage, or a *first* turkey-stage bordering on the last trout-stage. This depends on the purported internal topological structure of the trout-turkey.

[15] This is made clear by Koslicki's concluding paragraph (29): "Sider's account has the consequence that there is really not much of interest that a *strictly ontological theory* can say about the persistence and nature of the familiar concrete objects of common sense.... Thus, the character of the whole enterprise in which we are engaged as metaphysicians has really shifted, as a result of Sider's position, in a way which we should resist, if we want to preserve the genuinely ontological character of certain central metaphysical questions" (italics mine).

borders are worldly, we can *legitimately* wonder why objects go in and out of existence, or change, when they do. Apart from this being something we need to discover where-and-when facts about, we'll additionally demand *explanations*. If they are projections, though, then the "some borders are miracles" puzzle Koslicki poses is a pseudo-puzzle in need of no explanation whatsoever.

9.5 The Principle of Indiscernibles

Important topics in metaphysics—that show up any introductory course in metaphysics—are these laws:

For all P, if $a = b$, then $Pa \equiv Pb$.

and

If for all P, $Pa \equiv Pb$, then $a = b$ follows.

Call the first "the indiscernibility of identicals"; call the second "Leibniz's law" (there are different nomenclatural traditions that clash over this language). Tangled philosophical issues arise for both, depending on what P is supposed to stand in for (e.g., properties, relations . . .), or instead predicates of various sorts (more or less inclusive ones, e.g., modal, extensional, or . . .). The first law seems to be violated by "opaque contexts," for example; the second has issues with relations (as opposed to properties) as well as issues about modal or dispositional properties. And (of course), bedeviling any philosophical analysis of these "laws" are the various and sundry conflicting metaphysical intuitions about particular versions of them.[16] I'll sometimes refer to both laws, in what follows, with the phrase "the L-laws."

Given object projectivism, we aren't going to discover which (refined) versions of these laws *actually* apply to worldly objects, and which don't. These laws, instead, are helpful guides to analyzing our many and complex practices of object projection. The primary insight I'll be developing in this chapter is that we often use these laws to design "objects": those items deemed to have such-and-such "properties."

---

[16] Citing literature is pretty hopeless because there is so much. I can at least mention Black (1952) and Kripke (1980). But the novice should go to the online *Stanford Encyclopedia of Philosophy* and look up "Leibniz's law" and "the indiscernibility of identicals."

An important qualification: "design" has to be understood appropriately. It isn't that we (collectively or individually) consciously project objects (and object boundaries). We don't manage this even when we're self-consciously engaged in talking about what we recognize to be *fictions* (when we know, for example, we're making up stories). For even in those cases, where our myth-making practices are most consciously undertaken, involuntary psychological processes nonetheless force us to think of our made-up fictional entities in "object-directed" ways. That is, the various ways we project *objects* are involuntary in the more general sense that our experience of the world induces thinking of objects in an automatic fashion that we're barely conscious of. This is the case even when object projection is arising not from psychological experience but instead from linguistic cues.

The point just made bears on a natural question. Is object projectivism compatible with our "ordinary" (non-philosophical) view of objects? An argument for compatibility is that the non-philosopher's notion of "object" is lightweight—metaphysically speaking. The non-philosopher, so this argument goes, sometimes recognizes that the "objects" being singled out aren't genuine. Against this is that (as discussed in chapters 2 and 7) non-philosophers take ontological borders seriously. Although they deny shrees exist, they take as completely genuine the ontological borders between lamps and the tables they're on, between people (when they're shaking hands), or between billiard balls being knocked about on a pool table. It's hard to see in what sense, therefore, they're supposed to nevertheless think these items are non-genuine, either in their being real or in their having exactly the ontological borders they are *seen* to have.

The aim of the rest of this chapter isn't to *exhaustively* characterize how we "manufacture" objects. It's to indicate some of the ways we do it, and to sketch how a philosophical approach to object borders is far more tractable when borders are approached as projections instead of as induced by metaphysical worldly facts that we need to discover. (So, we're to see, e.g., issues of "constitution" as studies in how we experience and talk, and not as studies of the mechanisms that genuinely make some items into an object in addition to those items that "compose" it.) Despite my use of "object," "property," and "relation" in what follows, only feature metaphysics is presupposed. To say, for example, that certain properties and relations are worldly only means that certain features are co-occurring, and the co-occurring spatial and temporal features are coordinates.

9.6 Creating Abstracta Out of Nothing (Ex Nihilo) in Mathematics

We regularly create nothing out of nothing. One aim of this section is to indicate the role of the L-laws in non-referring *language*. But the usual warnings should be stressed about talk of "the creation" of nonexistent objects. A mathematician creating abstracta isn't like a potter creating a vase because there is something (clay) the potter shapes into a statue in a straightforward sense of the word "shape." It's confused to claim something similar occurs with abstracta—that (say) we "shape" concepts into new ones. No doubt mathematical invention involves the manipulation, modification, and evolution of concepts—both mathematical and non-mathematical. But concepts aren't the relata of mathematical terms. The concept of "1" isn't 1. On the nominalist view taken here, "1" doesn't refer at all. So when I describe mathematicians as "inventing" new mathematical objects, this must be recognized for the sheer metaphor it is; to speak of mathematical objects being invented is to (strictly) speak falsely. If there are no such objects, then *they* cannot be invented.

Why not avoid these metaphors altogether, especially in philosophical contexts where they so easily mislead? One reason not to is that, ultimately, any *systematic* attempt is hopeless. Sentences with non-referring terms are indispensable. We must accept that there are no ontological implications to our saying true things "about" nonexistent objects and attributing properties to them. (Recall the discussion of this in chapter 4.) This warning in place, recall the idealized picture of mathematics in section 4.5. This idealization in terms of explicit axiom systems won't mislead here, and so I'll use it again. In brief, inventing mathematical abstracta is stipulating the properties of a collection of objects axiomatically.

One mark of the *imaginary* nature of mathematical abstracta (that they're "made up") is that systematic identity questions about them are *always* left open. This is because when mathematical objects are characterized, necessary and sufficient conditions are restricted to the context of a *subclass* of other mathematical objects. For example, the real numbers are linearly ordered, and so a neat "identity condition" for them in terms of other real numbers is possible: A real number F is a real number G if and only if $F \leq G$ and $F \geq G$. This formulation, of course, doesn't say whether a *real number* F is identical to one or another particular *set* G. As Benacerraf (1965) makes clear, there are many good answers to *that* question. Talk of "adequate" necessary and sufficient conditions in the case of mathematics is misleading if it means such conditions specify identity conditions with respect to *all* mathematical objects—let alone anything else. This is why it doesn't violate mathematical practice to suggest that mathematical entities *actually are* physical entities or social objects of some sort—as some do.

That distinctions between mathematical entities are axiomatically stipulated piecemeal is widely exploited in twentieth- and twenty-first-century mathematics.[17] The examples most philosophers know best are the already mentioned identifications of numbers with sets. It doesn't matter to mathematicians that these identifications apparently give numbers properties they weren't seen as having before, because those properties and relations aren't relevant to the number-theoretic theorems preserved by the identifications. Although different subset relations among numbers are induced, and they similarly gain other mathematical properties depending on what mathematical object they are identified with—this is always ignored.

Perhaps anyone other than a deflationary nominalist faces metaphysical quandaries and hard decisions because of this practice. The deflationary nominalist (joining forces with formalists)[18] explains everything I've just described in terms of benefits for mathematical theorem-proving, and without invoking metaphysics. Metaphysicians, on the other hand, who endow mathematical abstracta with one or another form of reality, notoriously face unpleasant (and philosophically irresolvable) problems. They can adopt the view that mathematical objects really do have the properties in question (ones nothing in mathematical practice itself dictates they have), or they can instead adopt a version of structuralism—a view that mathematical objects are intrinsically incomplete in some way.[19]

I won't rehearse this further—in particular, I won't now oppose these substantial metaphysical views with arguments for nominalism. My purpose, instead, has been only to note that the application of the L-laws to fictions doesn't *require* identity-condition completeness; characterizations of these objects can remain open to (or indifferent about) all sorts of properties and relations—whether or not these objects have them or not. It can similarly remain open about whether these objects—described in such-and-such a way—are the same as those objects (described in some different way).

The last point to make is that our ways of leaving the properties/relations of mathematical abstracta open-ended doesn't just enable the application

---

[17] The technique is ubiquitous because it neatly brings mathematical theories to bear on one another. Map a certain group structure into the topological transformations on a space, and many results about those transformations are immediately provable by group theory alone.

[18] See Azzouni (1994) for one way to manage this marriage.

[19] See Resnik (1997) for one attempt at this.

of mathematical theories to other mathematical theories. It also enables empirical applications of mathematics by the identification of a domain of phenomena with mathematical objects—so that we can then treat those phenomena as obeying mathematical theorems as well as additional physical laws/regularities. An example of this is the reconstrual of physical objects (and the spaces they reside in) in terms of manifolds of various sorts.[20]

9.7 Creating Artifacts Out of Something Else by Specifying the Set of Properties and Relations They Are to Have

Our mathematical practice with manufactured abstracta is a clean case because relations and properties are made up (along with the objects). The other cases I'll discuss in the rest of this chapter aren't like this because there are important interactions with real features that must be accommodated.

I'll begin with a general description. We first indicate—usually roughly—a relevant set S of relations and properties that correspond to features. Then we craft "objects" by imposing the L-laws on those "objects" in relation to S. We're often quite conscious (or can easily be made conscious) that the chosen properties and relations are a subset of the properties and relations that we take as operative in the domain we're crafting a group of objects in terms of. It's in these cases that we most naturally describe (or experience) the crafted objects as "artifacts." It's also in those cases that we're most conscious (or can be made conscious) that we're ignoring or not focusing on *all* the properties and relations that these objects (often) possess.

However (and I'll illustrate this later), if we mistakenly adopt a worldly-objects perspective toward the items that have been crafted in terms of the set S, we'll face irresolvable philosophical puzzles because the relevant set S isn't the *entire* set of relations and properties that such items either do exhibit or can—in principle—exhibit. Some failures of bivalence, in particular, arise directly from doing this. One point I want to stress is that many of the intuitions that philosophers reach for when grappling over philosophical questions about L-laws can also be recognized to arise directly from these object-crafting practices. (I'll indicate these points when relevant.)

Consider chess. This is a game that's—often but perhaps not always—physically embodied: a material board and chess pieces. (I qualify "embodied" because many people play chess "in their heads," and doing so perhaps

---

[20] See Azzouni (2004a, chapters 8 and 9), and Azzouni and Bueno (forthcoming).

isn't to physically embody the game in the sense I have in mind.) These (physical) items are "conventionally stipulated" in some of their properties. Chess pieces move only in certain ways, and not others: they have certain stipulated "powers." Furthermore, their possible positions on the board are similarly stipulated. They're always on specific squares, and can only move to other specific squares. They're never on the borders of two squares (even if it looks like this).

This is similar to the macro-/micro-discs case of chapter 8—how a pattern at a certain ontological focus is identified by excluding some of what's real. A chess game is a macro-pattern (a series of events in space) extracted from a larger pattern—a larger pattern that in this case we're completely aware of—by ignoring otherwise real aspects of that larger pattern, as well as "empty space." Excluded additionally are many things that happen during chess games—for example, that a piece is knocked aside by accident and then put back where it was, that different amounts of time occur between moves, that fingers are used to move pieces, and so on. None of these are "essential" to the game.

Chess pieces, nevertheless, are experienced as a type of object. Those of us familiar with chess from a young age involuntarily see certain items as chess pieces—especially if they're arranged on a board or traditionally shaped. Other items—Star Wars figures, for example, or irregularly jagged pieces of granite—are items we have to be told are chess pieces; we won't otherwise *recognize* this.

We can give *definitions* of chess pieces—for example, a pawn is a physical item (used in a game) with such-and-such *powers*. Chess pieces even within a game aren't (fully) individuated by definitions of this sort, of course: their individuation conditions are inherited from their physical instantiations. That is to say, when we distinguish chess pieces from one another, we do so by presupposing the individuation relations that carved physical objects already have.[21] Like all artifacts, actually, chess pieces are individuated in terms of properties and relations singled out from the full set of properties and relations those objects have. In particular, chess pieces are required to

---

[21] Well, not exactly. The individuation conditions of carved objects raise standard philosophical problems of the statue/clay sort. I discuss this momentarily. Individuation conditions also get a little weird when two people play chess in their heads: certain questions don't make sense. Are these chess pieces the same ones they used when they were playing (the same game of) chess in their heads yesterday? Notice, however, that the pieces (pawns for example) being "used" in a mental game of chess are individuated from one another for the purposes of the game. They are, perhaps, individuated by their historical (mental) trajectories starting from their original "positions" in the game.

retain their shapes: metal ones that have been melted and reshaped into something else (metal bars for prisons, say) are no longer chess pieces.

This raises a set of famous problems in the metaphysics of composition.[22] Goliath is a statue made from a lump of clay; call it "Lump." In our world, Lump precedes Goliath because (let's say) there is a time when Lump exists but Goliath doesn't yet exist. There are, however, (nearby) possible worlds in which Lump continues to exist although Goliath doesn't; there are also possible worlds, perhaps, in which Goliath continues to exist although Lump doesn't; and there are further away possible worlds in which Goliath exists before Lump does. In our world (let's say) the artisan crushes Goliath back into a lump of clay: Goliath is gone, Lump remains.

Goliath and Lump can have different temporal contours (in our world)—perhaps they can have different spatial contours. They certainly seem to have different modal profiles. Is this a problem? The literature contains conflicting views that variously invoke temporal parts, constitution or composition relations, denials or affirmations of the identity (or nonidentity) of Goliath and Lump, and differences in non-categorical (although not categorical) properties.

My purpose in revisiting this complex of problems is narrower. There are no worldly ontological boundaries. Therefore, to acknowledge a way of speaking that distinguishes Goliath and Lump as objects isn't to give rise to the requirement that these objects be characterized as metaphysically distinctive.[23] Left are only these concerns: Are ordinary ways of speaking of Goliath and Lump as (distinct) objects consistent? In particular, are they consistent with other ways we speak? Some of the metaphysical issues of the literature may remain in mutated form after object metaphysics is recast as feature metaphysics. Reassurance by object projectivists that these don't pose difficulties is therefore required.

For example, some philosophers assert that no two objects can exist at the same time in the same place;[24] some philosophers assert further that this is a law of physics—although it's not. Presupposed, perhaps, by these

---

[22] See Wasserman (2015) for a survey of some of this (gigantic) literature, and specifically a classification of some of philosophical responses to these problems.

[23] Distinguishing Goliath and Lump doesn't require, say, characterizing an irreflexive, asymmetric constitution relation that portions of clay have to statues, as Thomson (1998) and so many others attempt. The object projectivist finds Wasserman's (2004, 704–05) "deflationary view of constitution" appealing: "there is no constitution, only coincidence." This is not to say, of course, that the object-border projectivism that the object projectivist uses to deduce a deflationary view of constitution as a corollary, is held by Wasserman.

[24] Wiggins (1967, 90) writes: "It is a truism, frequently called in evidence and confidently relied upon in philosophy that two things cannot be in the same place at the same time."

philosophers is that anything that's an object must be described in the language of physics (whatever language *that is*, exactly). When put this way, the issue translates (for the projectivist) into a claim about the potential clash between two kinds of discourse: ordinary commonsense discourse and the rarified discourse of scientific physics.

However: to talk of Lump and Goliath as two distinct objects, and as two distinct objects that (for a time) overlap in space, *doesn't* endanger the compatibility of ordinary talk with scientific talk. If we describe Goliath as an object (which we surely do) and if we describe the clay as an object (which we can, but is artificial), there's nothing untoward or peculiar about this talk or about these objects overlapping. This is a perfectly common way of talking about what's in the world, it's a perfectly common way to *experience* what's in the world, and it's internally consistent as well as not violating physical laws, or physical assumptions, of any sort.

In chapter 8, I described the exclusionary intuitions about objects induced by close-up and zoom-back visual scenarios. We seem unable to experience objects and their parts *simultaneously* as objects. But these intuitions shouldn't be turned into general conditions on object projection (let alone metaphysical principles) because it's only *particular* context-specific (visual) cues that generate them. In other circumstances, when we simultaneously talk, for example, about regiments and the solders of those regiments, or about "transformer" toys that are vehicles that can be snapped apart into pieces (and reassembled—using all the same pieces) into a humanoid-shaped robot or something else, we have no trouble thinking of different objects as simultaneously occupying the same time and place.[25]

It may be thought that formalizing or regimenting these ways of talking of overlapping objects faces problems. A standard assumption in formal

---

[25] Object-experience intuitions are compartmentalized. They're sensitive to *very* subtle contextual cues. Consider some cartoon scenarios. An artisan makes clay into a statue. She's *created* a statue (this is the intuition). Another artisan weaves a single long straw into a hammock. In the same way as with the statue, we experience this as the creation of a *hammock*. Imagine instead a long slender snake with the same visual (physical) contours as the straw (except, maybe, for a small chunk of snake head at one end—little beady eyes and some fangs sticking out of a small smirking mouth). The unsuspecting artisan weaves this *snake* into a hammock! Has she created a *hammock*? Not everyone will experience the scenario that way. Imagine a cartoon in which a snake has been so weaved into a hammock, or imagine instead that it weaves itself into a hammock to catch unsuspecting nappers. Many watching this cartoon will experience not a hammock but a snake *disguised* as a hammock—this will be so even if the snake's visual contours are identical to those of a long straw. Suppose that the snake breathes a little or flexes itself, and the "hammock" moves subtly in a way an actual hammock would never move. (But the squirrel stretching out for a nap in the hammock, alas, doesn't notice this. . . .) To construct these cases, I've perversely warped an example from van Inwagen (1990, 126, 127).

mereology, after all, is that parthood is both reflexive and anti-symmetric. This assumption, when coupled with the additional standard assumption that any object is a part of itself, leads to the result that two objects that overlap in both time and space are identical. The solution to this conundrum is obvious: deny the second standard assumption that any object is a part of itself. Some may worry that the resulting family of mereological systems is awkward. *So what?* If non-awkward mereological systems don't apply to our ordinary ways of speaking, this doesn't show that our ordinary ways of talking are inconsistent; it doesn't even show that those ways of talking are troubled. Any mereological system, after all, is only a branch of (pure) mathematics. Nothing *requires* a branch of pure mathematics to be applicable to an empirical domain; nothing requires a branch of pure mathematics that's particularly simple in its principles to be applicable to an empirical domain.

It may be thought the threat looms of numerous objects with the same modal, spatial, and temporal contours. If *two* material objects exist in the same time and space (and are composed of the same stuff), what stops *dozens* of objects in the same time and space (and composed of the same stuff)? Only metaphysicians committed to worldly object boundaries face this problem. Only these metaphysicians face the question: What is it *about the world* that allows only two objects to be in the same place during the same time (and composed of the same material) but not seventeen?

The object projectivist has a tamer problem: she must explain why we talk of (or experience) two objects but not seventeen. This question is answered in terms of why we find it valuable (for example) to distinguish a created artifact from the object/stuff we've created it from, and why we don't find it valuable (if we don't) to talk about other "objects" that we would have spoken of instead (given, that is, an alternative evolutionary or cultural history). For example, it could have been (although for us it isn't) that just as material *can* compose a statue if and only if it possesses certain properties, that same statue could compose an "Italifact" if and only if it's owned by an Italian. (An Italifact comes into existence when an Italian citizen gains ownership of it, and goes out of existence as soon as Italian ownership ceases.) In this case, *three* sorts of objects can overlap in time and space, and not just two.

It may be thought that allowing "non-physical" objects like Goliath to be spoken of and to have distinct ontological boundaries from the clay making them up creates problems for either the view that "everything is physical", or less dramatically, for the potential application of physical laws to everything there is.[26] It doesn't. Drawing ontological boundaries in crisscrossing

---

[26] Gibbard (1975, section II) raises this issue.

ways doesn't cause problems for the sciences as long as (i) no metaphysical assumptions are entertained because of the practice and (ii) the crisscrossing doesn't induce inconsistency.

9.8 Different Modal Profiles and the Manufacturing of Relations and Properties in Order to Satisfy L-Laws

Let's imagine, as Gibbard (1975) does, that Lump and Goliath share all their worldly properties and relations. Both the statue and the lump of clay are brought into existence when the bottom half of a statue is joined with the upper half of a statue so that Lump (the *whole* lump of clay) and Goliath (the *whole* statue) begin to exist at the same time; their existence ends at some subsequent same time, and they are both brought into being by an artist who has *exactly* the same intentions about both of them.[27] If these two objects differ because they differ in at least one of their properties or in their relations to other objects, there must be one or another non-categorical property or relation (to others) that they differ in. But these differing non-categorical properties or relations (as some philosophers sometimes put it) can't be *grounded* in their categorical differences. Here's how that issue arises. Start with the question: Must we identify these objects because they agree on all the properties and relations they *manifest*? Well, no—and here I'm describing a resource the non-philosopher is as likely to invoke as the philosopher is. Lump and Goliath are different objects because their spatial and temporal contours *could have been* different from the way they actually are: Lump *could have* survived Goliath's demise or vice versa.

Are there, therefore, *modal* properties that these objects differ on? Well, perhaps, but we often describe their differences in ways that aren't *obviously* modal: Goliath is fragile and Lump *isn't*. Well, okay, but isn't fragility a disposition, and therefore a modal property? Let's say it is. Still, we can easily wonder: What sort of properties are modal properties? And we can easily wonder: Do modal properties correspond to *features*?

In certain scientific contexts, we *like* the idea that the propensities or the dispositions of things are grounded in categorical (or manifest) properties of those things. An example: We like the idea that the solubility of sugar—a disposition that sugar exhibits, *all things being equal*, whenever sugar is

---

[27] This condition is always stated—and it's essential to making the example pose the philosophical issues it poses; but it's hard to believe it's possible. Nevertheless, along with everyone else (in this literature), I'll pretend it *is* possible—to make the example work.

dissolved in tea—is due to properties that sugar molecules actually manifest (that they structurally possess). But grounding the dispositions of objects (or substances like sugar) in substructural (or other) categorical properties that those things or substances (or their parts) exhibit only goes so far. Quarks and electrons, for example, have propensities that presumably can't be grounded in substructural properties that quarks and electrons exhibit. Many quarks, we think, would have done thus-and-so things under such-and-so circumstances. These *propensities* of quarks and electrons are ones those specific quarks and electrons never exhibit; these propensities can't be grounded in anything actual.[28]

In any case, this won't help with Goliath and Lump. They overlap completely in space and time, so it seems that whatever categorical properties Goliath (or whatever is in Goliath) exhibits, Lump (or whatever is in Lump) exhibits as well.

What is the intuitive basis for our impression that Goliath and Lump differ in at least one non-categorical property or relation? One thing, surely, is the close resemblance Goliath/Lump has to other objects. Goliath-like objects that overlap with Lump-like objects break regularly and deviate in their temporal/spatial contours from the Lump-like objects they (for a time) overlap with. This suggests invoking a (higher-order categorical) relation that Goliath-like objects share with all and only other Goliath-like objects, and a correspondingly different higher-order categorical relation that Lump-like objects share with all and only other Lump-like objects. Such a higher-order relation is exhibited by all and only such objects, and it therefore can provide the categorical relation that (on some views) is required for grounding the differing modal properties that Goliath and Lump exhibit in this world.

Will this work? Suppose someone says: "Wait a minute. *Lump*, by virtue of its overlap with Goliath, bears the higher-order relation to all the other Goliath-like objects *too*. So this doesn't appropriately distinguish Goliath from Lump." "You are begging the question against the Goliath/Lump distinguisher," we can respond. That proponent can assume that Goliath and Lump are distinct, and only *then* undertake the burden of finding a categorical

---

[28] Perhaps science will progress, and substructural properties for quarks and electrons will emerge. Regress looms. At any stage in scientific progress, there will always be items with categorically ungrounded propensities. We might (metaphysically) posit an infinite descent of the following sort: all propensities (in the infinite fullness of time) will be grounded categorically. But why assume this? One motivation is a kind of methodological intuition that all propensities *must be* grounded categorically. Everything in the world that does happen, or can happen, must be explicable in terms of properties that things (categorically) have. But this seems to be an entirely empirical matter—not something to be *argued* for.

property (or relation) that one of these objects—but not the other—bears to other objects. And these just-invoked higher-order relations are exactly what are needed for this.

Well, okay (although there's something really *annoying* about this response), but still—our world *could be* poor in the needed additional Goliath-like objects. Suppose, that is, that there are *no other* objects that either Goliath or Lump respectively resemble in the needed way. (Oddly—and sadly—there are no other statues in the world, no other lumps of clay; more dramatically, there are no other artifacts of any sort.) Then there are no higher-order relations exhibited by all and only such objects, ones that suffice to allow that there is at least one relation that the actual Goliath and Lump exhibit a difference with respect to.

Never mind how we might as a result fail to know (in this empty-ish world) that Goliath could have failed to survive Lump, or vice versa. They are still different objects, in this case, because they differ (so one thinks) in their modal properties, a difference (in this world) that can't be grounded in anything categorical.

Let's grant this, and let's call this issue *the grounding objection*.[29] Does this objection pose a problem for the object projectivist? As it's normally posed, the grounding objection is a metaphysical constraint on properties and relations of objects: non-categorical (dispositional and modal) properties and relations of objects must be grounded in their categorical (manifest) properties and relations. For the object projectivist, the grounding objection must be recalibrated into the following demand: no properties or relations can be invoked unless they correspond to actual features.

But why? Why can't the object projectivist invoke the acceptability of *manufacturing properties and relations*? Why, that is, can't the object projectivist assert that a practice—that we've already seen at work in section 9.5 with respect to abstracta—is also at work here? After all, as we saw, manufactured along with abstracta are relations and properties attributed to those abstracta. Both objects *and* relations and properties attributed to those objects are manufactured in this case; the whole package is *made up*.

It may be protested that Lump and Goliath aren't made up the way *abstracta* are. Indeed, at the beginning of section 9.6, thinking of the creation of abstracta as similar to the creation of statues was criticized as confused. Response: Okay, it's true there is this important difference in the two cases. Lump/Goliath is a locale of the world that exhibits feature. This isn't

---

[29] As Wasserman (2015, 7) does. For discussion, see further references from Wasserman's article.

true of the number 2. *Nevertheless*, we can still make up a property that prevents Leibniz's law from being violated by Lump and Goliath. This posited property (e.g., fragility) is "made up" in the sense that it doesn't correspond to a feature. Nevertheless, we distinguish Lump and Goliath by means of that made-up property that we take one to have but not the other.

First worry about this move: doesn't it resurrect metaphysical primitivism? To invoke a relational/propertied difference that doesn't correspond to features in order to distinguish two objects certainly sounds like an "ontological border" is being drawn between two objects that isn't (really) being underwritten by anything actual. The quick answer is no. The claim being made *isn't* that there *are* worldly ontological borders that aren't (simultaneously) features corresponding to relational or propertied differences. The claim, instead, is that we (sometimes) make up properties and relations, and attribute them to (projected) objects that otherwise couldn't be described as differing in their properties and relations. Metaphysical primitivism is a claim about worldly ontological borders. This is an issue about *projected* object borders.

The second worry about this move: describing these properties—fragility, in particular—as "made up" looks *wrong*. There are (powerful) intuitions that Goliath and Lump really *do* differ insofar as Goliath *is* fragile and Lump *isn't*. And this difference *is* modal: under certain possible circumstances Goliath *will* cease to exist although Lump won't. To describe this difference as "made up"—to say that a difference in properties is *manufactured* to codify this difference—doesn't seem to do justice to the *metaphysics*. There is a genuine metaphysical distinction to be made here, one overlooked by talk of "manufacturing properties and relations": how the world *would have* gone under certain circumstances. Here's another way to put it: there is a truth-maker fact involved here, the fragility of Goliath versus the sturdiness of Lump. That difference *isn't* made up; so talk of manufacturing properties and relations is misleading.

At work here is the implicit role of a specific grounding requirement: that Goliath and Lump could have diverged in their spatiotemporal trajectories must be because of something categorical about *them*—some structural difference, say, between them. But, further, it's clear what those structural facts are; Lump's continued existence is less sensitive to rearrangements of its parts than Goliath's is. Put another way: Goliath is more sensitive to entropy than Lump. It's not that Goliath is more organized than Lump (they're, after all, equally organized). It's that Goliath won't survive subpersonal rearrangements that Lump *will* survive.[30]

---

[30] And vice versa: Lump won't survive loss of bits that Goliath will survive (see Thomson 1998 or Wasserman 2004).

This difference can be used to explicate why Lump bears a different higher-order relation to its fellow Lumps than Goliath, who (in turn) bears a narrower higher-order relation to its fellow Goliaths. Still, this won't supply differing categorical higher-order relations in worlds without fellow Goliaths or Lumps. So we're again forced to acknowledge what must be described as a *modal* difference between them.

A kind of "conventionalist" reconstrual of this "modal difference" is available, though.[31] The modal difference between Goliath and Lump can be explained away not as a metaphysical difference of some sort between Goliath and Lump but instead as due to how we stipulate (in some extended sense of "stipulate") differences between when we apply "statue" and when we apply "lump"—and (therefore) in particular, "Goliath" and "Lump." We understand these words so that the set of arrangements of materials that "statue" is to apply to is much smaller (and contained in) sets of arrangements of materials that we call "lumps." The view is conventionalist because it focuses on the application of the *terms* "statue" and "clay" (and so, derivatively, of "Goliath" and "Lump"). It doesn't turn, that is, on what's in the world that "statue" and "lump" apply to; it turns on the differing properties of the words "statue" and "lump."

Modality, of course, deserves an extended analysis. I'm not trying to do that. Apart from the suggestion made in the last paragraph, I won't further address the important question about whether modal intuitions about Goliath and Lump reveal legitimate metaphysical demands that need to be satisfied—by, say, invoking the metaphysics of possibility in some rather strong sense (i.e., the reality of possible worlds containing alternative feature presentations).

What I need to do instead is indicate how this issue fully survives a redescription that doesn't presuppose it's about finding facts that distinguish the worldly *objects* Lump from Goliath—*even in possible worlds*. If a redescription is possible, then the object projectivist can be neutral about the outcome of an analysis of modality. In particular, the object projectivist needn't sign on to the conventionalist story I gave in the last paragraph about Goliath and Lump. Here's how the object projectivist can be a realist about possible worlds. What remains of the differences between Goliath and Lump (after

---

[31] I'm sympathetic to—in a broad way—the "conventionalist" approach to modality offered by Sidelle (1989). Exactly how my own approach to modality will differ from his goes far beyond what can be discussed in this book, although a number of relevant differences will be obvious to that reader who has read both Sidelle (1989) and this book.

discarding questions about how the *objects* Goliath and Lump could differ) is this: we recognize that the trajectory of feature over time and space *could have* been different.

Object projectivism, thus, is indifferent between grounding genuine possibility metaphysically in what's actual and (alternatively) grounding it in terms of *possible worlds*. A metaphysically rich worldview that recognizes possible worlds need no more accept the cogency of *other-worldly* ontological boundaries than it need accept the cogency of worldly ones or the cogency of trans-worldly questions about object identity or feature identity. There are issues—of course—about how we talk (or should talk), or about how we experience objects when raising issues about how things *might have gone*. And, similarly, there are questions about our talking practices of identifying (or not identifying) objects across possible worlds (as it's put). But this requires other-worldly object boundaries no more than it requires worldly ones.

9.9 Some Concluding Remarks

The conditions for features being worldly are weak in one sense: we can treat a feature pattern as exhibited in the world even if to do so isn't to take account of *everything* that's so featured. (Recall the discussion of this in section 8.8.) The modal considerations raised in the last section reveal the possibility that we attribute properties and relations to objects that don't correspond to features even in this weak sense. There are other cases, too, where it's (perhaps) more reasonable to say that we're attributing manufactured properties and relations to what's real, rather than claiming instead that (somehow) the properties and relations so attributed correspond to features. Worldly abstracta—such as borders—are one clear example because even the acceptance of the reality of Euclidean (or some other kind of) space isn't, I've argued, to accept the reality of Euclidean points or lines. I've also indicated the existence of such cases in this chapter while discussing games—specifically chess. Other important cases, which I must delay discussion of until a future occasion, are the many items studied in social ontology—groups, institutions of various sorts, cities, countries, and so on.

In any case, if there are manufactured properties and relations (properties and relations that don't correspond to features exhibited by the world), the motivation for such manufacturing is—at least in part—an adherence to L-laws. If we must speak of two objects, this is usually because we need distinct topics distinguished by relations and/or properties. This motive is also at work when we're talking about what doesn't exist at all, for example, in mathematics. We don't introduce a mathematical theory of a kind of abstracta unless we also take them to be (in principle) distinguishable from other kinds of abstracta. But an adherence to the L-laws looks purely verbal—without even an attempt to generate predicational/relational content—in at least one case: with respect to *some* of our talk of entities when telling fictional stories.

Consider the story "Sixteen Sisters," which I'll give in full: *Once upon a time there were sixteen sisters. They didn't get along. Things ended badly for all of them. The End.*[32] There are fiction journals that have published stories rather like this one. When we talk *about* the characters in this story, we'll talk about sixteen *distinct* sisters. But there are no properties or relations that distinguish them. In adhering to bivalence when talking about these sisters, of course, we may allude to an indefinite number of facts that we don't know for sure but that we officially assume *could* distinguish these sisters. (For example, we can speculate that the sisters looked different in various ways, that they did different things to undermine one another, certainly that they took up different space during the same time, and so on.) Along with our adherence to bivalence about these sisters comes an adherence to L-laws—as I just indicated.

An interesting question is: *Why* are our practices like this? *Why* do we (psychologically) feel constrained to honor the L-laws? This question has a complex answer, I think. A rough answer, in the right neighborhood, has to do with why it matters to us (evolutionarily speaking) to distinguish objects at all. We need to do this because the resulting chunkings of the world (generally) enable local methods of affecting the world (or maneuvering out of the ways that it can locally affect us)—for example, escaping a predator cat that's chasing us, or hunting down a coconut for dinner. But this requires there being feature that distinguishes local bits from what's around them. Notice this explanation is cognitively deep (I've hardly scratched the surface of how it's supposed to go; how, that is, our experience of objects is shaped by factors like this) but metaphysically shallow. That's exactly how explanations in this domain should be if object projectivism is right.

---

[32] This story was originally published in Azzouni (2010a, 132 n. 50). *Flash fiction*, as the genre is called, flourishes nicely in footnotes.

General Conclusion

Hume's remarks about metaphysics are probably as famous as anything ever gets in philosophy:

> When we run over libraries ... what havoc must we make? If we take in our hand any volume; of divinity or school metaphysics, for instance, let us ask, *Does it contain any abstract reasoning concerning quantity or number?* No. *Does it contain any experimental reasoning concerning matter of fact and existence?* No. Commit it then to the flames: for it can contain nothing but sophistry and illusion.

The particular tool he used to determine which books were to be burnt is one many of us can't take seriously any longer: the exhaustive division of propositions between matters of fact and connections among ideas. Nevertheless, metaphysics has remained an activity viewed with suspicion. As recently as the middle of the last century, it was treated disdainfully by a substantial portion of the best "analytic philosophers."

This is no longer so; but the reasons, I think, aren't obvious. "Analytic philosophy" has been incredibly successful, and in intellectual culture the unpleasant reward for success is balkanization. Contemporary metaphysics and metametaphysics are actively studied by contemporary philosophers in a bewilderingly large number of active subdisciplines, the practitioners of which barely ever cite or read one another. There are, of course, contemporary ontologists and metaontologists who troll in the topics of traditional ontology (composition, identity, the nature of time, etc.), Grounding (or, instead, grounding with a small "g" (Wilson 2014)) the substantial/insubstantial nature of debates about these topics. But in addition there are contemporary practitioners of philosophy of logic—in particular, those worried about truth and reference; there are philosophers of language who busily read off ontological commitments from semantic theories; there are the many subdisciplines in philosophy of science (e.g., philosophers worried about species, or about the metaphysical implications of general relativity, special relativity, various quantum theories, loop theory, string theory, etc.), as well as philosophers of mathematics. Finally there is a large crowd of non-philosophers actively engaged in metaphysics as well. Some of these are physicists in full standing—but there are many others, from other academic disciplines, or from no specific academic discipline at all. Only those freakishly widely read are even going to know about the existence of all this stuff, let alone be able to comment on it successfully or incorporate any insights found there into their own work.[1]

In "analytic philosophy," narrowly construed, balkanization leads to a strange combination of technical, specialized, and sophisticated argument with a concurrent naiveté about otherwise related material. Philosophers, for example, will offer complex arguments about the composition conditions of concreta while at the same time overlooking obvious facts about the logical properties of those conditions, or while making what look like undergraduate-level remarks (or blunders) about, say, induction or scientific practice.

Kant (1783, 121) seems to have predicted (and feared) this state of contemporary metaphysics:

> There will ... be metaphysics in the world at every time, and what is more, in every human being, and especially the reflective ones; metaphysics that each, in the absence of a public standard of measure, will carve out for themselves in their own manner.

I've interpreted his worry about "a public standard" as about the possibility of a failure to acknowledge the best argumentation available in the (various) philosophical literatures. Metaphysics—there is no way around this—requires rigorous *as well as broad* training: and one of the easiest ways not to meet this standard is to have narrow philosophical resources.

---

[1] Carus (2007, 5–6) writes, "[Philosophy] has less importance in the wider world of academic or educated discourse than at any time since the 1920s, and much less than competing forms of general thought or reflection—whether or not these describe themselves explicitly as 'philosophy.'"

No doubt there are complicated sociological reasons for this. But one factor is the rampant (and unprincipled) metaphysics that many non-philosophers—in physics, for example—are engaged in. They don't exactly ignore philosophy, especially contemporary analytic metaphysics; *they aren't aware it's relevant*. In addition, the extreme balkanization of philosophy itself is invisible to many of its practitioners—no doubt because they read narrowly. One is surprised when Sider (2009, 386), for example, talks about sensing a silent majority "watching from the sidelines" current debates among metaontologists.

Perhaps, then, it is no surprise that contemporary analytic metaphysicians usually don't *argue* for their "first principles." Van Inwagen (1990, 36), when speaking against the metaphysical theory Contact, writes:

> It is a basic conviction of mine that this theory is wrong and that its being wrong is in no sense a matter of convention. I cannot prove this thesis, for I know of no propositions more plausible than itself from which it could be derived. I can only say that I shall try to display in this book the fruits of agreeing with me about this and various similar theses. I will content myself for the present by pointing out that if you disagree with me about *Contact*, you face a host of metaphysical problems that I avoid.[2]

He adds:

> Nevertheless, it is not in order to avoid difficulties that I have adopted the position that the coming into contact of two human beings is without metaphysical issue. I have adopted it because it seems to me, on reflection, to be true.

Sider (2009, 385) writes about "contemporary ontologists":

> Their methodology is rather quasi-scientific. They treat competing positions as tentative hypotheses about the world, and assess them with a loose battery of criteria for theory choice. Match with ordinary usage and belief sometimes play a role in this assessment, but typically not a dominant one. . . . Theoretical insight, considerations of simplicity, integration with other domains (for instance science, logic, and philosophy of language), and so on, play important roles.

Close inspection, however, shows this process is only remotely scientific. Contemporary metaphysics is speculative: a system of principles is described and, pretty much like van Inwagen does, one is invited to inspect it for its "fruits."[3]

I've approached this topic area differently. I avoid stating any metaphysical principles at all—neither ones that strike me as "plausible" nor ones I claim to be a priori.[4] Instead, I start (in part I) with quantifiers and other

---

[2] What follows are descriptions of issues like the ones Koslicki (2003) raises against Sider (2001). See my discussion of this in section 9.4.
[3] In particular, there is a lot of infighting over strongly held ("plausible") principles on the basis of mutual recriminatory charges of ad hocness, lack of simplicity, and other problems. This isn't what *successful* science looks like.
[4] Hirsch (2009, 222 n. 3), commenting on the work of contemporary ontologists, and on John Hawthorne's suggestion that such philosophers "do not appeal primarily to a priori arguments," expresses bewilderment over Hawthorne's term "a priori." Hirsch employs charity: "What Hawthorne must mean is that revisionary ontologists often adopt the speculative tone of high-level theorists rather than the tone of philosophers engaged in straightforward conceptual or linguistic analysis."

apparently referential devices, both in natural and in formal languages, because their purported role is so central to contemporary metaphysics and metametaphysics. I aim to establish their actual properties—in particular, that they don't require (or impose) worldly metaphysical tissue of any sort. The primary result disentangles our understanding of these devices from the kinds of metaphysical theses that they traditionally are made to support.

The reason for this focus on language is that a primary—if not *the* primary—tool in metaphysics is one or another version of an indispensability argument, an argument of the form "Ontological commitments to such-and-such entities of such-and-such types are indispensable for language or for theories—either scientific language or scientific theories, or commonsense language or commonsense views." A notable version of such an argument uses Quine's criterion for what a discourse is committed to. But they arise in many disguised ways; it's important to track these down and determine their soundness.

Hunting down (and killing off) indispensability arguments happens a lot in this book. When I consider, in section 9.2, whether numeral persistence is required for induction, I'm evaluating an indispensability argument. When I criticize Cortens, O'Leary-Hawthorne, Strawson, and Turner for assuming that introducing quantifiers into a feature-placing language induces ontology, I'm evaluating an indispensability argument. And, of course, Sider's (2011) grand package of "structure" being required to explain the success of scientific theories is another indispensability argument. I don't want to suggest that philosophers who ply indispensability arguments are deluded about this. But I do think they surprisingly often beg the question against those who oppose these arguments as unsound.

There is no doubt that minimalist metaphysics becomes difficult (if not impossible) if indispensability arguments succeed. But proponents of indispensability arguments face difficulties too—ones similar to difficulties faced by scientists when they recognize that a quantifier posit of one of their theories must be taken to be real. A host of (empirical) questions arises for scientists—in a phrase, what are these things *like*? For philosophers (contrastively), it's just at this stage in the argumentative flow that maneuvers like van Inwagen's make the most sense. We have established the existence of a kind of object or structure (or whatever). What are *they* like? If we've reached this point, why not speculate a little, and see if the objects fit with the speculations? Were object projectivism blocked by an indispensability argument, I would face the same project. There *are* objects with such-and-such contours. Now try to describe the *metaphysical* principles that govern these things.

But what options are there for *arguments* for worldly ontological boundaries? Not many. One set of arguments include the ones I've just discussed: indispensability arguments arising from considerations of language or the nature of explanation or theory virtues. A second set are epistemic arguments like "We have (perceptual/theoretical) *evidence* for worldly boundaries of such-and-such a sort."

I've pursued the topics of this book in the way I have because philosophical arguments are relatively opaque. Let me explain. Debating situations arise in philosophy and in ordinary life that almost never arise in fields (like mathematics) with more transparently checkable reasoning: good-looking arguments for both A and $\neg A$. If this *weren't* the case, the book would have been *much* shorter. As it is, part I establishes that indispensability arguments don't work, and then the master argument of chapters 6 and 7 establishes that no metaphysical sense can be made of ontological borders. Subsidiary arguments have to be addressed, however; otherwise, even if philosophers are convinced of the foregoing, it won't sway them. Thus, it also has to be shown that, contrary to appearance, perception and scientific theorizing don't *show* that there are worldly ontological borders. Notice: if, contrary to my arguments, these practices did show the reality of worldly ontological borders (or if indispensability arguments did work), this coupled with the master argument would put us in an unhappy situation. Established would have been that our interaction with the world presupposes a commitment to a metaphysical "we know not what," a required "thing in itself" that we can know nothing about.

Most people *are* wrong about the metaphysics of our world. They take ontological borders to be worldly—thus the acceptance of trees and the rejection of shrees. More generally, our experience of the world has the projection of object borders built into it, in a sense that I've tried to explain. But these misapprehensions that there are such object borders are *intellectually* excisable. We're not cognitively trapped in a false metaphysics; we can *think* ourselves past this. (We can, anyway, if what I've argued in this book is right.)

One may worry that feature metaphysics is hard to understand.[5] I don't think so. That it's *unfamiliar* is surely right. But if contemporary analytic metaphysics shows anything, it shows that with careful thought it becomes clear how puzzling our ordinary notions of object and property are. Not everyone is equally sensitive to the peculiar tensions and asystematic aspects of these notions, but the master argument stresses something right: we don't

---

[5] My thanks to a referee for raising this concern.

understand what objects and properties can be. When we analyze the ideas, we run up against perennial puzzles. Running up against perennial puzzles is what always happens when we're in the presence of a myth: *Something doesn't add up.* (And it *keeps on* not adding up. Forever.)

Feature metaphysics, by comparison, is clear. We may have an urge to push it in directions we're not metaphysically licensed to go in: we may want to resolve identity questions (like, for example, when we should conclude that we have two features that resemble one another perfectly, as opposed to when we should conclude we have the same one). But that nothing about features tells us what this difference could amount to should indicate (to us) that there is something badly wrong with the *question*.

The other half of object projectivism—the *projectivism*—has barely been sketched in this book. There is an enormous amount to say and find out here—and not just by philosophers. In this regard, it should be stressed that the cognitive (and social) processes that project object boundaries are *not* conceptual tissue to be analyzed by the philosophical tool of "conceptual analysis." It's interesting how so many philosophers, who resist worldly metaphysical structure in one way or another, offer instead something in the ballpark of conceptual analysis.[6] On my view, conceptual analysis can have only a tiny role, at best—for at least two reasons. First, as I illustrated in chapter 2, our "concepts" are open-ended and defeasible. That means that very little is fixed about their conceptual contours—in particular, their "analytic entailments" are thin. But, second, the empirical facts about how we project objects into the world involve psychological/sociological factors that go beyond anyone's possession of a (possibly innate) collection of "concepts." Rather, there are numerous *prompts*—perceptual ones, linguistic ones, ones cued by background social facts—all of which induce our dealing with bits of the world "as objects." There is plenty more to study about this.

One important lacuna in this book, therefore, is any discussion of what's currently described as social ontology.[7] A lot of the tools I develop in this book provide fresh ways to look at the ontology of institutions, for example. I realized, however, (i) that to appropriately say what's called for requires several chapters (and maybe another book), and (ii) that this book is big enough already.

So, a promissory note: I intend to write about this stuff eventually.

---

[6] Sidelle (1989) is a good illustration—with his explicit invocation of "analyticity." Thomasson's views—criticized in chapter 2—exhibit the same tendency. Chalmers (2012), not discussed in this book for reasons of space, is yet a third example.
[7] See Epstein (2015) for important work in this, as well as a valuable survey of the area.

BIBLIOGRAPHY

Adams, Robert M. 1979. Primitive thisness and primitive identity. *Journal of Philosophy* 76, 1: 5–26. Reprinted in Kim, Korman, and Sosa (eds.) 2011, 109–21. Page references are to the reprint.
Asay, Jamin. 2010. How to express ontological commitment in the vernacular. *Philosophia Mathematica* III, 18: 293–310.
Austin, J. L. 1962. *Sense and sensibilia*. Oxford: Oxford University Press.
Azzouni, Jody. 1994. *Metaphysical myths, mathematical practice: The ontology and epistemology of the exact sciences*. Cambridge: Cambridge University Press.
———. 1997. Applied mathematics, existential commitment and the Quine-Putnam indispensability thesis. *Philosophia Mathematica* III, 5: 193–209.
———. 2000. *Knowledge and reference in empirical science*. London: Routledge.
———. 2004a. *Deflating existential consequence: A case for nominalism*. Oxford: Oxford University Press.
———. 2004b Theory, observation and scientific realism. *British Journal for the Philosophy of Science* 55: 371–92.
———. 2006. *Tracking reason: Proof, consequence, and truth*. Oxford: Oxford University Press.
———. 2008a. Alternative logics and the role of truth in the interpretation of languages. In (Douglas Patterson, ed.) *New essays on Tarski and philosophy*, 390–420. Oxford: Oxford University Press.
———. 2008b. The compulsion to believe: Logical inference and normativity. In (Gerhard Preyer and Georg Peter, eds.) *Philosophy of mathematics: Set theory, measuring theories, and nominalism*, 73–92. Frankfurt: Ontos Verlag.
———. 2009a. Evading truth commitments: The problem reanalyzed. *Logique et Analyse* 206: 139–76.
———. 2009b. Why do informal proofs conform to formal norms? *Foundations of Science* 14: 9–26.
———. 2010a. *Talking about nothing: Numbers, hallucinations and fictions*. Oxford: Oxford University Press.

———. 2010b. Ontology and the word "exist": Uneasy relations. *Philosophia Mathematica* III, 18: 74–101.

———. 2011. Nominalistic content. In (Carlo Cellucci, Emily R. Grosholz, and Emiliano Ippoliti, eds.) *Logic and knowledge*, 33–51. Newcastle upon Tyne: Cambridge Scholars Publishing.

———. 2012a. Simple metaphysics and "ontological dependence." In (Fabrice Correia and Benjamin Schnieder, eds.) *Metaphysical grounding: Understanding the structure of reality*, 234–53. Cambridge: Cambridge University Press.

———. 2012b. Responses to Gabriele Contessa, Erin Eaker, and Nikk Effingham. *Analysis* 72, 2: 366–79.

———. 2012c. Taking the easy road out of Dodge. *Mind* 121, 484: 951–65.

———. 2013a. *Semantic perception: How the illusion of a common language arises and persists.* Oxford: Oxford University Press.

———. 2013b. Hobnobbing with the nonexistent. *Inquiry: An Interdisciplinary Journal of Philosophy* 56, 4: 340–58.

———. 2014a. A new characterization of scientific theories. *Synthese* 191, 13: 2993–3008.

———. 2014b. Freeing talk of nothing from the cognitive illusion of aboutness. *Monist* 97, 4: 443–59.

———. 2015. The challenge of many logics: A new approach to evaluating the role of ideology in Quinean commitment. *Synthese*, doi:10.1007/s11229-015-0657-9.

———. 2017. *The rule-following paradox and its implications for metaphysics.* Dordrecht: Springer.

———. Forthcoming. Deflationist truth. In (Michael Glanzberg, ed.) *Handbook of truth.* Oxford: Oxford University Press.

Azzouni, Jody, and Bradley Armour-Garb. 2005. Standing on common ground. *Journal of Philosophy* 102, 10: 532–44.

Azzouni, Jody, and Otávio Bueno. 2008. On what it takes for there to be no fact of the matter. *Noûs* 42, 4: 753–69.

———. Forthcoming. True nominalism: Referring versus coding. *British Journal for the Philosophy of Science.*

Bayne, Tim, and Michelle Montague (eds.). 2011. *Cognitive phenomenology.* Oxford: Oxford University Press.

Benacerraf, Paul. 1965. What numbers could not be. *Philosophical Review* 74: 47–73.

Bennett, Karen. 2009. Composition, collocation, and metaontology. In (David J. Chalmers, David Manley, and Ryan Wasserman, eds.) *Metametaphysics: New essays on the foundations of ontology*, 38–76. Oxford: Oxford University Press.

Black, Max. 1952. The identity of indiscernibles. Reprinted in *Problems of analysis* (1954), 204–16. Ithaca, New York: Cornell University Press.

Blackburn, Simon. 1984. *Spreading the word.* Oxford: Oxford University Press.

Braudel, Fernand. 1986. *Civilization and capitalism: 15th–18th century, vol. 3, The perspective of the world.* New York: Harper and Row.

Braun, David. 2005. Empty names. *Noûs* 27: 443–69.

———. 2012. Hob, Nob, and mythical witches. In (W. Kabasenche, M. O'Rourke, and M. Slater, eds.) *Reference and referring, vol. 10, Topics in contemporary philosophy*, 149–87. Cambridge, MA: MIT Press.

Bueno, Otávio. 2010. Philosophy of mathematics. In (Fritz Allhoff, ed.) *Philosophies of the sciences*, 68–91. Oxford: Wiley-Blackwell.

———. 2014. Nominalism in the philosophy of mathematics. In *Stanford encyclopedia of philosophy* (Spring 2014 edition), ed. Edward N. Zalta, http://plato.stanford.edu/entries/nominalism-mathematics.

Burge, Tyler. 1979. Individuation and the mental. In *Foundations of mind* (2007), 100–150. Oxford: Oxford University Press.

Calvino, Italo 1968. *Cosmicomics*. New York: Harcourt Brace.

Cameron, Ross. 2010. Quantification, naturalness, and ontology. In (Allan Hazlett, ed.) *New waves in metaphysics*, 8–26. Houndmills, Basingstoke, Hampshire, Great Britain: Palgrave Macmillan.

Carey, Susan. 2009. *The origin of concepts*. Oxford: Oxford University Press.

Carey, Susan, and Fei Xu. 2001. Infant knowledge of objects: Beyond object files and object tracking. In (Brian J. Scholl, ed.) *Objects and attention*, 179–213. Cambridge, MA: MIT Press.

Carnap, Rudolf. 1956a. *Meaning and necessity: A study in semantics and modal logic*. Chicago: University of Chicago Press.

———. 1956b. Empiricism, semantics, and ontology. In *Meaning and necessity: A study in semantics and modal logic*, 205–21. Chicago: University of Chicago Press.

———. 1963. Quine on logical truth. In (Paul Arthur Schilpp, ed.) *The philosophy of Rudolf Carnap*, 915–22. La Salle, IL: Open Court.

Cartwright, Richard. 1960. Negative existentials. Reprinted in *Philosophical essays* (1987), 21–31. Cambridge, MA: MIT Press.

———. 1987. Ontology and the theory of meaning. In *Philosophical essays*, 1–12. Cambridge, MA: MIT Press.

Carus, A. W. 2007. *Carnap and twentieth-century thought: Explication as enlightenment*. Cambridge: Cambridge University Press.

Casullo, Albert. 1988. A fourth version of the bundle theory. *Philosophical Studies* 54: 125–39.

Chalmers, David J. 2009. Ontological anti-realism. In (David J. Chalmers, David Manley, and Ryan Wasserman, eds.) *Metametaphysics: New essays on the foundations of ontology*, 77–129. Oxford: Oxford University Press.

———. 2012. *Constructing the world*. Oxford: Oxford University Press.

Chomsky, Noam. 1986. *Knowledge of language*. New York: Praeger.

———. 2000. Explaining language use. In *New horizons in the study of language and mind*, 106–33. Cambridge: Cambridge University Press.

Collins, John. 2011. *The unity of linguistic meaning*. Oxford: Oxford University Press.

———. Forthcoming. *The grades of variable involvement*. Oxford: Oxford University Press.

Colyvan, Mark. 2010. There is no easy road to nominalism. *Mind* 119, 474: 285–306.

Contessa, Gabriele. 2012. Sweet nothings. *Analysis Reviews* 72, 2: 354–66.

Correia, Fabrice, and Benjamin Schnieder (eds.). 2012. *Metaphysical grounding: Understanding the structure of reality*. Cambridge: Cambridge University Press.

Craig, William Lane. 2011. A nominalist perspective on God and abstract objects. *Philosophia Christi* 13: 305–18.

Crane, Tim. 2013. *The objects of thought*. Oxford: Oxford University Press.

Daly, Chris, and David Liggins. 2014. In defense of existence questions. *Monist* 97, 4: 460–78.
Dasgupta, Shamik. 2009. Individuals: An essay in revisionary metaphysics. *Philosophical Studies* 145: 35–67.
Davidson, Donald. 1984. *Inquiries into truth and interpretation*. Oxford: Oxford University Press.
———. 2005. *Truth and predication*. Cambridge, MA: Harvard University Press.
Dennett, Daniel C. 1991a. Real patterns. In *Brainchildren* (1998), 95–120. London: Penguin Books.
———. 1991b. *Consciousness explained*. New York: Little, Brown.
DiSalle, Robert. 2016. Space and time: Inertial frames. *The Stanford encyclopedia of philosophy* (Winter 2016 edition), ed. Edward N. Zalta, http://plato.stanford.edu/archives/win2016/entries/spacetime-iframes.
Dorr, Cian. 2005. What we disagree about when we disagree about ontology. In (Mark Eli Kalderon, ed.) *Fictionalism in metaphysics*, 234–86. Oxford: Oxford University Press.
Dummett, Michael. 1973. *Frege: Philosophy of language*. Cambridge, MA: Harvard University Press.
Dupré, John. 1981. Natural kinds and biological taxa. *Philosophical Review* 90: 66–90.
Eddington, A. S. 1929. *The nature of the physical world*. New York: Macmillan.
Effingham, Nikk. 2012. Talking about something (but really talking about nothing). *Analysis Reviews* 72, 2: 329–40.
Eklund, Matti. 2008. The picture of reality as an amorphous lump. In (Theodore Sider, John Hawthorne, and Dean W. Zimmerman, eds.) *Contemporary debates in metaphysics*, 382–96. Oxford: Blackwell Publishing.
———. 2009. Carnap and ontological pluralism. In (David J. Chalmers, David Manley, and Ryan Wasserman, eds.) *Metametaphysics: New essays on the foundations of ontology*, 130–56. Oxford: Oxford University Press.
Elder, Crawford. 2011. *Familiar objects and their shadows*. Cambridge: Cambridge University Press.
Epstein, Brian. 2015. *The ant trap: Rebuilding the foundations of the social sciences*. Oxford: Oxford University Press.
Everett, Anthony. 2013. *The nonexistent*. Oxford: Oxford University Press.
Fine, Kit. 2009. The question of ontology. In (David J. Chalmers, David Manley, and Ryan Wasserman, eds.) *Metametaphysics: New essays on the foundations of ontology*, 157–77. Oxford: Oxford University Press.
Fodor, Jerry A. 1981. The present status of the innateness controversy. In *Representations*, 257–316. Cambridge, MA: MIT Press.
Friedman, Michael. 1983. *Foundations of space-time theories*. Princeton: Princeton University Press.
Frigg, Roman, and Stephan Hartmann. 2012. Models in science. *The Stanford encyclopedia of philosophy* (Fall 2012 edition), ed. Edward N. Zalta, http://plato.stanford.edu/archives/fall2012/entries/models-science.
Gasparri, Luca, and Diego Marconi. 2016. Word meaning. *The Stanford encyclopedia of philosophy* (Spring 2016 edition), ed. Edward N. Zalta, http://plato.stanford.edu/archives/spr2016/entries/word-meaning.

Geach, Peter. 1967. Intentional identity. Reprinted in *Logic matters* (1972). Oxford: Blackwell.
Gibbard, Allan. 1975. Contingent identity. *Journal of Philosophical Logic* 4: 187–221.
Goodman, Nelson. 1983. *Fact, fiction and forecast*, 4th edition. Cambridge, MA: Harvard University Press.
Gregory, Richard L. 2009. *Seeing through illusions*. Oxford: Oxford University Press.
Griffiths, Paul L., and Karola Stoltz. 2007. Gene. In (David L. Hull and Michael Ruse, eds.) *The Cambridge companion to the philosophy of biology*, 85–102. Cambridge: Cambridge University Press.
Hawley, Katherine, and Fiona MacPherson. 2011. *The admissible contents of experience*. Malden, MA: Wiley-Blackwell.
Hawthorne, John. 2006. Plenitude, convention, and ontology. In *Metaphysical essays*, 53–70. Oxford: Oxford University Press.
Hawthorne, John [O'Leary-] and Andrew Cortens. 1995. Towards ontological nihilism. *Philosophical Studies* 79: 143–65.
Heim, Irene. 1992. Presupposition projection and the semantics of attitude verbs. *Journal of Semantics* 9: 183–221.
Heller, Mark. 1990. *The ontology of physical objects: Four-dimensional hunks of matter*. Cambridge: Cambridge University Press.
Hirsch, Eli. 1982. *The concept of identity*. Oxford: Oxford University Press.
———. 1993. *Dividing reality*. Oxford: Oxford University Press.
———. 1999. Objectivity without objects. In *Quantifier variance and realism: Essays in Metaontology* (2011), 36–44. Oxford: Oxford University Press.
———. 2002. Quantifier variance and realism. In *Quantifier variance and realism: Essays in metaontology* (2011), 68–95. Oxford: Oxford University Press.
———. 2003. Against revisionary ontology. In *Quantifier variance and realism: Essays in metaontology* (2011), 96–123. Oxford: Oxford University Press.
———. 2004. Sosa's existential relativism. In *Quantifier variance and realism: Essays in Metaontology* (2011), 132–43. Oxford: Oxford University Press.
———. 2005. Physical-object ontology, verbal disputes, and common sense. In *Quantifier variance and realism: Essays in metaontology* (2011), 144–77. Oxford: Oxford University Press.
———. 2009. Ontology and alternative languages. In *Quantifier variance and realism: Essays in metaontology* (2011), 220–50. Oxford: Oxford University Press.
———. 2011a. *Quantifier variance and realism: Essays in metaontology*. Oxford: Oxford University Press.
———. 2011b. Introduction. In *Quantifier variance and realism: Essays in metaontology* (2011), xi–xvi. Oxford: Oxford University Press.
Hofweber, Thomas. 2007a. Innocent statements and their metaphysically loaded counterparts. *Philosophers' Imprint* 7, 1: 1–33.
———. 2007b. Review of *Deflating existential consequence: A case for nominalism*, *Philosophical Review* 116: 465–67.
———. 2009. Ambitious, yet modest, metaphysics. In (David J. Chalmers, David Manley, and Ryan Wasserman, eds.) *Metametaphysics: New essays on the foundations of ontology*, 260–89. Oxford: Oxford University Press.

Horgan, Terence E., and Matjaž Potrč. 2008. *Austere realism*. Cambridge, MA: MIT Press.

Hudson, Hud. 2001. *A materialist metaphysics of the human person*. Ithaca, NY: Cornell University Press.

Hume, David. 1958. *An enquiry concerning human understanding*. La Salle, IL: Open Court.

———. 1961. *A treatise of human nature*. Garden City, NY: Doubleday.

Kahneman, D., A. Treisman, and B. J. Gibbs. 1992. The reviewing of object files: Object-specific integration of information. *Cognitive Psychology* 24: 174–219.

Kant, Immanuel. 1783. *Prolegomena of any future metaphysics that will be able to come forth as science* (1997), ed. Gary Hatfield. Cambridge: Cambridge University Press.

Kaplan, David. 1969. Quantifying in. In (D. Davidson and J. Hintikka, eds.) *Words and objections*, 178–214. Dordrecht: Reidel.

Keenan, E. L., and D. Westerståhl. 1997. Generalized quantifiers in linguistics and logic. In (Johan van Benthem and Alice ter Meulen, eds.) *Handbook of logic and language*, 837–93. Cambridge, MA: MIT Press.

Kim, Jaegwon, Daniel Z. Korman, and Ernest Sosa (eds.). 2011. *Metaphysics: An anthology*, 2nd edition. Malden, MA: Wiley-Blackwell.

Korman, Daniel Z. 2009. Eliminativism and the challenge from folk belief. *Noûs* 43, 2: 242–64.

———. 2010. The argument from vagueness. *Philosophy Compass* 5, 10: 891–901.

———. 2016. Ordinary objects. *The Stanford encyclopedia of philosophy* (Spring 2016 edition), ed. Edward N. Zalta, http://plato.stanford.edu/archives/spr2016/entries/ordinary-objects.

Koslicki, Kathrin. 2003. The crooked path from vagueness to four-dimensionalism. *Philosophical Studies* 114: 107–34.

———. 2008. *The structure of objects*. Oxford: Oxford University Press.

Kripke, Saul. 1980. *Naming and necessity*. Cambridge, MA: Harvard University Press.

———. 1982. *Wittgenstein on rules and private language*. Cambridge: Harvard University Press.

Landau, L. D., and E. M. Lifshitz. 1976. *Mechanics*, 3rd edition. New York: Pergamon Press.

LaPorte, Joseph. 1996. Chemical kind term reference and the discovery of essence. *Noûs* 30: 112–32.

Lewis, David. 1983. New work for universals. In *Papers in metaphysics and epistemology* (1999), 8–55. Cambridge: Cambridge University Press.

———. 1984. Putnam's paradox. In *Papers in metaphysics and epistemology* (1999), 56–77. Cambridge: Cambridge University Press.

———. 1986. *On the plurality of worlds*. Oxford: Basil Blackwell.

———. 1990. Noneism or allism? In *Papers in metaphysics and epistemology* (1999), 152–63. Cambridge: Cambridge University Press.

Lewis, David, and Stephanie Lewis. 1983. Holes. In *Philosophical papers*, vol. 1, 3–9. Oxford: Oxford University Press.

Lowe, E. J. 2012. Against monism. In (Philip Goff, ed.) *Spinoza on monism*, 92–112. Houndsmills, Basingstoke, Hamshire, England: Palgrave-Macmillan.

Lynch, Michael P. 2001. *The nature of truth*. Cambridge, MA: MIT Press.

Machery, E., R. Mallon, S. Nichols, and S. P. Stich. 2004. Semantics, cross-cultural style. *Cognition* 92: B1–B12.

Maddy, Penelope. 1997. *Naturalism in mathematics*. Oxford: Oxford Univerity Press.

Malvern, Lawrence E. 1969. *Introduction to the mechanics of a continuous medium*. Upper Saddle River, NJ: Prentice-Hall.

Marr, D. 1982. *Vision*. New York: W. H. Freeman.

Marx, Karl. 1967. *Capital, vol. 1: A critical analysis of capitalist production* (ed. Frederick Engels). New York: International Publishers.

Matthews, Gareth. 1972. Senses and kinds. *Journal of Philosophy* 69: 149–57.

Mattuck, R. 1976. *A guide to Feynman diagrams in the many-body problem*, 2nd edition. New York: Dover.

McDaniel, Kris. 2009. Ways of being. In (David J. Chalmers, David Manley, and Ryan Wasserman, eds.) *Metametaphysics: New essays on the foundations of ontology*, 290–319. Oxford: Oxford University Press.

McNally, Louise. 2011. Existential sentences. In (C. Maienborn, K. von Heusinger, and P. Portner, eds.) *Semantics: An international handbook of natural language meaning*, vol. 2, 1829–48. Berlin: De Gruyter Mouton.

McTaggart, J. M. E. 1908. The unreality of time. *Mind* 18: 457–84.

———. 1921. *The nature of existence*, vol. II. Cambridge: Cambridge University Press.

Melia, J. 1995. On what there's not. *Analysis* 55, 4: 223–29.

Merricks, Trenton. 2001. *Objects and persons*. Oxford: Oxford University Press.

Michotte, A. 1963. *The perception of causality*. New York: Basic Books.

Moore, George Edward. 1903. *Principia ethica*. Cambridge: Cambridge University Press.

Nagel, Ernest. 1960. *The structure of science: Problems in the logic of scientific explanation*. New York: Harcourt, Brace and World.

O'Leary-Hawthorne, John, and Andrew Cortens. 1995. *See* Hawthorne, John, and Andrew Cortens 1995.

Parent, T. 2014. Ontic terms and metaontology, or: On what there actually is. *Philosophical Studies* 170, 2: 199–214.

Paul, L. A. 2012. Building the world from its fundamental constituents. *Philosophical Studies* 158: 221–56.

———. 2013. Categorical priority and categorical collapse. *Proceedings of the Aristotelian Society Supplementary Vol.* LXXXVII, 89–113.

Peñaranda, Juan José Lara. 2013. Ontology: Minimalism and truth conditions. *Philosophical Studies* 162, 3: 683–96.

Perry, John, ed. 1975. *Personal identity*. Los Angeles: University of California Press.

Peters, Stanley, and Dag Westerståhl. 2006 *Quantifiers in language and logic*. Oxford: Oxford University Press.

Pietroski, P. 2005. Meaning before truth. In (Gerhard Preyer and Georg Peter, eds.) *Contextualism in philosophy: Knowledge, meaning, and truth*, 255–302. Oxford: Oxford University Press.

Pitt, David. 2004. The phenomenology of cognition, or, what is it like to think that P? *Philosophy and Phenomenological Research* 69: 1–36.

Plato. 1963. Parmenides. In *Plato: The collected dialogues*, 920–56.

Pollock, James. 1974. *Knowledge and justification*. Princeton: Princeton University Press.

Price, Huw. 2009. Metaphysics after Carnap: The ghost who walks? In (David J. Chalmers, David Manley, and Ryan Wasserman, eds.) *Metametaphysics: New essays on the foundations of ontology*, 320–46. Oxford: Oxford University Press.

Priest, Graham. 2011. Review of *Talking about nothing*. *Philosophia Mathematica* III, 19: 359–63.

———. 2014. *Sein* language. *Monist* 97, 4: 430–42.

Pryor, James. 2000. The skeptic and the dogmatist. *Noûs* 34, 4: 517–49.

Putnam, Hilary. 1975. The meaning of "meaning." In *Mind, language and reality: Philosophical papers*, 2nd edition, vol. 2, 215–71. Cambridge: Cambridge University Press.

———. 1987. *The many faces of realism*. La Salle, IL: Open Court.

———. 1990. Truth and convention. In *Realism with a human face*, 96–104. Cambridge, MA: Harvard University Press.

Pylyshyn, Zenon W. 2003. *Seeing and visualizing: It's not what you think*. Cambridge, MA: MIT Press.

Quine, W. V. 1951a. Ontology and ideology. *Philosophical Studies* 2: 11–15.

———. 1951b. On Carnap's views on ontology. In *The ways of paradox*, revised and enlarged edition (1966, 1976), 203–11. Cambridge, MA: Harvard University Press.

———. 1953. On what there is. In *From a logical point of view* (1980), 1–19. Cambridge, MA: Harvard University Press.

———. 1956. Quantifiers and propositional attitudes. In *The ways of paradox*, revised and enlarged edition (1966, 1976), 185–96. Cambridge, MA: Harvard University Press.

———. 1960a. Variables explained away. In *Selected logic papers* (1966), 227–35. Cambridge, MA: Harvard University Press.

———. 1960b. *Word and object*. Cambridge, MA: MIT Press.

———. 1969. A symposium on Austin's method. In (K. T. Fann, ed.) *Symposium on J. L. Austin* (II: W. V. O. Quine), 86–90. London: Routledge and Kegan Paul.

———. 1976. Algebraic logic and predicate functors. In *The ways of paradox and other essays*, 2nd edition, 238–307. Cambridge, MA: Harvard University Press.

———. 1981. What price bivalence? In *Theories and things*, 31–37. Cambridge, MA: Harvard University Press.

———. 1981b. Things and their place in theories. In *Theories and things*, 1–23. Cambridge, MA: Harvard University Press.

———. 1986. *Philosophy of logic*, 2nd edition. Cambridge, MA: Harvard University Press.

———. 1995. *From stimulus to science*. Cambridge, MA: Harvard University Press.

Raley, Yvonne. 2009. Deflating existence away? A critique of Azzouni's nominalism. *Philosophia Mathematica* III, 17: 73–83.

Raley, Yvonne, and Richard Burnor. 2011. The predicate approach to ontological commitment. *Logique et Analyse* 54: 359–77.

Resnik, Michael D. 1997. *Mathematics as a science of patterns*. Oxford: Oxford University Press.

Rorty, Amélie Oksenberg, ed. 1976. *The identity of persons*. Los Angeles: University of California Press.

Rosen, G., and Dorr, C. 2002. Composition as a fiction. In (Richard Gale, ed.) *The Blackwell guide to metaphysics*, 151–74. Oxford: Blackwell.
Russell, Bertrand. 1912. *The problems of philosophy*. Oxford: Oxford University Press, 1959.
Ryle, Gilbert. 1949. *The concept of mind*. London: Hutchinson.
Salmon, Nathan. Forthcoming. The philosopher's stone and other mythical objects.
Schaffer, Jonathan. 2009. On what grounds what. In (David J. Chalmers, David Manley, and Ryan Wasserman, eds.) *Metametaphysics: New essays on the foundations of ontology*, 347–83. Oxford: Oxford University Press.
———. 2012. Why the world has parts: Reply to Horgan and Potrč. In (Philip Goff, ed.) *Spinoza on monism*, 77–91. Houndmills, Basingstoke, Hampshire, England: Palgrave Macmillan.
Scholl, Brian J. 2002. Objects and attention: The state of the art. In (Brian J. Scholl, ed.) *Objects and attention*, 1–46. Cambridge, MA: MIT Press.
Sidelle, Alan. 1989. *Necessity, essence, and individuation: A defense of conventionalism*. Ithaca, NY: Cornell University Press.
Sider, Theodore. 2001. *Four-dimensionalism: An ontology of persistence and time*. Oxford: Oxford University Press.
———. 2004. Precis of four-dimensionalism. *Philosophy and Phenomenological Research Research* 68: 642–47.
———. 2009. Ontological realism. In (David J. Chalmers, David Manley, and Ryan Wasserman, eds.) *Metametaphysics: New essays on the foundations of ontology*, 384–423. Oxford: Oxford University Press.
———. 2011. *Writing the book of the world*. Oxford: Oxford University Press.
Sider, Theodore, John Hawthorne, and Dean W. Zimmerman. 2008. *Contemporary debates in metaphysics*. Malden, MA: Blackwell.
Siegal, Susanna. 2010. *The contents of visual experience*. New York: Oxford University Press.
Simons, Peter. 1994. Particulars in particular clothing: Three trope theories of substance. *Philosophy and Phenomenological Research* 54, 3: 553–75.
———. 1998. Farewell to substance: A differentiated leave-taking. *Ratio* XI, 3: 235–52.
Sosa, Ernest. 1999. Existential relativity. In (Peter A. French and Howard K. Wettstein, eds.) *Midwest studies in philosophy 23: New directions in philosophy*, 132–43.
Spar, Jessica. 2015. 20 foods (and drinks) that aren't what they seem: Everything you thought about these foods has been wrong. Accessed December 27.
Spiegel, Aison. 2014. These everyday foods aren't what you think they are. *Huffington Post*, April 9.
Stalnaker, Robert. 2011. *Mere possibilities: Metaphysical foundations of modal semantics*. Princeton, NJ: Princeton University Press.
Stein, Howard. 1967. Newtonian space-time. *Texas Quarterly* 20: 174–200.
Strawson, Peter F. 1953-54. Particular and general. In *Logico-linguistic papers* (1971), 28–52. London: Methuen.
———. 1959. *Individuals*. London: Methuen.
Strawson, Galen. 1994. *Mental reality*. Cambridge, MA: MIT Press.

Tarski, Alfred. 1983a. The concept of truth in formalized languages. In (J. H. Wooder and John Corcoran, eds.) *Logic, semantics, metamathematics*, 152–278. Indianapolis: Hackett.

———.1983b. Foundations of the geometry of solids. In (J. H. Wooder and John Corcoran, eds.) *Logic, semantics, metamathematics*, 24–37. Indianapolis: Hackett.

Thomasson, Amie L. 2007. *Ordinary objects*. New York: Oxford University Press.

———. 2009. Answerable and unanswerable questions. In (David J. Chalmers, David Manley, and Ryan Wasserman, eds.) *Metametaphysics: New essays on the foundations of ontology*, 444–71. Oxford: Oxford University Press.

Thomson, Judith Jarvis. 1998. The statue and the clay. *Noûs* 32, 2: 149–73.

Turner, Jason. 2011. Ontological nihilism. In (Karen Bennett and Dean W. Zimmerman, eds.) *Oxford studies in metaphysics*, vol. 6, 3–54. Oxford: Oxford University Press.

Truesdell, C. 1991. *A first course in rational continuum mechanics*, vol. 1. Boston: Harcourt Brace Jovanovich.

Truesdell, C., and K. R. Rajagopal. 2000. *An introduction to the mechanics of fluids*. Berlin: Birkhäuser.

Unger, Peter. 1979. Why I do not exist. In *Philosophical papers*, vol. 2 (2006), 36–52. Oxford: Oxford University Press.

———. 1980. The problem of the many. In *Philosophical papers*, vol. 2 (2006), 113–82. Oxford: Oxford University Press.

Van Cleve, James. 1985. Three versions of the bundle theory. *Philosophical Studies* 47: 95–107.

van Inwagen, Peter. 1983. Fiction and metaphysics. *Philosophy and Literature* 7: 67–77.

———. 1990. *Material beings*. Ithaca, NY: Cornell University Press.

———. 1996. Why is there anything at all? In *Ontology, identity, and modality: Essays in metaphysics* (2001), 57–71. Cambridge: Cambridge University Press.

———. 2001. Creatures of fiction. In *Ontology, identity, and modality: Essays in metaphysics*, 37–56. Cambridge: Cambridge University Press.

———. 2009. Being, existence, and ontological commitment. In (David J. Chalmers, David Manley, and Ryan Wasserman, eds.) *Metametaphysics: New essays on the foundations* of ontology, 472–506. Oxford: Oxford University Press.

Venclova, Tomas. 1983. The game of the Soviet censor. *New York Review of Books*, March 31.

Walker, Ralph C. S. 1989. *The coherence theory of truth: Realism, anti-realism, and idealism*. London: Routledge.

Walton, Kendall L. 2003. Restricted quantification, negative existentials, and fiction. *Dialectica* 57: 241–44.

Wasserman, Ryan. 2004. The constitution question. *Noûs* 38, 4: 693–710.

———. 2015. Material constitution. *The Stanford encyclopedia of philosophy* (Spring 2015 edition), ed. Edward N. Zalta, http://plato.stanford.edu/archives/spr2015/entries/material-constitution.

Westerståhl, D. 2011. Generalized quantifiers. *The Stanford encyclopedia of philosophy* (Winter 2016 Edition), ed. Edward N. Zalta, https://plato.stanford.edu/archives/win2016/entries/generalized-quantifiers/.

Wiggins, David. 1967. *Identity and spatio-temporal continuity*. Oxford: Oxford University Press.

———. 1980. *Sameness and substance*. Cambridge, MA: Harvard University Press.
Williams, Edwin. 1984. *There*-insertion. *Linguistic Inquiry* 15: 131–53.
Williams, J. Robert G. 2007. Eligibility and inscrutability. *Philosophical Review* 116: 361–99.
Williamson, Timothy. 1994. *Vagueness*. London: Routledge.
Wilson, Jessica M. 2014. No work for a theory of grounding. *Inquiry* 57, 5–6: 535–79.
Wittgenstein, Ludwig. 1958. *Philosophical investigations*, 3rd edition. New York: Macmillan.
Yablo, Stephen. 1998. Does ontology rest on a mistake? In *Things: Philosophical papers*, vol. 2 (2010), 117–144.

INDEX

@, 177–193
  characterization of, 177
  why it is not predication, 179
  See also is at relation
@-ication, 182–183, 185
@-languages, 182–186
aboutness illusions, xi–xiii, xxxiv
absolute space, 160, 218
  See also space
actual quantifier variance, 43–44
  See also quantifier variance
Adams, R.M., 155n17, 169, 170n31
Adrian, A., vii, xxiiin15, 137n2, 164n27
"amorphous lumpism," xv, xvn9
  See also mereological universalism
anti-realism, xi, 10n13, 11, 47n20
  See also reality/irreality distinction
argument from optimal theorizing, the, 148–149, 158–166, 221
argument from phenomenology, the, 148–152, 156–158
argument from the description of the setup, the, 160–162
arguments from arbitrariness, xvn7
arguments from bruteness, xvn7
arguments from explanatory redundancy, xvn7
Aristotle, xxiin15, 127, 192
Armour-Garb, B., xxxivn28
Armstrong, D., 173–174n1

Arntzenius, F., 101n1
Asay, J., xxxvn30
Austin, J.L., 8n7, 38n9, 121–122, 130n3
average entities, 107–108

Bach, E., 129n2
Baldwin, T., 216n29,
Bayne, T., 150n8
"being depicted in such-and-such work," 106
"being presented as." *See* "being depicted in such-and-such work"
Benacerraf, P., 326
Bennett, K., 3, 11n14, 21n22, 102n2
Benz, Karl, 32
bivalence, 74, 83–89, 200, 202, 238, 249
  in the context of identity statements, 123–126
  See also vagueness
Black, Max, 169n30, 173–174, 177, 234n16
Blackburn, S., 88n18
blobjects, xviii–xixn14
borders. *See* ontological borders
Boolos, G., 5n2
Boscolo, S., vii
Braun, D., 118, 118n29, 119n30, 121, 121n32
Braudel, F., 116n24

broad ignorance thesis, the, 83, 85–87,
    86n17, 88, 123, 200
  See also bivalence
Bueno, O., vii, x, xxxiv n29,
    47n20, 85n15, 101n1, 111–112n17,
    214n26, 238n20
bundle theories, xxiii, 176–178, 186
burden of proof
  in ontological debate, x, 58,
    164, 225n4
Burnor, R, xxxivn29, 71n15

calculated nonentities, 108–109
Calvino, I., 125n34
Cameron, R, xi n4, xviii n13, xxv n17,
    xxvii, 81, 81n10, 149
Carey, S., 151n10, 205n19
Carnap, R., xi, xin1, xxii, 3–12, 15–16, 24,
    26, 32n2, 38n9, 68, 123
Carné, P., vii
Carter, N., vii, xxvi n18, 137n2
Cartwright, R., xi, 10
Carus, A.W., 4n1, 251n1
"carving" metaphor, xvii, xviin1, xviii,
    xviiin13, 26, 148–149, 152, 164, 165,
    226, 228, 239, 239n21, 249
  See also quantifier domains;
    ontological borders
Casullo, A., 176n3
"causal picture of reference," the,
  objections to, 39–40
  See also Kripke, S.; Putnam, H.;
    public meaning
center of mass, 109–110, 110n15,
    230–232
challenge from folk belief, the, 137n1,
    156–158
Chalmers, D., 64n10, 255n6
charity, 17, 48, 252n4
  See also Hirsch
chess, philosophical significance of,
    238–239, 248
Chisholm, R., 141
Chomsky, N., xxxii, 80–81n8,
    129–130, 129n2

"chunking". See "carving" metaphor
coarse-grained truth-conditions, 13,
    18, 18n20
  See also sentence-sentence
    mappings; Hirsch
co-featuring,
  characterization of, 176,
  See also feature presentation
coherence. See theories of truth,
    coherence
Collins, J., vii, xxxiv n29, 80n8, 129n2,
    147n7, 183n8, 193n15
Colyvan, M., x
composition questions, 139–140n5,
    144n1, 153n14, 198–202
  See also general composition
    questions; special composition
    questions; statue/clay puzzles
compositional nihilism, 144n1,
    153n14, 157
  See also metaphysical nihilism;
    ontological nihilism
compositional truth-conditions
  requirement, 13, 13–14n15
  See also theories of truth,
    compositional
conceptual analysis,
  objections to, 255, 255n6
conceptual relativism, xi, xviin11, xix
  See also existential relativism;
    ontological relativism
constitution of objects, xxi
  issues of, 235, 240, 240n23
Contact, 252
Contessa, G., 113n22, 116, 117n27, 118
contour questions, 138, 145–146, 149,
    164–165, 169, 173, 176, 187, 192,
    194, 197–198
contour illusions, 146n5
  See also feature presentation;
    ontological contours
co-occurrence of features, 176, 191,
    194–195, 195n2, 202–203, 209, 212,
    217, 235
  See also bundle theories

coordinate systems, 141, 159–163, 171–172, 175–176, 181, 191, 195, 212, 223
 See also empty space
coordinatization, a,
 Cartesian, 159
 characterizations of, 159, 160n23, 177
 polar, 159
coordinatizing colored landscapes, 159–162
 See also argument from optimal theorizing, the; argument from the description of the setup, the
Correia, F., 81n10
correspondence notion of truth, the, xxvii, 194n1
 See also external discourse demand, the
correspondence question, the, 26–29, 198
Cortens, A., xxvi, 136–137, 164n26, 183–184, 188, 200n10, 253
"cosmic exile", the impossibility of, 7n6, 8, 8n6, 11
 See also Quine, W.V.O.
Craig, W.L., ixn1, xxxivn29
Crane, T., xxxivn29
criterion for what exists, 54, 213
 de facto vs de jure, 40, 45–46
 See also mind- and language-independence; Quine's criterion
criterion immanence. See criterion transcendence vs criterion immanence
criterion transcendence, 147, 148
 strong-retroactive property of, 41, 42
 defeasibility of, 50–51
 See also criterion transcendence vs criterion immanence
criterion transcendence vs criterion immanence, 38–46
 characterization of, 37
 See also public meaning, entailments

Daly, C., 112n20
Dasgupta, S., xxiiin15, 144
 underdetermination argument of, 168–169
Davidson, D. xxxiin26, 16–17, 147n7, 192–193, 193n15
Dean, E., vii, xxxvn31, 42n13, 42n14
deep ontology, xxi, xxiv
definitional primitivism, 140n5, 145
deflationary metaphysics, x, xn2, xxvi
 See also pure deflationary metaphysics
deflationary nominalism, x, 80, 82, 82n12, 237
 See also nominalism
deflationary view of constitution, the, 240n23
deflationary view of existence, the. See existence deflationism
deflationary view of truth, the. See theories of truth, deflationary
demonstrative expressions, xxxi, xxxin25
Dennett, D.C., 203n15, 207n21
depth perception, 151n10
designing objects, 234–248
Dethier, C., vii, 137n2
differential equations, 109–110, 230–231
DiSalle, R., 169n29
discourse, coherence condition on, xxvii, 74, 80, 84, 90, 93, 97
 characterization of, 83–84
 See also theories of truth, coherence
discourse, truth-value induced, 90, 91, 91n21
 characterization of, 83–84
discovery picture of reference, the, 43
 objections to, 39–40
 See also criterion transcendence; Kripke, S.; Putnam, H.
"distinguished structure", xviii
 See also Sider, T.; ontological borders
distribution of features. See feature distribution
"domain metaphysics", xii
domains. See quantifier domains
Dorr, C., xv, 8n6, 101n1, 144n1

Dummett, M., xvn9, xviin11
Dupré, J., 40n11
"dynamic cohesion" relations, xxi

Eddington, A.S., 141n6
Effingham, N., xxvii, 79n7, 82n12
Eklund, M., xv, 3, 4n1, 13n15, 15–16, 16n19, 17, 20
Elder, C., 190, 225–226, 226n5
eliminativist metaphysics
   characterizations of, xv, xvi, xxiiin15, 142, 157
   replacement views. *See* compositional nihilism; monism
   pure eliminativist views. *See* object projectivism
empty space, 207–211, 210n24, 239, 141
   See also space
empty terms, 108, 113, 115
   See also predicative intensional form; vacuous terms
endurantism, 156
   contrast with perdurantism, 188
Epstein, B., 255n7
Everett, A., 112n20
"exist,"
   absence of ambiguity, polysemousness or nonliterality of, 64–67
   ambiguity views about, xxxii
   criterion transcendence of, 34, 37–38, 42–48
   ontological committing role of, 33–34, 62, 187
   regimentation of, 70–72
existence deflationism, 69, 69n14, 70
existence pluralism, 68–69
existential relativism, xviii, xviiin14, 189
   See also conceptual relativism; ontological relativism
experience of objects, the. *See* object-experiences
explanation, xiv, 87–88, 229–230, 232–234, 161–164, 204–205, 232–234
explanatory Occam's razor principle, 168–169

"explosionism," xv
   See also mereological universalism
external discourse demand, the, 108, 112, 112n18, 113, 194n1, 195n3

"feature"
   used as a mass term, 176
feature-characterizing languages, 191–192
   isomorphism to first-order languages, 191
   See also feature-placing languages; feature-presentation languages
feature distribution, xviii, xxv, 160, 162–163, 167, 169, 218
   See also features; properties and relations
feature metaphysics, 144, 167, 173–177, 180, 183n8, 184, 190–191, 195, 212, 214n26, 235, 240, 254–255
feature-placing boundary problem, the, 202–203
feature-placing languages, 136, 140–141, 147, 147n7, 175–183, 183n8, 184–193, 212, 253
feature-placing sentences, xvii
feature-placing terms, 174
   See also feature-characterizing languages; feature-presentation languages
feature presentation, 164, 174–180, 186–187, 191, 195, 197, 197n5, 198, 200–201, 206, 212, 219, 222, 224, 226–228, 247
   as a characterization of the real, 194
feature-presentation languages, 168
   See also feature-characterizing languages; feature-placing languages
features, xiv, xvii, xix–xx, xxii, 139n4, 144, 164, 166, 167, 172, 176–182, 185–189
   individuation conditions for, xxiii–xxiv, 168, 173–176
   distinction between real and unreal, 189–191
Field, H., 101n1
Fine, K., xxxivn29, 64n10, 71n15,

focus. *See* ontological focus
Fodor, J.A., 98n28
four-dimensionalism, 20–22
free logic, xxxiv, 106n6
Friedman, M., 169n29
Frege, G., 147n7, 192
Frigg, R., 108n11
fundamental structure, 132
fundamentalist language projects, 149

Gasparri, L., 36n7
Geach, P.,
  Hob-Nob problem, the, xxxiv, 113, 118–122, 126–128, 185
  Geach sentences, 118, 118n29
general composition questions, 200
  See also composition questions
generalized quantifiers,
  xxviii–xxx, 56–58
Gibbard, A., 242n26, 243
Gibbs, B.J., 151n10
Glanzberg, M., viii, 8n8, 14n15, 33n3, 35n4, 121n34, 124n33, 145n4, 150n9, 183n8, 216n29
God, ontological debate over, 32–33, 58, 63, 69, 70, 104–105
Gödel's theorem, 84–85, 90
Goliath. *See* Goliath/Lump
Goliath/Lump, 240–248
Goodman, N., xxii, 224–225, 225n1, 225n3
Gottlieb, D., vii, 137n2
grain invariance, 197–198, 198n6, 203
Gregory, R., 146n5
Gricean implicature, 33
Griffiths, P.L., 150n9
grounding problem, the, 243–246
grounding projects, xxvi–xxvii, 81–82, 250
grounding objection, the
  characterization of, 245
group theory, 237n17
grue, xxi, 36n5, 138, 225n3
  definition of, 225

Hartmann, S., 108n11
Hawley, K., 150n8

Hawthorne, J., 13n15, 15–18, 20, 26–29, 252n4
  See also O'Leary-Hawthorne, J.
Heidegger, M., 69n14
Heim, I., 113n21, 114
Heisenberg "uncertainty",
  195n2, 202n14
Heller, M., xvin10
Hirsch, xi, xin3, xin4, xx–xxi, 3, 4, 4n1, 9n10, 10n12, 10n13, 12–29, 34–37, 43n17, 45–48, 51, 53–55, 103–104, 131–132, 138, 144n1, 151–152, 152n12, 154–155, 187, 196, 200n11, 226, 252n4
Hirsch visions, 154–155
  characterization of, 154
Hob-Nob case. *See* Geach, Hob-Nob problem, the
Hofweber, T., xxxvn30, 34, 64n10, 64n12, 65, 65n13
holes, 82, 94–96, 198, 210, 215–218
Horgan, T.E., xv, xv n7, xvii n11, xix n14
Hudson, H., 102n2
Hume, D., 143n1, 250

idealized entities, 108
identity,
  conditions of, 122–128, 156, 201, 236–237
  relativity of questions of to coordinate systems, 177–179
identity of indiscernibles, the, 145n3
ignorance, expressions of, 83, 85–88, 91, 95, 200, 202
  See also bivalence; vagueness
incars/outcar examples, 14–15, 20, 22, 24–25, 28, 48, 51, 103–104, 187, 196
indexicals, xxxi, xxxin25
indispensability arguments, x, xviin11, 67, 101–104, 105n4, 107, 112n17, 112n19, 113, 115, 128, 132, 136, 141–142, 146, 158–160, 162–163, 167, 199n7, 253–254
induction, 141, 224–230, 251, 253
is at relations, xxii
  See also @

inventing abstracta. *See* designing objects
Italifacts, 242

Jackendoff, R., 129n2
Jenkins, C., 216n29

Kahneman, D., 151n10
Kant, I., xxi, xxii, 11, 32n2, 69, 85, 251,
Kaplan, D., 113n21
Kaniza figures, 146n5
Keenan, E.L., xxxn24,
Koon, J., vii, 137n2
Korman, D.Z., xvn7, 137n1, 137n3, 140n5, 144n1, 156–57
Koslicki, K., 200n12, 233–234, 252n2
Krifka, M., 129n2
Kripke, S., 38, 38n9, 39–41, 43, 52, 105, 125n35, 190n13, 234n16

L-laws, 236–249
 characterization of, 234
 See also laws
Landau, L.D., 110n15
LaPorte, J., 40n11
Laprade, D., vii, 83n13, 137n2
lawlike patterns, 220–221
 characterization of, 220
 See also micro-/macro-disc examples
laws, 108, 110, 110n15, 141, 163–165, 203–206, 210, 221–222, 224, 226–234, 238, 241–242
 See also induction
Leibniz's law, 141, 155, 224, 246
 characterization of, 234
lexical meaning, 25, 36, 38
 See also public meaning
Lewis, D., xxxivn28, 5n2, 96n24, 139n5, 144n1, 156n20, 173–174n1, 189–191, 201n13, 225n2, 226n5, 233
Lifshitz, E.M., 110n15
Liggins, D., 112n20
"linguistic division of labor," the, 40n11
location conditions, 135–137, 139n4, 142, 182

Lowe, E.J., xv, n7, xix n14
Lump. *See* Goliath/Lump
Lynch, M., 95n23

mind- and language-criterion. *See* mind- and language-independence
Machery, E., 36n6, 38n10
MacPherson, F., 150n8
Maddy, P., 108
Mallon, R., 36n6, 38n10
Malvern, L.E., 111n16, 231n11
Marr, D., 151n10, 158n22
master argument, the, 137, 139–140, 143–170
 directed towards individuation conditions for properties, 173–176
Mattuck, R., 109n12
Marconi, D., 36n7
Marx, K., 42n14
mathematical structuralism, motivations for, 237
Matthew, G., 69n14
Max Black universes, 169n30, 173–175, 177
McConnell, J., vii
McDaniel, K., 69n14
McNally, L., xxxii–xxxiii
McTaggert, J.M.E., 188, 188n12
Meinongianism, x, xn2, xi, xiii, 10, 81, 122–123, 215
Melia, J., 107, 108
mereological essentialism, 20–22
mereological sums, xvi, xxiii, 14–16, 24, 147, 196, 228
mereological universalism, xv, xvn9, xvi, 25, 137, 138, 144, 144n1, 144n2, 147n6, 150, 199n8,
mereology, 241–242
Merricks, T, xv, 199n8
metalanguage quantifiers, xii–xiii, xxix, 6
 See also object-language quantifiers
metaphysical debate. *See* ontological debate

metaphysical focus. *See* ontological focus
metaphysical nihilism, 102, 199, 199n7
   See also ontological nihilism
metaphysical primitivism, 139–140n5, 143n1, 145–147, 164–165, 168, 202–203, 233, 246,
   characterization of, 139
metaphysical simples, 102, 144n1, 163n25, 199n7
metaphysical stability positions, characterizations of, xiv–xvi, 137–139
   See also mereological universalism; monism; nihilism
metaphysical unfactorability, xxii,
metaphysician's dream come true, the, 163
metaphysics, contemporary state of, 250–253
Michotte, A., 205n19
micro/macro disc examples, 203–209, 220–221, 239
mind- and language-independence, 43, 54, 194, 218
   characterization of, 214–216
   metaphysical character of, 216–217
misfit problem, the, 202
modal profiles, 240, 243–248
modal properties, grounding problem of. *See* grounding problem, the
modality, conventionalist approach to, 141, 247, 247n31
monism, xv–xvi, xviiin14, 136–139, 142, 157
Montague, M., 150n8
Moore, G.E., xxv, 43n16, 152
Moorean fact strategy, 137, 151, 154n15, 156–157
motion and change, the reality of, 188, 231
mottle-properties, 196

Nagel, E., 81n9,
natural features, xx, 190, 226
natural kinds, 42, 52, 189–190, 225–226
   See also natural kind terms
natural kind terms, 38n9, 39, 43
neutralism. *See* quantifier neutralism
neutral quantifiers. *See* quantifier neutralism
new theory of reference, the. *See* discovery picture of reference, the
Nichols, S., 36n6, 38n10
nihilism. See ontological nihilism
Nolan, D., 215n27, 216n29
nominalism, x, 16, 16n19, 22, 25–26, 28, 80, 82, 82n12, 100–101, 101n1, 103–104, 142n7, 215, 236–238
   reformulation of in terms of the feature presentation, 194–195
nontology, 107
numerical persistence, 225, 225n4

object-based/truth-based property attribution distinction, 171, 191
   characterization of, 107
   See also property attributions
object boundaries, xiv–xxiii, 140–159, 165–169, 173–175, 190–193, 199–200, 203, 206, 235, 242, 246, 248
   conditions on being worldly, 150
   experience of, 152–156, 254
   irrelevance of to induction, 224–231
object borders. *See* object boundaries
object experiences, xiv, xxvi, 148–150, 150n8, 151n10, 152–157, 166, 199n9, 201, 204–205, 239, 241, 241n25,
   characterization of, 150
   polka dot examples of, 155
   possible, 153–156
object-intuitions, 203n16, 204–206, 221–222, 230–231, 241, 241n25
   characterization of, 150
   conditions on object-intuitions corresponding to worldly objects, 150
   that motivate metaphysical nihilism, 199
object-language quantifiers, xii, 56, 75
   See also metalanguage quantifiers
"objects," neutral use of, 63

objects-parts mappings, 13–15, 18–20, 197–198, 227n6
object projectivism, xiv, xv n7, xvi–xxiii, xxvi–xxvii, 141–142, 157–158, 187–188, 255
    characterizations of, 135–136, 143, 255
objectual semantics, xii, xxix
    See also Tarskian semantics
objectual truth conditions for quantifiers, xii
Occam, 155n17
Occam's razor, 139, 164, 168, 169
    See also explanatory Occam's razor principle
    See also simple-minded Occam's razor principle
O'Leary-Hawthorne, J., xxvi, 136–137, 164n26, 183–184, 188, 200n10, 253
    See also Hawthorne, J.
ontologese, 8n6, 34, 64n11, 81, 130
ontological borders, xv–xvi, xvi–xvii, xviii–xx, 29, 132, 135, 143, 145–146
    constituted of relations and properties, 147–151, 158–165
    commonsense notion of, xvi, xxi
    nonexistence of, 188–189
    transcendental argument for brute worldly, 146
    See also object boundaries
ontological boundaries. See object boundaries
ontological commitment, x, xiii, xviii, xxvii–xxxii, 5, 22, 28, 29, 31
    assertions and denials of, 30, 32–34, 37, 53, 59–64, 122
    See also "exist"; Quine's criterion
ontological contours, xiv
    questions about, xv
    See also ontological borders
ontological debate test, the
    applications of, 37–38, 43, 46, 52
    definition of, 35
ontological debate, x, xi, 4, 11, 23–29, 33, 48, 53–54, 59, 67–70, 100–107, 130–131
    characterization of, 23
    purely verbal vs. substantial, 12, 16n19, 17
ontological focus, 195, 207–210, 223, 231, 239
    characterizations of, 208, 213, 219
    See also micro/macro disc examples
ontological incommensurability, xi
    See also ontological debate
ontological nihilism, xxvi, 136, 183, 188, 194, 199n7, 200n10,
ontological projectivism. See object projectivism
ontological realism, 11
    See also reality/irreality distinction
ontological relativism, 132
    See also conceptual relativism; existential relativism
ontological saturation, 75–84, 87–98
    characterization of, 74
ontological scales, 196–197, 203–206
    See also grain invariance

package-deal objection, the, 140, 144, 146–147, 168–169
    See also predication
Parent, T., 129n1
Paul, L., xxiin15,, 144,
Peñaranda, J.J.L., 7n5,
perdurantism, 18n20, 20, 156, 187n10, 188
    See also endurantism
persistence conditions of objects, xxi, 14, 200n10, 223n15
    "numerical persistence" and induction, 225, 225n4, 253
    See also incar/outcar examples; objects-parts mappings; tree/shree examples
Perry, J., 125n36
Peters, S., xxx n24, 57n3
Pietroski, P., 80–81n8
Pitt, D., 150n8
pixel analogies, xviin12, 155, 219–220
placement apparatus, 211–212
    See also coordinate systems
Plato, 127, 147n7, 192
Platonism, x, 16, 101, 103, 104, 111

Pollock, J.L., 151n11
Potrč, M., xv, xvn7, xviiin11, xixn14
predication, xxii, 168–169, 171–176,
    179–185, 192–193
  See also package deal objection, the
predicative intensional form, 113–118
  characterization of, 113
Price, H., 10n11, 69n14
Priest, G., 59n5, 79n7, 90n19, 98
primitive thisness relation,
    169–170, 170n31
primitivism. See metaphysical
    primitivism; definitional primitivism
principle of indiscernibles, the,
  characterization of, 234
  See also identity of indiscernibles
properties and relations, xvii
  individuation conditions for, 167–168,
    173–174n1
  See also features
property attributions, 51, 87, 95, 124
  See also object-based/truth-based
    property attribution distinction
Pryor, J., 151n11
public meaning, 40, 46, 51, 52, 63, 148
  contrast with lexical meaning, 35–37
  entailments of, 38, 42–43
  See also criterion-transcendence
pure deflationary metaphysics, x,
    xn2, xxvii
  See also deflationary metaphysics
Putnam, H., xi n3, xvii n11, xxii, 4n1, 10n13,
    12, 16, 25, 38, 38n9, 39–41, 52, 190n13
  on stereotypes, 48–51
Pylyshyn, Z.W., 146n5, 149n8, 151n10

"quantificational joints" metaphor, xviii,
    xviiin13
  See also object boundaries; ontological
    borders; "carving" metaphor
quantifier, context-restricted use of,
  definition, 3
quantifier, context-unrestricted use of,
  definition, 3
quantifier domains, xi–xiii, xviii,
    xxviii–xxxi, 4–6, 9–20, 24–31, 35–37,
    47, 53–57, 68, 74, 79n7, 81, 87, 91,
    99–113, 118, 128–131, 149, 159–166,
    172, 176, 181–203
quantifier immanence, 4, 5–12, 25–26,
    27, 29, 37, 53, 55
  definition of, xviii
  See also quantifier transcendence
quantifier indifference, 224, 226
quantifier-meaning relativism. See
    quantifier relativism
quantifier relativism, 131n4, 226
quantifier neutralism, ix–x, xi, xiii, xxv,
    xxviii, xxxiii–xxxv, 29, 55–64,
    100–128, 171–172, 181,
  advantages in ontological debate
    about, 100–107
  advantages in science of, 107–111
  characterization of, 55–56
quantifier onticity, 4, 72, 113, 118, 123, 128
  characterization of, 55
  See also ontological saturation
quantifier transcendence, 5–12,
    23–25, 29, 47
  as a consequence of Quine's
    naturalism, 7–8
  definition of, 3
quantifier variance, xi, 4, 10n13, 27–28,
    35, 48, 104–105, 131–132
  independence from realism/
    anti-realism, 10–11
  See also actual quantifier variance;
    quantifier immanence
quantifiers, contouring portions of the
    real, 192
quantifiers, generalized. See generalized
    quantifiers
quantifiers, natural language,
    30, 56–58
Quine, W.V.O., xi, xxii, 3–5, 5n3, 7–12,
    78n5, 113n21, 123, 133
  on bivalence, 84–85
  on identity conditions, 124
  on ontological commitment, 5n2, 30–32
  on predicate functorese, 184n9
Quine's criterion, xi, xxvii–xxviii, 1, 5,
    6–7, 165, 253

Rajagopal, K.R., 111n16
Raley, Y., vii, xxxiv n29, xxxv n30, 36n5, 71n15, 225n1
realism. *See* reality/irreality distinction
reality/irreality distinction, 10–11, 131, 180, 182, 186–187, 189–191, 194, 207–213
reduced mass, 109–110, 230–231
reification, xiv, 135, 175
"reference,"
   conventions for in this book, 75
reference achievement, 75
reference magnetism, 190, 190n13
regimentation, xiiin5, 129, 130, 183–184
   See also "exist," regimentation of
relational occurences. *See* properties and relations
"relative to",
   talk of, xix
Resnik, M., 237n19
Rorty, A., 125n36
Rosen, G., 144n1
Routley, R., xxxivn28
Russell, B., 97n26, 147n7, 192
Ryle, G., 66–67

Salmon, N., 120n31, 122
Schaffer, J., xixn14, xxvii, xxxvn30, 63n8, 69n14, 81, 81n10, 112n20,
Schnieder, B., 81n10, 216n29
Scholl, B.J., 151n10, 158n22
scope, 113–118
semantic objection, the, 15–18, 23
semantics, Tarskian. *See* Tarskian semantics
semantics, neutral interpretation of, xxvii–xxxi, 74–77, 80
sentence-to-sentence mappings, 12–15, 20–23, 24, 48, 227n6
   characterization of, 12
   finite characterization objection to, 18–20
   for purposes of evaluating debates, 16–17
   term independence of, 16
shrees. *See* tree/shree examples
Sidelle, A., 190, 226n5, 247n31, 255n6

Sider, T., xviii, xviiin13, 3, 8n6, 10n13, 26, 29, 47n20, 102n2, 132, 139–140n5, 144n1, 149, 166–167, 190, 201n13, 216n29, 225n2, 226n5, 233–234, 251n1, 252–253
Siegal, S., 150n8
Simons, P., xxii–xxiii n15, xxiv n16, 144
simples. *See* metaphysical simples
simple-minded Occam's razor principle, 168
   See also Occam's razor
singular terms, x, 106
Sixteen Sisters, 249
"slicing". *See* "carving" metaphor
Smith, G.E., vii
social ontology, 248, 255
Sosa, E., xv, xviii, 144n1, 189, 226
space, 141, 151n10, 159–169, 208–214
   See also empty space
space and time,
   as coordinates, 177–178
   as features, 176,
   two roles of, 177
Spar, J., 39
special composition questions, 153n24, 200
   See also composition questions; general composition questions
Spiegel, A., 39
stability positions. *See* metaphysical stability positions
Stalnaker, R., 123, 124
statue/clay puzzles, 70, 137, 169n30, 239n21, 240–248
   See also Goliath/Lump
Stein, H., 169n29
Stich, S., 36n6, 38n10
Stoltz, K., 150n9
Strawson, G.
Strawson, P.F., xvii, 136, 150n8, 183, 253
stuff metaphysics, xvn9, 136
   See also stuffs
stuffs, xiv, xv, xviii, xix, 136, 209,
   individuation conditions for, 187
   See also stuff metaphysics
supervenience, 8n9

Tarski, A., 5n4, 160n23
Tarskian semantics, xi, x, xxvii–xxviii, 5, 17–18
  See also theories of truth, Tarskian
theories of truth,
  coherence, 95–98
  compositional, 19n21
  deflationary, 73–74, 77–79
  finitary, 13–14,
  Tarskian, 16, 18–20
"there is". See "exist"
"the thing in itself", xxi
thisness relation. See primitive thisness relation
Thomasson, Amie, 34, 49–53, 54, 64n11, 69n14, 112n20
  on sortals, 49–50, 51n26, 68, 255n6
Thomson, J.J., 240n23, 246n30
tree/shree examples, 14, 25, 29, 33, 45, 47n21, 48, 131–132, 144n1, 151–152
Treisman, A., 151n10
tropes, xxii–xxiii, xxiii n15, 32, 167, 173–176, 214n26
  "bundling", xxii
  See also features; properties and relations
trout-turkey, 233, 233n14
Truesdell, C., 111n16
truth based vs. object based. See object-based/truth-based property attribution distinction
truth conditions, neutral interpretation of, 80
truth inducing, coherence model of, 95–98
truth values, mechanisms for determining, 79–98
Turner, J., xxvi, 136–137, 183–186, 188, 253
  his "pegboard model" of quantification, 211–212, 218

underdetermination arguments, 169–170
Unger, P., xv, 43
"universalism," xv
  See also mereological universalism

urelements, 76
  characterization of, 76n2
  usage evidence for quantifier neutralism, ix, xiii, 34, 45, 56

vacuous terms, 95, 106–109, 113, 116, 118, 122, 124
  See also empty terms
Van Cleve, J., 176n3
van Inwagen, P., xv, xv n7, xv n8, xvii n11, 5n2, 67, 102n2, 112n19, 113, 144n1, 153n14, 199n7, 199n8, 200n10, 200n11, 201n13, 241n25, 252, 253
vagueness, xiv–xv, xxi, 84–86, 139n5, 201–203
  See also bivalence; ignorance, expressions of
Venclova, T., 67
Voltolini, A., 112n20

Walker, R.C.S., 86, 95n23
Wasserman, R., 102n2, 240n22, 240n23, 245n29, 246n30
Walton, K., 112n20
weather reports, 180–183, 183n8, 210–211
Westerståhl, D., xxx n24, 57n3
Wiggins, D., 199n8, 240n24
Wilhelm, I., vii, 137n2
William of Ockham. See Occam
Williams, E., xxxii
Williams, J.R.G., 190n13
Williamson, T., 86
Wilson, J., 250
Wittgenstein, L., 147n7, 190n13, 192
worldly borders, xviii, 146, 150–151, 163–164, 191, 194, 199–200, 217, 224, 226–230, 233–234, 254,
  regimentation of, 187–188

Xu, F., 151n10

Yablo, S., 9n9,

zebra-wires, 228–229

Index | 279

www.ingramcontent.com/pod-product-compliance
Ingram Content Group UK Ltd.
Pitfield, Milton Keynes, MK11 3LW, UK
UKHW042005230426
12048UKWH00009B/575